"Dr. Alcántara first makes a convi.... ....p ....
America through this century, but our churches will look very different. Then he
makes a compelling case that anyone who is going to survive as a preacher has
to learn new skills in order to proclaim the gospel to an intercultural society. Best
of all, he lets the amazing preacher Dr. Gardner Taylor show us how it is done."

M. Craig Barnes, president, Princeton Theological Seminary

"Dr. Jared E. Alcántara's *Crossover Preaching* dazzles in its contribution to homiletics and assessment of seldom-studied facets of Gardner C. Taylor's ministry.
Weaving scholarship in race theory, intercultural studies and performance
studies, Alcántara has produced a new tapestry of homiletics, with Gardner C.
Taylor's contribution resting at its center. In doing so, he has created a template
by which others may successfully engage in crosscultural preaching. Written in
a sophisticated yet accessible style, *Crossover Preaching* calls gospel proclaimers
to become passionate instruments of God who share God's word with all
human beings. Readers of *Crossover Preaching* will be intellectually stimulated
by its scholarship, moved by its accurate analysis of Gardner C. Taylor's
preaching, spiritually elevated by its thoughtfulness and persuaded to heed Dr.
Alcántara's call to preach a gospel that transcends human boundaries."

Edward L. Taylor, editor, The Words of Gardner Taylor Series and *Faith in the Fire*

"On Easter Sunday 2015, Gardner C. Taylor left this world for a better one. But
his long and productive life casts a long shadow, and his extraordinary pulpit
work merits the kind of close analysis Alcántara offers in this book. Taylor
emerges here as a paradigmatic 'crossover' preacher, prescient and prophetic, a
watchman on the wall with a word from the Lord for his time and for ours."

Timothy George, Beeson Divinity School of Samford University, general editor of
the Reformation Commentary on Scripture

"Christian preaching in the twenty-first century will need to be what Alcántara
calls intercultural, and his *Crossover Preaching* bridges oral and literary cultures,
racial and ethnic divides, and theory and practice. May the exemplar of Alcántara's analysis here inspire many to improvise homiletically under the power of
the Spirit for the next generation."

Amos Yong, Fuller Theological Seminary

"As the United States moves toward its 2040 demographic change from a white majority nation, Jared Alcántara's study of Gardner C. Taylor provides a timely guide for preachers emerging into the intercultural world in which America's churches are increasingly situated. Readers will find both inspiration and instruction through Alcántara's depiction of Taylor as one who boldly 'crossed over' to address audiences well beyond those of his own Concord Baptist Church in Brooklyn. Highlighting Taylor's improvisational adeptness and contextual awareness, Alcántara brings to the fore Taylor's contribution to an intercultural homiletic, and one that still holds promise for the church today."

James F. Kay, Princeton Theological Seminary

"There are those who live within their times with the insights and knowledge necessary for a time yet to come. Alcántara has captured the prophetic wisdom of a preacher whose life modeled for us how to navigate, as a disciple of Christ, intercultural and interracial currents. His proclamation was a teaching that serves to guide us in our times and sets the standards of kingdom values for living as a holy people in our times. With a sharp mind and the craft of an artist and practical theologian, Alcántara analyzes the text, the preacher and the art of Gardner C. Taylor's sermons, pointing to how they impart a timeless education for the making of our sermons and for the formation of the preacher for such a time as now in the Christian global church. As a preacher for over thirty years I was fascinated by how much I learned from and was refreshed by this book."

Elizabeth Conde-Frazier, Eastern University

"Dr. Alcántara has truly produced a first-rate work of contemporary importance in *Crossover Preaching* by brilliantly drawing from one of the most significant preachers of the twentieth century, the luminary figure of Gardner C. Taylor. Not only will preachers and students of preaching benefit from Dr. Alcántara's work in order to minister to an intercultural church and society, but also, his analysis should have a positive contribution in shaping the future of seminary education and informing theological educators as they aim to prepare church leaders for intercultural witness to the world. The depth and breadth of scholarship in this book is impressive. It is bound to enlighten, challenge and inspire those who thoughtfully engage it and seek to apply it in their preaching and teaching ministries. I recommend that all who take the future of the twenty-first-century church seriously to read it."

Patrick T. Smith, Gordon-Conwell Theological Seminary

STRATEGIC INITIATIVES IN EVANGELICAL THEOLOGY

CROSSOVER PREACHING

INTERCULTURAL-IMPROVISATIONAL HOMILETICS IN CONVERSATION WITH GARDNER C. TAYLOR

JARED E. ALCÁNTARA

◆

IVP Academic

An imprint of InterVarsity Press
Downers Grove, Illinois

InterVarsity Press
P.O. Box 1400, Downers Grove, IL 60515-1426
ivpress.com
email@ivpress.com

InterVarsity Press® is the book-publishing division of InterVarsity Christian Fellowship/USA®, a movement of students and faculty active on campus at hundreds of universities, colleges and schools of nursing in the United States of America, and a member movement of the International Fellowship of Evangelical Students. For information about local and regional activities, visit intervarsity.org.

Scripture quotations, unless otherwise noted, are from the New Revised Standard Version of the Bible, copyright 1989 by the Division of Christian Education of the National Council of the Churches of Christ in the USA. Used by permission. All rights reserved.

Cover design: Cindy Kiple
Interior design: Beth McGill
Images: Baptist Rev. Gardner C. Taylor: Ted Thai /The Life Picture Collection /Getty Images

ISBN 978-0-8308-3908-7 (print)
ISBN 978-0-8308-9902-9 (digital)

Printed in the United States of America ∞

Library of Congress Cataloging-in-Publication Data
Alcántara, Jared E., 1979-
  Crossover preaching : intercultural-improvisational homiletics in conversation with Gardner C. Taylor / Jared E. Alcántara.
    pages cm. -- (Strategic initiatives in evangelical theology)
  Includes bibliographical references and index.
  ISBN 978-0-8308-3908-7 (pbk. : alk. paper)
  1. Preaching. 2. Intercultural communication--Religious aspects--Christianity. 3. Taylor, Gardner C. I. Title.
  BV4211.3.A4225 2015
  251--dc23

                                                                                                    2015027307

P 23 22 21 20 19 18 17 16 15 14 13 12 11 10 9 8 7 6 5 4 3 2 1

Y 34 33 32 31 30 29 28 27 26 25 24 23 22 21 20 19 18 17 16 15

To Jen,

My Anchor and Sail

CONTENTS

◆

ACKNOWLEDGMENTS

◆

Only one name appears on the title page of this book, but the one who has written it knows that more than one name should appear. Numerous people shaped and guided its completion: teachers, friends, mentors, clergy, colleagues, and family members. Throughout this whole process, countless people have advised me, come alongside me, opened doors for me, supported me, challenged me, and encouraged me. For that, I am humbled and most grateful.

At the outset, I should note that some of what is written in these pages has already appeared at annual homiletics conferences as a way of testing the value of some ideas over against others. For instance, selected portions of chapter two appear in a paper titled "Improvisational Preaching" that I delivered at the 2013 meeting of the Academy of Homiletics in Louisville, Kentucky. Selected portions of chapter four appear in a paper titled "Toward an Intercultural Homiletic" that I delivered at the 2012 meeting for the Evangelical Homiletics Society in New Orleans. The feedback and pushback from people in these venues and others shaped my thinking indelibly. Thank you!

Special thanks are due to Rev. Dr. Gardner C. Taylor, the inspiration for this book. Dr. Taylor's preaching continues to bless people from many different walks of life and church traditions, and it continues to bless me. I will remember the precious moments I spent with him in informal interactions and formal interviews for the rest of my life. Dr. Taylor passed away on Easter Sunday, April 5, 2015. Thank you to the Taylor family, especially his wife, Phillis Taylor, and his daughter, Martha Taylor LaCroix, for allowing me to spend time with him in his final years of life. Thank you for sharing him with so many of us.

I would like to thank the members of my dissertation committee for their wise counsel, commitment to academic rigor, and generous support. Drs. Michael A. Brothers and Cleophus J. LaRue pointed me to helpful resources that supported my work, and they directed me to key people to interview. They also provided me with valuable feedback on my writing. A special word of thanks is due to the chairperson of my committee, James F. Kay, who was generous with his time and thoughtful with his feedback. His wise counsel, constant encouragement, and editorial skill were all sources of help and inspiration. Without a doubt, he pushed me to do my best work.

Also, to some of my current colleagues and mentors at Trinity Evangelical Divinity School—Elizabeth Sung, Greg Scharf, Peter Cha, Steve Roy, Craig Ott, Tite Tiénou, and Donald Guthrie—thank you for reading draft revisions and providing feedback and support. Thanks also to Jimmy Roh, my graduate assistant.

I am also indebted to two organizations in particular that have invested their time, energy, and resources toward this book's completion. The Hispanic Theological Initiative has been invaluable as a source of theological deepening, academic training, Latin@ solidarity, and professional networking. Thank you to the whole staff at the HTI, especially the director, Joanne Rodriguez, along with two of my HTI mentors: Dr. Elizabeth Conde-Frazier and Ulrike Guthrie. Also, the Louisville Institute provided me with financial funding, emotional support, and academic training in the final year of my studies through their dissertation fellowship program. Their support has also been invaluable.

I would be remiss if I did not also thank the congregation at Central Baptist Church in Ewing, New Jersey, and its pastor, Richard Gay. Their love, care, and support were steadfast and life giving during our days at Princeton Theological Seminary.

Thanks as well to David Congdon at IVP Academic for his editorial support and guidance.

Finally, I want to thank my family. Thank you to my parents, José and Susan, who have supported me in too many ways to count and have made innumerable sacrifices toward my education; my sisters and brothers; my children, who are a constant source of joy; and my extended family, whose presence in my life blesses and enriches me in more ways than they know. Most of all, thank you to my wife, Jennifer. She is a loving companion, a constant friend, a tireless encourager, a spiritual bulwark, and a beautiful sign of God's grace in my life.

Reflecting on God's faithfulness through such a lengthy, challenging, and rewarding process, I resonate with these ancient words attributed to King David: "Who am I, O Lord God, and what is my house, that you have brought me thus far?" (2 Sam 7:18).

ABBREVIATIONS

NYAN   *New York Amsterdam News*

NYT   *New York Times*

WGT   Gardner C. Taylor. The Words of Gardner Taylor. Edited by
Edward L. Taylor. 6 vols. Vol. 1, *NBC Radio Sermons, 1959–
1970.* Vol. 2, *Sermons from the Middle Years, 1970–1980.* Vol. 3,
Quintessential Classics, 1980–Present. Vol. 4, *Special Occasion
and Expository Sermons.* Vol. 5, *Lectures, Essays, and Interviews.* Vol. 6, *50 Years of Timeless Treasures.* Valley Forge, PA:
Judson Press, 2004.

"TIME IS FILLED WITH SWIFT TRANSITION"

*In 1900, fully 90 percent of Christians lived
in Europe or the United States. Today 60 percent live in
Asia, Africa, and Latin America, and that figure will probably
rise to 67 percent by 2025. About 1975, Christianity
ceased to be a "Western" religion.*

HARVEY COX, *The Future of Faith*

It was a spring day in Princeton, New Jersey, in April 2001. The speaker was noted missiologist Andrew F. Walls, who was there to deliver the Stone Lectures on Missions at Princeton Theological Seminary. Walls chose as his theme the recent history of Western mission and its connection to world Christianity in the twenty-first century, and he emphasized two phenomena in particular: the exponential rise of Western Protestant missionary expansion in non-Western nations, especially in the late nineteenth and early twentieth centuries, and the demographic transformation of the church to the southern and eastern hemispheres over that same time span. In just over one century, Walls argued, Christianity had undergone a tectonic shift from being a predominantly Western religion to being a predominantly non-Western religion.[1]

---

[1]Andrew F. Walls, "From Christendom to World Christianity: Missions and the Demographic

It was not that Christianity was never Eastern. Walls reminds us: "There was nearly a millennium and a half of active and expansive Christianity in Asia . . . [and] Christian communities in Africa that could claim a continuous history from sub-apostolic and early patristic times."[2] Rather, Christianity was *statistically* Western when the twentieth century began. In the centuries leading up to the twentieth, Christianity's numerical representation had receded in the southern and eastern hemispheres and expanded in the northern and western hemispheres.[3] For example, in 1893, 80 percent of the world's Christians lived either in North America or Europe.[4] It appeared that Christianity had become Western by the end of the nineteenth century, at least statistically speaking. Walls explains:

> Circumstances dictated that Christianity became more European than it had ever been before, and did so just at the point when Europe became more Christian than it had ever been before. Events so welded Christianity and the West together, and the domestication of Christianity in the West was so complete, the process of acculturation there so successful, that the faith seemed inseparable from the categories of European life and thought.[5]

Christianity and the West were so intertwined that it was difficult for Western Christians to imagine one without the other. The two "seemed inseparable."

Many of the late nineteenth and early twentieth-century reactions to the marriage between Christianity and Western civilization were bold and declarative. Some concluded that the economic rise of the European con-

Transformation of the Church," *The Princeton Seminary Bulletin* 22, no. 3 (2001): 306-30. Walls published this same essay in Andrew F. Walls, *The Cross-Cultural Process in Christian History: Studies in the Transmission and Appropriation of Faith* (Maryknoll, NY: Orbis Books, 2002). Walls's essay and subsequent book chapter were a transcription of a lecture he delivered at Princeton Theological Seminary. For the audio lecture, see Andrew F. Walls, *From Christendom to World Christianity: The Demographic Transformation of the Church [Audio Recording]*, Students' Lectureship on Missions: Lecture 4 (Princeton, NJ: Princeton Theological Seminary, Educational Media, 2001).
[2]Walls, "From Christendom to World Christianity," p. 307.
[3]Historical events such as the Protestant Reformation in Europe and Islamic expansion in the Middle East undoubtedly contributed to these demographic shifts. The reasons for this shift are complex.
[4]Walls, "From Christendom to World Christianity," p. 322.
[5]Ibid., p. 307.

tinent was part of God's providential plan. As European life, thought, and economic power ascended, so also Christianity would ascend, at least so it was thought. Strong ties between Christianity and the West led the French writer Hilaire Belloc to declare in 1920: "The Faith is Europe, and Europe is the Faith."[6] In the world that Belloc inhabited, the church's destiny was bound together with the destiny of Europe. Without the church there was no Europe, and without Europe there could be no church. Others reacted with excitement over the impact Western Christianity could have on the entire world. Many Western missionaries responded with eagerness and exhilaration about the future, especially in regard to the church's potential expansion into the non-Western regions of the world.

Several leaders of the modern (Western) missions movement responded with a mood of optimism, triumphalism, and even martialism. "God has chosen American Christians to be the saviors of Christianity in the East," exclaimed the Rev. Dr. James S. Dennis, a Presbyterian missionary to Beirut, Lebanon, when he presented the first Students' Lectures on Missions at Princeton Theological Seminary in 1893.[7] Eight years earlier, in 1885, the American reformer and clergyman Josiah Strong declared, "It is *fully* in the hands of the Christians of the United States, during the next fifteen or twenty years, to hasten or retard the coming of Christ's kingdom in the world by hundreds, and perhaps thousands, of years." In his book *Our Country*, Strong referred to the United States as "the Gibraltar of the ages which commands the world's future" and described the generation in which he lived as having "the power to mold the destinies of unborn millions."[8] Then, in 1910, during

---

[6]Hilaire Belloc, *Europe and the Faith* (Rockford, IL: TAN Books and Publishers, 1992), p. 2.

[7]James S. Dennis, *Foreign Missions After a Century*, Students' Lectures on Missions, Princeton Theological Seminary 1893 (New York: Fleming H. Revell, 1893), pp. 126-27; as cited in Walls, "From Christendom to World Christianity," p. 309.

[8]Josiah Strong, *Our Country: Its Possible Future and Its Present Crisis* (New York: Baker & Taylor, 1885), p. 180 (emphasis added). Strong's bestselling missions manifesto "propelled him into national prominence as a writer, religious reformer, and missions advocate." Wendy J. Deichmann Edwards, "Forging an Ideology for American Missions: Josiah Strong and Manifest Destiny," in *North American Foreign Missions, 1810–1914: Theology, Theory, and Policy*, ed. Wilbert R. Shenk (Grand Rapids: Eerdmans, 2004), pp. 163-91; quote on p. 163. *Our Country* was an instant bestseller nationally and internationally. It sold 175,000 domestic copies and was translated into German and Dutch. For an overview of the popularity of *Our Country* and an assessment of Strong's legacy in modern Western missions, see Deichmann Edwards, "Forging an Identity."

the closing address of the Edinburgh Missionary Conference, an event dedicated to the evangelization of the non-Western world within the century, John R. Mott, the chairman of the convention, proclaimed: "The end of the Conference is the beginning of the conquest. . . . The end of the planning is the beginning of the doing."[9] A prevailing sense of excitement was in the air.

Not even the most perceptive or prescient missiologist could have predicted the unforeseen outcomes and seismic shifts that were set to take place in Christianity, and in the world, for that matter, over the course of the next century. The world that most Christians occupy today is markedly different from the one Western Christians occupied in the early twentieth century. One decade into the twenty-first century, the shortsightedness of Belloc's assertion, Dennis's prediction, Strong's declaration, and Mott's proclamation, is in plain view—*the West is no longer Christian, and Christianity is no longer Western.* The Christian faith is withering in its former centers and growing in its previous peripheries. As Walls notes, "Christianity began the twentieth century as a Western religion, and indeed, *the* Western religion; it ended the century as a non-Western religion, on track to become progressively more so."[10]

Around 1910, approximately eleven million Christians lived in Africa. Around 2010, the number of African Christians exceeded 490 million.[11] When Walls lectured at Princeton in 2001, more than 60 percent of the world's Christians lived in Africa, Asia, Latin America, and the Pacific— it stood at 20 percent in 1900.[12] As a consequence of these trends and others like them, more and more Western systems and structures linked to Christendom are moving to the periphery as new ways of being the church emerge. Alister McGrath suggests that "the Protestant denomination is essentially a European phenomenon" that will probably meet

---

[9]John R. Mott, "Report of Commission: World Missionary Conference, Edinburgh 1910," in *The History and Records of the Conference, Together with Addresses Delivered at the Evening Meetings.*, vol. 9 (Des Moines, IA: LBS Archival Products, 1990), as cited in Walls, "From Christendom to World Christianity," p. 321.

[10]Walls, "From Christendom to World Christianity," p. 322.

[11]For statistics on the rise of African Christianity over the last one hundred years, see "Christianity in Africa, 1910–2010," in Todd M. Johnson and Kenneth R. Ross, eds., *Atlas of Global Christianity: 1910–2010* (Edinburgh: Edinburgh University Press, 2009), pp. viii-ix.

[12]Walls, "From Christendom to World Christianity," p. 322.

its demise by the end of the twenty-first century.[13] Philip Jenkins observes: "The era of Western Christianity has passed within our lifetimes, and the day of Southern Christianity is dawning. The fact of change itself is undeniable: it has happened, and will continue to happen."[14]

It would be unrealistic and counterproductive to expect that this shift will somehow reverse its course. Likewise, it would be premature and even unhelpful for Western Christians to abandon ship out of fear that they have nothing worthwhile left to offer. Neither willful ignorance nor nihilistic escapism is a realistic option. What is required is reorientation and recalibration. At such a time, theological reflection on a course of action is not only warranted but urgent. The church may have shifted, but it is also growing in surprising and exciting ways and expanding to unexpected places. To quote again from Walls, "At the end of the story and the beginning of our century, Christendom is dead or almost so, but Christianity is alive and well without it."[15]

Not everyone shares Walls's sense of optimism concerning the prospects for Western Christianity moving forward. In significant ways, the West is post-Christian and Christianity is post-Western. Statistically, and even symbolically, Europe is no longer the Christian heartland. The faith is *not* Europe and Europe is *not* the faith. In some corners of Europe, for example, church attendance is at record lows. In the United Kingdom, where weekly church attendance stood at around 50 percent in the mid-nineteenth century, church attendance in 2005 hovered at around 6.5 percent. Walls also notes: "There are now far more Muslims in England than there are Presbyterians in Scotland."[16] Even in Edinburgh, within a one-mile radius of the site of the great missions conference of 1910, there are at least four churches that have been converted into coffee

---

[13]Alister E. McGrath, *The Future of Christianity* (Malden, MA: Wiley-Blackwell, 2002), p. 40. Perhaps McGrath is right, or perhaps the denomination as we know it and understand it today is more of an American phenomenon. It is difficult to know for sure. For more on denominations as phenomena, see H. Richard Niebuhr, *The Social Sources of Denominationalism* (Hamden, CT: Shoe String Press, 1954).

[14]Philip Jenkins, *The Next Christendom: The Coming of Global Christianity* (New York: Oxford University Press, 2002), p. 3.

[15]Walls, *From Christendom to World Christianity: The Demographic Transformation of the Church [Audio Recording]*.

[16]Walls, "From Christendom to World Christianity," p. 323.

shops or tourism bureaus. Travel a bit farther out, and you find churches converted into homes, pubs, performance venues, and climbing walls.

Some argue that the prospects for Christianity in the United States are equally perilous, the recession of Christian faith from society a foregone conclusion. In *Christianity After Religion* (2012), Diana Butler Bass suggests that "the first decade of the twenty-first century in the United States could rightly be called the Great Religious Recession."[17] "Christian belief and practice," she claims, are experiencing a precipitous decline, and "general belief in God has eroded in the last thirty years."[18] Not only does Bass cite recent polls in *USA Today* and statistics that highlight the rapid numerical decline in traditional mainline denominations, but she also notes the sizable increase among those who self-identify as "religiously unaffiliated," "atheist," or "agnostic" compared to a generation ago. The writing is on the wall for American Christianity, she suggests. Even Walls acknowledges that statistics like these coupled with other trends in society at large should *at least* cause American Christians to pause before making optimistic generalizations about Christianity in their own nation. Add to these trends the complexities of secularization,[19]

---

[17]Diana Butler Bass, *Christianity After Religion: The End of the Church and the Birth of a New Spiritual Awakening* (New York: HarperOne, 2012), p. 20.

[18]Bass bases her argument not only on data collected by *USA Today* but also on the writings of other sociologists of religion. Bass writes: "Since the mid 1990s . . . observers of contemporary religion have increasingly argued that Christian belief and practice are eroding even in the United States" (p. 14). Later in the same chapter, she notes the statistical rise of unaffiliated atheists (p. 16). In fairness to Bass, it seems that she is focused on the emergence of secular society. See ibid., pp. 14, 16.

[19]The debate over secularization—its theoretical underpinnings, definition, and applicability or lack thereof in a global context—is too lengthy, complex, and nuanced to describe here. For mainstream defenses of secularization theory, see Peter Berger, *The Heretical Imperative* (New York: Doubleday, 1979); Harvey Cox, *The Secular City: Secularization and Urbanization in Theological Perspective* (New York: Macmillan, 1965); and Charles Taylor, *A Secular Age* (Cambridge, MA: Belknap Press of Harvard University Press, 2007). For recent discussions of secularization, see Michael Warner, Jonathan VanAntwerpen, and Craig J. Calhoun, eds., *Varieties of Secularism in a Secular Age* (Cambridge, MA: Harvard University Press, 2010); Mary Eberstadt, *How the West Really Lost God: A New Theory of Secularization* (Radnor, PA: Templeton Press, 2013); and Philip S. Gorski, "Historicizing the Secularization Debate: An Agenda for Research," in *Handbook of the Sociology of Religion*, ed. Michele Dillon (New York: Cambridge University Press, 2003), pp. 110-22. For critiques of secularization theory, what is sometimes referred to as "postsecularization theory," see Rajeev Bhargava, ed., *Secularism and Its Critics* (New York: Oxford University Press, 1998); Monica Duffy Toft, Daniel Philpott, and Timothy Samuel Shah, *God's Century: Resurgent Religion and Global Politics* (New York: W. W. Norton, 2011), pp. 1-8; and Berger's reversal of his previous stance in Peter L. Berger, *The Desecularization of the World: Resurgent Religion and World Politics* (Grand Rapids: Eerdmans, 1999). For discussions on the impact of secularization on the Millen-

globalization,[20] and polarized perspectives on immigration,[21] and pessimism seems like a more tenable option than optimism. Walls writes: "Many signs are visible in the United States now that marked Europe when its own rapid retreat from Christianity began."[22]

But what if the task of reorientation and recalibration required a more nuanced and textured approach, one that complicated and problematized the data? What if traditional binaries such as Western Christianity/ world Christianity, Christian West/post-Christian West, were too simplistic and reductive? How might the narrative change concerning these statistics if there were also countervailing data supporting an alternate

nial generation, see David Kinnaman, *You Lost Me: Why Young Christians Are Leaving Church— And Rethinking Faith* (Grand Rapids: Baker Books, 2011); and George Barna and David Kinnaman, *Churchless: Understanding Today's Unchurched and How to Connect with Them* (Austin, TX: Tyndale Momentum, 2014). For a discussion of the impact of secularization on Christian preaching, see David J. Lose, *Preaching at the Crossroads* (Minneapolis: Fortress, 2013), pp. 49-64.

[20] For treatments of globalization as a phenomenon, see Arjun Appadurai, *Modernity at Large: Cultural Dimensions of Globalization* (Minneapolis: University of Minnesota Press, 2005); Peter Beyer and Lori Beaman, eds., *Religion, Globalization and Culture* (Boston: Brill, 2007); Nayan Chanda, *Bound Together: How Traders, Preachers, Adventurers, and Warriors Shaped Globalization* (New Haven, CT: Yale University Press, 2008); Roland Robertson, *Globalization: Social Theory and Global Culture* (Thousand Oaks, CA: Sage, 1992); and Robert J. Schreiter, *The New Catholicity: Theology Between the Global and the Local* (Maryknoll, NY: Orbis Books, 1997). For an account of globalization's influence on missiology, see Craig Ott, "Globalization and Contextualization: Reframing the Task of Contextualization in the Twenty-First Century," *Missiology: An International Review* 43, no. 1 (2014): 43-58. For an analysis of how globalization shapes North American homiletics, see Eunjoo Mary Kim, *Preaching in an Age of Globalization* (Louisville: Westminster John Knox, 2010).

[21] In the last ten years especially in the United States, scholars have given greater attention to establishing theologies of immigration and reflecting on the dangers of anti-immigrant sentiment. See Amos Yong, *Hospitality and the Other: Pentecost, Christian Practices, and the Neighbor* (Maryknoll, NY: Orbis Books, 2008), pp. 159-77; Daniel G. Groody and Gioacchino Campese, *A Promised Land, A Perilous Journey: Theological Perspectives on Migration* (South Bend, IN: University of Notre Dame Press, 2008); Amos Yong, *The Future of Evangelical Theology: Soundings from the Asian American Diaspora* (Downers Grove, IL: IVP Academic, 2014), pp. 187-216; and Carmen Nanko-Fernández, *Theologizing En Espanglish: Context, Community, and Ministry* (Maryknoll, NY: Orbis Books, 2010), pp. 110-52. One of the insights that Jehu Hanciles brings into focus is that the United States is at one and the same time a "nation of immigrants" and a nation of anti-immigrant sentiment, such as is found in the writings of Rev. Josiah Strong. This anti-immigrant bias goes at least as far back as one of the nation's founders, Benjamin Franklin, who disdained German immigrants to Philadelphia. For Hanciles's treatment of Josiah Strong, see Jehu Hanciles, *Beyond Christendom: Globalization, African Migration, and the Transformation of the West* (Maryknoll, NY: Orbis Books, 2008), pp. 165-66, 229-32, 276-77. Another book that discusses anti-immigrant bias is an ethnographic work on prejudice and racism toward undocumented migrant farmers and the racial hierarchy that exists among them; see Seth M. Holmes, *Fresh Fruit, Broken Bodies: Migrant Farmworkers in the United States* (Berkeley: University of California Press, 2013).

[22] Walls, "From Christendom to World Christianity," p. 323.

conclusion, data, say, that highlighted a significant connection between Christianity's move south and east and the demographic transformation of the population in the United States?

Almost everyone acknowledges that Christianity is growing at an exponential rate in the Global South. The data is irrefutable and probably conservative in its estimates. Statistically speaking, Africa and Latin America are *now* the Christian heartlands. Instead of Wittenberg and Geneva, think São Paulo and Jakarta. The majority of the world's Christians live in the eastern and southern hemispheres. However, here is what is so surprising: *few people have observed the significant connection between Christianity's shifts southward and eastward and the demographic shifts taking place among the general population of the United States.* If Christianity is moving south and east, then what do we make of the fact that the majority of immigrants who come *to* the United States, as well as the subpopulations *within* the United States that are growing the fastest, happen to come from these regions?

Take the matter of immigration and the trends today versus the trends fifty years ago. In the 1960s, persons from Europe, Canada, and Oceania (Australia, New Zealand, etc.) accounted for 49 percent of US immigrants "obtaining lawful permanent residence," and those coming from Latin America, Asia, and Africa accounted for 49 percent, with the other 2 percent referred to as "unspecified" or "Other America." By contrast, in 2013, the latest year these statistics were available, percentages were markedly different. European, Canadian, and Oceanic immigrants accounted for just under 12 percent of the nation's immigrant population, and Latin America, Asia, and Africa accounted for just over 86 percent of the nation's immigrants (Asia: 40 percent, Latin America: 38 percent, Africa: 10 percent), with just under 2 percent reporting as "unspecified."[23]

---

[23]The demographic shifts are remarkable when one contrasts the 1960s with 2013. The statistical breakdown of immigration in the 1960s is as follows: 3,213,749 total immigrants, with 35 percent from Europe, 13 percent from Canada, .007 percent from Oceania, 11 percent from Asia, 38 percent from Latin America, and .007 percent from Africa. Contrast that with the statistical breakdown of immigrants in 2013: 990,553 total immigrants obtaining lawful permanent resident status, with 9 percent from Europe, 2 percent from Canada, .006 percent from Oceania, 39 percent from Asia, 37 percent from Latin America, and 10 percent from Africa. It is worth noting that, at least statistically speaking, more Asian immigrants obtained permanent resident status in the United States in 2013 than Latin American immigrants. However, these figures do not account

These demographic shifts are not just remarkable; when examined more closely, they constitute a counternarrative to challenge Bass's thesis and that of others. Moreover, they provide American Christians with a unique opportunity to rethink their theological and homiletical agendas as they discover new ways of being the church.

Put differently, Christianity's geographical shift *positively* affects the church in the United States. Three demographic trends in particular are significant. First, over the next forty years, there will be a steady increase in the overall population of the United States. As some European nations are confronted with the problem of indigenous depopulation, the overall population in the United States is set to grow larger each year. In 1950, European nations accounted for eight of the twenty most populous nations. In 2000, the number was three out of twenty. By 2050, only one nation—the Russian Federation, projected to rank eighteenth—will remain. According to projections, dwindling populations and low birth rates will hit European countries like Italy and Spain especially hard. By contrast, the United States is projected to grow by approximately two million people per year between now and 2050. In the United States, ranked the third most populous nation after China and India in 2000, the trends will be opposite to trends in Europe. The United States will have 408.7 million people in 2050 (in 2000: 285 million) and retain its status as the third most populous nation, with India projected to be first ahead of China on account of China's former one-child policy.[24] Barring a major economic meltdown or an isolationist renaissance, it is probable that the US church will also grow in line with these projections. Yet, *how*

---

for the annual influx of undocumented immigrants. Current estimates place the undocumented immigrant population at just under 12 million people. Note also two other rapid changes: (1) the change in African immigration between the 1960s at less than 1 percent and the year 2013 at just under 10 percent and (2) the rapid change in Asian immigrants seeking permanent legal residence between the 1960s at 11 percent and the year 2013 at 39 percent. See the *Yearbook of Immigration Statistics: 2013* on the Department of Homeland Security's website. For the specific statistics contrasting the data from the 1960s and the data from 2013, see Department of Homeland Security, *Table 2: Persons Obtaining Legal Permanent Resident Status by Region and Selected Country of Last Residence: Fiscal Years 1820 to 2013*, last modified June 16, 2014, www.dhs.gov/yearbook-immigration-statistics-2013-lawful-permanent-residents.

[24]Statistics from the United Nations' report *World Population to 2300* (New York: The United Nations Department of Economic and Social Affairs: Population Division, 2004), pp. 42, 112-18, last modified March 2, 2014, www.un.org/esa/population/publications/longrange2/WorldPop 2300final.pdf.

the church will grow and the demographic the church will represent is what is of vital importance, which leads to the next significant demographic shift.

Second, there will be a significant rise in the nonwhite population *within* the United States over the next forty years, partly due to non-Western immigration and partly on account of high birth rates among nonwhite ethnic groups. On the matter of immigration, Christians from the eastern and southern hemispheres will immigrate to the United States at much higher rates and in larger numbers than non-Christians. In fact, this has already happened. In his 2013 book, *From Times Square to Timbuktu*, Wesley Granberg-Michaelson observes:

> An estimated 214 million people in the world today are migrants, living in a country different from where they were born. Nearly half of these migrants are Christians—about 105 million, far more than the proportion of Christians in the world, which is about 33 percent. And for these Christians who are on the move, the *United States* is their chief destination; they presently account for about 32 million, or 13 percent of the Christian community in the United States. *That percentage will continue to rise.* These new immigrant Christians are changing America's religious landscape.[25]

Granberg-Michaelson's claim can be statistically substantiated by at least one other reputable source. According to the Pew Forum on Religion and Public Life, in the year 2010, there were forty-three million foreign-born residents living in the United States, approximately one in eight people. About *74 percent* of these forty-three million were Christian, 5 percent Muslim, 4 percent Buddhist, and 3 percent Hindu.[26] In other words, three of every four foreign-born residents living in the United States self-identified as Christian. By 2050, the number of foreign-born residents will increase to one in five people. As it pertains to population projections, both the Asian and Latin@ populations will *triple* in size between now and 2050. By contrast, the number of those who self-

---

[25]Wesley Granberg-Michaelson, *From Times Square to Timbuktu: The Post-Christian West Meets the Non-Western Church* (Grand Rapids: Eerdmans, 2013), p. 83 (emphasis added).

[26]Pew Forum on Religion and Public Life, "Faith on the Move: The Religious Affiliation of International Migrants," last modified February 19, 2014, www.pewforum.org/2012/03/08/religious-migration-exec/.

identify as white will drop from 67 percent to 47 percent. In 1960, whites accounted for 85 percent of the population.[27]

Third, in 2050, the white population in the United States will be older than the nonwhite population, and it will also be smaller. The year 2010 was the first year that more nonwhite babies were born in the United States than white babies. In 2012, four states and one municipality—California, New Mexico, Hawaii, Texas, and Washington, D.C.—already had populations in which minorities were the majority. In that same year, statisticians also observed the significant differences between the median age of whites and that of nonwhites. In 2012, the median age for whites was about forty-two, for African Americans and Asians about thirty-two, and for Latin@s about twenty-eight. Differences in median age also account for the rapid shift in the ethnic makeup of children enrolled in public schools in the United States. The academic year 2014–2015 was the first that public schools had a nonwhite majority of children enrolled. Only twenty years ago, in the mid-1990s, white children accounted for 65 percent of public school students. Today, that number is less than 50 percent and is set to drop to 45 percent by the mid-2020s.[28] The year 2042 is now the latest projected year in which nonwhites will become the overall, general-population majority in the United States and whites the minority.[29]

These three demographic shifts also mean that seminary classrooms in general and homiletics classrooms in particular will change. In fact, the ethnic and cultural makeup of the seminary classroom has *already* changed dramatically since 2001. Barbara G. Wheeler, an independent

[27]Statistics found in Haya El Nasser, "U.S. Hispanic Population to Triple by 2050," *USA Today*, February 12, 2008, www.usatoday.com/news/nation/2008-02-11-population-study_N.htm.

[28]Sean Coughlan, "US Schools to Have Non-White Majority," *BBC News*, August 26, 2014, accessed January 31, 2015, www.bbc.com/news/education-28937660.

[29]William H. Frey observes: "The Census Bureau's new projections through 2050 portend a more accelerated transformation of the nation's population on race-ethnic dimensions than was previously supposed. These new projections show that the minority majority tipping point—the year when the white population dips to below half of the total—will occur in 2042, 8 years sooner than in the Bureau's projections just 4 years ago." See William H. Frey, "The Census Projects Minority Surge," *The Brookings Institution*, August 18, 2008, accessed January 23, 2015, www.brookings.edu/research/opinions/2008/08/18-census-frey. Statistics on minority babies, median age, and the year 2042 are available in Carol Morello and Ted Mellnik, "Census: Minority Babies Are Now Majority in United States," *The Washington Post*, May 17, 2012, www.washingtonpost.com/local/census-minority-babies-are-now-majority-in-united-states/2012/05/16/gIQA1WY8UU_story.html.

researcher who works in consultation with Auburn Seminary's Center for the Study of Theological Education, spoke in depth about these trends and their impact on seminaries between now and 2040 in an April 2013 consultation address for the Forum for Theological Exploration. She explains:

> The enrollment of groups other than whites has been growing fast and will continue to increase at high rates, because those are the groups that are growing in the population as a whole. The religious segment of the population is changing even faster in its make-up. Whites are disaffili-ating from organized religion, but other groups are doing so much more slowly, so the part of the population that is religiously observant and adherent is diversifying faster. In religious America, 2040—the year that there is predicted to be no racial or ethnic majority in the United States—will occur well before 2040.[30]

Wheeler's claims are grounded in the Association of Theological Schools' (ATS) recent statistics on enrollment in North American seminaries over the last decade. Since the year 2005, white student enrollment has dropped by 17 percent from its peak; African American student enrollment has increased by 7 percent; and Latin@ student enrollment has grown by 26 percent since 2005 and a remarkable 100 percent (i.e., doubled in size) since 1996. Asian American student enrollment has dropped by 7 percent since 2005, but when the focus shifts from microtrends to macrotrends, the data show us that Asian American student enrollment has increased by 3 percent since 2002 and 13 percent since 1996. It is also significant that these figures do not include enrollment by international students from Asian coun-tries, a demographic that has grown significantly in the last two de-cades. At least one more statistic on trends is worth mentioning. In 2008, the first year ATS gathered data on students who self-identified as multiracial (people like myself), they counted 123 students in this category. In 2011, the last year these projections were made available,

---

[30]Barbara G. Wheeler, "Consultation Address," in Anne Joh and Dori Baker, *Time to Choose, Time to Change: A Report on the 2013 FTE Consultation on Doctoral Theological Education* (Decatur, GA: The Forum for Theological Exploration, October 2013), p. 56, last modified February 13, 2014, http://fteleaders.org/resources/Doctoral-Report.

that number had risen to 448, an increase of 364 percent.[31]

Based on these data (national and educational), we can posit that over the next one to two generations Christians born *in* the Global South or with ethnic and cultural ties *to* the Global South will be a major force in the preservation, reshaping, and renewal of the US church and its mission. The nonwhite, non-Western population will do more than join the church's ranks; it will lead the church into an "intercultural" future.[32] Herein lies the significance of the connection between global Christianity's shift and the projections for the overall population in the United States: *If the church in the United States bears even a remote resemblance to the overall population, it will be an intercultural church with an intercultural witness to an intercultural society.* An ancillary claim can also be made about the homiletics classroom: *If the homiletics classroom in the United States bears even a remote resemblance to the overall population, those who teach them will need to develop pedagogies that account for and engage with an intercultural church with an intercultural witness to an intercultural society.*

An intercultural future is knocking on the church's door, and the preachers and homileticians of today and tomorrow must answer it. The danger of doing nothing is too great. If we cannot or, worse yet, will not rethink our theological and homiletical agendas in light of these projections, we will soon discover that no one is listening or paying attention. Our so-called audience will be disinterested and dissuaded by us, and our homiletical strategies will be better suited to a museum than a classroom.

INTRODUCTION TO THE PRIMARY CLAIM

In this book, I argue that the way to bring homiletics into congruence with demographic shifts in the church is to develop a *crossover homiletic* that engages with and accounts for difference. By *crossover homiletic* I

---

[31]Barbara G. Wheeler and Anthony T. Ruger, "Sobering Figures Point to Overall Enrollment Decline," *In Trust* 24, no. 2 (Spring 2013): 9. For figures on the 1996 head count enrollment according to race and ethnicity, see *2000–01 Annual Data Tables* (Pittsburgh: The Association of Theological Schools, 2001), www.ats.edu/resources/institutional-data/annual-data-tables.

[32]The words *intercultural* and *multicultural* are often used interchangeably. Some churches prefer the term *multiethnic* because it emphasizes the fact that every church member has an ethnicity. Recently, at least in many academic circles, the word *intercultural* has carried more currency and so will be the word used most frequently. On occasion, the words *multicultural* and *multiethnic* will also be used for stylistic variation.

mean a homiletic that effectively deploys performative and metaphorical improvisation-as-intercultural-negotiation. This approach constitutes an alternative way of thinking about preaching practice and homiletical strategy with a specific aim in mind: to foster dispositional commitment to improvisational-intercultural proficiency as a way of being and acting. To construct this approach, we will engage in a case study of one of America's premier twentieth-century preachers: Gardner C. Taylor, pastor emeritus of Concord Baptist Church of Christ in Brooklyn, New York. Taylor's preaching functions as a way by which the improvisational-intercultural homiletic that I propose becomes visible and viable. The reason I chose Taylor as opposed to other preachers of the past or present becomes clear in chapter one.

Moving toward the advent of an improvisational-intercultural homiletic does not have to mean starting from scratch. It assumes that we can learn lessons from the past and, in particular, from past preachers who embodied and actualized improvisational and intercultural proficiency. Taylor displayed these two proficiencies in his preaching, and it is my contention in this book that these are the same two proficiencies homileticians need in the future to meet the demands of an intercultural church. The thesis I propose is as follows: *An analysis of Gardner C. Taylor's preaching reveals an improvisational-intercultural approach that, in light of recent developments in improvisational and intercultural theory, illumines his contemporary significance to preaching and homiletics in the United States now and in the future.*

It should be stated at the outset that this book is *not* a biblical or systematic theology of preaching. It is a case study on a particular individual's contemporary significance at a particular point in time and the bearing his improvisational-intercultural approach might have on today's context. It assumes that preachers and homileticians already strive to be gospel centered, biblically tethered, exegetically proficient, theologically competent, and spiritually mature, and that they are also committed to other significant aspects of Christian proclamation. The focus here is much more specific and narrow. It studies an individual preacher from whom we can learn, and it is a proposal as to what we can learn from him. Most everyone who preaches understands the importance of these other commitments, and they have studied and gained competency in them. As a result, they recognize the importance of attending to the timeless dimensions of preaching and the character of Christian faithfulness. Although these are important and even crucial to a robust understanding of proclamation, this book is designed to provoke thought and initiate dialogue around issues of contextual timeliness and homiletical fittingness in twenty-first-century churches and seminaries on account of rapid demographic changes in both of these spaces.

In the first part, we will provide a rationale for why we can refer to Taylor as a "crossover preacher," and we will discuss performative and metaphorical improvisation. Performance theory and race theory are emerging fields that provide us with tools for describing how improvisation functions in Taylor's preaching. I argue that improvisation is both a practice in which one riffs on one's tradition (performative) *and* an ability to negotiate across racial, ethnic, and ecclesial difference with protean reflexivity (metaphorical). First, I point to performative instances, that is, occasions on which improvisation appears in Taylor's sermons, and I discuss his own acknowledgment that his preaching has improvisational dimensions. While Taylor does not use the word *improvisation* to describe some of his preaching practices, it will become evident that these practices *are* improvisational, at least in the way I define the term.[33] Then, I make the bolder claim that Taylor's social location is both a condition of and catalyst for improvisation at a metaphorical level. Put differently, I argue for a connection between Taylor's social location and his adeptness at improvising in the broader sense of communicating across cultural difference.[34]

---

[33] I should note that in my discussion of improvisation, I do not an attempt to enter into wider discussions concerning the family resemblances between systematic theology and improvisational performance. Though these discussions are useful and even important, they are somewhat peripheral to this book's aims. Some of the systematic theologians who make connections between improvisational performance and theology are as follows: Kevin J. Vanhoozer, *Faith Speaking Understanding: Performing the Drama of Doctrine* (Louisville: Westminster John Knox, 2014); Vanhoozer, *The Drama of Doctrine: A Canonical-Linguistic Approach to Christian Theology* (Louisville: Westminster John Knox, 2005); Peter Heltzel, *Resurrection City: A Theology of Improvisation* (Grand Rapids: Eerdmans, 2012); Nathan Crawford, *Theology as Improvisation: A Study in the Musical Nature of Theological Thinking* (Boston: Brill, 2013); Nicholas Lash, *Theology on the Way to Emmaus* (London: SCM Press, 1986); and Yong, *Hospitality and the Other*, pp. 47-56.

[34] Some educational theorists refer to metaphorical improvisation from a linguistic vantage point as

Then, in the second part, we will examine intercultural competence and pedagogy. Here I enlist intercultural and education theory as inter-locutors. Like performance theory and race theory, these theories are descriptive tools that situate Taylor's practices and effectuate strategies for the future. In this section, I will not leave the language of improvisation entirely behind; rather, I foreground the language of *intercultural competence* (IC), by which is meant *the cultivation of knowledge, skills, and habits for effectively negotiating cultural, racial, and ecclesial difference.* I survey intercultural competence theorists, suggest ways these theorists can deepen our understanding of Taylor's approach, and provide a threefold model for attaining IC proficiency. The educational theory I appeal to is more specific rather than general. It is educational theory in conversation with performance and intercultural theories.

Although we will foreground improvisation in chapters one through three and intercultural theory in chapter four, neither has logical priority; they are symbiotically related. The two categories—intercultural and im-provisational—are two sides of the same coin. Taylor's homiletical approach is *both* improvisational and intercultural. To be intercultural in preaching is to be improvisational and to be improvisational is to be intercultural.

Throughout this book, we will use the metaphor of *crossing over* in order to describe an improvisational-intercultural approach to preaching. We will also use phrases such as "crossover preacher" and "crossover preaching" to visually depict the dispositional dimensions to this ap-proach.[35] The point in doing so is neither to lift up a reductive binary nor to imply a facile or sterile action. The aim is to provoke thought, initiate dialogue, and recommend action.

Crossing over is a salient and fecund metaphor for a number of

---

"code switching" or "code meshing." They investigate the ways that some African Americans change their language and grammar when navigating majority culture contexts, in particular public school settings. For more on this research, see Vershawn Ashanti Young, Rusty Barrett, Y'Shanda Young-Rivera, and Kim Brian Lovejoy, *Other People's English: Code-Meshing, Code-Switching, and African American Literacy* (New York: Teachers College Press, 2013). See also Charles E. DeBose, "Codeswitching: Black English and Standard English in the African-American Linguistic Reper-toire," *Journal of Multilingual and Multicultural Development* 13 (1992): 157-67.

[35]Cleophus LaRue uses the phrase "crossover preacher" to describe "one who intentionally seeks to have broad appeal to as wide and diverse an audience as possible," in Cleophus J. LaRue, *I Believe I'll Testify: The Art of African American Preaching* (Louisville: Westminster John Knox, 2011), p. 32.

reasons. First, it conceptualizes Taylor's ability to negotiate racial, ethnic, and ecclesial difference effectively, a phenomenon we will discuss in greater depth in chapter one. Taylor was a crossover preacher in the sense that he engaged with and negotiated across difference so as to be well received in diverse contexts. Second, crossing over reflects an important reality, namely, that both improvisational performers and interculturally proficient persons are known for their commitment to crossing borders and transgressing boundaries. For the former, these are usually boundaries of convention and tradition in theater and music and, for the latter, these are boundaries of otherness and normativity in intercultural dialogue. Third, crossing over is action oriented. Twenty-first-century preachers must be willing to *act* improvisationally and interculturally, not just think about or talk about improvisation or discuss interculturality. In addition to thinking and speaking, crossover preachers have a bias toward action; they transgress boundaries and cross borders inside and outside the pulpit. Fourth, in the Latin@ theological circles in which I participate, the imagery of crossing over resonates on account of its migratory, diasporic connotations.[36] Finally, the imagery implies both risk and possibility. Those who cross borders, whether literal, performative, metaphorical, or intercultural, are willing to risk much, sometimes even their lives, to discover the promise of something better and to experience what is new. Borders are the places where danger and possibility meet, where risk and reward come together, where the threat of transgression converges with the promise of new life.[37] In this book, preachers and homileticians are invited to be border crossers, to become *crossover preachers*, who are willing to risk much in order to discover the promise of something better, in order to experience what is new.

---

[36]For example, see Gloria Anzaldúa's widespread use of the border as a metaphor in *Borderlands=La Frontera* (San Francisco: Aunt Lute Books, 1999). See also Ada María Isási-Diaz's discussion of one-way traveling across borders of difference in *La Lucha Continues: Mujerista Theology* (Maryknoll, NY: Orbis Books, 2004), p. 77.

[37]Journalist Anne Fadiman, who works with Hmong immigrants acclimating to and sometimes colliding with a new culture in the United States, discusses her fascination with borders as both exciting and dangerous places in Anne Fadiman, *The Spirit Catches You and You Fall Down: A Hmong Child, Her Doctors, and the Collision of Two Cultures* (New York: Farrar, Straus and Giroux, 1997), p. x. Robert C. Dykstra draws on Fadiman's fascination with borders and connects border crossing to preaching in Robert C. Dykstra, *Discovering a Sermon: Personal Pastoral Preaching* (St. Louis: Chalice, 2001), p. 105.

THE STRUCTURE OF THE BOOK

Chapter one addresses three questions that pertain to the case study for the primary claim: (1) *Who is Gardner C. Taylor?* (2) *Why choose Taylor as a case study in crossover preaching?* and (3) *What is a crossover homiletic, or, what characterizes a homiletic that is improvisational and intercultural?* To answer the first two questions, I will look at a biographical sketch of Taylor, and I demonstrate the ways Taylor was a crossover preacher in different phases of his life and ministry. To answer the third question, I delimit my terminology (i.e., what I mean by *improvisational* and *intercultural*) by surveying recent developments in improvisational and intercultural theory, and I provide a rationale as to why current homiletical literature requires revision in light of demographic shifts in the United States in general and homiletics in particular.

Chapters two through four analyze Taylor's preaching in conversation with three academic disciplines: performance theory (chap. two), race theory (chap. three), and intercultural theory (chap. four). Chapter two sets forth improvisation as a performative phenomenon in Taylor's preaching. It bears witness to actual instances where improvisational moves can be *seen* and *heard*. Not only does Taylor's preaching sound differently depending on context and occasion in much the same way that performances sound differently when a jazz musician plays or an *improvisateur* acts in the theater, likewise his approach to preaching also parallels the approaches of improvisational performers. Taylor's practice of performative improvisation is demonstrable in at least three ways: (1) observable differences between the sermon-as-prepared and the sermon-as-preached, (2) a commitment to attuning to the space where he preaches, and (3) the use of oral formulas or "tropes" in sermons much like improvisational performers draw from templates, familiar melodies, or formulas in practice and performance. Chapter two also draws on performance theory in order to place Taylor's practice of performative improvisation in conversation with current discussions in performance studies. In addition to surveying the literature in the field, I set forth my own definition of performative improvisation. Then, I highlight the connections or family resemblances between performative improvisation and Christian preaching. Last, I describe the practices mentioned previously—differences between the sermon prepared and the sermon preached, attunement to the space, and the use of tropes.

Chapter three explores the larger metaphorical extensions of improvisation vis-à-vis Taylor. I argue for a connection between Taylor's social location and his adeptness at operating in an improvisational mode. Improvisation as a metaphor for one's stance in the world is not new to critical race theory, nor is it unfamiliar to African American studies. In *Race Matters*, Cornel West argues that improvisation is integral to the black experience in America. It is a *"mode of [black] being in the world . . . of protean, fluid and flexible dispositions."*[38] In *Open Mike: Reflections on Philosophy, Race, Sex, Culture and Religion*, sociologist Michael Eric Dyson claims that improvisation is the "great next" for African American discourse in the twenty-first century. Throughout their history, he argues, African Americans have improvised with "leftovers" and "fragments" from the dominant culture. Dyson invokes the image of the "bricolage" (a metaphor borrowed from Claude Lévi-Strauss) in claiming that African Americans have historically used the disparate cultural materials at hand to recreate and reinvent themselves through improvisation.[39]

Instead of making the bolder claim of West or Dyson that improvisation is characteristic of the African American experience, I appropriate their arguments to make a narrower claim: *Gardner C. Taylor's experience of being black in the United States was a central but not sole factor in accounting for his protean reflexivity.* Taylor's social location is not a single-strand but a multistrand phenomenon. His race constitutes a necessary but not sufficient cause in understanding his improvisational-intercultural approach. To make this claim and, thus, problematize potentially reductive categories such as "authentic blackness" and "authentic black preaching," I criticize the views of James H. Cone and Henry H. Mitchell, and I engage critically with the works of J. Kameron Carter, Brian Bantum, and Victor Anderson. Carter critiques "hermetically sealed" essentialist definitions of blackness that remain "beholden to the

---

[38]Cornel West, *Race Matters* (Boston: Beacon, 1993), pp. 104-5.

[39]Michael Eric Dyson, *Open Mike: Reflections on Philosophy, Race, Sex, Culture and Religion* (New York: Basic Civitas Books, 2003), p. 206. For Claude Lévi-Strauss's discussion of bricolage, see *The Savage Mind* (Chicago: University of Chicago Press, 1966), pp. 17-35.

[oppressive] logics of modern racial reasoning."[40] According to Bantum, Cone's famous dictum that "Jesus is black" promotes an unnecessary and limiting "enclosure of Christ's redemptive moment" that may actually harm rather than help the cause of black theology.[41] Anderson warns of the dangers of "metaphysical" or "ontological blackness." Narrow understandings of blackness, he claims, lead to a dangerous and counterproductive reification of race as *the* exhaustive category for identity.[42] Through enlisting Carter, Bantum, and Anderson as conversation partners, I challenge reified definitions of "authentic blackness" and "authentic black preaching." My aims are to complexify Taylor's social location, add requisite layers to improvisation as a metaphor of identity, and contribute to ongoing debates concerning what makes black preaching distinctive.

Chapter four claims that Taylor's adeptness at metaphorical improvisation is another way of describing what communication theorists refer to as *intercultural competence* (IC).[43] Once again, by *intercultural competence* I mean the cultivation of knowledge, skills, and habits for effectively negotiating cultural, racial, ethnic, and ecclesial difference. It would not be at all presumptuous to say that Taylor—like Martin Luther King Jr.—was highly proficient at acquiring and wielding the skill of intercultural competence. The ease with which Taylor preached across racial, ethnic, and ecumenical difference uniquely positions him as a pioneer in the sort of intercultural proficiency required for the twenty-first-century church of the present and the future. After defining intercultural competence in conversation with intercultural theory, I recommend a

---

[40]J. Kameron Carter critiques James Cone especially (and Albert J. Raboteau to a lesser extent) for what he describes as a "hermetically sealed," essentialist definition of blackness. See J. Kameron Carter, *Race: A Theological Account* (Oxford: Oxford University Press, 2008), p. 158.

[41]Brian Bantum, *Redeeming Mulatto: A Theology of Race and Christian Hybridity* (Waco, TX: Baylor University Press, 2010), p. 5.

[42]Like Carter and Bantum, Victor Anderson challenges James Cone's theology of blackness. See Victor Anderson, *Beyond Ontological Blackness: An Essay on African American Religious and Cultural Criticism* (New York: Continuum, 1995), esp. pp. 10-15.

[43]This term is common parlance among education and communications theorists. See James W. Neuliep, *Intercultural Communication: A Contextual Approach* (Thousand Oaks, CA: Sage, 2012); Myron W. Lustig and Jolene Koester, *Intercultural Competence: Interpersonal Communication Across Cultures* (Boston: Allyn & Bacon, 2009); Gerhard Neuner, *Intercultural Competence*, ed. Michael Byram (Strasbourg, France: Council of Europe, Language Policy Division, 2003).

threefold framework for intercultural competence attainment that consists of acquisition, aptitude, and action, or a "3A Model of Intercultural Competence Proficiency." In this chapter, Taylor's preaching serves as an "interpretive guide" for intercultural competence proficiency.[44] At present, the stakes for homileticians to prepare seminarians to preach in ways that are demonstrably effective, theologically astute, and interculturally faithful are higher than ever. As the church becomes more intercultural, preachers and those who teach them must develop intercultural competence proficiency; they must learn to cultivate knowledge, habits, and skills that account for and engage with difference.

Chapter five concludes the argument by "climbing down the ladder of abstraction," to borrow a phrase from the semantic theorist S. I. Hayakawa.[45] This chapter will provide readers with concrete strategies for the pulpit *and* for the homiletical classroom. While we have already established that both the church and the homiletical classroom in the United States are undergoing a seismic demographic shift—this fact is undeniable—the onus remains on homileticians to develop concrete preaching and homiletical-pedagogical strategies that account for and engage these changes. The strategies I recommend are drawn from three sources: insights from Gardner C. Taylor's homiletical approach, homiletical literature in which improvisation and intercultural competence

---

[44]In *An Introduction to Pastoral Care*, Charles V. Gerkin proposes a new model for pastoral leadership: pastor as "interpretive guide." The image first appears in his *The Living Human Document* and is developed further in his *Widening the Horizons* (1986), chap. 5. He also develops this image in *Prophetic Pastoral Practice* (1991). See Charles V. Gerkin, *An Introduction to Pastoral Care* (Nashville: Abingdon, 1997), pp. 113-14; Gerkin, *The Living Human Document: Re-Visioning Pastoral Counseling in a Hermeneutical Mode* (Nashville: Abingdon, 1984); Gerkin, *Widening the Horizons: Pastoral Responses to a Fragmented Society* (Philadelphia: Westminster, 1986), esp. chap. 5; Gerkin, *Prophetic Pastoral Practice: A Christian Vision of Life Together* (Nashville: Abingdon, 1991).

[45]S. I. Hayakawa argues that one of the best ways for a communicator's ideas to gain traction with an audience is to "climb down the ladder of abstraction," that is, to be as concrete as possible. For instance, in *Language and Thought in Action*, Hayakawa describes how moving from abstraction to concreteness works. Wealth is an abstract concept. One must ask, "What kind of wealth?" when talking about a subject as broad as wealth. Hayakawa climbs down the ladder in order to concretize an abstract concept. A way to describe wealth more concretely would be to talk about assets. To be more specific, one could talk about farm assets or, to be more specific, livestock, or to be more specific, cows, or to be even more specific, "Bessie, the cow." At the top of the ladder is wealth, an abstract concept, and at the bottom of the ladder is "Bessie," a concrete example of what wealth might look like. According to Hayakawa, speaking concretely helps to make abstract ideas more tangible and memorable to one's listeners. See S. I. Hayakawa, *Language: In Thought and Action* (London: George Allen & Unwin, 1964), pp. 84-95.

are discussed, and developments from improvisational and intercultural theory.

In my conclusion, we will examine why an improvisational-intercultural homiletic such as the one I have proposed will become more rather than less important to the US church context in the future, I suggest possibilities for further research, and I describe the dispositional commitments of crossover preachers.

Before arriving at this destination, however, at least two questions must be asked: *Why Taylor?* and *Why crossover preaching?* These are the questions we answer in the first chapter and to which we now turn.

1

GARDNER C. TAYLOR

CASE STUDY IN CROSSOVER PREACHING

The believer standing where Jesus stands
is not someone who can only be "at home" in a specific
bit of this worldly territory. He or she has become a
person at home everywhere and nowhere.

ROWAN WILLIAMS, *Christ on Trial*

◆

The venue was Abyssinian Baptist Church in New York in 1960; the gathering was a regional Baptist Ministers Conference; and the occasion was a fundraiser for the Martin Luther King Defense Fund. White and nonwhite clergy and laypeople gathered there because they wanted to raise $10,000 to cover expenses for King's legal defense in Alabama. Dr. Taylor, knowing that some in the audience had pockets deep enough to cover King's legal fees, aware that King's name was well known and widely regarded, took the podium and said the following to those gathered for the fundraiser, "I feel like a mosquito in a nudist colony. I know what I'm here for, but I don't know where to start." The place erupted in laughter, and the financial goal was met.

This story provides a brief snapshot into what makes Taylor a unique case study in crossover preaching: his attunement to space, attentiveness to listeners, capacity for humor, and rhetorical timing. But the actual claim of this book is that Taylor was more than just a good joke teller or public speaker. His contemporary significance to homiletics centers on two proficiencies in particular that mark him out as a forerunner, a harbinger of preaching's future: *improvisational proficiency and intercultural proficiency.* These proficiencies are not only neglected in historical-homiletical assessments of Taylor but, of greater import to homiletics, they are the same proficiencies that preachers and homileticians need now more than ever to serve a church with an intercultural future here in the United States.

At least two questions are worth considering at the outset of this chapter: *Why choose Gardner C. Taylor?* and *Was Gardner C. Taylor really a crossover preacher?*

As to the first: Is studying a preacher from a bygone era worth so much time and energy, especially if the aim is to chart a course for the future? Perhaps an analysis of Taylor's preaching is better suited to an honorific entry in an encyclopedia of preaching or a journal entry in a church history periodical. Moreover, is not the setting for his preaching ministry anachronistic? A number of signs point to this conclusion. Gone is the age of building neo-Gothic church cathedrals. Generally speaking, congregations in the United States no longer build cathedral-like structures as Harry Emerson Fosdick did when he built the Riverside Church with John D. Rockefeller's money, or Taylor did when his congregation rebuilt the Concord Baptist Church of Christ in Brooklyn. While congregations still build large structures today, these buildings look nothing like the neo-Gothic architecture that once exemplified Western-establishment Christendom. Likewise, gone is the heyday of the nationally and internationally prominent radio preacher. Although some preachers today have successful radio ministries, their listening audiences do not rival the national and international audiences who listened to Taylor and other preachers on the *NBC National Radio Pulpit* or *The Art of Living* in the mid-twentieth century.[1] Gone also is the golden age of preaching in New York City—the 1940s and 1950s—when preachers such as Harry Emerson Fosdick, Adam Clayton Powell Jr., Sandy F. Ray, George Buttrick, Ralph W. Sockman, and Paul Scherer

---

[1]For more on the era of radio preaching in the United States in the mid-twentieth century, see Jolyon P. Mitchell, *Visually Speaking: Radio and the Renaissance of Preaching* (Edinburgh: T & T Clark, 1999), pp. 143-74.

were household names in the city and, in some cases, prominent at the national level.[2]

To be sure, the pulpit prince, the neo-Gothic church cathedral, the nationally and internationally prominent radio preacher, and the national preaching circuit that Taylor traveled are long gone. So too are the days of Jim Crow–era segregation, white numerical hegemony, and mainline liberal Protestantism at the controlling centers of US society.[3] So then what does a preacher who belongs to a bygone era contribute to an intercultural church with an intercultural future? The answer lies not in what marks out Taylor's time period as a product of the past; rather, it lies in what distinguishes Taylor in the present from the other pulpit princes of his day. *Taylor was an improvisational-intercultural preacher who lived ahead of his time, a harbinger of crossover preaching proficiency.*

This leads to the second question—*Was Gardner C. Taylor really a "crossover preacher"?* Did he engage with and account for difference? Do not the data suggest otherwise? How can one claim that Taylor was an improvisational-intercultural preacher who crossed borders of racial and ecumenical difference when Concord Baptist, the church he served for forty-two years, was more than 98 percent African American during his tenure there? If Taylor was both improvisational and intercultural, then why wasn't Concord more racially and ethnically diverse when he was pastor? Wouldn't a preacher with a racially and ethnically diverse congregation be a more suitable alternative? If we confined the list of candidates to New York City, more recent names would come to mind, such as James Forbes during his tenure at the Riverside Church, or Jim Cymbala at the Brooklyn Tabernacle Church. These two churches are more diverse than Concord was, and these two pastors were and are

---

[2]For Taylor's discussion of these preachers, see "Gardner Calvin Taylor: Oral History Memoir, Interview 3," interview by Joel C. Gregory, Baylor University Institute for Oral History, March 17, 2008, p. 19. For a survey of the preaching ministries of Fosdick, Scherer, Sockman, and Buttrick, see William B. Lawrence, *Sundays in New York: Pulpit Theology at the Crest of the Protestant Mainstream, 1930–1955* (Lanham, MD: Scarecrow, 1996).

[3]In an interview with Touré, African American writer and producer Greg Tate comments specifically on changes in white numerical hegemony. As Tate observes, "whiteness is becoming less relevant as a marker of power, authority, and civilization." See Touré, *Who's Afraid of Post-Blackness? What It Means to Be Black Now* (New York: Free Press, 2011), p. 216.

committed to diversity and inclusion. Is Taylor the best person on whom to confer the crossover preacher designation?

Another problem arises when we use crossover language and decouple it from the contexts in which Taylor crossed over. When one considers examples of crossing over such as Taylor's broadcasts on the *NBC National Radio Pulpit*, his involvement on the board of education in New York City, his presidency of the local chapter of the National Council of Churches, and his delivery of the Beecher Lectures at Yale in 1976, all of which were predominantly white organizations at the time, *Would these data support my claim that Taylor crossed over boundaries of difference, or would they support a counterclaim that predominantly white organizations crossed over boundaries of difference in reaching out to Taylor?* Who is doing the crossing over, and why are they doing it? Is it predominantly white organizations, Taylor, or both? Who was being improvisationally and interculturally proficient: an African American preacher deciding to participate in predominantly white organizations, or white organizations asking an African American preacher to work alongside them?

The question as to whether whites embodied improvisational-intercultural proficiency is indeed a fascinating one. Perhaps the answer is yes. Perhaps no. How can we know for sure? Do we know the motivations among whites at NBC, the NCC, the New York City School Board, or at Yale? Can we know? Were their motivations guided by a desire for friendship, veiled forms of racism and tokenism, or a combination of both? Are there data that support or refute a conclusion in one of these directions? Other questions arise concerning majority/minority power differentials, giving and receiving hospitality, and structural and systemic change. Although an investigation into these questions and others would no doubt be beneficial, it is also beyond the scope of this project. The question under consideration for this book is *not* whether white organizations were embodying improvisational-intercultural proficiency, but whether Taylor was. Likewise, the question is *not* whether the crossover preacher designation can be applied to other preachers besides Taylor, preachers like Forbes, Cymbala, or others; it is whether the designation can be applied to him. The answer to both of these questions is yes. To answer the latter question, the data will be our guide.

As this chapter unfolds, it will become clear why *crossover preacher* is a more-than-apt description for Taylor. This designation will reveal new dimensions to understanding Taylor's preaching, dimensions that have not been previously considered, and it will also frame his contemporary significance to homiletics. If Taylor was an improvisational-intercultural preacher who lived ahead of his time, then an analysis of his preaching not only sheds new light on past understandings of Taylor's contribution *to* preaching; it also illumines a path for the future *of* preaching.

To support my argument and authorize the crossover designation, we will answer three questions in particular: *Who is Gardner C. Taylor? Why choose Taylor as a case study in crossover preaching? What is an intercultural-improvisational homiletic?* First, I provide a brief biographical sketch of Taylor designed to introduce the reader to his life and ministry. Second, I provide data to support my thesis that Taylor was a crossover preacher. Third, I delimit the key terms in the model I propose (e.g., What do I mean by *improvisational?* What do I mean by *intercultural?*) so as to provide parameters for the crossover designation, and I interface these key terms with current homiletical literature. Our answer to the third question will demonstrate that, although some important homiletical literature has already been written, much work remains.

QUESTION 1: WHO IS GARDNER C. TAYLOR?

Gardner Calvin Taylor was born on June 18, 1918, in Baton Rouge, Louisiana. He was the only child of a well-known Baptist preacher, the Reverend Washington ("Wash") Monroe Taylor, and his well-educated wife, Selina Gesell Taylor. Washington Taylor served as pastor at one of the largest churches in Louisiana, the Mt. Zion Baptist Church in Baton Rouge, and he was the vice president-at-large of the National Baptist Convention, U.S.A., Inc. (NBC).[4] Despite not having finished high

---

[4]Washington Taylor's position as vice president-at-large in the National Baptist Convention signaled the beginning of a long connection between the Taylor family and Martin Luther King Jr.'s family. King's grandfather, A. D. Williams, was the treasurer of that same convention, and he and Wash Taylor were good friends. As a result, Williams's son-in-law, Martin Luther King Sr., preached at Wash Taylor's church in Louisiana. Thus Taylor's friendship with Martin and with his family was an inherited friendship dating back to the 1920s. See "Gardner Calvin Taylor: Oral History Memoir, Interview 2," interview by Joel C. Gregory, Baylor University Institute for Oral History, March 17, 2008, p. 14.

school, Taylor's father was well read and widely respected, and his preaching ministry extended "far beyond the bounds of his local church."[5] Moreover, he had a gift for pulpit eloquence. "I do not know where my father got it," Taylor recounts, "but there was a peculiar construction of language with which I think he was born."[6] In *African American Preaching: The Contribution of Dr. Gardner C. Taylor*, Gerald Lamont Thomas notes, "This father-son relationship became a cornerstone in the personal development and faith of Gardner Taylor."[7] Years of listening to Sunday morning sermons from a highly skilled preacher—even if he happens to be your father—do not hurt one's chances for becoming a skilled preacher. When Taylor's father died in 1931, he was only thirteen.

His mother Selina was a bright woman whom he described as having "an almost intimate feeling for the transactions of Scripture."[8] She was also well read and passed on to her son an abiding love for the English language.[9] During Taylor's early years, his mother did not work outside the home. However, this arrangement changed after her husband died. For financial reasons, she took a job as a public schoolteacher in order to produce income for the family. In an era of segregated schools, she worked at the all-black Perkins Road School and, with her gone all day, Dr. Taylor's great-aunt Gerty moved in to help raise him.[10] Those days

---

[5]Timothy George, "Introduction: Honor to Whom Honor Is Due," in *Our Sufficiency Is of God: Essays on Preaching in Honor of Gardner C. Taylor*, ed. Timothy George, James Earl Massey, and Robert Smith Jr. (Macon, GA: Mercer University Press, 2010), p. x.

[6]"Gardner Calvin Taylor: Oral History Memoir, Interview 1," Interview by Joel C. Gregory, Baylor University Institute for Oral History, January 22, 2007, pp. 2-3.

[7]Gerald Lamont Thomas, *African American Preaching: The Contribution of Dr. Gardner C. Taylor* (New York: Peter Lang, 2004), p. 84.

[8]"Gardner Calvin Taylor: Oral History Memoir, Interview 1," p. 2.

[9]Taylor describes how both his parents shaped his love for language. Although his father had not finished high school and his mother had not finished college, he explains that they had a "natural feel for the essential music of the English language wedded to an intimate and emotional affection for the great transactions of the Scriptures." See Gardner C. Taylor, *How Shall They Preach? The Lyman Beecher Lectures and Five Lenten Sermons* (Elgin, IL: Progressive Baptist Publishing House, 1977), p. 13.

[10]Gerald Lamont Thomas describes the history and nature of Taylor's relationship with his great-aunt Gerty in the following way: "After the death of his father, a great aunt, Miss Gerty, moved in to assist with the raising of the precocious lad. Taylor described her as a rough-speaking little woman who virtually 'ruled' their neighborhood, which was white and black. Outside of his father, she was the only one who could keep young Gardner straight. 'She saw a little meanness in me, and did not mind or excuse laying her hands on me.' Later, a foster sister, Theresa, came to live with them and helped his aunt and mother care for Gardner and persons who roomed at their home." See Thomas, *African American Preaching*, p. 82.

were challenging, as he recounted: "We were land poor; we had some land but no money and the land was not worth anything back then. She [his mother] had to go to work and she did, supporting the two of us [Taylor and Aunt Gerty]."[11]

Dr. Taylor's formative years might be described as a juxtaposition of constraints and contingencies, restrictions and open doors. He grew up during Jim Crow segregation in the South. His mother received a lower salary than white schoolteachers. They were poor, and throughout his childhood he attended underresourced, nonaccredited, all-black schools. Even so, despite segregationist laws at the local, state, and national levels, the street where he grew up was integrated. People of Italian, German, Cajun, and African descent lived alongside one another and, for the most part, got along well. To use Taylor's words, in this neighborhood he received "early training in race relations."[12] His father's church attracted upwardly mobile African American educators and community leaders, *and* it attracted old, poor people, some of whom had been former slaves.[13] At one point, Taylor's grades were so low that one of his teachers described him as a "good mind going to waste."[14] At another point, in fourth grade, he took a statewide IQ test and received "the top IQ rating of any elementary child, *black or white*, in Louisiana during the mid-1920s."[15] By the time he graduated, he had turned his grades around. He was valedictorian of his class and captain of the football team.

After high school, he received a football scholarship to attend Leland College, an all-black, unaccredited school twelve miles outside Baton Rouge. While at Leland, his vocational plan was to become a lawyer. But all of that changed suddenly. His life was radically altered on one day in particular when, during his senior year, he was in a near-fatal car accident. He writes: "My quick brush with death that afternoon . . .

---

[11] Thomas, *African American Preaching*, p. 83.
[12] "Gardner Calvin Taylor: Oral History Memoir, Interview 1," p. 2.
[13] Timothy George describes the dynamic between Taylor and former slaves in the community: "As a young man, Gardner Taylor knew personally many of those who had survived the dark night of slavery. Their stories of heartbreak and hope, of struggling but not losing, inspired and informed Taylor's view of the world and gave him a social conscience that would shape his life's work." See George, "Introduction: Honor to Whom Honor Is Due," p. x.
[14] Thomas, *African American Preaching*, pp. 95-96.
[15] Ibid., pp. 85-86 (emphasis added).

turned me imperiously toward consideration of the meaning of my life
and the ultimate purpose of human existence."[16] It was then that he
answered the call to pastoral ministry just as his father had done before
him. At the recommendation of Dr. J. A. Bacoats, the president of
Leland College, he enrolled at the Oberlin (Ohio) Graduate School of
Theology in 1937.

At Oberlin, Taylor spent countless late nights in the library reading
homiletics periodicals; these journals contained sermons by nationally known preachers such as Frederick Norwood, Paul Scherer,
George Buttrick, and Harry Emerson Fosdick.[17] Long before Taylor
was regarded as a "great preacher," he read the sermons of great
preachers. At Oberlin, he also met his future wife, Laura Scott, to
whom he was married for fifty-four years before she died in a bus
accident in 1995. When he completed his degree in May 1940, Taylor
became only the third African American to graduate from the School
of Theology at Oberlin.[18]

Before becoming the senior pastor at Concord, Taylor served at three
different churches: part time at Bethany Baptist in Oberlin, during
seminary (1938–1941), full time at Beulah Baptist in New Orleans (1941–
1943), and full time at Mt. Zion Baptist in Baton Rouge (1943–1947), the
same church his father had served years earlier. In each place, he
preached as much as possible. Especially at Mt. Zion, he built a solid
reputation as a pastor and preacher. He gained a large following among
students and professors at Southern University (an all-black school in
Baton Rouge), he began a radio ministry, and he either preached or
delivered addresses at a variety of church services, school chapels, and
graduations. Commenting on the Baton Rouge years, Gerald Lamont
Thomas observes: "The preaching success of Taylor along with his in-

---

[16]Gardner C. Taylor, "Why I Believe There Is a God," in *Why I Believe There Is a God; Sixteen Essays
by Negro Clergymen*, ed. Howard Thurman (Chicago: Johnson, 1965), p. 86. More than likely,
theologian James E. Loder would describe a traumatic event like this as a "transforming moment."
See James E. Loder, *The Transforming Moment* (Colorado Springs: Helmers & Howard, 1989).

[17]"Gardner Calvin Taylor: Oral History Memoir, Interview 1," p. 20.

[18]In an interview with Joel C. Gregory, Taylor recounted that he was only the second or third
Louisiana Baptist (in the National Baptist Convention) *ever* to attend seminary. The opportunities
for African Americans to receive a theological education, especially in the South, were rare. See
"Gardner Calvin Taylor: Oral History Memoir, Interview 3," p. 15.

stant popularity took the Mt. Zion congregation to higher heights, as the largest church in the city."[19]

Taylor also received more regional and national exposure. He was considered a rising star in the NBC.[20] In September 1946, while Taylor was attending an NBC meeting in Atlanta, Rev. Dr. James B. Adams, the pastor of the prestigious Concord Baptist Church of Christ, one of the oldest and largest black Baptist churches in Brooklyn, approached him and said, "I want you to preach the centennial celebration of our church."[21] Shortly after this invitation, just a few weeks later, Dr. Adams died tragically and unexpectedly. Still reeling from this loss but wanting to celebrate Adams's memory, Concord's leaders wanted to honor their pastor's last wishes by inviting Taylor to preach at their centennial celebration in 1947. When Taylor came to Concord, his sermon was so well received that he was invited back twice more that year and, in 1948, they called him to be their next pastor. At the state convention of the NBC in Louisiana that same year, Taylor announced to the delegates, "God has called me to preach at the crossroads of the world. I must go."[22] His church in Baton Rouge was devastated by the decision, as was his mother. During his farewell sermon, the church had standing room only, and radios throughout the black community were tuned to his weekly radio program. One of the black community's favorite sons in Baton Rouge was heading north.

When he and Mrs. Taylor arrived in New York in 1948, Concord already had five thousand members. It had a large facility, a proud history, several ministry programs, a solid record on civil rights, and a long tradition of preaching pastors. As Timothy George puts it, Taylor stepped into "one of the most prestigious pulpits in the country."[23] Although this might intimidate most thirty-year-old ministers, Taylor recounts: "The more I preached the more they began to trust me and

---

[19]Thomas, *African American Preaching*, p. 96.
[20]He represented the NBC as a delegate to the United Nations in 1945. Also, he preached at the Second Church of Copenhagen during the Seventh Baptist World Congress in Copenhagen, Denmark, in 1947.
[21]The fuller story can be found in Thomas, *African American Preaching*, p. 97.
[22]WGT 1:4.
[23]George, "Introduction: Honor to Whom Honor Is Due," p. xiv.

realize my talents not only as a preacher but also as a pastor."[24] One church congregant named Anna Belle recalled his first sermon at Concord: "When he came that first Sunday morning, he electrified the congregation with his mastery of the English language.... He had us on our feet."[25]

Also, early in his tenure, Taylor became politically active. As church historian Clarence Taylor observes, "Taylor became the most noted black minister in the Democratic Party [in New York]."[26] Most African American ministers in the city were still Republican when Taylor arrived. In addition, eleven months into his pastorate, he was nominated to serve on the local school board in Brooklyn.[27] Then he became the second African American ever to serve on the citywide board of education, and for at least part of his tenure, he was the *only* African American on the board of education.[28] Later, he served as a member of the Commission for Integrated Schools. For a time, he also chaired the Democratic Party in King's County, one of the most powerful county organizations in the United States after Cook County in Chicago.[29] At the same time in Harlem, Adam Clayton Powell Jr. was building a political machine for the Democrats.[30] Taylor and Powell became political allies and good

---

[24] Thomas, *African American Preaching*, p. 98.

[25] "Interview with Anna Belle," in ibid.

[26] Clarence Taylor, *The Black Churches of Brooklyn* (New York: Columbia University Press, 1994), p. 118.

[27] "Concord Pastor Sworn in as School Board Member," *NYAN*, May 7, 1949, p. 7.

[28] In a newspaper article published in 1958, Taylor is described as "the only Negro [*sic*] member of the city's Board of Education." See "Negro Pastor Honored: Legion Post Gives Award to Dr. Taylor of Brooklyn," *NYT*, September 15, 1958.

[29] Edward L. Taylor, "Introduction," WGT 1.

[30] Adam Clayton Powell Jr. was senior pastor of the historic Abyssinian Baptist Church in Harlem from 1938 to 1971. In 1950, Abyssinian had approximately fifteen thousand members. According to journalist Nora Holt, it was the "largest Protestant church in the world." In addition to his responsibilities as pastor, in 1944, Powell Jr. became only the second African American to win a seat in the House of Representatives, a position he held until 1970. In his book *Black Religious Leaders*, Peter J. Paris describes Powell's influence this way: "For over a quarter of a century the names Abyssinian Baptist Church and Adam Clayton Powell Jr., were virtually household terms throughout Black America. In many respects the religious institution and its pastor had come to symbolize the political struggle for racial justice in this country." See Peter J. Paris, *Black Religious Leaders: Conflict in Unity* (Louisville: Westminster John Knox, 1991), p. 152. See also Nora Holt, "Abyssinian Baptist Largest Protestant Church in the World," *NYAN*, December 2, 1950. For more on Powell's life and ministry, see Charles V. Hamilton, *Adam Clayton Powell, Jr.: The Political Biography of an American Dilemma* (New York: Atheneum, 1991); and Adam Clayton Powell Jr., *Adam by Adam: The Autobiography of Adam Clayton Powell, Jr.* (New York: Dial, 1971).

friends. Taylor would attend civil rights functions at Abyssinian Baptist (where Powell was pastor), and he lent him his public support, even when the two disagreed over Powell's support of Dwight D. Eisenhower's reelection bid.[31]

Taylor's church was growing larger and his influence expanding. Many of Taylor's constituents in Brooklyn saw promise in him and encouraged him to run for higher political office. However, according to Taylor, when his wife informed him one day that his preaching was "getting very thin," he decided *against* running for political office.[32]

In point of fact, there were likely various reasons why Taylor chose not to seek public office. One possible reason was that his mother chided him for becoming too entangled politically. "I told you never to get involved in politics," she exclaimed.[33] That his close friend Sandy F. Ray, an African American pastor at Cornerstone Baptist Church, five miles down the road from Concord, had decided to opt out of seeking public office after experiencing the double-edged sword of political involvement on several occasions may also have influenced Taylor. Timothy George suggests that Taylor decided early on in his pastorate that he could "make a greater difference in the lives of his people through his ministry of influence as their pastor" than he could as a politician.[34]

In a 1995 interview with Michael Eric Dyson, Taylor acknowledged that his decision not to seek political office meant that he would have to make peace with his ministry not being as visible to the general public. "I recognized early that the [kind of] work I do is not attention-grabbing," he said.[35] In the same article, James Earl Massey suggests a possible

---

[31]Referring to attempts to discipline Powell after his Eisenhower endorsement, Hamilton writes, "The Reverend Gardner C. Taylor of New York joined a group from that city in telegrams to the New York political leaders saying: 'The Negro community may not agree with Congressman Powell but will look upon this [attempt to impose party discipline] as an anti-Negro move.' They threatened retaliation at the polls in future elections." See Hamilton, *Adam Clayton Powell, Jr.*, p. 277.

[32]George, "Introduction: Honor to Whom Honor Is Due," p. xv.

[33]Taylor's mother's quotation is found in the essay "The Pastor and Political Realities" in WGT 5:78. This essay originally appeared in Samuel D. Proctor and Gardner C. Taylor, *We Have This Ministry: The Heart of the Pastor's Vocation* (Valley Forge, PA: Judson Press, 1996).

[34]George, "Introduction: Honor to Whom Honor Is Due," p. xv.

[35]Michael Eric Dyson, "Gardner Taylor: Poet Laureate of the Pulpit," *Christian Century* 112, no. 1 (January 4, 1995): 14.

explanation why Taylor's ministry was neither politically impressive nor "attention-grabbing." He writes: "Taylor has been stuck with the church. He has been busy handling the themes of the gospel and seeking to affect society in ways that are consonant with the gospel purpose. This is not newsworthy like leading a sit in."[36]

On October 2, 1952, Taylor faced perhaps his biggest leadership challenge: Concord's church building was destroyed by fire. In a personal conversation with Dr. Cleophus J. LaRue, a homiletics professor at Princeton, Taylor recounted that the incident took place in the early (predawn) hours of a Sunday morning and that the smoke billowing from the church could be seen all the way from Queens.[37] In just one night, one of Brooklyn's oldest and largest black Baptist congregations went from being prominent and successful to being homeless. Fortunately, churches in the New York metropolitan area sprang into action on hearing this news. Within three days of the incident, fifteen Protestant churches and leaders of other faiths not only offered their condolences and prayer support, but also promised to provide financial help for Concord to rebuild. It was ecumenical cooperation at its best.[38] Soon after the fire, Taylor held a meeting in his home and told his congregation: "We are going to go forward because I have a community of baptized believers who believe in me and in what I have said in the four years of my preaching here and with them and their faith in God and my leadership, we cannot fail."[39]

For four years, Concord remained without a building; they rented space. It was a long period for a large congregation, but the church persevered. On April 1, 1956, they marched into their new $1.7 million facility at 833 Marcy Avenue. One of Taylor's closest friends in Brooklyn, Dr. Sandy F. Ray of Cornerstone Baptist, was the guest preacher that day.[40]

---

[36]See ibid.

[37]Recounted in a personal conversation with Cleophus J. LaRue in January 2014.

[38]"Aid Offered to Church," *NYT*, October 4, 1952, p. 12.

[39]"Interview with Anna Belle."

[40]Sandy F. Ray was the pastor of Cornerstone Baptist Church in Brooklyn, New York, from 1944 until his death in 1979. Not only was he one of Taylor's closest friends, but he also had a reputation as one of the great preachers of his day. Describing Ray's impact on Cornerstone, Milton K. Curry writes: "He transformed it into one of the truly great churches of the nation while remaining active in politics and developing a close personal friendship with top government officials."

It was a defining moment for the church and for Taylor as their leader. On the occasion of his ten-year anniversary in 1958, the local paper described him as a "born leader" who "towered as a giant" in the rebuilding of Concord, a man with high "esteem among his members and the citizens of Brooklyn and New York."[41] In the new building, Taylor brought Concord to new heights. By January 1960, its membership was tallied at 13,500 people, a net growth of 8,500 over a twelve-year span.

Taylor's ministry at Concord was both exciting and challenging in the decades from 1960 until his retirement in 1990. Although he held no political office, he publicly supported and raised money for Martin Luther King Jr. and was a mentor to him while King was a student in Boston. King looked to Taylor as a role model and father figure.[42] The two families vacationed together in Jamaica, Puerto Rico, and elsewhere.[43] One of the biggest challenges he faced (besides the Concord fire of 1952) was a 1961 battle with J. H. Jackson over the presidency of the NBC. According to Gerald Lamont Thomas, J. H. Jackson was at one time "the most powerful Black man in the United States."[44] However, Jackson was also vulnerable to the Taylor constituency on account of his conservative views, opposition to Martin Luther King Jr., and soft stance on civil rights. In 1961, Jackson defeated Taylor in the battle for the presidency of the NBC, but did so amid widespread confusion at the time the votes were cast and accusations of vote tampering. When Jackson was awarded the presidency, and the moderate

---

When Taylor delivered Ray's funeral eulogy in 1979, he referred to Ray as a "president of preaching" and a "crown prince of the pulpit." "This pulpit was his throne," Taylor said, "and he made it to ring with good news and glad tidings." Recalling the quality of his preaching, Taylor said, "It was hard to tell whether one heard music half spoken or speech half sung. And when the glad thunders of that voice reached its climactic theme, the heavens seemed to open and we could see the Lord God on his throne." See Milton K. Curry Jr., "Foreword," in Sandy F. Ray, *Journeying Through a Jungle* (Nashville: Broadman, 1979), p. 12. See also WGT 4:140-41.

[41]"Taylor Completes Decade at Concord," *NYAN*, May 31, 1958, p. 20.

[42]As Richard Lischer notes, "What King and many young preachers besides would have learned from Taylor was the genius of channeling evangelical doctrine and the great stories of the Bible into socially progressive and prophetic utterance." See Richard Lischer, "Gardner Taylor," in *Concise Encyclopedia of Preaching*, ed. William H. Willimon and Richard Lischer (Louisville: Westminster John Knox, 1995), p. 466.

[43]"Gardner Calvin Taylor: Oral History Memoir, Interview 3," p. 15.

[44]Thomas, *African American Preaching*, p. 100. See also Taylor Branch, *Parting the Waters: America in the King Years, 1954–63* (New York: Simon and Schuster, 1988), pp. 335-39, 502-7.

delegates who supported Taylor were unable to find recourse for action within the NBC, they decided to form a new denomination: the Progressive National Baptist Convention, Inc. (PNBC). Taylor served as president of the PNBC from 1966 to 1969, and he influenced the denomination to such an extent that some still refer to him as the "Father of the PNBC."[45]

While maintaining a vibrant preaching ministry at Concord, Taylor and his wife established the Concord Elementary School for children grades one through six. Drawing no salary, Mrs. Taylor served with distinction as the school's president for thirty-two years. The Taylors also oversaw the construction of a 121-bed nursing home, a seniors' residence, and the Concord Credit Union, with assets exceeding $1.8 million. They established a million-dollar "Christfund Endowment" for African American children and for community uplift.[46] On February 5, 1995, when his wife died in a bus accident, Taylor was heartbroken. A year and a half later, on July 30, 1996, he married his second wife, Phillis Strong, a woman whom he had baptized at Concord fifty years earlier in 1946. Taylor has a daughter from his first marriage named Martha Taylor La-Croix, who lives in California and is a professional vocalist.

Taylor retired from Concord in 1990 after serving as its pastor for forty-two years. By then, he had cemented his place as one of the premier preachers of the twentieth century. At its height, the church had over fourteen thousand members, though active membership was closer to five thousand when he retired.[47] In the 1990s and 2000s, he continued preaching and teaching in churches and seminaries both nationally and internationally. In August 2000, Taylor received the Presidential Medal of Freedom, one of the highest honors a civilian can receive, from then-president Bill Clinton. He received numerous awards, distinctions, and honorary degrees, and until recently, his name was frequently included

---

[45]Thomas, *African American Preaching*, p. 101.

[46]Ibid., p. 100.

[47]A *NYT* article published in 1990 offers the following description of Concord Baptist Church in Brooklyn: "With about 5,000 active members, Concord Baptist operates a credit union worth $1.8 million, a 121-bed nursing home, a senior citizens' residence, an elementary school and a clothing exchange." See "Brooklyn's Exceptional Preacher," *NYT*, June 30, 1990, last modified January 22, 2009, www.nytimes.com/1990/06/30/opinion/brooklyn-s-exceptional-preacher.html.

on the lists of top preachers in the English-speaking world. He died on Easter Sunday, April 5, 2015, in Durham, North Carolina.

QUESTION 2: WHY CHOOSE TAYLOR AS A CASE STUDY IN CROSSOVER PREACHING?

The second question is, *What makes Taylor an ideal case study in crossover preaching?* Was it his historical contribution? None would deny that he was an important figure in the history of twentieth-century preaching. In 1979, *Time* magazine conferred on him the title "dean of the nation's black preachers."[48] In 1996, Baylor University named him as one of the twelve "most effective preachers in the English-speaking world."[49] In 1997, Henry H. Mitchell, a dean of black homileticians in his own right, described Taylor as "the Prince of the *American* pulpit."[50] More recently, in 2011, Cleophus J. LaRue claimed that Taylor is "regarded by many as one of the greatest preachers of the twentieth century."[51] While the category "great preacher" is problematic theologically, as a sociological or media term, its cultural currency is undeniable. Few would question Taylor's status as one of the great preachers of the last hundred years and, therefore, worthy of study.

Perhaps the reason to study Taylor is that there are still spaces open for further homiletical reflection. Standard encyclopedias of preaching are somewhat cursory. In Hughes Oliphant Old's seven-volume work on the history of preaching, Taylor only gets two sentences.[52] In O. C. Edwards's 870-page history of preaching, Taylor gets three pages.[53] Edwards and Old are not intentionally neglectful of minoritized preaching in the United States or abroad. Both of them devote an entire chapter to the history of African American preaching in the United States. The main

---

[48]"American Preaching: A Dying Art?," *Time*, December 31, 1979, p. 67.

[49]Study conducted by Baylor University. See "Baylor Names the 12 Most Effective Preachers," *Baylor University Media Communications*, last modified April 23, 2012, www.baylor.edu/media-communications/news.php?action=story&story=1036.

[50]Henry H. Mitchell, "African American Preaching," *Interpretation* 51, no. 4 (October 1997): 372 (emphasis original).

[51]Cleophus J. LaRue, *I Believe I'll Testify: The Art of African American Preaching* (Louisville: Westminster John Knox, 2011), p. 17.

[52]See Hughes Oliphant Old, *The Reading and Preaching of the Scriptures in the Worship of the Christian Church: The Modern Age* (Grand Rapids: Eerdmans, 2007), 6:356, 85.

[53]O. C. Edwards, *A History of Preaching* (Nashville: Abingdon, 2004), pp. 714-16, 721.

issue is that their commentaries on Taylor are cursory. Besides, other homileticians have taken up the baton through sustained homiletical reflection. Since Taylor's retirement from Concord in 1990, four major scholarly works have been written: L. Susan Bond's work on Taylor and eschatology, Jerry M. Carter's work on homiletical sacramentality, Gerald Lamont Thomas's dissertation and subsequent book on rhetorical theory, and a recent study by Alfonza W. Fullwood on Taylor's theology/theory of preaching and the implications for homiletical pedagogy.[54]

Even so, there is still important work left to do. To date, no one has written a definitive biography on Taylor. Moreover, in 2008, Taylor donated the bulk of his sermons and other writings to the Robert W. Woodruff Library of the Atlanta University Center. This collection houses 1,148 manuscripts of sermons, lectures, speeches, eulogies, and prayers, but is primarily made up of sermons. Most of these materials were previously inaccessible and are now available for analysis.[55]

But one could take a contrarian point of view in light of these data. Not every preacher has had four dissertations written about him. Standard encyclopedias of preaching may not do him justice, but at least they mention him rather than neglect him altogether. Also, in 2010, homileticians took an important step toward further reflection by publishing a *Festschrift* in Taylor's honor.[56] Edward L. Taylor, the editor of the six-volume *Words of Gardner Taylor* series, is working on a definitive biography of Taylor's life. Although there is important work left to do, important work has already been done and will be done.

---

[54]See L. Susan Bond, "To Hear the Angel's Wings: Apocalyptic Language and the Formation of Moral Community with Reference to the Sermons of Gardner C. Taylor" (PhD diss., Vanderbilt University, 1996); Jerry M. Carter, "The Audible Sacrament: The Sacramentality of Gardner C. Taylor's Preaching" (PhD diss., Drew University, 2007); Gerald Lamont Thomas, "African American Preaching: The Contribution of Gardner C. Taylor" (PhD diss, Southern Baptist Theological Seminary, 1993); Gerald Lamont Thomas, *African American Preaching: The Contribution of Dr. Gardner C. Taylor* (New York: Peter Lang, 2004); and Alfonza W. Fullwood, "A Study of Gardner C. Taylor's Theology of Preaching as a Decisive Factor Shaping His Theory of Preaching: Implications for Homiletical Pedagogy" (PhD diss., Southeastern Baptist Theological Seminary, 2012).

[55]The Woodruff Library works in partnership with the Interdenominational Theological Center (ITC) to preserve Taylor's legacy in written, audio, and video formats. In 2007, the ITC opened the Gardner C. Taylor Archives and Preaching Laboratory. It is a multimedia teaching and learning lab in which researchers can access audio and video media content associated with Taylor, videoconference, and take advantage of other teaching and learning technologies.

[56]See George, Massey, and Smith Jr., *Our Sufficiency Is of God.*

That Taylor was historically significant to twentieth-century preaching and that there could still be gaps in homiletical reflection are not the *primary* reasons for choosing him as an ideal case study. The main reason for choosing Taylor over against other exemplars, and the reason for choosing a different trajectory than other major studies of Taylor, is as follows: unlike most of his contemporaries, he was a crossover preacher whose improvisational-intercultural approach anticipates the needs of twenty-first-century preaching. This reason reveals his *contemporary* significance to homiletics.

In addition to the crossover image, another pertinent image of Taylor is that of a *forerunner*—a pioneer—whose historical contribution to twentieth-century preaching has been widely noted, but whose contemporary significance to twenty-first-century homiletics has not yet been sufficiently considered. Taylor was a forerunner or harbinger in this sense: he was improvisational and intercultural before these categories had wide currency. Prior to the popularization of academic discussions about improvisation in performance studies, ethnomusicology, and some corners of homiletics, Taylor was already an *improvisateur*. Prior to academic discussions about interculturalism in education and communication theory, Taylor already demonstrated skill in what theorists refer to as "intercultural competence"—a skill that will receive more attention in chapter four. While it is impossible to fully capture or describe a decades-long, multifaceted preaching ministry, what one can do is this: enlist Taylor as a discussion partner in working toward a model of preaching that recognizes his contemporary significance while also making an original contribution to the field of homiletics. As it is my conviction that preachers and homileticians must learn to be *both* improvisational and intercultural, Taylor's approach is well suited to our aims.

But how do we know that Taylor was a forerunner and pioneer, a man ahead of his time? What is it specifically that makes him an ideal case study? How do we know that *he* was a crossover preacher? Let us examine six possible reasons.

1. Providing leadership in predominantly white organizations: Secular and religious. One way that Taylor crossed over racial divides was through taking on leadership positions in predominantly white organizations. Some of these organizations were secular. As stated earlier, he served on the local school board in Brooklyn starting in 1949, on the citywide board of education later in the 1950s (where, during his tenure, he was the only African American on the board), and as a member of the Commission for Integrated Schools. In these specific leadership positions, Taylor often spoke out as the lone minority voice in a white majority-run organization, and he usually used that voice to advocate for integrated, equal opportunities in education for both white and black children.

Taylor also took on leadership in predominantly white *religious* organizations. Even if these organizations were becoming integrationist before he joined them, it is still significant that he provided leadership rather than participation. In the early 1950s, he was the president of the Brooklyn Division of the Protestant Council of New York City.[57] Then, in 1958, he became the first African American to serve as the president of the Protestant Council of Churches in New York, a local branch of the National Council of Churches.[58]

In 1959, Taylor took on leadership in a different capacity when he became the first African American ever to preach for the *NBC National Radio Pulpit* broadcast.[59] He began preaching for NBC on July 5, 1959, and was the preacher-in-residence there for thirteen consecutive weeks.[60] In doing so, Taylor added his name to an esteemed company of preachers on the broadcast. The program started in the late 1920s with Harry Emerson Fosdick, the pastor of the Riverside Church in Manhattan, a man whose radio ministry had at one time reached two million people na-

---

[57]In a *NYT* article written in 1953, journalist George Dugan refers to Taylor as the "former president of the Brooklyn Division of the Protestant Council of New York City." See George Dugan, "Churches Scored as Race Conscious," *NYT*, May 26, 1953, p. 27.

[58]See "Negro [*sic*] Pastor Honored: Legion Post Gives Award to Dr. Taylor of Brooklyn," *NYT*, September 15, 1958, p. 19.

[59]Gerald Lamont Thomas writes: "From 1959 through 1960 he [Taylor] served as the first black minister to preach weekly for the National Pulpit Radio Broadcast." See Thomas, *African American Preaching*, p. 100. Also, in an April 1959 article in *The Afro-American*, the columnist writes: "Dr. Taylor will be the first colored [*sic*] person to serve on this famous religious program during its 31-year history." See "Dr. Taylor Will Preach on Radio," *The Washington Afro-American*, April 21, 1959, p. 7.

[60]For the announcement in the local Brooklyn newspaper that Taylor was preaching for NBC, see "Dr. Taylor on Radio Pulpit for 13 Weeks," *NYAN*, June 27, 1959, p. 25.

tionally and internationally.[61] Although Taylor only met Fosdick once and did not know him personally, he did get to know some of the other prominent white pastors in the city through the broadcast. Paul Scherer, the well-known Lutheran pastor-preacher, also appeared on the program several times. Taylor's immediate predecessor was Ralph W. Sockman, the nationally known pastor of Christ Church Methodist in Manhattan. When Taylor began at NBC, the program received more than twenty thousand letters per week in connection with the sermons broadcasted.[62] Taylor preached intermittently for various programs on NBC from 1959 to 1970.[63]

2. Building strategic partnerships with white mainline preachers in New York. Early on at Concord, Taylor demonstrated a commitment to building strategic partnerships with white mainline preachers. The timing was also in his favor. He came to New York at a time when white churches were becoming more integrationist. As Taylor recounts, "I came to New York at a very fortunate, blessed time. There was an opening for black participation. And I was a new boy on the block and black, and

---

[61]Keith D. Miller writes: "On a given Sunday he [Fosdick] enjoyed a national and international congregation of well over two million listeners, including Larry Williams and the teenage M. L. King Jr. At times a couple in, say, Iowa would make once-in-a-lifetime trip to New York City to see Babe Ruth or Joe DiMaggio swat a home run and hear their beloved radio minister in person." See Keith D. Miller, *Voice of Deliverance: The Language of Martin Luther King, Jr., and Its Sources* (New York: Free Press, 1992), p. 48. Taylor did not know Fosdick personally, but he did get an opportunity to hear him speak at a luncheon. When Taylor arrived in New York, Fosdick was nearing retirement at Riverside. Fosdick retired in 1955, and Taylor heard him speak at the luncheon after he had finished his tenure at Riverside. In a 1999 interview with Kirk Byron Jones, Taylor comments: "I knew McCracken [pastor of the Riverside Church] but I did not know Fosdick. I heard Fosdick once, but only at a luncheon engagement." See WGT 5:297. In a 1978 lecture delivered at Duke University titled "The Preaching of the Black Patriarchs, Part 2," Taylor indicates his high regard for Fosdick and his ministry: "Dr. Fosdick's years at Riverside did more as far as the pulpit ministry of this country is concerned to liberate the American pulpit, certain segments of it surely, than any other ministry which we have known in this country. Dr. Fosdick has been grievously misunderstood. This man was no ascriptural, antifaith liberal assaulting the great doctrines of the faith. If you really study Dr. Fosdick's work you discover a deep piety and great loyalty to the mighty transactions of the faith. He did see that this was being obscured by a kind of rigid fundamentalism and a kind of inflexible literalism, and he did a great deal to liberate the American pulpit from that." See WGT 5:217.

[62]According to a 1959 newspaper article, Taylor was Sockman's replacement. In the same article, we read: "Each week NBC receives more than 20,000 letters in connection with sermons heard on the program." See "Dr. Taylor Will Preach on Radio," p. 7.

[63]Taylor also preached on another program called *The Art of Living*. The whole first volume of the six-volume The Words of Gardner Taylor series is made up of NBC radio sermons. See WGT 1.

so a lot of invitations came to me that I never would have had otherwise."[64]

Taylor befriended three well-known white pastors in particular through his involvement with the NBC broadcast and with the National Council of Churches: Ralph W. Sockman of Christ Church Methodist, George A. Buttrick of Madison Avenue Presbyterian Church, and Paul E. Scherer of Holy Trinity Lutheran Church.[65] Years earlier, when he was a student at Oberlin, Taylor would read Scherer and Buttrick's sermons in the library. He was only forty-one years old when he started preaching on NBC radio, a generation younger than the white counterparts he admired. On at least one occasion, Taylor referred to Paul E. Scherer as his "preaching idol."[66]

In various lectures, books, and interviews, Taylor makes clear his high regard not only for these three individuals, but also for the other renowned preachers of that day in New York. Taylor also befriended prominent African American preachers such as Sandy F. Ray at Cornerstone Baptist Church and Adam Clayton Powell Jr., the controversial senior pastor at Abyssinian Baptist Church and US congressman.[67] In a 1983 lecture, Taylor refers to all of these New York preachers as "titans" and suggests that they were some of the "best known preachers in America" at the time. He continues: "That I was privileged to be a colleague of this shining company continues to fill me with pride and thankfulness."[68]

Although the original sources reveal that Taylor admired these preachers, they also reveal that Taylor was their colleague rather than their protégé. Although he was young when he arrived in Brooklyn (thirty years old), it is unlikely that he was seen as a novice preacher or a wistful onlooker. Church membership tallies are not always the best indicators of gospel fidelity, but it is illuminating to say the least that

---

[64]"Gardner Calvin Taylor: Oral History Memoir, Interview 2," p. 10.

[65]For an overview of these three men and their ministries as well as an overview of Fosdick's ministry, see Lawrence, *Sundays in New York*.

[66]WGT 5:176.

[67]Taylor also shows regard for Samuel D. Proctor, the man who came after Adam Clayton Powell Jr. Bear in mind that Proctor came later than the other preachers. Proctor began at Abyssinian in the 1970s. The other preachers were already established in New York when Taylor arrived. For Taylor's comments on Proctor, see WGT 5:266-67.

[68]"The Preacher's Trinity of Needs: The Messenger." Lecture delivered in the 1983 Sprinkle Lectures at Atlantic Christian College in Wilson, North Carolina. See WGT 5:264.

Taylor's church membership in the late 1950s—close to 13,500 members—was larger than the memberships at Riverside, Holy Trinity, Christ Church, and Madison Avenue. The only church that was larger at the time was Abyssinian. In other words, Taylor was not an entry-level pastor when he met these men. And he knew it. In a 1983 chapter for the book *Preaching Biblically* he noted that "In my years in the city of New York some of the most notable preachers of our generation have been *my colleagues*, and their memories are still a benediction to me."[69] In other places, he uses the word "mentor" or "idol," but in this particular instance, he uses the word "colleagues." It is likely that he saw himself as a preaching colleague rather than as a neophyte, and as in no way inferior.

The data also support the conclusion that he was a colleague. In a 1996 lecture, Taylor comments almost in passing that he preached with Sockman.[70] Throughout the 1950s, Taylor went on various preaching tours with Buttrick.[71] He never states that he preached with Scherer on the regional and national circuit or that he was a guest preacher at Holy Trinity, but it is not unreasonable to conjecture that he did. Taylor's lectures *are* filled with numerous anecdotes about Scherer, descriptions of Scherer, and quotes from Scherer. It is not uncommon for Taylor to begin a sentence, "Dr. Scherer used to say . . ." Also, on at least one occasion, Taylor recounts something Scherer said to him in a private conversation. When he responded, Scherer offered a witty retort.[72] Clearly the two of them were friends rather than acquaintances.

In addition to his friendships, Taylor also maintained acquaintanceships, including one with Robert McCracken, who succeeded Fosdick at Riverside, and one with Norman Vincent Peale at Marble Collegiate, and he preached as well as lectured at the Riverside Church on several

---

[69]Originally published as Gardner C. Taylor, "Shaping Sermons by the Shape of Text and Preacher," in *Preaching Biblically*, ed. Don M. Wardlaw (Philadelphia: Westminster Press, 1983), pp. 137-52. See also WGT 5:44. Emphasis added.

[70]Taylor comments: "Ralph Sockman was at Christ Church. I remember many telling statements he made, but we were preaching once up in Rochester." Then he shares a personal anecdote about Sockman. See "Great Preachers Remembered." Lecture originally delivered in 1996 at the E. K. Bailey Conference on Expository Preaching in Dallas, Texas. See WGT 5:115.

[71]In a 2008 interview, he recounts: "I preached along with him [Buttrick] in the East. There was a Lenten circuit in the east: Syracuse, Buffalo, Rochester, all around." See "Gardner Calvin Taylor: Oral History Memoir, Interview 2," p. 10.

[72]WGT 5:93-94.

occasions.[73] For instance, on July 31, 1960, when Taylor was running for the presidency of the National Baptist Convention, he preached at Riverside as the "guest of Dr. Robert J. McCracken."[74] In a 1999 interview with Kirk Byron Jones, Taylor also indicates that he was acquainted with the well-known Jewish theologian Abraham Heschel and the prominent Protestant theologian Reinhold Niebuhr.[75] No doubt Taylor was a key figure in the fraternity of preachers and theologians in New York during that time period.

We also know that Taylor preached at predominantly white churches when he was the president of the Protestant Council of Churches in New York in 1959. According to Gerald Lamont Thomas, Taylor preached "either the Easter morning sermon or the Christmas sermon in the pulpits of council members' churches for many years."[76] Since Scherer's church was a member of the Protestant Council of Churches, we can infer that Taylor almost certainly preached at Holy Trinity.

The fact that Taylor maintained strategic partnerships with white preachers does not mean that he did not have close relationships with African American preachers. I have already mentioned his friendship with Sandy F. Ray at the nearby Cornerstone Baptist, five miles down the street, his mentoring role in the life of Martin Luther King Jr., his friendship with Adam Clayton Powell Jr., and his willingness to raise money for him. This is to say nothing of his connections in the NBC and later in the PNBC. It is not that Taylor said yes to friendships with white preachers and no to friendships with black preachers, but that he said yes to both. Taylor was willing to cross racial boundaries during a turbulent time in race relations in the United States. He added his voice to

---

[73]In a 2008 interview with Joel Gregory, Taylor talks about his personal friendship with Norman Vincent Peale. See "Gardner Calvin Taylor: Oral History Memoir, Interview 2," p. 10. In a 1999 interview with Kirk Byron Jones, Taylor says, "I knew McCracken, but I did not know Fosdick." See WGT 5:297.

[74]"Dr. Taylor Speaking at Riverside Ch.," *NYAN*, July 30, 1960, p. 22. In addition to the sermon in 1960, which was titled "A Dialogue in Depth," the Riverside Church also has a written record of Taylor preaching there on the following dates and subjects: "The Hazard of the Uncommitted (Aug. 31, 1969)," "When the Wagons Come (February 18, 1973)," "A Life Worth Wanting (Aug. 10, 1975)," "Untitled (Aug 15, 1976)," and, "Father and Son Story (June 21, 1998)."

[75]Taylor comments: "I knew Abraham Heschel. He and I and Reinhold Niebuhr signed, together, a plea about Martin King for the *New York Times*." See WGT 5:292.

[76]Thomas, *African American Preaching: The Contribution of Gardner C. Taylor*, p. 100.

the mix of prominent New York preachers. Moreover, his friendships with the likes of Scherer, Sockman, and Buttrick as well as his association with other white preachers benefited them just as much as these friendships benefited him.

3. Preaching at predominantly white conventions and conferences. Taylor also crossed over boundaries of racial difference by preaching at predominantly white conventions and conferences. His ministry across racial difference actually started the year before he came to Concord. In 1947 he traveled to Copenhagen as both a delegate and guest preacher for the Baptist World Alliance. Timothy George notes:

> On the Sunday morning of that meeting, he preached at the Second Baptist Church of Copenhagen, a remarkable honor for a twenty-nine-year-old. In subsequent years, Taylor would speak at four consecutive meetings of the Baptist World Alliance, in Cleveland, London, Miami Beach, and Tokyo. His work on behalf of Christian unity and human rights found an eager response within the world community of Baptists.[77]

As he became an internationally recognized preacher in his own right through the Baptist World Alliance, Taylor also built lasting friendships with foreign white preachers (as we will see in our section "Offering Hospitality at Concord"). Gerald Lamont Thomas notes that Taylor received a thunderous round of applause and a standing ovation after his 1950 address, "They Shall Ask the Way," delivered before the Baptist World Alliance in Cleveland.[78] Although the Alliance was more diverse and integrated than some of the subsequent examples in this section, it is still significant that Taylor, a young minority voice in his twenties and thirties, addressed an international delegation as early as the 1940s and 1950s, a delegation in which older whites were the majority. It is also illuminating that Taylor became an internationally known preacher

---

[77]George, "Introduction: Honor to Whom Honor Is Due," p. xxii. George fails to mention that Taylor also delivered an address titled "The Minister in Today's World" at the Baptist World Alliance meeting in Rio de Janeiro, Brazil, in June 1960. See WGT 4:67-73.

[78]Thomas, "African American Preaching: The Contribution of Gardner C. Taylor," p. 99. Robert Smith Jr. indicates on his "Curriculum Vitae of Gardner Calvin Taylor" that Dr. Taylor preached at the Golden Jubilee of the Baptist World Alliance in London in 1955. For the reference to Taylor preaching in London in 1955, see George, Massey, and Smith Jr., *Our Sufficiency Is of God*, p. 6.

willing to reach across national, cultural, and racial differences *before* he went to New York.

Starting early in his time at Concord, Taylor preached on a regular basis for the annual conference of the American Baptist Convention (ABC). At the time the ABC was an almost entirely white denomination of northern US Baptists. In May 1953 he delivered a sermon on race and civil rights titled "There Is Power in That Cross" at the ABC's annual conference in Denver.[79] At this conference as well as on other occasions, Taylor made it known that, as a member of the NBC, he did not think that Baptists in general and the NBC/ABC in particular should be cast along racial lines. His concern was for unity, solidarity, and partnership. For instance, he exclaimed at a 1958 luncheon in New York in which twenty-five city pastors from the NBC and the ABC were present: "If we're going to be Christian, we've got to look to the day when there will be no [separate] National Baptist Convention and American Baptist Convention."[80]

Henry H. Mitchell shares an important story about Taylor's commitment to crossover preaching. When Taylor preached before the annual conference of the ABC in Denver in May 1953, it was a time of great tension and unrest over racial inequality in America. Taylor himself describes 1953 as a "tortured time in American race relations."[81] Mitchell attended the ABC conference in Denver that year and remembers Taylor delivering a stirring conclusion to his sermon. Mitchell writes:

> He painted a vivid picture straight out of the Book of Revelation (7:9 KJV), where it mentions every kindred and people and tongue. As 10,000 American Baptists (mostly white and not enthusiastic about civil rights) prepared for Holy Communion, a feast in heaven was portrayed, with all these ethnic and lingual identities. . . .
>
> Following the sermon, those whose throats would allow it joined in

---

[79]See WGT 4:27-35. Taylor delivered addresses for the annual conference of the ABC in Denver in May 1953; Cincinnati in June 1958; San Francisco in May 1965; Seattle in May 1969; and Portland in June 1985. Four out of five of these addresses can be found in WGT 4:27-55. The fifth address, titled "A New Creation" and delivered in Seattle in May 1969, is available at several theological libraries in audiocassette format.

[80]"Ties Sought in City by Baptist Groups," *NYT*, July 31, 1958.

[81]See Taylor's note in the subscript on the first page of this address in WGT 4:27.

the spiritual "Let Us Break Bread Together." The rest just choked up and sobbed, but every eye . . . seemed moist with tears. The greatly distinguished C. Oscar Johnson (a white pastor from St. Louis) arose from his seat on the platform and lifted Dr. Gardner C. Taylor of Brooklyn from the floor with a powerful hug. Each being tall and large, it is hard to imagine a more powerful witness for justice and against racial discrimination. . . . [The delegates] had just been gently led to *experience* vicariously the very kingdom of God, and had yielded to it with spiritual joy and gladness. And surely none of them left as they came.[82]

Here we see some of Taylor in action as a crossover preacher. In situations like this, he did not simply impress his predominantly white audience with rhetorical flash and poetic sophistication. He did something more significant. By God's grace and with God's help, he invited his mostly white listeners into a transformative experience, a Christ-centered and cross-focused divine encounter designed to break down racial barriers of separation.

There are many other examples of Taylor crossing over racial divides in predominantly white convention/conference contexts. For the sake of brevity, I will mention just a few. In 1959, at the age of forty, he was a traveling preacher in Australia for six weeks. Over that span, he delivered 102 sermons and addresses in predominantly Australian churches and other monocultural venues as well as engaged in talks with ministers of education on topics such as urban decay, juvenile delinquency, and education.[83] In 1961 he was an "exchange preacher" in England and Scotland and traveled throughout those two countries for an extended period.[84] Last, in 1978, he delivered lectures and preached sermons at the Fosdick Ecumenical Convocation on Preaching at Riverside Church.[85]

---

[82]See Henry H. Mitchell, "Preaching as Experience of the Gospel: An Insight with Roots in the Wisdom of Gardner C. Taylor," in George, Massey, and Smith Jr., eds., *Our Sufficiency Is of God*, p. 149.

[83]According to a 1959 *NYT* article written *before* his trip to Australia, he and his wife, Laura, were scheduled to make stops in Dublin, Athens, Cairo, Beirut, Jerusalem, New Delhi, and Singapore on their way to Australia. They were also scheduled to engage in talks with Israeli Prime Minister David Ben Gurion during their stopover in Israel. See John Wicklein, "Taylor to Preach for Australians," *NYT*, July 26, 1959, p. 50.

[84]See Robert Smith Jr.'s "Curriculum Vitae" in George, Massey, and Smith Jr., *Our Sufficiency Is of God*, p. 7.

[85]See WGT 5:96-99.

Again, the point here is *not* that Taylor avoided preaching in black Baptist circles like the NBC and PNBC conventions or conferences like the Hampton Institute, or even other venues that were predominantly or exclusively African American, before, during, and after his tenure at Concord. The data support this conclusion as well. He preached in black congregations all over the city and the country. Instead, the point in this instance is that he preached in *both* places, in black and nonblack settings, and was well received in both. That Taylor crossed over into predominantly white convention/conference contexts as a young minority preacher during a time in US history when such opportunities were limited and relations between many black and white Americans were strained is not a small accomplishment. The fact that that he was so well received instead of being rejected is just one of the indications that he was improvisationally-interculturally proficient.

4. Teaching and lecturing at predominantly white theological institutions. Throughout the late 1960s and 1970s, Taylor gained experience as a guest lecturer and teacher in predominantly white theological seminaries. He held several adjunct professor positions in homiletics at schools such as Colgate Rochester Divinity School (1969–1972), Union Theological Seminary in New York (1973–1974), and Harvard Divinity School (1975–1976), all of which were predominantly white at the time. The story of how Taylor originally guest lectured at Colgate Rochester in 1952 is a peculiar addition to Colgate's history, but it bears repetition.

Samuel McKinney, an African American Baptist student at Colgate who was set to graduate that same year, passed along Taylor's name to Wilbert E. Saunders, then president of the school. McKinney knew of Taylor's reputation because of his involvement in black Baptist circles. President Saunders had attended Union Seminary in New York and had done his field education at the same church address where Concord was located. However, when President Saunders was a student, the church was called Marcy Avenue Baptist Church, and the church members were white. Saunders assumed Taylor was white based on his fieldwork experience and, according to McKinney, "the white fellows [in my class] assumed he was white because it was the same church building." Mc-

Kinney continues: "And when he showed up they said, 'You tricked us,' and I said, 'Keep your mouths shut and you will learn something.' He [Taylor] talked about a 'Divine Ultimatum.' Taylor went on that night and 'toned the bell in Zion.' Later, two white guys with tears in their eyes said, 'You were right.'"[86]

We can surmise that Taylor's other interactions at predominantly white seminaries were not quite as peculiar. What is interesting about Colgate is the transformation: closed-mindedness among whites beforehand (to the extent that they assumed McKinney needed to trick them) and open-mindedness afterward, resistance giving way to repentance. Perhaps more stories like this one exist from other visits Taylor made to predominantly white theological institutions. Bear in mind that, for many students as well as professors, Taylor's guest lectures and adjunct teaching were the only access they had to theological education by an African American lecturer or professor in a formal seminary environment. It appears that Taylor left a lasting impression at Colgate and at other schools. Several years later, Taylor was the first African American person to serve on Colgate Rochester's Board of Trustees.[87]

The best-known example of Taylor serving as a guest lecturer dates back to 1976 when Yale Divinity School invited him to speak at the hundredth anniversary of the prestigious Lyman Beecher Lectures, which he later published in his book *How Shall They Preach?*[88] According to O. C. Edwards, Yale originally asked Taylor to team up with Henry H. Mitchell to deliver the 1974 Beecher Lectures, but Taylor respectfully declined. Yale invited Mitchell to go first since Mitchell was better known in academic circles than Taylor at the time.[89] When it was his turn, Taylor did not disappoint. He delivered four lectures without notes and received an enthusiastic response from his predominantly white audience. After the lectures were over, some of those gathered learned that Taylor had spent countless hours prior to this occasion in the library at

---

[86]Samuel McKinney, in an interview with Gerald Lamont Thomas in Thomas, *African American Preaching: The Contribution of Gardner C. Taylor,* pp. 102-3.

[87]See ibid., p. 103.

[88]Taylor, *How Shall They Preach?.*

[89]See Edwards, *History of Preaching,* p. 714.

Union Theological Seminary reading every word of the previous ninety-nine lectures in the series.[90]

Taylor was also a guest preacher, lecturer, and adjunct professor at many other predominantly white theological institutions. Examples abound.[91]

5. Offering hospitality to white preachers. An analysis of Taylor's years at Concord reveals a steadfast commitment to providing hospitality by inviting white preachers to preach and white parishioners to attend Concord. In other words, Taylor did not just accept invitations from white preachers to preach at their churches and deliver addresses at their conventions or seminaries. *Taylor extended invitations.* Crossover preaching is not just about accepting invitations to sit at the table from those who are racially, ethnically, or ecclesially different. Although this involves risk, it is also a form of one-way traveling. Crossover preaching requires extending hospitality to those who are racially, ethnically, or ecclesially different by inviting them to join you at your table, to cross over into your domain of comfort. This is another form of transgression

---

[90]George, "Introduction: Honor to Whom Honor Is Due," p. xix. Carolyn Knight also reports that this is a true story in Dyson, "Gardner Taylor," p. 14.

[91]For instance, Taylor was a speaker at the seventy-second convocation at Bangor Theological Seminary in January 1977. He also preached at Princeton Theological Seminary in 1977 at the special invitation of his personal friend Conrad H. Massa. Massa was a member of the board of trustees at the time. Also, at Princeton, he guest lectured and preached multiples times, such as in 1990, 1992, and 2002, and he was an adjunct professor for a brief time after he retired from Concord in 1990. In February 1978 he delivered the James Sprunt Lectures at Union Theological Seminary in Richmond, Virginia. In April 1979 he preached as part of the second annual Mordecai Johnson Lectures at Colgate Rochester. In February 1979 he delivered the Mullins Lectures at the Southern Baptist Seminary of Louisville. He delivered a series of lectures at Golden Gate Baptist Theological Seminary in April 1980; he delivered the Sprinkle Lectures at Atlantic Christian College (now Barton College) in Wilson, North Carolina, in 1983; and he preached and delivered lectures at the Lutheran Theological Seminary at Philadelphia in June 1984 and June 1986. He delivered lectures at Midwestern Baptist Theological Seminary in Kansas City, Missouri (September 1988), the Iliff School of Theology in Denver (November 1989), Louisville Presbyterian Seminary in Louisville (1992, February 1998), and The Methodist Theological School in Delaware, Ohio (April 1998). In the local paper in Bangor, Maine, the announcement reads: "Dr. Gardner C. Taylor, pastor, Concord Baptist Church of Christ, Brooklyn, NY, will be the David Newton Beach Quiet Hour leader. His general theme will be 'Bearers of an Incredibly Rich Gospel.'" See "72nd Convocation Set at Bangor Seminary," *Bangor Daily News,* January 21, 1977, p. 23. Audio recordings of Taylor's sermons and lectures at Princeton are available at the library of Princeton Theological Seminary. Some of the years in which one finds recordings are 1977, 1990, 1992, and 2002. Besides the Bangor and Princeton examples, the dates and locations of these audio recordings were found on www.worldcat.org.

that involves risk, perhaps more risk, and, as we will see, it is a form of transgression that Taylor embraced.

As early as 1950 (!), Taylor invited white preachers to Concord. In fact, Taylor invited white preachers to share his pulpit on several occasions in the 1950s. It is not every day that the senior pastor of one of the largest black churches in New York hands his pulpit over—let alone to a white preacher. Few nationally known white preachers offered to share their pulpits with African Americans during this era in race relations in the United States.

In August 1950 Taylor invited a Danish pastor, the Rev. A. Baungaard Thomson, to preach at Concord. Thomson was a forty-year-old pastor from Copenhagen, and he was someone whom Taylor had met through the Baptist World Alliance. While Thomson and his family traveled through New York on their way back to Denmark, they stayed with James Farrar, the Concord church clerk. Then Thomson preached at Concord on August 27, 1950.[92]

Two more examples of offering hospitality to white preachers took place within a few months of each other in the same year. In May 1957 Taylor invited a white British pastor from London, Dr. F. Townley Lord, to come and be the *featured* preacher at Concord's 110th anniversary celebration.[93] Taylor had befriended Lord ten years earlier in 1947 at the Baptist World Congress in Copenhagen. It is noteworthy that he invited him to preach at a significant moment in Concord's history as a church.

In July 1957 Taylor cohosted an event with Rev. Dr. Sandy F. Ray at Cornerstone Baptist, where Ray was the senior pastor. Together they invited the famous evangelist Billy Graham, who had preached to eighteen-thousand-plus crowds at Madison Square Garden over a several-week span. Ray invited Graham to preach a sermon outside the steps of Cornerstone on a Sunday afternoon, and Taylor cohosted the event. This was a symbolic and courageous move. Ray and Taylor were taking a risk to invite a white evangelist to Brooklyn, and Graham was undoubtedly alienating some members of his constituency to accept the invitation. Graham preached a surprising, politically charged sermon in which he

---

[92]"Copenhagen Minister Preaches Sunday at Concord," *NYAN*, August 26, 1950, pp. B4, B12.
[93]"Concord to Mark 110th Anniversary," *NYAN*, May 4, 1957, p. 20.

spoke openly against racist and segregationist laws and called for changes to legislation at the national level.[94] Over twenty local pastors and leaders supported the event, and more than three thousand people attended.[95]

In a 2008 interview with Joel C. Gregory of Truett Theological Seminary, Taylor offers another example of offering hospitality to a white preacher at Concord. In that interview, Taylor recalls Paul Scherer's visit:

> He [Scherer] preached for me once in the Concord Church, and our people in that day, much more than now, would give a vocal response to the preacher. And Scherer told, I think, Jim Forbes, who later came to the Riverside Church as pastor, but who was a student of Scherer's then at Union [Seminary in Manhattan], that Scherer liked the attachment of the responses.[96]

Taylor does not specify the date that Scherer preached at Concord, but if Scherer were still teaching at Union, which he did from 1945 to 1960, and Taylor started at Concord in 1948 and at NBC in 1958, then Scherer probably spoke in the late 1950s.

Taylor also offered hospitality to white *parishioners*. In December 1955 Taylor's church and a white Methodist church in Brooklyn participated together in a "pilot project" to bridge the racial divides between them. Taylor and the Concord Church congregation invited fifty white parishioners from Hanson Place Central Methodist Church down the street to "share their fellowship," and one hundred members of the Concord Church were "welcomed by the Rev. Dr. John E. Zeiter at Central Methodist." The goal of the exchange was to "promote racial understanding" between the two congregations.[97] At least two points are worth mentioning about this event. First, it is an example of crossing over both racial *and* ecclesial differences. This particular congregation was not a Baptist congregation. Both congregations were engaging in racial *and* ecclesial boundary crossing. Second, this event is a window into an important dynamic at Concord, perhaps one that is not immediately ap-

---

[94]"Billy Graham: Heaven Won't Let Racists In," *NYAN*, July 20, 1957, p. 9.
[95]For more on this significant event in the history of Brooklyn, see ibid.
[96]"Gardner Calvin Taylor: Oral History Memoir, Interview 2," p. 8.
[97]"Brooklyn Tests Racial Exchange," *NYT*, December 12, 1955, p. 36.

parent: although Concord was 98 percent African American, it was neither insular nor isolationist. Even in the 1950s, it was a congregation that was opening the doors instead of circling the wagons. It seems that Taylor was at the forefront of this ecclesial shift. In fact, he was trying to lead the way. Two years earlier in Denver, at his ABC convention speech on race and civil rights, Taylor lamented the fact that Concord was not as integrated as it could or should be. "I stand before you tonight smitten with shame," Taylor confessed, "that in my own beloved borough, in Brooklyn, my own church, all black, is less Christian, at least in appearance, than the baseball diamond at Ebbets Field in the same borough."[98] In this address, delivered in 1953, Taylor shines the mirror back on his own community, stating, "The suspicion and the resentment and the bitterness in this country are not confined to people of lighter hue."[99] Even if Concord was not as diverse as other churches, we should not conclude that Taylor did not want it to be. He was committed to crossing over *outside* nonblack contexts, and he was committed to offering hospitality *inside* black contexts to nonblack preachers and parishioners. He makes his intentions clear in conference confessions like the one in 1953, church exchanges like the one in 1955, and, again, by hosting white preachers at Concord throughout the 1950s.

6. Practicing crossover preaching. Taylor's preaching also reveals a peculiar commitment to crossover preaching. In addition to other crossover practices, we also see a commitment to an improvisational-intercultural stance in the sermons and lectures themselves. What I mean by stance is this: Taylor maintained high levels of protean reflexivity. Moreover, his sermons were a performative pastiche of various sources and influences from both white and nonwhite preaching traditions.

Taylor's protean reflexivity becomes clear when one reads the Beecher Lectures. The majority of his quotations, anecdotes, sermon reading recommendations, and illustrations come from white American or white British preachers such as John Jowett, Frederick W. Robertson, Paul

---

[98]See the convention address, "There Is Power in That Cross," in WGT 4:31. The mention of Ebbets Field is a reference to Jackie Robinson being the first African American to play professional baseball with the Brooklyn Dodgers. For more on this convention address, see also Dugan, "Churches Scored as Race Conscious," p. 27.

[99]WGT 4:31.

Scherer, and Charles Spurgeon, among others. In fairness, Taylor does share at least one anecdote about Martin Luther King Jr., and he briefly commends several African American preachers to his audience, including his old nemesis, J. H. Jackson.[100] But it is still true that almost all of his references are to white American or white British preachers. What do we make of this rhetorical move? Was Taylor adapting, as the apostle Paul recommends in 1 Corinthians 9:19-23? To paraphrase Paul's point, was he becoming "like a Jew in order to win the Jews" (1 Cor 9:20)? Although adaptation is a part of what it means to engage in crossover preaching, there is nothing novel about it. It is a hallmark of ancient classical rhetoric. Taylor definitely knew his audience. Although this is the simplest explanation, it may not be the only or the best one.

Taylor was arguably doing something more than adapting to context and occasion. One might ask: Was Taylor supposed to be representing black preaching, not representing black preaching, or representing preaching in general on this occasion? And did anyone tell Taylor that he *had* to represent black preaching or, for that matter, transfer preaching wisdom from black preachers of the past? Perhaps Taylor was refusing to be defined as a black preacher citing black preachers and speaking on behalf of all black preachers, past and present. This is not to suggest that he was embarrassed in any way by his preaching tradition and heritage. Clearly he wasn't. Rather, it may be the case that he was defying circumscription by his own volition, that is, he was refusing to be defined through categorization as a "black preacher" representing black preachers and speaking on behalf of black preaching. In many ways, Taylor's decision can be seen as a countermove to Mitchell's 1974 lectures on black preaching.

Crossover speakers not only show adeptness at crossing over racial, cultural, and ecclesial difference in lecturing and preaching, but they also show adeptness at performing improvisation and intercultural competence. To practice crossover preaching is to break free from traditional modes of classification. For example, in his 1976 Beecher Lectures, Taylor

---

[100]Taylor tells an anecdote about King in the lecture "Preaching the Whole Counsel of God." See WGT 5:192-93. Taylor commends several African American preachers, names like John Jasper, Sandy F. Ray, and J. H. Jackson in his lecture "Building a Sermon." See WGT 5:176.

breaks free from oppositional categories like black preaching versus *not* black preaching, black preacher versus *not* black preacher, black preaching's historian versus *not* black preaching's historian.

Performative pastiche might sound complex, but it is quite simple. Taylor's preaching is a unique blend of various traditions. In chapter three, it will become clear that his style of preaching resists the traditional classifications often found in African American homiletical textbooks. The point here is that his preaching does not fit in any of the traditional boxes. Perhaps the literature requires revision, or, perhaps more to my point, Taylor's preaching does not fit *because* of its improvisational and intercultural dimensions. Another way of thinking about performative pastiche is through the suggestion that Taylor is a bricoleur, that is, he is one who puts together seemingly disparate strands from various traditions and creates out of those strands a bricolage.[101] Bricolage is a helpful image to get at what it means to practice crossover preaching. One stands among various preaching traditions yet refuses to be circumscribed by them. The preacher appropriates various traditions in new contexts; she discovers her own authentic voice *within* traditions in order to create new patterns *of* tradition. One is plurivocal rather than univocal, traditioned and traditioning.

At least one well-known homiletician agrees with my claim that Taylor escapes the confinements of traditional classification. James Earl Massey suggests in a 1995 interview that Taylor's preaching has improvisational-intercultural dimensions, even if he does not use the language of improvisation or intercultural competence to do so. Massey suggests that Taylor's preaching is actually a blend of some of America's greatest preachers

---

[101]Michael Eric Dyson uses the terminology of bricoleur and bricolage to describe African American improvisation in the majority culture in Michael Eric Dyson, *Open Mike: Reflections on Philosophy, Race, Sex, Culture and Religion* (New York: Basic Civitas Books, 2003), p. 206. In his discussion of bricolage, Dyson accesses language familiar to postmodern discussions of identity construction, and draws on "bricolage" language that originates with Claude Lévi-Strauss, *The Savage Mind* (Chicago: University of Chicago Press, 1966), pp. 17-35. Princeton sociologist Robert Wuthnow suggests that being a "tinkerer" or "bricoleur" is a defining characteristic of young adults, especially as it pertains to their religious expression. Tinkerers sift through ideas and practices from a variety of places, and they construct a unique "bricolage" when engaging in identity construction. See Robert Wuthnow, *After the Baby Boomers: How Twenty- and Thirty-Somethings Are Shaping the Future of American Religion* (Princeton, NJ: Princeton University Press, 2007), pp. 13-16, 134-36.

from the past. In his judgment, Taylor possesses Henry Ward Beecher's "prolixity to spin words," Phillips Brooks's "earnestness of style and breadth of learning," and Harry Emerson Fosdick's "ability to appeal to the masses yet maintain a dignity in doing so." The characteristics of all of these preachers, Massey notes, "Taylor has brought into one person."[102] To a certain extent, Massey identifies the same phenomenon we have seen and continue to see throughout this book: Taylor's proficiency in improvisation and intercultural competence is not only visible in his symbolic actions as a pastor, but also in his practices as a preacher. He is committed to protean reflexivity and performative pastiche.

QUESTION 3: WHAT IS A CROSSOVER HOMILETIC?

Since I have already used the terminology of crossover preacher with Taylor, and I have suggested that these two proficiencies are important to the future of homiletics, now a third question is in order: *What exactly is an improvisational-intercultural or crossover homiletic?*

Improvisational proficiency. Improvisation has wide currency across an array of disciplines like psychology,[103] business,[104] education,[105] and

---

[102]See Dyson, "Gardner Taylor," p. 13.

[103]The most popular psychologist of improvisation is R. Keith Sawyer. In *Creating Conversations*, Sawyer argues, contra Erving Goffman, that our everyday performances are unscripted rather than scripted, and fused with more spontaneity than Goffman was willing to concede. Rather than opting for Goffman's scripted drama metaphor as a way to describe daily human interaction, Sawyer opts for the metaphor of improvisational performance. According to Sawyer, and in contrast to Goffman's claim, we are *more* spontaneous than we like to think rather than less spontaneous. See R. Keith Sawyer, *Creating Conversations: Improvisation in Everyday Discourse* (Cresskill, NJ: Hampton Press, 2001), pp. 1-4, 7-15. For more on how improvisation and psychology interact, see Sawyer, *Improvised Dialogues: Emergence and Creativity in Conversation* (Westport, CT: Ablex, 2003). For more on how improvisation interacts as a form of "social emergence" in psychology *and* sociology, see Sawyer, *Social Emergence: Societies as Complex Systems* (New York: Cambridge University Press, 2005), esp. pp. 170-88. For Goffman's discussion of spontaneity and script, see Goffman, *The Presentation of Self in Everyday Life* (Garden City, NY: Doubleday Anchor Books, 1959), pp. 72-74.

[104]See Dusya Vera and Mary Crossan, "Improvisation and Innovative Performance in Teams," *Organization Science* 16, no. 3 (June 2005): 203-24; cf. also Mary Crossan and Marc Sorrenti, "Making Sense of Improvisation," in *Advances in Strategic Management*, ed. J. Walsh and A. Huff (Greenwich, CT: Jai Press, 1997), 14:155-80.

[105]See David Wright, "The Mythopoetic Body: Learning Through Creativity," in *Pedagogies of the Imagination: Mythopoetic Curriculum in Educational Practice*, ed. Timothy Leonard and Peter Willis (New York: Springer Books, 2010), pp. 93-106; and R. Keith Sawyer, "Creative Teaching: Collaborative Discussion as Disciplined Improvisation," *Educational Researcher* 33, no. 2 (March 2004): 12-20.

Christian ethics.[106] The term has come to mean so many different things to different people that it requires delimitation. Many of the scholars in the aforementioned disciplines draw extensively from the same well from which we will draw: performance, in particular, music and theater. My interest in improvisation is threefold: to discover how the word is used in performance settings in theater and music, to discern its potential function in Taylor's preaching, and to draw attention to both its performative occurrences and metaphorical extensions.

Although improvisation has garnered attention recently in a number of disciplines, its roots are in musical and theatrical performance. Homileticians such as Kirk Byron Jones, Eugene L. Lowry, and others have noted the connections between preaching and musical performance, jazz music specifically. Although I interact with their homiletical contributions later in this section, the focus of this chapter is improvisation in *performance theory* rather than jazz music theory. Instead of tilling the same soil as previous homileticians, I move into new terrain in homiletical discussion through engagement with a different field: improvisational performance theory.

Since various definitions of improvisation exist *within* (and not just outside) performance studies, still further delimitation is required. One way to get at what is meant is to begin with what is *not* meant by the term. Often the word is used to describe getting caught unprepared, as in, "We ran out of gas so we had to improvise." Some performance theorists use it in this way in order to describe unprepared artistic creation ex nihilo. Mick Napier, the founder of Chicago's *Annoyance Theatre*, defines the word as "getting on a stage and making stuff up as you go along."[107] However, improvisation-as-unprepared-invention is neither what is meant in this book, nor is it an adequate way of describing the practices of the preacher under consideration. Taylor was not an ad-hoc preacher. He was highly prepared. Spontaneity arose out of intense

---

[106] Anglican ethicist and preacher Samuel Wells argues that for a church community to be faithful ethically, it must learn to "improvise within its tradition." Wells continues: "Improvisation means a community formed in the right habits trusting itself to embody its tradition in new and often challenging circumstances; and this is exactly what the church is called to do." See Samuel Wells, *Improvisation: The Drama of Christian Ethics* (Grand Rapids: Brazos, 2004), p. 12.

[107] Mick Napier, *Improvise: Scene from the Inside Out* (Portsmouth, NH: Heineman, 2004), p. 1.

preparation and memorization. His manu*script* was more like a manu-*template* from which improvised sermonic discourse could emerge.

One of the clearest definitions of improvisation, one that narrows the term while also conceptualizing Taylor's approach, comes from performance theorist Amy Seham, who defines improvisation as "inventiveness within limitation."[108] As with improvisational performance, Taylor's sermons were fused with possibilities for spontaneity (inventiveness), but, unlike extemporaneous preachers, he insisted on writing and memorizing his sermon manuscripts (limitation). Seham contends that improvisation is a space where contingency and constraint coexist; the performer invents and creates but always within the framework of rehearsal and structural adherence.[109] To be an expert performer, then, means that one creates unique sounds and maintain an individuated style within established systems and structures and not apart from them. One leverages an established system in order to create "free spaces within the framework," to use Italian director Roberto Ciulli's phrase.[110] Although some performance theorists (such as Napier) espouse the belief that artistic improvisation occurs ex nihilo, such a view remains untenable according to Seham's definition. More important, it is inconsistent with Taylor's sermonic practice. For Taylor, there is no such thing as a blank canvas, and there is no place for an extempore speech in preaching. This is not to say that Taylor could *not* deliver an eloquent, articulate speech at a moment's notice, which he was sometimes called on to do and did with excellence. Rather, it means that Taylor did not practice or encourage extemporaneous preaching.

Performative improvisation, a subject we will return to in chapter two,

---

[108]Amy E. Seham, *Whose Improv Is It Anyway? Beyond Second City* (Jackson: University Press of Mississippi, 2001), p. xx.

[109]Theologian and music enthusiast Jeremy Begbie uses the language of "constraint" and "contingency" in Jeremy Begbie, *Theology, Music, and Time* (Cambridge: Cambridge University Press, 2000), p. 185.

[110]Roberto Ciulli explains that opportunities for freedom are always present, but that these opportunities never exist apart from larger systems and structures in which they can appear. Ciulli writes: "You always have this situation of having to create free spaces within the framework, within the given constraints so that individual creativity can unfold, a creativity which does not destroy everything, but which, on the contrary, enriches it" (Malgorzata Bartula, Stefan Schroer, and Roberto Ciulli, *On Improvisation: Nine Conversations with Roberto Ciulli*, trans. Geoffrey V. Davis [New York: Peter Lang, 2003], p. 38).

represents only one strand of a multistrand phenomenon. In Taylor's preaching, improvisation does not just function at a performative level, but at a metaphorical level as well. It is more than a performative practice; it is a commitment to protean reflexivity born partly from necessity and partly from volition. By *protean reflexivity* I mean improvisational aptitude and action across racial and cultural difference. This reflexivity is born out of necessity in that, as a member of an oppressed community facing the daily realities of racism, his social location *required* proteanism. It is volitional in the sense that strategic deployment of improvisational speech is arguably an emancipatory act. In chapter three, I claim that the primary (but not sole) factor that fostered this ability to be protean was being racialized-as-black in the United States—a lived reality, then and now, that entails or affords a commitment to improvisational speech as a form of intercultural negotiation. Thus Taylor's social location and his adeptness at improvisational preaching are correlative.

Yet, it would be misguided to imply or assert that social location as a category is simplistic or reductive. It is not a fixed point but a complex matrix. Just as improvisation is not reducible to a single strand, so also social location is not reducible; it requires a multistrand description. Taylor's race constitutes a necessary but not sufficient cause for his improvisational adeptness. Other factors such as growing up in the South during segregation, attending Oberlin College, ministering in an urban metropolis, and building strategic friendships across racial difference are also relevant. Taylor's social location is more fluid than it is static, more of an interstitial matrix than a fixed point on a map. I discuss the complexity of social location in greater depth in chapter three. I problematize and challenge simplistic, essentialist descriptions of Taylor's social location, especially the category of race, in favor of a more nuanced account.

In homiletics, improvisation as a metaphor is not new. It has been used before to talk about preaching. Homileticians such as Charles L. Campbell, Eugene L. Lowry, Kirk Byron Jones, and Robert C. Smith Jr. make use of this metaphor in their published works. Campbell and Lowry use it to a lesser extent, while it plays a more central role in books by Jones and Smith. In *Preaching Jesus*, Charles L. Campbell criticizes the preaching-as-translation model in which method and technique are central, opting rather for a "preaching as linguistic improvisation model" in which immersion in and imitation of the *language* of the faith community are central.[111] In Campbell's framework, improvisation refers to immersion in the language world of one's community for the sake of celebrating, enriching, and building that community. The preacher does not "translate" the biblical text into a sermon but, like a jazz musician, decides to "go on" with the text. Campbell writes: "Jazz musicians do not translate that text [of music] into a new language, but rather 'go on' with the language of the text in new ways for new contexts."[112] Instead of translating a text, an improvisational preacher "goes on" with the text in service to the faith community.

In *The Sermon: Dancing on the Edge of Mystery*, Eugene L. Lowry argues that the sermon's conflict-resolution pattern should be just as complicated and intricate as the irresolution-resolution pattern in great jazz music. For Lowry, jazz music functions as an analogy for conflict-resolution in the sermon. There should be enough conflict and irresolution in the sermon, Lowry argues, that it seems chaotic at times, but this is always for the purpose of lifting up the sheer beauty of gospel resolution. Drawing on the work of Leroy Ostransky, who argues that the key to great jazz is not an elaborate resolution, but the "inherent intricacy of the irresolution," Lowry pushes preachers to complicate the sermon in order to sustain narrative tension.[113] He invites us to "release our grip on the known," to allow the "itch to move farther toward chaos" in order for the scratch, the resolution of the gospel, to be heard in a clear and compelling way.[114] Lowry also makes similar connections between preaching and jazz in his 2012 book *The Homiletical Beat*. As he does in *The Sermon: Dancing on the Edge of Mystery*, Lowry notes similarities

---

[111]Charles L. Campbell, *Preaching Jesus: New Directions for Homiletics in Hans Frei's Postliberal Theology* (Grand Rapids: Eerdmans, 1997), p. 231.

[112]Ibid., p. 236. Drawing from George Lindbeck's postliberal theology, Campbell casts preaching within the framework of a larger "cultural-linguistic model." See George A. Lindbeck, *The Nature of Doctrine: Religion and Theology in a Postliberal Age* (Louisville: Westminster John Knox, 2009), pp. 32-40.

[113]See Leroy Ostransky, *The Anatomy of Jazz* (Seattle: University of Washington Press, 1960), p. 83, as cited in Eugene L. Lowry, *The Sermon: Dancing on the Edge of Mystery* (Nashville: Abingdon, 1997), p. 69.

[114]Lowry, *The Sermon*, p. 105.

between tension-resolution in jazz and the need for tension-resolution in the sermon.[115] He also notes other possible resonances between jazz and preaching besides this, such as "spontaneous creativity," call and response between the artist and the audience, and risk and vulnerability in artistic creation.[116]

In *The Jazz of Preaching*, Kirk Byron Jones draws lessons from jazz music in order to infuse more creativity and originality into sermon preparation and delivery. Principles from jazz improvisation, he argues, illumine the poetics of preaching performance. He writes: "Musicians play notes; preachers play words."[117] Great jazz artists like Wynton Marsalis, for example, understand how to prepare, create, adapt, and respond musically. They know that the sound and shape of the notes are important. Like jazz musicians, wise preachers understand that the sound and shape of their words are important. Improvisational preaching involves creativity in preparation, openness in delivery, and precision in content concerning what words are used and how they are used. Jones highlights four principles from jazz improvisation that are also applicable to preaching: playfulness, variation, risk taking, and mastery.[118] Concerning the principle of *playfulness*, Jones suggests: "To a large extent, the spirit of improvisation is the spirit of playfulness."[119] Preachers who "cultivate playfulness in preaching" discover God's divine humor in what so often seems too serious, and God's divine handiwork in what so often seems like the mundane.[120] Concerning *mastery*, Jones notes the link between improvisational excellence in performance and endless hours of practice/rehearsal (referred to as "shedding" or "wood-shedding" in jazz).[121] In his definition of improvisation, he writes: "Improvisation is spontaneity infused by preparation. . . . Improvisational surrender

---

[115]Eugene L. Lowry, *The Homiletical Beat: Why All Sermons Are Narrative* (Nashville: Abingdon, 2012), p. 20.

[116]Ibid., p. 21. Lowry also talks about the differences between horizontal and vertical jazz music in ibid., pp. 37-38.

[117]Kirk Byron Jones, *The Jazz of Preaching: How to Preach with Great Freedom and Joy* (Nashville: Abingdon, 2004), p. 30.

[118]Ibid., pp. 79-95.

[119]Ibid., p. 82.

[120]Ibid., p. 88.

[121]Ibid., p. 85.

happens on the backside of arduous preparation."[122] To illustrate his point, he tells the story of jazz great Wynton Marsalis, who practiced for two hours every day as a child growing up in New Orleans. As Marsalis got older, he lengthened the number of hours he practiced and deepened his "emotional and professional commitment to his craft." When an interviewer asked Marsalis about the many hours he spent practicing, Marsalis responded: "One thing about excellence, it's an exclusive club. And it's only for those who really want to pay dues."[123]

Of the four principles, *mastery* is probably the one that applies most to Taylor's homiletical approach. Taylor practiced constantly and labored over the precise wording and phrasing of his sermons, lectures, and addresses. He believed that a preacher should "pay his dues" through practice, and he was fond of quoting Paul Scherer's dictum: "Inspiration is 10 percent genius and 90 percent firm application of the seat of the pants to a chair."[124] This is the most obvious link between Taylor and jazz musicians. In both instances, the focus is on careful preparation as the primary pathway to spontaneity, originality, and innovation. One masters a tradition through rehearsal and practice *before* he or she can riff on it.

Second to mastery would be *playfulness*, but Taylor's "spirit of playfulness" is arguably different from Jones's definition. Taylor's playfulness centers more on play in biblical interpretation. His preaching practices reveal an interest in playing with the dynamics of the biblical text: its nuances, its time and place, its main characters, and its connections to modern life.[125] In a 1983 book chapter for *Preaching Biblically*, Taylor talks about playing with the imaginary line between past text and present circumstance. He writes:

> A wise preacher of another generation ago suggested that one ought to "walk up and down the street where a text lives." The surrounding terrain ought to be taken into account. What is the block like on which the text

---

[122]Ibid.

[123]Touré, "Wynton Marsalis," *Icon Thoughtstyle Magazine* (August 1997), as cited in Jones, *Jazz of Preaching*, p. 86.

[124]From lecture 3, "Building a Sermon," in the Lyman Beecher Lectures of 1976. See WGT 5:172.

[125]Robert C. Dykstra also uses the metaphor of play and the language of "playing with the text," in Robert C. Dykstra, *Discovering A Sermon: Personal Pastoral Preaching* (St. Louis: Chalice, 2001), pp. 13-21.

is located?. . . Does one hear light and merry music in the neighborhood
of the text or are there solemn cadences of some sad and mournful time?[126]

When one leverages one's imagination in order to see the sights and
smell the smells of the ancient biblical world, to walk up and down the
street where a text lives, as it were, one is set free to make connections
more readily between that world and this world.

Taylor was also skilled at playing with the sounds and shapes of words
in order to communicate ideas. So, he *does* fit Jones's definition of playfulness in a sense. Recall Jones's axiom: "Musicians play notes; preachers
play words." Taylor built a solid reputation on his ability to turn a phrase.
His adeptness at poetic playfulness was the main reason Michael Eric
Dyson referred to him as the "poet laureate of the pulpit."[127]

In Robert Smith Jr.'s *Doctrine That Dances*, he follows in Jones's footsteps by defining improvisation as "spontaneity infused by preparation."[128]
Smith conceives of improvisational preaching as meticulous preparation
of the *planned* sermon for the sake of contingent spontaneity in the *live*
sermon. Just as jazz musicians know what the notes on the page are, but
are prepared to play the unforeseen notes that are *not* on the page during
a *live* performance, likewise, preachers who prepare a sermon with meticulous precision can improvise according to the unforeseen movement
of the Holy Spirit during the *live* sermon. In his preaching classes, Smith
has his students write down every word of a sermon manuscript in order
"to let the Holy Spirit turn the ink of the manuscript into the blood of
spiritual passion."[129] He insists that his students internalize the manuscript so that, when they preach in class without a manuscript, they will
be attuned to the Spirit's movement rather than preoccupied with repeating verbatim what they prepared.

Of all the aforementioned homileticians, Smith comes closest to describing Taylor's actual preaching practices. In particular, Smith discusses internalization of the manuscript in order to improvise on it, a

---

[126]"Shaping Sermons by the Shape of Text and Preacher," in WGT 5:45-46.

[127]Dyson, "Gardner Taylor."

[128]Robert C. Smith Jr., *Doctrine That Dances: Bringing Doctrinal Preaching and Teaching to Life*
(Nashville: B & H Academic, 2008), p. 152.

[129]Ibid., p. 153.

theme that Jones, Lowry, and Campbell do not discuss in their published works. As was mentioned previously, Taylor prepared and memorized sermon manuscripts, but these functioned more as manu-*templates* from which free spaces for improvisation could emerge. He internalized the manuscript before the sermon, but also allowed for improvisational moments within the sermon, whether these meant call and response, unplanned illustrations and anecdotes, or spontaneous detours, all of which we will discuss in chapter two. Smith comes closest to describing Taylor's practice of sermon preparation and delivery. To borrow from Smith's analogy, Taylor prepared notes on the page in order to be ready to play notes off the page.

There is much to affirm about the works of Campbell, Lowry, Jones, and Smith, and their homiletical interaction with improvisation in jazz music. These publications have moved the discussion forward in positive directions. That stated, each of these works is more allusive than theoretical. They point in the direction of a phenomenon, but do not conceptualize or concretize the phenomenon's theoretical dynamics. In some cases, they simply miss the mark. For instance, in both of Lowry's books, *The Sermon* and *The Homiletical Beat*, he picks and chooses principles from jazz music that suit his claim that the core of every sermon should be narrative. When preachers prepare a sermon, he argues, they should think about time rather than space. He states, "Too often it is space that seems to be the underlying assumptive image regarding the sermon."[130] He uses phrases like "homiletical plot" and "movement in time" to talk about why movement rather than space is most important. Ironically, improvisational performers care deeply about space. While they also care about movement in time from irresolution to resolution, they also believe that space is indispensable to performance. Their thinking is spatial in addition to being narratival. In chapter five, I discuss the significance of space in improvisational performance, in particular attunement to space in conversation with two theorists: Viola Spolin and Keith Johnstone. I only note Lowry here to support my overall point that improvisational

---

[130]Lowry, *Homiletical Beat*, p. 8.

performance theory is more complex and nuanced than focusing only on narratival patterns might suggest.

Moreover, none of the surveyed homiletical texts touches on improvisation outside jazz music. In fairness, it may be their intent to keep the discussion as narrow as possible. While there are arguably lessons that can be learned from jazz music—important lessons—improvisation is also a wider phenomenon than jazz music. Improvisation is the genus; jazz music is the species. In each of these cases, the writers tend to flip the distinction around so that jazz music is the genus and improvisation the species. What will become clear in the performance theory discussion in chapter two and the race theory discussion in chapter three is that there is much more to improvisation than is currently featured in homiletical literature.

Intercultural proficiency. Like improvisation, interculturalism also has wide currency across an array of disciplines such as psychology,[131] communication,[132] business,[133] ecclesial practice / missiology,[134] theology,[135]

---

[131]See Walter J. Lonner and Susanna A. Hayes, "Understanding the Cognitive and Social Aspects of Intercultural Competence," in *Culture and Competence: Contexts of Life Success*, ed. Robert J. Sternberg and Elena L. Grigorenko (Washington, DC: American Psychological Association, 2004), pp. 89-110.

[132]See Igor Klyukanov, *Principles of Intercultural Communication* (New York: Pearson, 2005). See also Darla K. Deardorff, "In Search of Intercultural Competence," *International Educator* 13, no. 2 (Spring 2004): 13-15; Brian H. Spitzberg and William R. Cupach, *Interpersonal Communication Competence* (Beverly Hills, CA: Sage, 1984); William B. Gudykunst, *Bridging Differences: Effective Intergroup Communication* (Newbury Park, CA: Sage, 1991); William B. Gudykunst and Young Yun Kim, *Communicating with Strangers: An Approach to Intercultural Communication* (New York: McGraw-Hill, 1997).

[133]P. Christopher Earley and Soon Ang, *Cultural Intelligence: Individual Interactions Across Cultures* (Stanford, CA: Stanford Business Books, 2003), p. 59. See also Miriam Erez and P. Christopher Earley, *Culture, Self-Identity, and Work* (New York: Oxford University Press, 1993); P. Christopher Earley, Soon Ang, and Joo-Seng Tan, *CQ: Developing Cultural Intelligence at Work* (Stanford, CA: Stanford Business Books, 2006).

[134]See Gary L. McIntosh and Alan McMahan, *Being the Church in a Multi-Ethnic Community: Why It Matters and How It Works* (Indianapolis: Wesleyan Publishing House, 2012). See also Franz Xaver Scheuerer, *Interculturality: A Challenge for the Mission of the Church* (Bangalore, India: Asian Trading Corp, 2001).

[135]For the emerging conversation in intercultural theology, see Orlando O. Espín, *Grace and Humanness: Theological Reflections Because of Culture* (Maryknoll, NY: Orbis Books, 2007); Mark J. Cartledge and David Cheetham, eds., *Intercultural Theology: Approaches and Themes* (London: SCM Press, 2011); María Pilar Aquino and Maria José Rosado-Nunes, eds., *Feminist Intercultural Theology: Latina Explorations for a Just World* (Maryknoll, NY: Orbis Books, 2007); Richard Friedli et al., eds., *Intercultural Perceptions and Prospects of World Christianity* (Frankfurt am Main: Peter Lang, 2010); Walter J. Hollenweger, *Interkulturelle Theologie*, 3 vols. (Munich: Kaiser, 1979–

and education.[136] As I mentioned in the introduction, we will use the term *intercultural* as opposed to *multicultural* or *multiethnic* because *intercultural* is the preferred term in current academic discussions in communication theory and education theory. The term(s) has a wide breadth of uses. Sometimes people use it to talk about racial and cultural diversity in the United States. Someone might say, "Every year, the US is becoming more intercultural or multicultural," or, "The city of Houston is far more intercultural or multicultural than it was fifty years ago." Other times the term refers to intercultural dialogue, whether such as a conversation between people of different races and ethnicities *within* a larger society, or a conversation between people of different races and ethnicities across national cultures like Americans studying abroad in Mexico or Ghana, for example, in phrases such as "intercultural dialogue" or "intercultural exchange." Our interest in interculturalism is narrower than these definitions, especially since engagement with the broad ideas represented in a field this large could take up another book entirely.

Our interest is in intercultural proficiency, what intercultural theorists refer to as *intercultural competence* (IC). Again, I define intercultural competence as *the cultivation of knowledge, skills, and habits for effectively negotiating cultural, racial, and ecclesial difference.* Later, in chapter four, we will unpack this definition and discuss different models of intercultural competence. In addition to demonstrating the ways that Taylor was a forerunner in IC proficiency, I propose my own model—the "3A Model of Intercultural Competence Proficiency Attainment." Now, however, we will discuss why IC proficiency is so important to preaching pedagogy in the US context, and interact with current homiletical literature so as to locate this work in a wider conversation.

In the introduction, we saw that churches and seminary classrooms in the United States have already undergone and will continue to un-

---

1988); Theo Sundermeier, "Erwägungen zu einer Hermeneutik interkulturellen Verstehens," in *Konvivenz und Differenz: Studien zu einer verstehenden Missionswissenschaft*, ed. Volker Küster (Erlangen: Verlag der Ev.-Luth. Mission, 1995), pp. 87-101; and, most recently, Orlando O. Espín, *Idol and Grace: On Traditioning and Subversive Hope* (Maryknoll, NY: Orbis Books, 2014).
[136] See David Esterline and Ogbu Kalu, eds., *Multicultural Theological Education: On Doing Difference Differently* (Louisville: Westminster John Knox, 2006). See also Barbara Wilkerson, ed., *Multicultural Religious Education* (Birmingham, AL: Religious Education Press, 1997).

dergo a dramatic demographic shift. The word *already* is intentional since, in many ways, the shift in theological education *has* happened. In a 2012 address to the Association of Theological Schools (ATS), executive director Daniel Aleshire observes,

> In 1981–82, African, Asian, and Hispanic descent students accounted for 8 percent of total enrollment. This past academic year [2011–2012], these students constituted 27 percent of total enrollment. Add visa students, who are almost all persons of color, and racial/ethnic students approached 34 percent. Racial/ethnic faculty members have increased from 6 percent of the total thirty years ago to 19 percent this past academic year.[137]

If we expand the data trajectory back to 1969, when nonwhite student enrollment was just under 3 percent, this means that the nonwhite percentage of total enrollment has grown 900 percent (from 3 to 27 percent) in the last forty-three years (1969–2012), or over 1,100 percent (from 3 to 34 percent) when one includes international students.[138] Here also is a brief summary of recent trends in ATS member schools in the last four years:

Table 1. ATS Trends by Racial/Ethnic Makeup: 2009–2013

Racial/Ethnic Group	2009 Total Head Count (THC)	2013 Total Head Count (THC)	Total Gains and Losses
White	44,186	39,713	-10%
African American	8,524	9,325	+10%
Hispanic	3,185	3,789	+20%
Asian	5,165	5,756	+11%
Visa (International)	6,198	6,319	+2%

For these figures, see "Table 2.12-A: Head Count Enrollment by Race or Ethnic Group, Degree, and Gender, 2013, All Members Schools," in *2013-14 Annual Data Tables* (Pittsburgh: Association of Theological Schools), accessed January 30, 2015, www.ats.edu/resources/institutional-data/annual-data-tables.

It is obvious from these figures that THC (total head count) enrollment among white students is still the largest percentage—62 percent

---

[137]See Daniel Aleshire, *Community and Diversity*, report delivered at the ATS Biennial Meeting (Pittsburgh: Association of Theological Schools, June 2012), p. 2, last modified January 18, 2014, www.ats.edu/resources/publications-and-presentations.

[138]Data on 1969 total student enrollment taken from the report *Folio: Diversity in Theological Education* (Pittsburgh: Association of Theological Schools, March 2002), last modified January 30, 2014, www.ats.edu/resources/publications-and-presentations.

in 2013—far higher than every other racial and ethnic group. What is more significant than this figure, however, is the changes and trends that can be observed even just in the last four years. THC enrollment among white students is down 10 percent since 2009, whereas, in every other category including international students on an F-1 visa, the numbers have increased. Also, the data show that the THC growth among every category of US-born nonwhite students is at between 10 and 20 percent, and that international student growth stands at 2 percent. From a macro perspective, THC enrollment among nonwhite and international students grew from 20,205 in 2009 to 25,189 in 2013, an increase of 25 percent.

This is a remarkable shift—one worth celebrating—especially if it means that seminaries are doing better at reflecting the ethnic and racial makeup of the overall US context, and that nonwhite and non-US-born students who've been excluded from higher education in past generations are gaining access to opportunities that were not previously afforded them.

The problem is neither with how seminaries have changed, nor with whether seminaries are or are not celebrating this change. The problem is with what seminaries are doing about this change. Most would agree that it is good for an institution to celebrate its diversity and that institutions that celebrate diversity are making a better decision than those that do not celebrate it. But is celebration enough? Is more required? What if celebration is a way of avoiding the hard work of institutional change? Are institutions really engaging with difference and diversity, or are they paying lip service to it? Tokenism is a lot easier than reconciliation.

The demographic shift that has already taken place and will continue taking place requires a requisite shift in institutional thinking and training. In my judgment, the way forward for institutions is to learn to *think* and *act* interculturally and to teach their students to do the same. The reason conversations and actions that move toward intercultural competence are so important is that they center on education and training of interculturally proficient students, faculty, administrators, and staff.

Others agree with me that an institutional shift in thinking and acting is required. In *Our Underachieving Colleges*, former Harvard University president Derek Bok points out that the vast majority of today's undergraduate students do not have the necessary skills required to "think interculturally" and thus succeed in the global marketplace. However, Bok also observes:

> The difficulty with this objective is not just that "thinking interculturally" is as yet imperfectly understood. It is also a skill (as the term *intercultural competence* implies), and many Arts and Sciences professors are reluctant to teach skills. Given the opportunity, they will often choose to "cover" a body of knowledge and concepts rather than help their students to develop a competence, whether it be writing with clarity or understanding another society. Thus courses on other cultures frequently turn into a series of detailed lectures on a foreign country, leaving students with much information about its history, institutions, and problems but with little capacity for understanding and adjusting to the different societies they will encounter in their later lives.[139]

To illustrate his point, Bok describes the shift that happened in law schools in the mid-twentieth century when professors had to change their pedagogical approach. Because the laws in all fifty states had become too diverse and numerous for them to "cover," these professors started teaching their lawyers how to "think like a lawyer."[140] The same shift, Bok argues, must also take place in the faculty meeting rooms and pedagogies of undergraduate and graduate institutions in the United States, namely, a shift to teaching students how to think interculturally instead of "covering" material in programs or colloquia. Although a shift of this nature will no doubt encounter resistance, especially in the humanities, given its aversion to skill acquisition, Bok claims such a shift is necessary and even urgent if American students hope to compete in the global marketplace.

In a move more specific to our genre of education, some theological educators are making similar claims. Like Bok, they identify the need for changes in the prevailing academic culture at institutions and in pedagogy specifically. For instance, in April 2013, the Forum for Theological Exploration (FTE) facilitated an academic consultation of pres-

---

[139]Derek Bok, *Our Underachieving Colleges: A Candid Look at How Much Students Learn and Why They Should Be Learning More* (Princeton, NJ: Princeton University Press, 2008), p. 250.
[140]Ibid.

idents, deans, professors, researchers, and doctoral students in order to work toward two goals: first, to catalyze the educational-experiential enrichment of nonwhite PhD candidates in seminaries and divinity schools, and, second, to spark change in the institutions that train them. When one reads the FTE's final report, "Time to Choose, Time to Change," it becomes clear that training in intercultural competence proficiency is a necessary and even urgent step for institutions. Practical theologian Peter T. Cha attended the consultation. Cha teaches at Trinity Evangelical Divinity School, and he works alongside churches in areas like inclusion, intercultural/multiethnic training, and racial/ethnic reconciliation, especially in Asian American contexts. Cha makes this observation:

> In my view, in order to nurture and raise the kind of faculty needed for tomorrow's church—a church that is already here—will take nothing short of *rethinking our academic culture*. It socializes our future teachers. It shapes how they think and how they feel and how they shape certain assumptions about what should take place at the seminary.[141]

Cha also observes the growing interest among young seminary graduates who either serve in racial/ethnic immigrant churches or interculturally diverse churches. Institutions that hope to meet this demand, he argues, must facilitate "a heightened level of *intercultural awareness* among the faculty who teach them."[142]

Frank Yamada, the president of McCormick Theological Seminary, also attended the FTE consultation. McCormick is thinking strategically about intercultural theological education and trying to train church leaders for a "church we cannot yet envision."[143] Yamada makes a similar point to that of Cha. He recommends "developing *cross cultural competencies* for current and future faculty and infecting academic guilds with the idea that this *skill* is fundamentally important for the future of theo-

---

[141]Peter T. Cha, quoted in Joh and Baker, *Time to Choose, Time to Change*, p. 17 (emphasis added).
[142]Peter T. Cha, quoted in ibid., p. 12 (emphasis added).
[143]McCormick uses the phrase "preparing leaders for a church we cannot yet envision" in some of its promotional materials. See Anna Case-Winters, "Multicultural Theological Education: On Doing Difference Differently," in *Shaping Beloved Community: Multicultural Theological Education*, ed. David Esterline and Ogbu Kalu (Louisville: Westminster John Knox, 2006), p. 45.

logical education."[144] Interestingly, all of the participants in the consultation identified "training for cultural competency as part of the skill set of all executive leaders, faculty, and doctoral students" as one of three constructive practices that can help offset institutional racism and contribute to individual flourishing among students.[145] They used the term *cultural competency*, a term that is almost synonymous with the term I use, *intercultural competence*.

If Yamada is correct that this skill is "fundamentally important to the future of theological education" and that we should "infect" academic guilds with it; if Cha is right that a greater number of seminary graduates need to learn this skill from interculturally proficient professors; and if everyone at the FTE consultation agreed that cultural competency is a constructive practice for dismantling racist systems and enriching the lives of all students, white and nonwhite, the next logical question is, *What is homiletics doing to meet this need and participate in this conversation?* Are homileticians doing constructive work to change their teaching and to prepare their students for the future?

Here is why Taylor's skill at intercultural competence uniquely positions him as a harbinger from whom homileticians can glean insights. His is not just a historical contribution. That Taylor was interculturally competent before academic discussions about intercultural competence makes him relevant to today's context. If he maintained IC proficiency in the way I have defined it, that is, he knew how to cultivate knowledge, skills, and habits for effectively negotiating cultural, racial, and ecclesial difference, his homiletical approach is not only relevant to today's context but important for the future as well. In chapter four, I discuss the ways that Taylor attained this IC proficiency. Now, however, it will be helpful for us to analyze what the current homiletical literature says about preaching and interculturalism.

In a 2001 publication *Preaching to Every Pew: Cross-Cultural Strategies*, James R. Nieman and Thomas G. Rogers discuss the results of their research interviewing pastors of intercultural churches over a two-year

---

[144]Frank Yamada as quoted in Joh and Baker, *Time to Choose, Time to Change*, p. 28 (emphasis added).
[145]Ibid.

period.[146] Grounding their work in a biblical-theological foundation of offering hospitality and loving one's neighbor, Nieman and Rogers contend that preachers should pay more attention to four cultural frames in particular—ethnicity, economic class, geographical displacement, and religion—frames they believe are operative in intercultural congregations. In chapters two through five, they describe these frames and discuss how each frame shapes listeners' experiences of sermons. One of the assets of this book is its practicality. Nieman and Rogers draw on actual interviews with pastors of intercultural churches concerning what works and doesn't work in their context, and the final chapter contains personal advice to the preacher, such as exploring one's own culture more deeply, finding a support group, and becoming more adaptive in one's preparation and delivery.[147] Their book also contains a list of suggested readings for pastors working in these contexts.[148]

In *One Gospel, Many Ears: Preaching for Different Listeners in the Congregation*, Joseph R. Jeter Jr. and Ronald J. Allen contend that "every congregation is multicultural" even if, at first glance, a local church pastor does not see it that way.[149] (They prefer the term *multicultural* instead of *intercultural*.) By expanding more traditional understandings of the word *multicultural* and its association with churches that are multiethnic or multilingual, Jeter and Allen seek to reach pastors who might falsely conclude that they serve a "culturally identical congregation."[150] In other words, they want pastors to recognize that their listeners are more diverse than they might think. To make their point more concrete, Jeter and Allen challenge Nieman and Rogers's four cultural frames (implicitly, not explicitly) with a more nuanced interpretation of congregational life. Their analysis focuses on the *multiple* factors that shape a listener's experience of sermons, factors such as gender, age, personality type, patterns of mental operation, ethnicity,

---

[146]Nieman and Rogers refer to these churches as "multicultural churches" rather than "intercultural churches."

[147]James R. Nieman and Thomas G. Rogers, *Preaching to Every Pew: Cross-Cultural Strategies* (Minneapolis: Fortress, 2001), pp. 139-57.

[148]Ibid., pp. 158-59.

[149]Joseph R. Jeter Jr. and Ronald J. Allen, *One Gospel, Many Ears: Preaching for Different Listeners in the Congregation* (St. Louis: Chalice, 2002), p. 112.

[150]Ibid.

class, race, and theological orientation.[151] Jeter and Allen do not ignore the significance of race and ethnicity to preaching. Not at all. In fact, they devote an entire chapter to preaching in intercultural settings in which they take *multicultural* to mean churches where various races and ethnicities are represented.[152] Rather, they complicate traditional understandings of culture and diversity in order to help *every* preacher see and understand the complex web of factors that make their listeners more diverse than they imagine.

In *Preaching in an Age of Globalization*, Eunjoo Mary Kim argues that preachers should shift their attention from an *intracontextual* approach to a *transcontextual* approach to preaching. By *intracontextual* she means an approach in which one's focus is primarily on the local context and the local congregation. Although she affirms the contributions made by intracontextual approaches to homiletics, nevertheless she criticizes the works of Nieman and Rogers, along with Leonora Tubbs Tisdale's work, for fixing too strong a gaze on the local.[153] By *transcontextual* Kim means an approach that "moves beyond particularity to reach interdependent relationships between one's own and the contexts of others."[154] She argues that one's local context and another's local context are not mutually exclusive on account of globalization. The temptation is for preaching to get "locked into its own local context."[155] However, preaching must be both local and global.[156] Kim lifts up a homiletical strategy that emphasizes the "interwovenness" of local and global, a phenomenon she believes

---

[151]In *Preaching*, Fred Craddock makes a similar claim to Jeter and Allen's when he writes: "No congregation is homogenous, not even the small rural one which consists basically of three 'main families.'... Some listeners have a totally uncritical stance toward all matters of Christian doctrine.... Others in the congregation will be trying to arrive at a faith of their own.... Still other parishioners do not take Christian beliefs and traditions seriously." See Fred B. Craddock, *Preaching* (Nashville: Abingdon, 1985), pp. 90-91.

[152]Jeter and Allen, *One Gospel, Many Ears*, pp. 103-28.

[153]Kim critiques Nieman and Rogers's *Preaching to Every Pew* and Tisdale's *Preaching as Local Theology and Folk Art* in Eunjoo Mary Kim, *Preaching in an Age of Globalization* (Louisville: Westminster John Knox, 2010), pp. 15-17.

[154]Ibid., p. 17.

[155]Ibid.

[156]Some prefer to use the word *glocal* to describe the symbiotic relationship between the local and the global. See Bob Roberts Jr., *Glocalization: How Followers of Jesus Engage the New Flat World* (Grand Rapids: Zondervan, 2007); Tormod Engelsviken, *The Church Going Glocal: Mission and Globalisation* (Eugene, OR: Wipf & Stock, 2011).

preachers can and should attend to in an age of globalization.[157]

Three additional publications, a book chapter by Eric H. F. Law, a dissertation by Woosung Calvin Choi, and a recent book by Lisa Washington Lamb are also part of the emerging conversation concerning interculturalism and preaching. (Some original research on interculturalism and congregational life has already been done in the wider field of practical theology.[158]) In *Word at the Crossings*, Eric H. F. Law devotes a chapter to preaching in intercultural churches, what he refers to as "preaching at the crossings."[159] In this chapter, he offers practical, hands-on advice to pastors preaching in "multi-ethnic" and "multi-generational" congregations. Most of his advice is anecdotal and based on lessons he learned serving a Chinese immigrant church in Boston just after seminary.

In 2013, Woosung Calvin Choi completed a dissertation on preaching in multiethnic churches (he uses the term *multiethnic*) in which he proposed a homiletical paradigm known as "positive marginality."[160] Choi supported his thesis by tracking a recurring theme of *marginality* in interviews he conducted with seven multiethnic church pastors in the United States, Great Britain, Canada, and other parts of the world. One of Choi's original contributions is that his research took place both inside and outside the US context, that is, he looked at phenomena that affect multiethnic churches on more than one continent.

---

[157]Kim coins this term as a descriptive image for the intercultural reality of today's world and the necessity of intercultural awareness in preaching. See Kim, *Preaching in an Age of Globalization*, p. 16.

[158]In *Places of Redemption*, Mary McClintock Fulkerson does ethnographic work on racial and ethnic identity in an intercultural United Methodist church in North Carolina. See Mary McClintock Fulkerson, *Places of Redemption: Theology for a Worldly Church* (Oxford: Oxford University Press, 2007). Also, Janice McLean completed a PhD dissertation at the University of Edinburgh on ethnic and religious tensions among Jamaican Pentecostal congregations in London and New York City. McLean teaches at City Seminary of New York. See www.cityseminary.org. These two projects are not homiletically oriented, but they are examples of practical theological research on intercultural congregations.

[159]See Eric H. F. Law, *The Word at the Crossings: Living the Good News in a Multicontextual Community* (St. Louis: Chalice, 2004).

[160]Choi defines positive marginality as "the ability to embrace two or more ethnic and/or cultural groups, engage in an intentional cross-cultural dialogue and establish relationships with others by fully utilizing the assets and strengths of those groups, and thereby, embody a communal identity and exhibit a renewed vision for society." See Woosung Calvin Choi, "Preaching to the Multiethnic Congregation: Positive Marginality as a Homiletical Paradigm" (PhD diss., London School of Theology, 2013), p. ix.

Finally, in her recent book *Blessed and Beautiful: Multiethnic Churches and the Preaching That Sustains Them*, Lisa Washington Lamb urges preachers to attend to the "neglected yet magnetic power of memory for forming congregations that dwell in the midst of ethnic and cultural diversity."[161] Just as appeals to shared memories and stories catalyze ethnic groups, claims Lamb, so also can appeals to shared memories and stories catalyze multiethnic Christian communities.[162]

Although these homiletical texts on interculturalism are useful, each of them deals with interculturalism-as-phenomenon, not -as-proficiency. While homileticians have written on preaching and interculturalism, it is significant, indeed unfortunate, that the literature on preaching and intercultural competence is *nonexistent*, especially since both secular and theological educators agree that intercultural competence is indispensible to education in the future. As churches move toward their intercultural future, intercultural proficiency among their preachers will become more rather than less important. Our concern is with intercultural competence as a dispositional proficiency, one that arguably is latent in Taylor's preaching and ministry practice but absent from the current homiletical discussion.

Undoubtedly, these homileticians make important connections between interculturalism as a phenomenon and the nature of the preaching task. Nieman and Rogers identify cultural frames; Jeter and Allen discuss ecclesial diversity in seemingly homogeneous settings; and Kim focuses on the impact of globalization. These connections are significant for at least two reasons: first, they help us think differently about sermon preparation and delivery, and, second, they force us to reconsider our homiletical assumptions about themes like homogeneous audiences (Jeter and Allen) or the impact of globalization (Kim). That stated, current homiletical literature does not provide a sufficient theoretical or theological framework for intercultural competence and preaching, and it does not recommend concrete practices for attaining and improving on this proficiency.

---

[161] Lisa Washington Lamb, *Blessed and Beautiful: Multiethnic Churches and the Preaching That Sustains Them* (Eugene, OR: Cascade, 2014), pp. viii-ix.
[162] Ibid., p. 2.

CONCLUSION

Taylor's approach reveals a commitment to improvisational-intercultural proficiency that is performative in practice, metaphorical in extension, and intercultural in scope. The next chapter deals with the ways his approach is performative in practice. We will see how recent developments in performance theory refine our understandings of Taylor's practice of improvisation. In subsequent chapters, we will see how developments in race theory deepen our analysis of Taylor's metaphorical improvisation and developments in intercultural competence theory expand our assessment of Taylor's intercultural competence.

Taylor's proficiencies as a crossover preacher are not only innovative and thought provoking, but more important to the discipline of homiletics, they anticipate the needs of churches and seminary classrooms now and in the future. An improvisational-intercultural approach, one that is demonstrated in Taylor's preaching as case study and contextualized to today's situational needs and opportunities, can help us meet this need. It can guide us toward becoming the sort of crossover preachers and teachers that the church in the United States will require in the days to come. The church has already changed. Now, it's our turn.

2

TURNING INK TO BLOOD

PERFORMATIVE IMPROVISATION

The art of improvising is not just a gift.
It is acquired and perfected by study.

JACQUES COPEAU
quoted in John Rudlin, *Jacques Copeau*

◆

To a request for permission to print his sermons, the eighteenth-century revivalist George Whitefield responded: "Well, I have no inherent objection, if you like, but you will never be able to put on the printed page the lightning and the thunder."[1] Indeed, published sermons and performed sermons are distinct from each other. The written sermon has a level of permanence to it; its appeal is more to the eye than the ear; in many ways, it is abstracted from its local place and time. To borrow language from linguistic and analytic philosophy, the written sermon primarily has a "locutionary" function.[2] The live sermon is ephemeral;

---

[1]As cited in D. Martyn Lloyd-Jones, *Preaching and Preachers* (London: Hodder and Stoughton, 1971), p. 58.

[2]In his article "Performative Utterances," analytic philosopher J. L. Austin argues that there are three primary functions of speech-acts: locutionary, illocutionary, and perlocutionary. Locutionary pertains to the act of saying something. Illocutionary is the way in which a locution is used. Perlocutionary is an act that occurs *by* saying something rather than an act *of* saying something (locutionary) or what occurs *in* saying something (illocutionary). A printed sermon primarily has a locutionary function in that the original way in which the locution was used (illocutionary) ended when the speech-act ended. For more on the three types of speech acts, see J. L. Austin, "Performative Utterances," in *Philosophical Papers* (Oxford: Clarendon Press, 1961), p. 222; and J. L. Austin, *How to Do Things with Words*, The William James Lectures 1955 (New York: Oxford

it is fused with gestures and sounds; it is oral and aural; its local situatedness marks it out as a particular word for a particular people in a
particular time and space. It has a locutionary, illocutionary, *and* perlocutionary function.[3] Although written sermons serve an important
function in society, most preachers do not need to be reminded that live
sermons are distinct. They understand Whitefield's lightning and
thunder argument. As D. Martyn Lloyd-Jones points out, "You can put
the sermon into print, but not the lightning and the thunder."[4]

In response to T. S. Eliot's dictum that the purpose of writing literature is to turn blood into ink, homiletician Charles L. Bartow suggests
that preaching does the opposite—it turns ink into blood.[5] The written
text is an "arrested performance" waiting to be set free through speech.[6]
Reading Scripture aloud in worship, Bartow argues, is an act infused
with gestures and sounds. Moreover, Christian leaders are commanded
in 1 Timothy 4:13: "give attention to the public reading of scripture." By
God's grace, the oral reading of Scripture can evoke God's divine
presence in a way that writing alone cannot.[7] In sacramental human

University Press, 1965), pp. 150-51. For more on speech acts and analytic philosophy, see John R.
Searle, *Speech Acts: An Essay in the Philosophy of Language* (London: Cambridge University Press,
1969); and Donald D. Evans, *The Logic of Self-Involvement: A Philosophical Study of Everyday
Language with Special Reference to the Christian Use of Language About God as Creator* (London:
SCM Press, 1963). For more on the connection between speech acts and homiletics, see James F.
Kay, *Preaching and Theology* (St. Louis: Chalice, 2007), p. 123.
[3]See previous footnote on the distinctions between speech-acts.
[4]Lloyd-Jones, *Preaching and Preachers*, p. 58.
[5]Charles L. Bartow, *God's Human Speech: A Practical Theology of Proclamation* (Grand Rapids: Eerdmans, 1997), p. 63. Bartow claims that the ink-into-blood metaphor for preaching originates with
William Brower, who taught speech at Princeton Theological Seminary.
[6]Beverly Long and Mary Hopkins describe the written text as an "arrested performance" in Beverly
Whitaker Long and Mary Frances Hopkins, *Performing Literature: An Introduction to Oral Interpretation* (Englewood Cliffs, NJ: Prentice-Hall, 1982), as cited in Bartow, *God's Human Speech*, p. 64.
[7]Richard F. Ward agrees with Bartow's claim that public reading of Scripture has the power to
evoke the presence of God. Ward writes: "The purpose of reading aloud is to give voice, bodily
shape, and expression to the 'presences' we find evoked in biblical texts." See Richard F. Ward,
Speaking of the Holy: The Art of Communication in Preaching (St. Louis: Chalice, 2001), p. 64. In
this same chapter, Ward acknowledges his indebtedness to the work of George Steiner, who argues
that words have the power to evoke real presence(s). According to Steiner, language in general and
aesthetic interpretation in particular is "underwritten by the assumption of God's presence." See
George Steiner, *Real Presences* (Chicago: University of Chicago Press, 1989), p. 3. That stated,
evocation of God's presence is only one part of the process: human agency. In divine agency, God
has the power to choose or not to choose a divine-human encounter through preaching or through
reading Scripture aloud.

speech in the public recitation of Scripture, God manifests God's presence. Bartow implies that sermons do this too, but stops his argument short at the oral reading of Scripture.

What if the sermon manuscript were also an "arrested performance" waiting to be set free through human speech? What if the move from a sermon manuscript to a live sermon, with all its ephemeral qualities, also turned ink into blood? And what would happen if the preacher, in a live sermon, riffed on what he or she had prepared in much the same way that blues musicians riff on melodies or improvisational performers draw from "ready-mades" in a scripted scene so that the sermon-as-preached were different from the sermon-as-prepared? In the context of the sermon-as-preached, what if free spaces emerged for the preacher to improvise on the sermon-as-prepared? We know that improvisational performers riff. What we will see is that Gardner C. Taylor riffs.

In this chapter, we will see that Taylor practices performative improvisation, and I point to significant connections between his preaching practices and improvisational performance. Taylor practices performative improvisation, first, through observable differences between the sermon-as-prepared and the sermon-as-preached; second, by attuning to the space in which he preached in person- and context-specific ways; and third, through using oral formulas or "tropes" in sermons in much the same way that improvisational performers use them.

One caveat to mention is that Taylor does not depart from the sermon-as-prepared in every instance. On some occasions, he sticks as closely to the manuscript as possible. In a 1981 interview with *Leadership* magazine, he explains that sometimes the best thing to do with a sermon is to "plow as straight a furrow as you can, finish, and leave the rest to God."[8] As a preacher, Taylor had a remarkable capacity for memorizing large portions of prepared text, and he was able to preach those portions almost verbatim. Although this is true, nevertheless, in many of his sermons, unforeseen and unplanned-for improvisational moments occur in real time. This chapter highlights his acknowledgment that this is the case along with the important family resemblances his homiletical ap-

---

[8]WGT 5:288.

proach shares with improvisational performance. First, I define what I mean by performative improvisation. Then, I *connect* my definition of performative improvisation by noting its parallels with Christian preaching. Last, I *observe* three of Taylor's preaching practices.

DEFINING PERFORMATIVE IMPROVISATION

Various definitions of improvisation have emerged in recent decades, especially in jazz music.[9] To support the aims of this chapter and to close a gap in homiletical discussion, however, our main focus will be on definitions of improvisation in performances studies. Performance theorists such as John Hodgson and Ernest Richards define *improvisation* as "the spontaneous response to the unfolding of an unexpected situation, and the ingenuity called on to deal with the situation."[10] Anthony Frost and Ralph Yarrow define it as "the skill of using bodies, space, all human resources, to generate a coherent physical expression of an idea, a situation, a character (even perhaps, a text); to do this spontaneously, in response to the immediate stimuli of one's environment, and to do it *à l'improviste*: as though taken by surprise, without preconceptions."[11]

Viola Spolin offers an extensive definition (abridged here). She suggests that improvisation is about: "Playing the game; setting out to solve a problem with no preconception as to how you will do it; permitting everything in the environment (animate or inanimate) to work for you

---

[9]Critical reflections on jazz improvisation—its history, definition, and prevalence—have increased greatly over the past few decades. The best place to begin is the oft-cited and highly acclaimed book by Paul Berliner, *Thinking in Jazz: The Infinite Art of Improvisation* (Chicago: University of Chicago Press, 1994). For a comprehensive overview of jazz improvisation and its development as a cultural and musical practice, see Bill Kirchner, ed., *The Oxford Companion to Jazz* (New York: Oxford University Press, 2000); and Mervyn Cooke and David Horn, eds., *The Cambridge Companion to Jazz* (New York: Cambridge University Press, 2002). For further reading, see also Bjorn Alterhaug, "Improvisation on a Triple Theme: Creativity, Jazz Improvisation, and Communication," *Studia Musicologica Norvegica* 30 (2004): 97-118; Daniel Fischlin and Ajay Heble, eds., *The Other Side of Nowhere: Jazz, Improvisation, and Communities in Dialogue* (Middletown, CT: Wesleyan University Press, 2004); Ingrid T. Monson, *Saying Something: Jazz Improvisation and Interaction* (Chicago: University of Chicago Press, 1996); and Gabriele Tomasi, "On the Spontaneity of Jazz Improvisation," in *Improvisation: Between Technique and Spontaneity*, ed. Marina Santi (Newcastle upon Tyne, UK: Cambridge Scholars Press, 2010), pp. 77-102.

[10]John Hodgson and Ernest Richards, *Improvisation* (New York: Grove Press, 1979), p. 2.

[11]Anthony Frost and Ralph Yarrow, *Improvisation in Drama* (New York: St. Martin's Press, 1990), p. 1.

in solving the problem."[12] Amy Seham provides the most succinct definition of improvisation as "inventiveness within limitation."[13] Despite variations on defining the term, a few common threads bind these definitions together, such as the importance of spontaneity, the need for adaptability, and the dialectical tension between freedom and limitation.

Let us define performative improvisation as *the ability to do a new thing in a new way as guided by convention, intuition, and interaction.* The first two words of my definition emphasize the interpreter's agency.

1. The interpreter exercises ability. Improvisation requires skill. Improvisers maintain a high level of *phronesis*, or, practical wisdom that informs what they do, when they do it, and how they do it.[14] As French director and theorist Jacques Copeau observes, "Improvisation is an art that has to be learned."[15] Performative knowledge involves the attainment of skills gained through practice and performance; it comes through honing one's abilities over time and critically reflecting on one's practices.

Lesa Lockford and Ronald J. Pelias suggest that specific forms of knowledge are needed for improvisational performance, what they refer to as "cognitive, affective, and intuitive capacities."[16] Some of these capacities are tacit and embedded in a performer's abilities, but most are

---

[12]Spolin's full definition of improvisation is as follows: "Playing the game; setting out to solve a problem with no preconception as to how you will do it; permitting everything in the environment to (animate or inanimate) to work for you in solving the problem; it is not the scene, it is the way to the scene; a predominate function of the intuitive; playing the game brings opportunity to learn theater to a cross-section of people; 'playing it by ear'; process as opposed to result; not ad-lib or 'originality' or 'making it up yourself'; a form, if understood, possible to any age group; setting object in motion between players as in a game, solving of problems together, the ability to allow the acting problem to evolve the scene; a moment in the life of people without needing a plot or story line for the communication; an art form; transformation; brings forth details and relationships as organic whole; living process." Viola Spolin, *Improvisation for the Theater* (Evanston, IL: Northwestern University Press, 1999), p. 361.

[13]Seham, *Whose Improv Is It Anyway?*, p. xx.

[14]For more on Aristotle's understanding of *phronesis*, see John E. Sisko, "Phronesis," in *Encyclopedia of Ethics: P-W*, ed. Lawrence C. Becker and Charlotte B. Becker (New York: Routledge, 2001), pp. 1314-16.

[15]Quotation in John Rudlin, *Jacques Copeau* (Cambridge: Cambridge University Press, 1986), p. 44, cited in Frost and Yarrow, *Improvisation in Drama*, p. 25.

[16]Lesa Lockford and Ronald J. Pelias, "Bodily Poeticizing in Theatrical Improvisation: A Typology of Performative Knowledge," *Theatre Topics* 14, no. 2 (September 2004): 439. Lockford and Pelias also argue that some of these capacities are embedded and embodied in a tacit sense. They write: "It is a place where performers sense what is right without, perhaps, being able to explain why. It is the place, as Michael Polanyi would have it, of 'tacit knowledge.'" Ibid., p. 436.

learned through rehearsal and performance. Sustained practice over time leads to a level of performative excellence that cognitive and behavioral theorists refer to as "automaticity," or higher-level actions and behaviors performed instinctively.[17] To return to Copeau's observation, improvisation is "acquired and perfected by study." It is not so much a gift that descends from heaven as it is a performative skill.

As is the case with preaching, improvisational performance requires an eclectic combination of gifting, experience(s), multiple intelligences, and skills. Even spontaneity, a trait that is often glorified in performance, does not take place ex nihilo.[18] The best moments of spontaneity arise when veteran performers draw from a reservoir of skill sets made accessible by years of study.[19] As theologian Stanley Hauerwas suggests,

---

[17]Behavioral studies suggest that automaticity, that is, deliberate practice over time, develops in the performer a high level of muscle memory and instinctiveness that are "central to the development of expertise." They contend that "practice is the means to automaticity." See Paul J. Feltovich, Michael J. Prietula, and K. Anders Ericsson, "Studies of Expertise from Psychological Perspectives," in *The Cambridge Handbook of Expertise and Expert Performance*, ed. K. Anders Ericsson et al. (New York: Cambridge University Press, 2006), p. 54. However, in a separate essay Ericsson cautions against practice without concerted deliberation and reflection. Without these, automaticity can actually become detrimental to the performer pursuing excellence and expertise. Ericsson writes: "The key challenge for aspiring expert performers is to avoid the arrested development associated with automaticity and to acquire the cognitive skills to support their continued learning and improvement. By actively seeking out demanding tasks—often provided by their teachers and coaches—that force the performers to engage in problem solving and to stretch their performance, the expert performers overcome the detrimental effects of automaticity and actively acquire and refine cognitive mechanisms to support continued learning and improvement." "The Influence of Experience and Deliberate Practice on the Development of Superior Expert Performance," in Ericsson et al., *Cambridge Handbook of Expertise and Expert Performance*, p. 696.

[18]Keith Johnstone, a key figure in improvisational performance, "tricks" students into believing that the content of the performance is not important in order to free up their creativity and promote the illusion that they're completely abandoning control. In reality, the students are learning both process and content in Johnstone's courses. They're learning to abandon control while also learning to exercise control. Johnstone writes: "I began this essay by saying that an improviser shouldn't be concerned with content, because the content arrives automatically. This is true, and also not true. The best improvisers do, at some level, know what their work is about. . . . You have to trick students into believing that content isn't important and that it looks after itself, or they never get anywhere. . . . In the end they learn how to abandon control while at the same time they exercise control." Keith Johnstone, *Impro: Improvisation and the Theatre* (New York: Routledge, 1992), p. 142.

[19]Study, experience, and *phronesis* are critical not only to improvisational performance in the theater; the same can be said of performers in jazz music. In an article on improvisation in musical performance, Philip Alperson comments: "The truth, of course, is that even the freest improviser, far from creating ex nihilo improvises against some sort of musical context. In fact, learning to improvise is often, in large part, learning to master that tradition." See Philip Alperson, "On Musical Improvisation," *Journal of Aesthetics and Art Criticism* 43, no. 1 (Autumn 1984): 22.

"Spontaneity . . . is but the outcome of years of training and practice and thousands of experiments."[20]

2. Doing a new thing in a new way. Performative improvisation is an exercise in controlled spontaneity. Though certainly improvisation requires ability—Seham writes: "the notion of *pure* spontaneity in improvisation is a myth"—this does not mean that spontaneity is unimportant or peripheral to improvisation itself.[21] Not only is it an essential ingredient in performance, but it remains central to most (if not all) definitions of improvisation.[22] Even the word *improvise* makes a nod to the importance of spontaneity in that it comes from the Latin *improvisus*, or "not foreseen." To be spontaneous, writes Gary Izzo, is "to summon an immediate, raw, unaltered creative impulse."[23] It is to act and react to new developments and unpredictable outcomes just as one would when playing a game. This means that improvisational performers commit to the unforeseen and the immediate. Those who embrace spontaneity participate in performances with high levels of unpredictability, what theologian Jeremy Begbie calls "contingency."[24] The only predictable thing is unpredictability.

Perhaps the most effective way to depict spontaneity is through metaphor, and so to borrow the central motif that guides Viola Spolin's

---

[20]Stanley Hauerwas, *Against the Nations: War and Survival in a Liberal Society* (Minneapolis: Winston, 1985), p. 52, as cited in Jeremy Begbie, *Theology, Music, and Time* (Cambridge: Cambridge University Press, 2000), p. 179. R. Keith Sawyer supports Hauerwas's claim with the following observation: "Creative improvisation depends on a lifetime of practice and rehearsal, and improvisers have a large body of material that they draw on during performance." See R. Keith Sawyer, *Creating Conversations: Improvisation in Everyday Discourse* (Cresskill, NJ: Hampton Press, 2001), p. 8.

[21]Amy Seham, "Play Fair: Feminist Tools for Teaching Improv," in *Radical Acts: Theatre and Feminist Pedagogies of Change*, ed. Ann Elizabeth Armstrong and Kathleen Juhl (San Francisco: Aunt Lute Books, 2007), p. 140 (entire quotation italicized in original text).

[22]Adam Blatner, Anthony Frost, and Robert Yarrow note the connection between spontaneity and psychotherapist J. L. Moreno's "psychodrama" movement in the 1920s in Vienna. Blatner notes that Moreno founded one of the first modern improvisational theater troupes. He called it "the Theatre of Spontaneity." See Adam Blatner, ed., *Interactive and Improvisational Drama: Varieties of Applied Theatre and Performance* (Lincoln, NE: iUniverse, 2007), p. xv. Frost and Yarrow show how spontaneity (along with other key ingredients) was integral to Moreno's therapeutic practices and to his definition of improvisational psychotherapy. See Frost and Yarrow, *Improvisation in Drama*, p. 145.

[23]Gary Izzo, *The Art of Play: The New Genre of Interactive Theatre* (Portsmouth, NH: Heineman, 1997), p. 145.

[24]Begbie, *Theology, Music, and Time*, p. 185.

work—the metaphor of play.[25] When children play games, claims Spolin, they engage in improvisational behavior, even if they play games they have played before. They agree on ground rules prior to playing, but they neither script out the playing, nor do they follow a timeline. Rather, they act and react according to events as they unfold. In a similar manner, seasoned improvisational actors know how to act and react spontaneously as the "game" of performance unfolds. Each game is different, and unpredictable outcomes are to be expected. Depending on the acting troupe and the philosophy that guides it, spontaneity might look like any one of the following: improvising on an established script, utilizing props in an impromptu manner, allowing the audience to guide the subject matter to be discussed, delivering an extempore speech, or, as Mick Napier puts it, "mak[ing] stuff up as you go along."[26] On account of this high level of contingency, some performance outcomes are not good. Thus there *is* such a thing as bad improvisational performance. However, in this particular genre, the focus is on the process rather than the outcome. Regardless of how a performance turns out, improvisational actors are willing to take the risk of trying. They understand the contingencies and unforeseen outcomes in performance. They realize that spontaneity is indispensible to improvisation.

3. Improvisation is guided by convention. Although levels of contingency are high, so also are levels of constraint. In fact, Begbie suggests that improvisation is "bound by a host of restraints."[27] Some argue that improvisational performance is unconventional on account of its interest in spontaneity and ambivalence toward Western models of composition,

---

[25]Spolin's work on play arose primarily out of her experiences in children's education with Neva L. Boyd. Boyd, a Chicago teacher, sociologist, and educational theorist, was Spolin's teacher. Boyd produced a book of children's games and was an innovator in creative group play. Working with illiterate immigrants and their children, she successfully produced nonverbal improvisations that were purposeful and educational. See Neva L. Boyd and Paul Simon, *Play and Game Theory in Group Work: A Collection of Papers* (Chicago: University of Illinois at Chicago, 1971). For more on the connection between Boyd and Spolin, see Spolin, *Improvisation for the Theater*, p. xlvii, and Frost and Yarrow, *Improvisation in Drama*, p. 50.

[26]Mick Napier, *Improvise: Scene from the Inside Out* (Portsmouth, NH: Heinemann, 2004), p. 1. Although Napier's definition is mentioned here, it is also lifted up in other places in this book as a negative example of defining improvisation without adequate appreciation for the tradition, rules, and practices embedded within improvisational performance itself.

[27]Begbie, *Theology, Music, and Time*, p. 185.

but, in many ways, it is profoundly conventional due to its constraints. Spontaneity has conditions that dictate what is acceptable and unacceptable to the community. Actors and musicians participate in traditions and communities that determine whether their *avant-garde* performances are acceptable or praiseworthy.[28] They are trained into these traditions and communities. Consciously or unconsciously, they draw from theorists and practitioners, and they abide by rules and regulations that govern their performance.[29] (Some of these rules in theater might include agreement, awareness, use of ready-mades, yes-and, and collaboration.[30]) Spontaneity is not born apart from restraints and limits; it is born *within* restraints and limits. As Stephen Nachmanovitch observes in *Free Play: Improvisation in Life and Art*, "Structure ignites spontaneity . . . [it] keeps it from wandering off course."[31]

Following all the rules perfectly in performance does not make one a great improviser, just as following all the rules of preaching does not make one a "great preacher," as misleading as that category is biblically and theologically (cf. 1 Cor 1:17-25; 2:1-5; 2 Cor 11:5-6; 12:11).[32] Rules are useful insofar as they are demonstrable during great performances. Gary Izzo observes: "The student of improv must not say, 'If I follow these rules, then I will be a brilliant improviser,' for that is not true. Rather, the student needs to say, 'When I am a brilliant improviser, these rules apply.'"[33]

---

[28]For instance, Berliner notes the ways that the jazz community functions in this capacity in that it remains committed to "producing, preserving, and transmitting musical knowledge." See Berliner, *Thinking in Jazz*, p. 37.

[29]For a helpful overview of the situational, formative, and other "rules" of improvisational performance, see Nicolas J. Zauenbrecher, "The Elements of Improvisation: Structural Tools for Spontaneous Theatre," *Theatre Topics* 21, no. 1 (March 2011): 52-54.

[30]For descriptions and definitions of each of these rules of theatrical improvisation, see Dusya Vera and Mary Crossan, "Theatrical Improvisation: Lessons for Organizations," *Organization Studies* 25, no. 5 (2004): 739-43.

[31]Stephen Nachmanovitch, *Free Play: Improvisation in Life and Art* (New York: Jeremy P. Tarcher/Putnam, 1990), p. 83.

[32]Also, unlike improvisational performance, preaching is a peculiar juxtaposition of divine action, human performance, spiritual gift, science, art, and sacramental ritual.

[33]Izzo, *Art of Play*, p. 138. For descriptions of improv pitfalls to avoid and rules to abide by, see ibid., pp. 155-58, 231-39. We find a similar observation on the part of Augustine in book IV, section 11 of *On Christian Teaching*. Augustine writes: "We find the rules of eloquence observed in the sermons and addresses of eloquent men, even though the speakers—whether conversant with them or entirely untouched by them—did not consider them either when preparing to speak or

Taylor makes a similar claim in one of his lectures on preaching. In a story about his preaching idol Paul Scherer, Taylor describes how the great Lutheran preacher used to say it was okay to break the rules of preaching so long as one was experienced enough to know what he or she was doing.[34]

Although improvisational performance grants actors opportunities to leverage their imaginations, embrace new possibilities, and risk success or failure, these opportunities are neither rule-less nor boundless. As Lockford and Pelias observe, "improvised moments also have boundaries to which the performer must be sensitive. Performers must follow linguistic rules, recognize theatrical conventions, and enact the given circumstances."[35] As biblical theologian N. T. Wright puts it, "spontaneity and freedom do not mean playing out of tune."[36]

Great improvisers not only know the rules; they also embody them in performance. Gabriele Tomasi, an expert in aesthetics and performance, describes this as "the *habitus* of the performer," that is, embodied knowledge of the conditions of a performance obtained through a combination of skill, practice, and attentiveness to the tradition and community.[37] If we borrow Tomasi's terminology, we might say that *im-*

---

when actually speaking. *They observe the rules because they are eloquent, they do not use them to become eloquent.*" See Augustine, *On Christian Teaching*, trans. R. P. H. Green (New York: Oxford University Press, 2008), p. 103 (emphasis added).

[34]Taylor writes: "Paul Scherer once said that all the rules of sermon preparation and delivery may be valorously violated if one knows what she or he is doing." See WGT 5:39.

[35]Lockford and Pelias, "Bodily Poeticizing," p. 435. Amy Seham agrees when she writes, "Improvisational performance, even the broadest improv-comedy, is not a free for all. It is created within a set of goals and guidelines-sometimes with lofty ideals, sometimes not with more commercial aspirations" (Seham, "Play Fair," p. 139).

[36]Wright was commenting on how the presence of rules in Christian homes as opposed to their absence leads to more freedom rather than less freedom. N. T. Wright, *The Epistles of Paul to the Colossians and to Philemon: An Introduction and Commentary* (Grand Rapids: Eerdmans, 1986), p. 146.

[37]Tomasi writes: "The point I want to emphasize is that spontaneity has conditions. To consider improvisation as spontaneous, since it is an unexpected action that has in some way an unconscious or groundless character, does not mean that it is automatic or instinctive, obtained without practice and preparation. Improvisation relies on what may be called 'blind' capacities, that is skills that have become a sort of *habitus* for the performer." See Tomasi, "On the Spontaneity of Jazz Improvisation," p. 87. *Habitus* as a concept extends beyond performance theory. It also figures prominently in the work of sociologist Pierre Bourdieu, among others. Bourdieu seeks to recover a more robust and thick understanding of practices as embodied, irregular, enculturated, and gendered, with a focus on *habitus* as improvisatory action. Rather than being programmatic and mechanical, *habitus* is more of a practical sense of how to perform "regulated improvisation" in a social world, and how to navigate, engage, and move in that world. For a snapshot of Bourdieu's discussion of

provisateurs display a performative *habitus* wherein rules are embedded as forms of embodied knowledge.

4. Improvisation is guided by intuition.[38] Both Viola Spolin and Gary Izzo suggest that the best moments in improvisational theater occur when actors go beyond the constrictions of established criteria or recycled material and instead opt to respond intuitively.[39] Great performers read one another, collaborate together, interact with their audience, assess the space, and follow specific cues. They follow hunches and attune to the various dynamics of the space.

Viola Spolin and Keith Johnstone are two performance theorists who attempt to free up actors to respond intuitively. They push their actors to listen, react, and respond instead of control, direct, and decide.[40] Through rehearsal exercises, Spolin's goal is to get her actors to a point where "you don't think, you *act!*"[41] She has them focus on what sociologists call *proxemics*, that is, attention to the space and to the dynamics of the space, and to the opportunities for play made available when one reads and responds to the space.[42] One of the phrases in Spolin's definition of improvisation reads: "permitting everything in the environment (animate or inanimate) to work for you in solving the problem."[43]

---

habitus, see Pierre Bourdieu, *Outline of a Theory of Practice* (New York: Cambridge University Press, 1977), or Pierre Bourdieu, *The Logic of Practice* (Stanford, CA: Stanford University Press, 1990). For a treatment of Bourdieu's sociology in which the author describes Bourdieu's understanding of *habitus*, see David Swartz, *Culture & Power: The Sociology of Pierre Bourdieu* (Chicago: University of Chicago Press, 1997). For an appropriation of Bourdieu's understanding of *habitus* in practical theology, see Mary McClintock Fulkerson, *Places of Redemption: Theology for a Worldly Church* (Oxford: Oxford University Press, 2007).

[38]The concept of intuition has also been grafted into business definitions of improvisation. Mary Crossan and Marc Sorrenti define improvisation from a business vantage point as "intuition guiding action in a spontaneous way." See Mary Crossan and Marc Sorrenti, "Making Sense of Improvisation," in *Advances in Strategic Management*, ed. J. Walsh and A. Huff (Greenwich, CT: Jai Press, 1997), 14:156, as cited in Vera and Crossan, "Theatrical Improvisation," p. 733.

[39]Spolin, *Improvisation for the Theater*, p. 3; Izzo, *Art of Play*, p. 139. Cf. also Lockford and Pelias, "Bodily Poeticizing," p. 436.

[40]Like Spolin and Johnstone, but to a lesser extent, Frost and Yarrow argue that a key discipline in improvisation is "to avoid the reflex of trying to make it [the performance] into something you think it *ought* to be, rather than letting it become what it *can* be" (Frost and Yarrow, *Improvisation in Drama*, p. 3).

[41]Spolin, *Improvisation for the Theater*, p. 370 (emphasis original).

[42]I explore proxemics in improvisational theater in the final chapter in my discussion of attunement.

[43]Spolin, *Improvisation for the Theater*, p. 361.

Similarly, in his book *Impro,* Johnstone tells actors: "You are not imaginatively impotent until you are dead; you are only frozen up."[44] The way actors free themselves to discover the "imaginative response in the adult" is through recovering the "power of the child's creativity."[45] Elsewhere in the same book, Johnstone suggests: "most children can operate in a creative way until they're eleven or twelve, when suddenly they lose their spontaneity, and produce imitations of 'adult art.'"[46] For both Spolin and Johnstone, the goal is similar: to unleash the imaginative, instinctive, and creative potential of improvisational artists, some of which remains tacit because of either lack of training or the suppression of creativity in adulthood.

Lockford and Pelias suggest that the best improvisational actors know how "to seek somatic signs, to follow hunches, and trust impulses."[47] Commitment to intuition gives actors permission to trust their instincts and react organically. Actors become active agents in leveraging creativity they *can* control while they navigate a host of constraints they *can't* control. According to Italian director Robert Ciulli, opportunities for freedom emerge when actors leverage their performative intuition: "You always have this situation of having to create free spaces within the framework, within the given constraints so that individual creativity can unfold, a creativity which does not destroy everything, but which, on the contrary, enriches it."[48] When actors leverage their intuition, new opportunities arise to "create free spaces within the framework." Intuition unleashes agency.

5. Improvisation is guided by interaction. In improvisational performance, the performer places a premium on connection with the au-

---

[44]Johnstone, *Impro: Improvisation and the Theatre,* p. 10.

[45]Ibid., p. 9. Johnstone tells the story of an ingenious art teacher whom he had as a young adult. His teacher, a man named Art Stirling, made the group of adult apprentice artists paint the tire marks of a clown car. He had them add color, texture, and patterns until the paintings were so bad that it was hard to tell what they were painting. Then Stirling pulled out paintings from the exact same exercise, but these were paintings done by eight-year-olds. The paintings were done, in Johnstone's words, "with such love and taste and care and sensitivity" that he was totally undone by the lesson (ibid., p. 19). In pastoral theology, Robert C. Dykstra also discusses the tendency among adults to "repress" the creativity that comes naturally in childhood. Robert C. Dykstra, "Unrepressing the Kingdom: Pastoral Theology and Aesthetic Imagination," *Pastoral Psychology* 61 (2012): 391-409.

[46]Johnstone, *Impro: Improvisation and the Theatre,* p. 77.

[47]Lockford and Pelias, "Bodily Poeticizing," p. 437.

[48]Malgorzata Bartula, Stefan Schroer, and Roberto Ciulli, *On Improvisation: Nine Conversations with Roberto Ciulli,* trans. Geoffrey V. Davis (New York: Peter Lang, 2003), p. 38.

dience. Put differently, the audience has an active rather than passive role. Several improvisational performance theorists emphasize the active agency and participatory function of the audience. Spolin suggests that the audience rather than the performer(s) is "the most revered member of the theater."[49] Improvisers see their audiences as participants rather than recipients, and hence use terminology like cocreators or inter-actors to describe them. To borrow a phrase from philosopher Hans Georg Gadamer's *Truth and Method*: "the spectator belongs essentially to the playing of the play."[50]

Brazilian theater director Augusto Boal's refers to the audience as a "spect-actor."[51] Louis-Martin Guay claims that audience-member-as-participant goes as far back as the radical thinking of French playwright and actor Antonin Artaud in the 1920s. Artaud conceived of the audience as an intermediary and presciently predicted: "People would come not so much to watch but to participate."[52] Réjean Dumouchel describes the nature of this shift: "The audience acquires a status equal of a character and plays in the drama as he [or she] plays in drama."[53] The recent rise of interactive theater is a fine example of the ways that improvisational performers esteem their audience.[54]

CONNECTING: FAMILY RESEMBLANCES BETWEEN IMPROVISATION AND PREACHING

The ability to do a new thing in a new way. Improvisation, at least as I have defined it, shares important family resemblances with Christian

---

[49]Spolin, *Improvisation for the Theater*, 13.

[50]Hans-Georg Gadamer, *Truth and Method* (New York: Continuum, 2006), p. 126. Elsewhere in this classic text, Gadamer suggests the presence of the audience brings the play into its "ideality." He writes: "It [the play] puts the spectator in the place of the player. He [the audience]—and not the player—is the person for and in whom the play is played" (p. 109).

[51]Boal writes: "The spect-actors, by acting out their ideas, train for 'real-life' action; and actors and audience alike, by playing, learn the possible consequences of their actions. They learn the arsenal of the oppressors and the possible tactics and strategies of the oppressed." Augusto Boal, *Games for Actors and Non-Actors* (New York: Routledge, 2002), p. 244.

[52]Antonin Artaud, *Ouevres Complète* (Paris: Gallimard, 1980), 2:12, as cited in Louis-Martin Guay, "Theatre of the Unexpected: When the Spectator Becomes Actor," trans. Jacqueline Dinsmore, *Canadian Theatre Review* 143 (Summer 2010): 7.

[53]Réjean Dumouchel, "Le Spectateur et le Contactile," *Revuecinemas.info*, 1.3.Web (October 2010), p. 6, as cited in ibid.

[54]See Izzo, *Art of Play*.

preaching. In many ways they diverge. My interest here is in the ways they converge. One of the family resemblances relates to the first part of my definition: *an ability to do a new thing in a new way*. While the interpreter's "ability" is unquestioned in improvisational performance, with reference to Christian preaching some feel nervous and uneasy about any word or phrase that emphasizes human agency. Is not preaching a spiritual gift from God that is anointed by God (cf. Rom 12:3-8; Eph 4:11; 1 Tim 4:13-14; 1 Pet 4:11)? Am I swimming in dangerous waters when I speak of human ability as integral to the preaching event?

Fearful that homiletics might turn into a glorified, horizontal branch of humanism, some point to Jesus' promise to the disciples that, if they are arrested and tried, the Spirit will give them the words to say (Mt 10:19). If Jesus himself promises nothing less than the Holy Spirit as a divine mouthpiece, they argue, does a preacher really need to focus on ability, to attend to preparation, practice, and skill? If preaching is a spiritual gift, which it is, questions about human ability invariably arise. Can a preacher really work on the craft of preaching without God's prior action? Does God's supernatural infusing of the spiritual gift of preaching come by way of *actio divina*, *homo performans*, or some combination of the two?

No doubt preachers and homileticians should pay careful attention to these questions and concerns in any and all conversations about human ability. Karl Barth contends that even in situations where it seems as if God is "absent, passive, non-responsible, or impotent," God is "always holding the initiative."[55] When preaching or homiletics becomes too horizontal, technique driven, or ability focused, it becomes solipsistic and humanistic. The sermon becomes an a-theological horizontal act, and homiletics evolves into reflection on preaching as if God were dead. The tendency to leave God's divine initiative out of discussions of preaching

---

[55]In the *Church Dogmatics*, Karl Barth writes, "This Lord is never absent, passive, non-responsible or impotent, but always present, active, responsible and omnipotent. He is never dead, but always living; never sleeping, but always awake; never uninterested, but always concerned; never merely waiting in any respect, but even where He seems to wait, even where He permits, *always holding the initiative*. In this consists His co-existence with the creature." See Karl Barth, *Church Dogmatics*, trans. Geoffrey William Bromiley (Edinburgh: T & T Clark, 1936), III.3, p. 13 (emphasis added).

is especially dangerous in some pockets of the post-Enlightenment West. Andrew F. Walls contends that a number of Western Christians ascribe to a "pared-down theology, cut and shaved-down to fit a small-scale universe."[56]

That stated, many preachers realize, especially those who endure long and arduous hours of sermon preparation, that human ability plays an integral if not central role to preaching itself. Recall that rule of 10 percent inspiration and 90 percent hard work. Trusting in God's divine action does not necessitate the abrogation of human ability and responsibility.[57] In 1 Thessalonians 2:9, the apostle Paul writes: "You remember our labor and toil, brothers and sisters; we worked night and day, so that we might not burden any of you *while we proclaimed to you the gospel of God.*" The nineteenth-century homiletician Alexandre Vinet puts it this way: "It is undoubtedly God who converts, but he converts man by means of man."[58] While overreliance on human ability is problematic, so also is underreliance. Although God always holds the initiative, God also uses particular human words and actions through particular human beings in particular communities.

On account of this tension, sermons are paradoxical: they involve ability and availability, *homo performans* and *actio divina*, biblical-exegetical faithfulness and homiletical fittingness, careful planning and faithful improvisation.[59] To say that preachers exercise ability does not mean that human agency is foregrounded and divine agency is backgrounded. Likewise, to say with Barth that God is "always holding the initiative" does not result in the cessation of human freedom. It *is* possible to maintain a commitment to divine and human agency by casting them in a noncompetitive relationship. In the *Church Dogmatics*, Barth

---

[56] Andrew F. Walls, "Christian Scholarship and the Demographic Transformation of the Church," in *Theological Literacy in the Twenty-First Century*, ed. Rodney L. Petersen and Nancy M. Rourke (Grand Rapids: Eerdmans, 2002), p. 177.

[57] For a discussion on human agency and divine agency through the Spirit coworking in a noncompetitive relationship, see Tanner's chapter "The Working of the Spirit," chap. 7 in Kathyrn Tanner, *Christ the Key* (New York: Cambridge University Press, 2010), pp. 274-301.

[58] Alexandre Vinet, *Homiletics*, trans. Thomas H. Skinner (New York: Ivison and Phinney, 1870), p. 36.

[59] Bartow uses the language of *homo performans* and *actio divina* to describe divine-human agency in Bartow, *God's Human Speech*, pp. 37, 95.

writes: "God's freedom does not compete with man's freedom."[60] In other words, human freedom and divine freedom can coexist in a non-competitive rather than competitive relationship.[61]

On the matter of the Holy Spirit functioning as a divine mouthpiece, even a superficial exegesis of Matthew 10:19 leads to the conclusion that it is taken out of its original context of persecution and prison and superimposed onto the context of sermon preparation and delivery.[62]

---

[60]Barth, *Church Dogmatics* I.2, p. 365. In writing on human freedom, Barth also states: "He (God) affirms and approves and recognizes and respects the autonomous actuality and therefore the autonomous activity of the creature as such." See ibid., III.3, p. 92. For Barth, human freedom is not so much limited by a lack of autonomy as it is by our own creatureliness. Freedom is something "which we cannot acquire for ourselves and which can be and actually is given us only by God, because He alone is originally free." See ibid., III.2, p. 194. On account of our creatureliness, Paul T. Nimmo suggests that human beings are "theologically circumscribed." See Paul T. Nimmo, *Being in Action: The Theological Shape of Barth's Ethical Vision* (London: T & T Clark, 2007), pp. 110-11.

[61]In *Christ the Key*, Kathryn Tanner describes the noncompetitive relationship between divine and human action in the following way: "Just as in the second account of the working of the Spirit, in Christ God does not evacuate the human or push it aside. Rather than forming competing powers like water and fire that extinguish or evaporate one another, humanity and divinity are present together in Christ. This lack of competitiveness from God's side, indeed, is the very prerequisite of incarnation: if the divine is to be one with the human in Christ, the presence of divinity cannot entail the removal of the human." See Tanner, *Christ the Key*, p. 296.

[62]In his classic book *Homiletics*, Alexandre Vinet pushes back against the ecclesial tendency to expect too little of homiletics by relying too heavily on the Holy Spirit to do all the work for us. He suggests that clergy and laity alike take Matthew 10:19 out of context in order to use it as a license to preach without adequate preparation, rhetorical training, or deep theological reflection. This passage, then, becomes an excuse for shirking one's responsibilities. Vinet does not mean to imply that there is no promised assistance offered to us by the Holy Spirit. Rather, he argues that the "promise of assistance is not against the use of human means." The preacher's gifts and abilities are valuable even if God is the one who does the supernatural work in people's lives. See Vinet, *Homiletics*, pp. 36, 39. The nineteenth-century American homiletician Robert Lewis Dabney makes a similar point in his discussion of unction and the Holy Spirit in preaching. Note the connection Dabney makes between unction and the preparation of the preacher while also acknowledging that unction is still guided by divine initiative. He writes: "To affect unction is manifestly impossible. It is, in short, a quality not merely intellectual or sentimental, but spiritual. . . . It cannot be taught by rhetoric alone. It cannot be acquired from imitation of others. But it is the Holy Spirit who communicates it to the cultivated mind and pure taste, *by enduing the soul which is thus prepared* with an ardent zeal for God's glory and a tender compassion for those who are perishing." Although Dabney is emphasizing spiritual preparation in this excerpt, elsewhere in his book *Sacred Rhetoric*, he emphasizes arduous, rational preparation in cooperation with God. See Robert Lewis Dabney, *Sacred Rhetoric: Or, a Course of Lectures on Preaching* (Richmond, VA: Presbyterian Committee of Publication, 1870), pp. 116-17.

Perhaps an anecdote will illustrate my point. Paul Scherer told of one preacher who went around informing people that his normal practice was to prepare the first half of the sermon. Then, in an act of faith, he trusted that God would reveal the second half of the sermon during the actual delivery. When a colleague heard the preacher's explanation, he answered back, "I congratulate you and want you to know that your part of the sermon was invariably better than God's part." In

While the New Testament writers indicate that preaching is indeed a divine gift, they do not imply that spiritual gifts come to God's people fully formed and completely fashioned. As has been mentioned, growing in the grace of spiritual gifts and participating in the task of Christian ministry is both *actio divina* and *homo performans*; it involves human action and divine action. In 2 Corinthians 6:1, the apostle Paul uses the phrase "God's fellow workers" to describe the divine-human relationship in the work of reconciliation discussed in 2 Corinthians 5. Although Paul makes clear, when he describes the work of reconciliation, that "all this is from God" (2 Cor 5:18) the one who initiated the work, he also makes clear that he is a fellow worker partnering with and participating in the work God is doing. He also uses the designation "fellow worker" in 1 Corinthians 3:9. Although God holds the initiative as Creator, and Paul operates from a position of contingency as creature, nevertheless, he describes his function as an apostle as working *with* God in the work that God is working out in the world.

In the two major passages on spiritual gifts, Romans 12 and 1 Corinthians 12, an analysis of the context reveals a broader concern for spiritual transformation for those who exercise them. Romans 12 begins with the charge not to conform to the pattern of this world, but to be transformed by the renewing of our minds (Rom 12:1). Just before enumerating the various spiritual gifts, Paul implores his readers to think of themselves with sober judgment, literally to exercise self-control or moderation as opposed to being high-minded (Rom 12:3). Immediately after listing the different spiritual gifts, Paul urges his readers to love one another, to honor one another, and to do good in the world (Rom 12:9-21). Paul's expectation is not just that preachers will exercise their gifts, for he assumes this; it is that they will grow their gifts through growing their character, that we will cultivate our gifts "according to the grace given to us" and in "proportion to faith" (Rom 12:6). This is one of the reasons why Jonathan Edwards makes a distinction between the gifts of the Spirit

---

other words, overreliance on Spirit-led inspiration is sometimes used as an excuse for careless exegesis and lack of preparation. Taylor recounted this story about Scherer in his lecture "The Foolishness of Preaching" during the Yale Beecher Lectures on Preaching in 1976. See WGT 5:160-61.

and the graces of the Spirit.[63] Those who possess the gifts of the Spirit without the graces of the Spirit have lost their way, according to Edwards. They claim to possess great gift and might even be able to demonstrate apparent evidence of it but, because they have not grown in the *grace* of that gift, they have moved away from the kingdom of heaven rather than toward it (Mt 7:21-23). This difference between possessing "extraordinary gifts" and "growing in grace" is essentially a difference between the Spirit's influence and impartation. Thus exercising one's gifts is not so much showcasing one's aptitude as it is cultivating the habits designed to grow the gift one has received.

In 1 Corinthians 12, Paul displays a similar concern for spiritual transformation and maturity. One chapter earlier, in 1 Corinthians 11, he chides the Corinthians for lacking spiritual maturity concerning the Lord's Supper. One person fails to wait for everyone else, another person gets drunk on wine, and still another humiliates those without means (1 Cor 11:20-22). All of these responses indicate a failure to exercise self-control and discernment, that is, a failure to be spiritually mature. Thus Paul urges the Corinthians to "wait for one another" when they come together and to eat their meals at home so as to avoid being judgmental (1 Cor 11:33-34). Two chapters later, in 1 Corinthians 13, Paul argues that the gifts *of* the Spirit are meant to be a sign that one is growing in the Spirit. Speaking in tongues, prophesying, gifts of knowledge, gifts of faith, and generosity to the poor are meant to be expressions of the larger command to love God and love people (1 Cor 13:1-3). If I fail to love, says Paul, "I am nothing" and "I gain nothing." Exercising the gifts of the Spirit flows naturally out of the cultivation of grace in the Spirit. To paraphrase the commentator James D. G. Dunn, grace in the Spirit (charisma) is the "fountainhead" from which gifts of the Spirit (charismata) flow.[64] First Corinthians 13 is not so much an excursus on the beauty of love as it is an exhortation for the Corinthians to grow up. Paul writes: "When I was a child, I spoke like a child, I thought like a child,

---

[63]See Edwards's discussion of the difference between gifts and graces of the Spirit in the sermon "Extraordinary Gifts of the Spirit Are Inferior to Graces of the Spirit," in Jonathan Edwards, *The Works of Jonathan Edwards: Religious Affections*, ed. John E. Smith (New Haven, CT: Yale University Press, 1959), 2:279-312.

[64]James D. G. Dunn, *Romans*, Word Biblical Commentary (Dallas: Word Books, 1988), p. 725.

I reasoned like a child; when I became an adult, I put an end to childish ways" (1 Cor 13:11). Practice and progress are necessarily conjoined here (with progress having the primacy): one practices and cultivates one's spiritual gifts as an expression of one's progress in spiritual maturity.

It is not wrongheaded to suggest that, as one matures spiritually and grows in practical wisdom, one's spiritual gifts also grow and mature. In the practice and exercise of one's gifts, God grows one's gifts. Although the spiritual gift of preaching is precisely that—a gift—one's response to God's divine initiative requires more than just gratitude. It requires growth: an appetite to practice and grow one's spiritual gifts, to "rekindle" (2 Tim 1:6) these gifts. When one exercises an ability to do a new thing in a new way, practice and progress conjoin in noncompetitive divine-human interaction.

As guided by convention, intuition, and interaction. Another family resemblance can be observed between the pattern of improvisation and preaching. Like improvisational performers, preachers are guided by convention, intuition, and interaction. At one level, preachers follow convention. They are "bound by constraints" in that they bend their own agenda to what the biblical text is saying and doing (at least in theory), and they are part of a tradition that started before them and will continue after they are gone. They also participate in communities that teach them boundaries, rules, and constraints, and validate or invalidate their preaching. They participate in an extant tradition while also playing a small role in generating new tradition. Their sermons are governed by other human constraints such as time, place, social location, and denomination that shape whether their sermons are deemed successes or failures, which is to say almost nothing about the sense of burden and responsibility they feel to be a spokesperson for God. In other words, preachers do not have freedom to do a new thing in a new way without learning the old things and the old ways. They have to learn a tradition before they can riff on it.

At another level, preachers follow intuition, at least in theory: their performances are free, spontaneous, and innovative. They follow hunches and trust instincts, thus exercising a level of freedom and agency not usually found in scripted performance. Although they learn from a community and are influenced by a tradition, their sermons are still new. To preach a sermon is to do a *new* thing in a *new* way. Although preachers operate from tradition, they also form tradition through new performance. While participating in a tradition, they bring high levels of contingency to the sermon by virtue of their unique voice, creativity, and agency. They are traditioned and traditioning.

At still another level, preachers practice interaction. They read and respond to their congregations. They interact with them as participants and inter-actors, or at least they should. In many black churches, for instance, preachers read and respond to specific cues from their congregation as a way to assess and reassess the quality of their sermons in much the same way that improvisers respond to audience cues in their performances.[65]

The form of improvisational preaching I argue for draws from convention, intuition, and interaction coexisting and cooperating in dynamic interplay. Improvisational preachers create "free spaces within the framework."[66] They abide by rules while also knowing how to "seek somatic signs, to follow hunches, and trust impulses."[67] As Nachmanovitch observes, "Creativity always involves a certain amount of discipline, self-restraint, and self-sacrifice. Planning and spontaneity become one. Reason and intuition become two faces of truth."[68] Preachers inter-act with the community with planning and spontaneity, reason and intuition; they respond in ways that demonstrate respect and concern for their listeners. Performative improvisation in preaching takes place at the intersection and interplay of all three levels mentioned: convention, intuition, and interaction.

An improvisational preacher abides by rules and constraints that govern the preaching event (convention); she trusts somatic hunches during the performance of the sermon (intuition); and she reads and

---

[65]For more on the "cues" exchanged between preacher and congregation in black preaching, see Evans E. Crawford with Thomas H. Troeger, *The Hum: Call and Response in African American Preaching* (Nashville: Abingdon, 1995). By making this claim, I do not mean to suggest that there are not also other contexts where preachers and audiences exchange verbal and nonverbal cues. Rather, I use it as an example of a scenario in which preacher-audience cues are more explicit and demonstrative.

[66]Bartula, Schroer, and Ciulli, *On Improvisation*, p. 38.

[67]Lockford and Pelias, "Bodily Poeticizing," p. 437.

[68]Nachmanovitch, *Free Play*, p. 189.

responds to a congregation that reads and responds to her as coparticipants or "spect-actors," to use Boal's term (interaction).[69] Once again,
the metaphor of play proves useful. Preacher and listeners alike "belong
to the playing of the play," to return to Gadamer's phrase.[70]

OBSERVING: THREE PRACTICES OF IMPROVISATION
IN TAYLOR'S PREACHING

An improvisational sermon grows out of the inter*play* of tradition and
innovation, careful preparation and real-time intuition, and prior
planning and contemporaneous interaction. This way of conceiving of
the sermon disrupts standard distinctions and binaries. The lines are
blurred between preacher and listener(s), scripted and unscripted, tradition and traditioning. Although an established framework exists, so
also does freedom, specifically the freedom to "create free spaces within
the framework."[71] The playing of the play enfleshes itself at the intersection of convention, intuition, and interaction, and in the free spaces
that such an intersection catalyzes.

In the next section, I claim that Taylor operated at the intersection of
this catalyzation. He did so in at least three concrete ways: by creating
free spaces within the framework, practicing attunement, and playing
with tropes.

Practice 1: Creating "free spaces within the framework." The first
practice of performative improvisation in Taylor's preaching is what I
call *the creation of free spaces within the framework.* Traditional interpretations of his preaching undervalue the amount of play between convention, intuition, and interaction as well as the free spaces that emerge
as a result of this play. More to the point, standard accounts of Taylor's
preaching overemphasize his reliance on convention and thereby fail to

---

[69]Boal, *Games for Actors and Non-Actors*, p. 244.
[70]Gadamer, *Truth and Method*, p. 126. Gadamer argues that the speaker and audience are not so
much subjects of the play as they are participants in the playing of the play (pp. 91-93). Rather
than the spectator standing "aloof at a distance of aesthetic consciousness," he is involved in the
"communion of being present" (p. 117). Elsewhere in *Truth and Method*, Gadamer claims that play
is the primary clue to ontological explanation. He notes that the German word for play, *Spiel*,
originally meant "to dance." He writes: "what is intended is to-and-fro movement that is not tied
to any goal that would bring it to an end . . . rather, it renews itself in constant repetition" (p. 104).
[71]Bartula, Schroer, and Ciulli, *On Improvisation*, p. 38.

acknowledge the ways that intuition and interaction also played a role in his crossover homiletic.

In *I Believe I'll Testify*, Cleophus J. LaRue puts Taylor in the category of "intellectual manuscript preacher," by which he means that Taylor was strident in his rejection of unprepared, extemporaneous speech. "Seldom, if ever, in public speaking did Taylor resort to any form of unadorned speech."[72] According to LaRue, Taylor labored over every word of his sermon beforehand. He wrote out a manuscript, memorized it, and preached it nearly word-for-word. Later in the same chapter, LaRue adds the following comment about the difference between folk preachers and intellectual manuscript preachers (like Taylor): "Spontaneity is central to the folk preacher's style, and the *appearance* of spontaneity is central to the intellectual preachers even though they have crafted their oration down to the word in pen and ink."[73]

LaRue is partly correct in his claims about Taylor. At least this much is true: Taylor did write out a sermon manuscript; he did craft each word meticulously; he did study his sermon manuscript; and he did internalize it so that he could preach without notes in the pulpit. Because he had an excellent memory, Taylor retained a significant amount of what he prepared beforehand. Thus he avoided "unadorned speech" in this sense: he rejected extemporaneous, uncritical spontaneity in favor of meticulous preparation. To put it in performance terminology, Taylor steered clear of Mick Napier's understanding of improvisation: "getting on a stage and making stuff up as you go along."[74] He rejected the idea of a sermon as an extempore speech.

---

[72]Cleophus J. LaRue, *I Believe I'll Testify: The Art of African American Preaching* (Louisville: Westminster John Knox, 2011), 86. By "unadorned speech" here, it is likely the case that LaRue is referring to unprepared, unplanned, ad-lib speech.

[73]Ibid., pp. 86-87. According to LaRue, even folk preachers are not being spontaneous in the purest sense of the word. He writes: "Folk (spiritual) preachers often engage in a heightened form of spoken language that is genuinely spontaneous, although they are drawing on oral formulas, memorized expressions, and standard phraseology that permeate the culture and can be inserted anywhere in the sermon." See ibid., p. 85. Interestingly, Henry H. Mitchell suggests that spontaneity—"the ability to respond to the movement of the Spirit among preacher and congregation and to express deep feeling without shame"—is a distinctive characteristic of African American preaching not only for preachers, but also for congregations. See Henry H. Mitchell, "African American Preaching," in *Concise Encyclopedia of Preaching*, ed. William H. Willimon and Richard Lischer (Louisville: Westminster John Knox, 1995), p. 3.

[74]Napier, *Improvise*, p. 1.

Problems arise, however, when we recall that Napier's definition of improvisation is one that most improvisational performers also reject. Also recall Amy Seham's dictum: "the notion of *pure* spontaneity is a myth."[75] Careful preparation prior to the sermon does not impede improvisation. Instead, it catalyzes it. In other words, preparation does not imprison or bind improvisational preachers; it sets them free. Perhaps LaRue's distinction between spontaneity and the appearance of spontaneity stems from a definition of spontaneity that is too narrow, from a Napier-like definition rather than a Seham-like one.

Although Taylor crafted his sermon "down to the word in pen and ink," to use LaRue's phrase, he freely admits that he practiced improvisation on a regular basis in the pulpit. The words meticulously prepared beforehand did not bind or imprison him. In addition to maintaining a commitment to the conventional methods of preparation, he also maintained a commitment to intuition and interaction in delivery. Since it is somewhat oxymoronic to refer to this way of preaching as "prepared spontaneity," instead, I appropriate Ciulli's phrase by suggesting that Taylor was committed to "creating free spaces within the framework" of the sermon.

In an interview with Terry Muck and Paul Robbins of *Leadership* magazine, published in the summer of 1981, Taylor talks in depth about going beyond the material he had prepared when he preached sermons on a weekly basis at Concord. For instance, when the interviewers ask him about how he prepares his manuscript, Taylor answers, "That's a weekly adventure. Once it comes, the sermon flows. Although I don't use it in the pulpit or memorize it, I write out a full manuscript of every sermon I preach. Some of the material is lost in the actual delivery, but *material I hadn't planned on comes to me while preaching.* The one makes up for the other."[76] When the interviewers ask him about how he stores and organizes his illustrations, Taylor freely admits that some illustrations come to him during preparation, while others come during the

---

[75]Seham, "Play Fair," p. 140. Entire quotation in italics in original essay.

[76]This interview originally appeared in *Leadership* magazine in the summer of 1981. See Gardner C. Taylor, "The Sweet Torture of Sunday Morning (Interview)," *Leadership* 2, no. 3 (Summer 1981): 16-29. See the full interview also in WGT 5:279 (emphasis added).

actual preaching of the sermon. He comments: "I admire people who do this [organize and store illustrations], and I think they have a great advantage, but I find illustrations just come back to me *as I'm preaching.*"[77]

By giving answers like these in the interview, Taylor makes at least two things clear about his approach. First, he is aware that differences exist between the sermon-as-prepared and -as-delivered, and, second, he believes these differences benefit rather than hinder his preaching. The gain of what comes to him during the live sermon more than makes up for the loss of what he is unable to recall from the prepared manuscript. Although his memory is such that he recalls most of what he prepared, he still incorporates unplanned, unforeseen insights and illustrations that come to his mind while preaching.

The interviewers also ask Taylor several questions about his interaction with the members of his congregation during the sermon, such as, "What role does the congregation play in your sermon delivery?" Taylor's response is illuminating: "I try to get very close to the congregation. . . . I have to feel they are right there with me."[78] He adds the following anecdote to illustrate his commitment to an interactive relationship with the congregation:

> In our black congregations, there is some vocal response, not as much as there was once, but there's still a good deal, and I enjoy it. We had a Canadian guest preacher here one Sunday when I was gone, Frank Zwackhammer, and Frank told me later that he must have been laboring a point a little too long because one of our deacons said out loud, "All right. We've got that. Go on." The point is that there's an *invisible interplay between pastor and people, and I can feel whether I'm getting to the people or not.*[79]

Does this "invisible interplay" ever result in actual practices of improvisation during the sermon, or is it more of a feeling or sense on Taylor's part?

When the interviewers ask him what he does when he feels like he's losing the people and needs to get them back on the same page, Taylor responds, "I may try to reach out to them again by repetition or di-

---

[77]WGT 5:280 (emphasis added).
[78]WGT 5:286.
[79]Ibid.

gression, or try to draw them closer with an unplanned illustration."[80] What Taylor describes as "invisible interplay," "digressions," and "repetition," I refer to as improvisational interactions between preacher and congregation. Taylor demonstrates a concern for connecting with his listeners while also displaying a willingness to riff on what he has prepared in order to keep his listeners engaged and involved in the sermon itself. In this sense, he sees his congregation as coparticipant, as spect-actor in the task of proclamation.

Answers like these demonstrate the three levels of interplay to which I refer. Taylor is conventional in the sense that he always prepares; there is nothing extemporaneous or ad hoc about his speech. Yet, he is also intuitive and interactive in that he trusts his instincts, and he reads and responds to his listeners in improvisational ways. If we return briefly to our definition, Taylor maintains a peculiar capacity for doing "a new thing in a new way" while also doing the conventional/traditional thing in preparing a manuscript beforehand. During the live sermon, he creates free spaces within the established framework. Put differently, Taylor's description of his preaching practices suggests a greater role for spontaneity than LaRue may have recognized.[81]

Perhaps the closest homiletical discussion we have to Taylor's creating free spaces within an established framework is found in Robert Smith Jr.'s *Doctrine That Dances*, a book we touched on briefly in chapter one.

---

[80]WGT 5:288.

[81]This does not mean that LaRue rejects improvisation as an option. In fact, LaRue leaves open the possibility that seasoned preachers can and should create free spaces within the framework of their sermons, albeit in tempered ways. Reflecting on the difference between the manuscript-as-prepared and the manuscript-as-preached, LaRue writes: "The manuscript is but an arrested performance that can only be brought to life through the living voice. Feel free to drop those pearls of great price as the imagination continues to produce even after you stand to preach, for even as you preach the sermon is yet pregnant with imaginative possibilities. Temper it, of course, so that you don't go off on a tangent, but a sentence or two of insight that comes to you while preaching enhances the sermon and honors the imagination as it continues to work and place itself at the service of the preached word" (p. 77). In a separate chapter in which he offers advice to preachers on how to enhance their imagination, LaRue explains that rich and fecund ideas come not just in the preparation time before one preaches, but also during the sermon itself. A seasoned preacher, LaRue argues, knows how to "skillfully employ fresh ideas that burst in on one's consciousness *while* the sermon is being preached" (p. 108). An important caveat he adds, however, is that fresh insights are better utilized in the hands of seasoned preachers, that is, experienced veterans who know what they are doing and not carelessly flitting about or chasing tangents during the live sermon. See LaRue, *I Believe I'll Testify*, pp. 77, 108 (emphases added).

Recall that Smith defines improvisation as "spontaneity infused by preparation."[82] Spontaneity is the outcome of practice and experimentation. Like Taylor, Smith is not interested in unadorned, extempore speech. In fact, he makes his preaching students memorize the core material of their manuscripts beforehand. He forces them to deliver their sermons from memory so that the Holy Spirit can "turn the ink of the manuscript into the blood of spiritual passion."[83] Rote memorization and verbatim recall of the manuscript is not what matters most. Rather, Smith wants his students to internalize core concepts in the manuscript so that they can attune themselves to the Holy Spirit's unforeseen, unpredictable action. The principle that undergirds Smith's argument, that careful preparation begets spontaneous innovation and conscious interaction, is the closest homiletical approach we have to Taylor's preaching practice of creating free spaces within an established framework.

Practice 2: Attunement to the space. The second practice of performative improvisation in Taylor's preaching is *attunement to the space.* Attunement means *an ability to achieve congruity with the space in which one preaches.*[84] In this section, what is important to remember about attunement is this: the preacher who shows adeptness at attunement understands that, as the space changes, the sermon changes. In other words, the preacher understands that sermons sound differently depending on the context in which they're preached. Although the architecture of the building is significant and should not be overlooked—whether one is preaching in a typical parish church, a storefront building, or a cathedral—achieving congruity with the space is more about the preacher's connection with the people than about the acoustics or architecture of

---

[82]Robert C. Smith Jr., *Doctrine That Dances: Bringing Doctrinal Preaching and Teaching to Life* (Nashville: B & H Academic, 2008), p. 152.

[83]Ibid., p. 153.

[84]*Congruity* is the word I have chosen to describe attunement. Congruity with the space means being in sync and in harmony with the physical and phenomenal dynamics of the space in which one preaches. In contrast to performance-studies homileticians Charles L. Bartow, Jana Childers, and Richard F. Ward, I emphasize congruity with context rather than congruity with content. Although Bartow, Childers, and Ward show an abiding concern for and commitment to context in preaching, even so they use words like *congruence* and *congruity* to describe the preacher's union with the text rather than the preacher's attending to the context. For more on how these homileticians use the words *congruity* and *congruence* in their published works, see my discussion of attunement in chapter five.

the building. The focus here is on the preacher's *interaction* with the congregation. Attunement to the space involves an approach that is person specific and context specific, a way of preaching that is interactive.

Taylor displays adeptness at the practice of attunement inside *and* outside African American church contexts.[85] In order to demonstrate what I mean by attunement, I will analyze a sermon he preached and repreached on various occasions and in different venues. Despite having the same Scripture text, Philippians 3:13-14, and the same central points, each sermon is slightly different, like a variation on the same theme in classical music or a riff on a melody in jazz music.[86] He preached the first sermon on September 8, 1996, in an African American church context: Galilee Baptist Church in Trenton, New Jersey; the second sermon in 1996 at New Rising Star Missionary Baptist Church, an African American church in Fort Worth, Texas; and the third on February 22, 1998, in a predominantly white Presbyterian context: Nassau Presbyterian Church in Princeton, New Jersey. The seed was planted for all three of these sermons on January 17, 1979, when Taylor preached a sermon at Concord Baptist Church called "The Christian Goal in Life."[87] In the January 1979 sermon, the text is the same and the themes are similar. In many ways, the three sermons I analyze are the progeny of the original sermon.

In each of the three sermons, Taylor takes the semimemorized manuscript and riffs on it in different ways. In the first two sermons, Taylor riffs on what he has prepared as a way of interacting with the dialogical "call back" responses of predominantly African American congregations. In the third sermon, Taylor riffs in a different way by making changes in the delivery, content, and structure of the sermon in a predominantly

---

[85]The role of race in improvisational performance, what I call *metaphorical improvisation*, is a theme I explore in chapter three. It is related but also distinct from the performative improvisation I refer to here.

[86]Taylor gives each sermon a different title as he repreaches them in different venues: "A Christian Plan for Living" (Sept. 8, 1996), "The Christian Goal in Life" (1996), and "A Formula for Christian Living" (Feb. 22, 1998). Taylor's changing the titles had more to do with stylistic variation than with altering the content. The template for the sermon remained virtually the same, but he changed the title slightly for the sake of variation. For a person who preached and repreached sermons all the time, a pragmatic and stylistic change like this was necessary if not beneficial.

[87]WGT 2:55-60.

white setting. Whether the riff is based on the dialogue between preacher and congregation or on reshaping the delivery, content, and structure of the sermon on account of context, in both instances Taylor shows adeptness at the practice of attunement. My analysis of the three sermons begins with a description of the first sermon, in particular its prophetic edge and celebrative conclusion.

The first sermon, "A Christian Plan for Living" (1996), takes place in an African American church context. This same sermon is also used as a model sermon in the Great Preachers series.[88] The theme centers on Paul's injunction to the Philippians to "Press on!" Like the apostle Paul, Christians must also realize that they have not *yet* arrived at the goal to which God has called them heavenward in Christ Jesus. Although the call is applicable to Christians in general, Taylor also directs his sights specifically at the black community. He argues that African Americans need to take responsibility for pressing on even if they feel held back by the larger society. In a prophetic and sharp critique of his own community, Taylor exclaims: "We need to stop saying to our young people that slavery is holding them back. There is some truth there. We ought to say it to other people, but not say it to ourselves. . . . We need to put that behind us and march on to what God has in store for us."[89] To be clear, Taylor is making a point about taking responsibility, a point he makes sure to emphasize in his own context. He does not blast society at large and wink at problems in his own community, but instead confronts these problems head on by challenging his listeners to press on toward a brighter future.[90] If we use homiletical terminology, Taylor's willingness to confront members of his own community falls under the domain of what LaRue calls "corporate concerns" in the African American preaching tradition, that is, preaching that pertains to "matters in black life that are best dealt with by other blacks."[91]

---

[88] *Great Preachers Series: Gardner C. Taylor* (Gateway Films/Vision Video; Odyssey Productions Ltd., 1997), video recording.

[89] WGT 3:79.

[90] In a 2008 interview, Joel C. Gregory asked Taylor whether there were some things that could be said in a black congregation that would not necessarily have to be said to a white congregation. Taylor answered: "Yeah, I think that's true." See "Gardner Calvin Taylor: Oral History Memoir, Interview 3," interview by Joel C. Gregory, Baylor University Institute for Oral History, March 17, 2008, p. 16.

[91] LaRue writes that some things, meaning some social issues that are of particular relevance to the

Perhaps the most powerful highlight of the first sermon is its climactic and celebrative conclusion. Taylor's inspiring ending to this message is available in both print and audio versions, and it is frequently mentioned as a highlight in conference and classroom settings where I have played or heard the audio version of this sermon. Taylor exclaims:

> I know what it is to have great sorrow. I know what it is not to know which way you are going sometimes. I know what it is to dampen the pillow some nights with one's own tears. I even know what it is to hope almost against hope not to wake up the next morning. Life can be very difficult. But press on! Today the battle shout, tomorrow the victor's song. Press on! We're bound for Emmanuel's land, where sickness and sorrow and pain and death are felt and feared no more. Press on! There's a bright side somewhere. Don't you rest until you find it. Press on! God's mercy stoops low, and his pity bows down to help us. Press on! Press on! Our eyes may be wet with tears sometimes, but the promise is that God shall wipe away all tears from our eyes. Press on! Your salvation is nearer than when you first begun [*sic*]. God wrought it! Christ brought it; the Holy Spirit taught it. Praise God my soul caught it.[92]

In many ways, the thunder and lightning are lost in the published version of this sermon. In the audio version, we hear Taylor crescendo as he reaches the final lines, the call back of the congregation, and the rhythmic cadence of the preacher attuned with his congregation. The power of the conclusion is found not just in the words that are spoken but also in their sound, that is, their tone, inflection, pacing, and volume.[93] This sermon is chosen as an exemplar for the Great Preachers series because both the content and the sound draw the listeners deeper into worship. The content is rich and poetic, and the sound is evocative, lyrical, and inspiring.

The second sermon, "The Christian Goal in Life" (1996), also takes

---

black community, "can best be said to blacks by other blacks." See Cleophus J. LaRue, *The Heart of Black Preaching* (Louisville: Westminster John Knox, 2000), p. 24.

[92]"A Christian Plan for Living," WGT 3:80.

[93]As academic theologian Stephen Webb points out, sound has the power to disfigure and reconfigure space, to echo the divine voice in the world, and to foreshadow the advent of the parousia. See Stephen H. Webb, *The Divine Voice: Christian Proclamation and the Theology of Sound* (Grand Rapids: Brazos, 2004), pp. 234-36.

place in an African American church context, this time in Fort Worth, Texas. The Scripture text is the same and the central themes are the same. Instead of memorizing the original 1979 sermon, Taylor prepared for this sermon by editing and internalizing the central points and pervasive themes from the previous message. Then he preached (without notes) a new iteration of the sermon. To use musical language, Taylor preached a variation on a theme: the melody of the sermon remained the same, but the notes were different. If we think of it in terms of improvisational performance theory, Taylor's approach is similar to that of the south Slavic *guslar* improvisational folk performers—he internalizes a "more or less stable core" of the sermon instead of memorizing a word-for-word fixed text verbatim.[94] The melodies and themes of the sermon remain the same, but the notes change slightly.

The main reason that "The Christian Goal in Life" is a fine example of Taylor's practice of attunement is that Taylor riffs on what he has prepared as a result of interacting through call and response. In the following excerpt, Raymond Bernard Spencer, a scholar who had access both to the manuscript and the audio version, highlights in bold the improvisational sections of Taylor's audio-recorded sermon:

> There are people who claim that they have already reached it [the goal]. Here, Paul says, I count not myself. . . . **And if you read the tenth or eleventh chapter of Second Corinthians, one of those, read them both, you need to read them both—not that I don't know what**

---

[94]Milman Parry traveled to the former Yugoslavia in the 1930s and discovered among south Slavic *guslar* performers an improvisational approach to performance that was rooted in the epic tradition, that is, in an approach to storytelling that precedes the narrative tradition. Parry discovered that the *guslari* internalized story templates rather than memorizing fixed texts, and that as a result their performances were never identical. Albert B. Lord, Parry's student and protégé, published Parry's findings in Albert B. Lord, *The Singer of Tales* (Cambridge, MA: Harvard University Press, 1960). In a follow-up article twenty-seven years after publishing *The Singer of Tales*, Lord explained his understanding of improvisation as internalizing a "more or less stable core" rather than rote, verbatim memorization of a fixed text. Lord writes: "Improvisation, in my view, is the opposite of memorization, which means a careful and conscious word-for-word recalling of a passage. . . . There is a 'more or less stable core' . . . but we should not equate a 'more or less stable core,' which can be remembered, with a *fixed* text to be memorized" (emphasis original). See Albert B. Lord, "Characteristics of Orality," *Oral Tradition* 2, no. 1 (1987): 66-67. For parallels to the south Slavic *guslar* performers in non-Western improvisation, among Balinese folk performers specifically, see Thérèse de Vet, "Context and the Emerging Story: Improvised Performance in Oral and Literate Societies," *Oral Tradition* 23, no. 1 (2008): 159-79.

chapter it is, you just read them both to find out what I'm talking about. [great laughter]

This man says that he has been beaten five times—with thirty-nine stripes. **And then, he says, I count not myself to have apprehended....** [response] And he says, "three times I've been stoned—left for dead." Once at Lystra and he turned up thirty miles away at Derbe, preaching the next day. "I count not myself to have apprehended.... [great response] I don't know any who have been stoned." He said, "Three times I've been shipwrecked, I've been in perils and danger from my countrymen on the highways of the empire"—**and yet, "I count not myself to have apprehended."**... [great response] Now who are we? What are we talking about, "I'll sacrifice for the Lord." But, this man says, "I have not yet reached my goal.... **I count not myself to have apprehended.**" [Tremendous response][95]

In a follow-up interview with Spencer, Taylor acknowledges that, after noticing the congregation's warm response to the phrase, "I count not myself to have apprehended," he decided to keep returning to it. Observing Taylor's preaching practice in this sermon, Spencer writes:

> Taylor acknowledges that a *pattern of improvisation* is developed from the favorable response of the audience to the statement, "I count not myself to have apprehended." Each time the phrase is repeated, following the details of Paul's experiences, the congregation increases the intensity of their response. This is a signal to the preacher that he has established a connection with the audience that needs to be *explored*.[96]

In this second sermon, we witness what Spencer refers to as a "pattern of improvisation." Taylor's acknowledgment that he reads and responds to his parishioners is significant. This sermon is a *concrete example* of him making improvisational decisions during the live preaching moment as he interacts with the congregation in call and response.

Taylor's practice of reading and responding to his listeners also demonstrates a commitment on his part to connecting with his listeners in

---

[95]See Raymond Bernard Spencer, "Imagery and Improvisation in African American Preaching: Resources for Energizing the Protestant Pulpit" (PhD diss., Southwestern Baptist Theological Seminary, 2001), p. 173. Emphasis added for the phrase *pattern of improvisation*.

[96]Ibid., p. 174 (emphasis original).

their own space. Attunement involves achieving congruity with the space in which one preaches—with *space* broadly defined. It is not just about attending to the architecture of the building; it also involves reading and responding to one's listeners as coparticipants or "spect-actors" in the sermon.[97]

What we find in Taylor's approach is straightforward: he improvises on the sermon-as-planned through dialogical interaction with his listeners. He riffs on the manuscript on account of the insights he gains through the live performance of the sermon. His "pattern of improvisation" is a demonstration of the respect he maintains for his listeners as coparticipants and collaborators in the sermon. As philosopher Bruce Benson points out, improvisational performance does not hold to a dichotomy that understands the performer vis-à-vis the audience; instead, it sees performance as an act of "communal collaboration."[98]

Taylor preached the third sermon, "A Formula for Christian Living" (1998), in a predominantly white Presbyterian setting in Princeton, New Jersey. The Scripture text is the same and the central themes are the same, but there are significant changes. Taylor practices attunement through changing his delivery and through making changes to the content of his sermon. His changes to delivery are immediately recognizable in the audio version of the sermon. In this context the characteristic call and response one finds in churches like Galilee Baptist or New Rising Star Baptist is nonexistent. Also, shouting in a sermon would be foreign to customary practice in this context. On account of these different performative expectations, Taylor attunes to the listening needs of his parishioners by changing the volume and pace of the sermon. It is quieter, slower, and more subdued in tone. Throughout his tone is reserved and conversational rather than loud and declaratory. For instance, instead of shouting, "There's a bright side somewhere! Don't you rest until you find

---

[97]Boal, *Games for Actors and Non-Actors*, p. 244.

[98]Bruce Ellis Benson, "The Improvisation of Hermeneutics: Jazz Lessons for Interpreters," in *Hermeneutics at the Crossroads*, ed. Kevin J. Vanhoozer, James K. A. Smith, and Bruce Ellis Benson (Bloomington: Indiana University Press, 2006), p. 196. For more on the relationship between hermeneutics and improvisation, see also Bruce Ellis Benson, "Improvising Texts, Improvising Communities: Jazz, Interpretation, Heterophany, and the Ekklesia," in *Resonant Witness: Conversations Between Music and Theology*, ed. Jeremy Begbie, Steven R. Guthrie, and Bruce Ellis Benson (Grand Rapids: Eerdmans, 2011), pp. 295-319.

it!" in the conclusion, as he did in the first sermon at Galilee Baptist in Trenton, Taylor barely raises his voice when he makes the same statement in the conclusion to the sermon in Princeton. Further, in the conclusion, Taylor does not crescendo as he does in the first two sermons. There is no loud, celebrative climax even though Taylor is still exhorting his congregants to "Press on!" There is no definitive cadence or metrical pacing in the Princeton sermon. He restrains himself in delivery. He is still forceful and passionate, but his volume is significantly turned down. As a seasoned preacher in this particular setting, we might surmise that Taylor knows that shouting sounds more like noise than conviction, and cadence sounds more like histrionics than sacramentality.

In addition to practicing attunement through changes in delivery, Taylor also attunes himself by making changes to the content of the sermon. For instance, at Nassau Presbyterian, he speaks about the plague of drugs on America in an abstract sense. He points out that drugs are not merely an inner-city problem; drugs are a ubiquitous epidemic that affects everyone. Instead of personalizing the problem to one specific community or another, he nationalizes it as a problem *all* Americans must confront. By contrast, in the first sermon, delivered before an African American audience in Trenton, he talks about the impact drugs have on the black community in particular. He personalizes the problem: "When we think of the plague of drugs that has spread through the land, which has so afflicted *our* own neighborhood, which has inflicted *upon them* so much damage, so much damage to *our* young people, we wonder why it is that a great nation like this cannot stop drugs from coming into *our* cities."[99] This subtle change, making the problem abstract in one setting and concrete in another, is another sign that Taylor attunes himself to his listeners. In the sermon delivered before a predominantly African American congregation in Trenton, drugs are a problem destroying the African American community—Taylor's community! In the sermon delivered before a predominantly white congregation in Princeton, drugs are a plague destroying the nation. In the Trenton sermon, Taylor is a comourner: drugs impact *our* cities and neighbor-

---

[99]WGT 3:76 (emphases added).

hoods, he says, whereas, in the Princeton sermon, Taylor is a prophet: drugs are not so much a black community or white community problem, but a national problem that affects everyone regardless of race.

Taylor also attunes to his listeners by finding common ground with them. In this sermon, he discusses recent changes in the Presbyterian denomination (PCUSA) to which Nassau Presbyterian belongs. Using humor as a way to connect to his listeners, he explains: "Some of our denominations are involved in Amendment A. I was down at Louisville Presbyterian Seminary the other week and they were talking about Amendment A. I don't know what it is. I'm a Baptist." Unlike in the other two sermons, Taylor establishes interdenominational rapport using humor. He pokes fun at being a Baptist while also indicating to his listeners that he knows the latest happenings in their denomination. Finding common ground and establishing rapport with white Presbyterian listeners may seem insignificant at first glance, but it is arguably another sign of Taylor's commitment to attunement through removing barriers and obstacles to communication. Not only does it win him credibility, but it signals to his listeners that he is genuinely interested in developments in their church. The importance of showing respect for other traditions in intercultural communication is a topic I discuss in chapter four on intercultural competence.

Practice 3: Playing with tropes. The third practice of performative improvisation in Taylor's preaching is the *use of tropes*. Of the three components involved in a dialectical interplay in improvisational preaching—convention, intuition, and interaction—the focus here is on the preacher's intuition. The word *trope* comes from the Greek τρέπειν, which means "to turn." In its most basic form, a trope is a figure of speech in word or phrase that *turns* away from the literal meaning of the word or phrase.[100] The change in literal meaning not only takes place in the word itself; it

---

[100]Tropes are related to figures and schemes in classical rhetoric. Tropes are usually construed as smaller units that may or may not be part of a larger figure or scheme. Preminger and Brogan argue that tropes could "appear to be a compressed instance of figures, and figures to be an expanded trope" (p. 409). In antiquity, a scheme was a "summary instance of the breadth and complexity of figurative language and its understanding" (pp. 410-11). The emphasis with schemes is on the broader "imagistic and figurative aspects" of thought and language (p. 411). See Alex Preminger and T. V. F. Brogan, eds., *The New Princeton Encyclopedia of Poetry and Poetics* (Princeton, NJ: Princeton University Press, 1993), p. 409.

also involves a change in signification.[101] A trope can be a simple non-literal figure of speech such as "the *leg* of a chair," a word or expression used in a different way than its literal meaning such as "Now, I can *die*," or a metaphorical refiguration of a literal thing or event such as, "In Christ, God leads us out of *exile*." A specific example from Scripture is "our *paschal lamb*, Christ, has been sacrificed" (1 Cor 5:7). Not only is the last example a metaphor, but it is also a trope. In each of these examples, the figure of speech causes the listener or reader to "turn away" from the word or phrase's literal meaning.

Language and communication theorists disagree as to how to define tropes. Richard A. Lanham, a noted scholar on the history of rhetoric, suggests that "any single definition would be prescriptive."[102] Sources as ancient as Quintilian and as modern as Kenneth Burke, Tzvetan Todorov, and Henry Louis Gates Jr. offer various definitions. Eighteenth-century Italian rhetorician Giambattista Vico contends that tropes are simplified figures of speech for "comprehending and performing signification."[103] Nineteenth-century French rhetorician Pierre Fontanier defines tropes as "the figures of discourse which consist of the divergent meaning of words, i.e., of a meaning more or less removed and different from their proper and literal meaning."[104] Communication theorists C. J. Gilbert and J. P. Rossing define them as "rhetorical stores or commonplaces that become common spaces of invention."[105] "To trope," write Gilbert and Rossing, "is to play on or with words, to turn meaning. They concurrently define and redefine, imagine and re-imagine."[106]

---

[101]See "trope" in Richard A. Lanham, *A Handlist of Rhetorical Terms* (Berkeley: University of California Press, 1991).

[102]Ibid.

[103]A summary of Giambattista Vico's definition of tropes can be found in Christopher J. Gilbert and Jonathan P. Rossing, "Trumping Tropes with Joke(r)s: The Daily Show Plays the 'Race Card,'" *Western Journal of Communication* 77, no. 1 (February 2013): 94. For Vico's discussion and definition of tropes, see Giambattista Vico, *The Art of Rhetoric: (Institutiones Oratoriae, 1711–1741)*, trans. Giorgio A. Pinton and Arthur W. Shippee (Atlanta: Rodopi, 1996).

[104]Quotation in Pierre Fontanier, *Les Figures Du Discours* (Paris: Flammarion, 1968). Citation of quotation in Preminger and Brogan, *New Princeton Encyclopedia of Poetry and Poetics*, p. 409.

[105]Gilbert and Rossing, "Trumping Tropes with Joke(r)s," p. 95.

[106]Ibid., pp. 94-95. Gilbert and Rossing also discuss the significance of "metatropes." Metatropes are more complex than tropes. When a performer uses a metatrope, she is using the creative power of one trope in order to offset and disrupt the destructive power of another trope. That is to say, the creative trope plays on and even trumps the destructive trope. Gilbert and Rossing

African American literary critic Henry Louis Gates Jr. suggests that tropes have a broader definition and usage in the literature and everyday discourse of African Americans than in ancient and even modern rhetoric. The importance of Gates and his understanding of tropes will become evident when we consider the function and significance of tropes in Taylor's preaching.

Gates uses the language of "Signifyin(g)" to describe the practice of "troping" in African American literary and quotidian discourse. Signifying converges with and diverges from traditional understandings of tropes. Although many African Americans use traditional tropes such as metaphor and synecdoche in writing and in speech, Gates contends that they also use nontraditional figures of speech. The emphasis is less on the figures of speech and more on the rhetorical practice. Gates writes:

> Signifyin(g) is a trope in which are subsumed several other rhetorical tropes, including metaphor, metonymy, synecdoche, and irony (the master tropes), and also hyperbole, litotes, and metalepsis (Bloom's supplement to Burke). To this list we could easily add aporia, chiasmus, and catachresis, all of which are used in the ritual of Signifyin(g).[107]

---

suggest that the judicious use of metatropes facilitates the destruction of "tropes that have hardened in meaning and become inflexible in unfamiliar contexts so as to articulate new meanings and explode discursive simplifications" (p. 98). For instance, ironic statements can be metatropological in that humor is used to parody the beliefs that need to be challenged. Gilbert and Rossing provide an example of the metatropological from television by arguing that the writers and performers on Comedy Central's *The Daily Show* use humor and "specifically irony" as creative metatropes designed to offset, disrupt, and refigure the destructive trope of "playing the race card." As the literary critic and historian V. Hayden White argues, "Irony is in one sense metatropological, for it is deployed in the self-conscious awareness of the possible misuse of figurative language. Irony presupposes the occupation of a 'realistic' perspective on reality, from which a nonfigurative representation of the world of experience might be provided. . . . It points to the potential foolishness of all linguistic characterizations of reality as much as to the absurdity of the belief it parodies." See V. Hayden White, *Metahistory: The Historical Imagination in Nineteenth-Century Europe* (Baltimore, MD: Johns Hopkins University Press, 1975), p. 37. Gilbert and Rossing draw from White's argument that irony is a metatropological device in their defense of *The Daily Show* as a show in which humor/irony is the way by which creative tropes trump destructive tropes. One of the ways Taylor utilizes metatropes is through refiguring the tropes of spiritual imprisonment and slavery to sin through the injection of metatropes designed to offset, disrupt, and refigure these metaphors. For more on metatropes, see Gilbert and Rossing, "Trumping Tropes with Joke(r)s," pp. 98-103.

[107]Henry Louis Gates Jr., *The Signifying Monkey: A Theory of Afro-American Literary Criticism* (New York: Oxford University Press, 1988), p. 52. Cf. also Henry Louis Gates Jr., "'Blackness of Blackness': A Critique of the Sign and the Signifying Monkey," *Critical Inquiry* 9, no. 4 (June 1983): 685-723.

Tropes are not so much figures of speech as they are a way of speaking. Gates emphasizes that a speaker uses individual tropes in the ritual of Signifyin(g) and wants to make clear that Signifyin(g) is in and of itself a trope, in fact, a trope that is distinctive (though not exclusive) to African American cultural practice.[108]

Put differently, Gates's emphasis is not so much on the thing signified (as in classical rhetoric) but on the practice of signifying. He writes: "One does not Signify some thing; one Signifies in *some way*."[109] Thus tropes are not a figure of speech, but a culturally situated rhetorical practice. In African American literature, for example, through practices such as revision, pastiche, and intertextual conversation, black writers Signify on other black writers. They invoke and revise tropes that recur in the black literary tradition. Gates lifts up Alice Walker's intertextual conversation with Zora Neale Hurston in Walker's book *The Color Purple* as an example of "tropological revision." This is an example in which "black texts 'talk' to other black texts."[110]

Tropes also take on additional connotations in modern performative contexts. In improvisational performance, tropes are usually the "rhetorical stores or commonplaces" that performers draw on and return to in order to communicate.[111] In improvisational theater, reliance on tropes reveals itself not only in the use of "ready-mades" learned in rehearsal and drawn from in performance, but also in the memorization of story templates. Similarly, in jazz music, tropes are the standard jazz melodies that performers memorize from a "fake book" so as to build up a repertoire of familiar tunes they can use in performance.[112] In theater and jazz

---

[108]Gates writes: "While linguists who disagree about what it means to Signify all repeat the role of indirection in this rhetorical strategy, none of them seems to have understood that the ensuing alteration or deviation of meaning makes Signifyin(g) the black trope for all other tropes, the trope of tropes, the figure of figures. *Signifyin(g) is troping*." See Gates, *Signifying Monkey*, p. 81 (emphasis added).

[109]Ibid., p. 78 (emphasis original). In *The Signifying Monkey*, Gates is not suggesting that *only* African Americans use signification, but that it is one of the central distinctives of African American literature and discourse. See "Introduction" in ibid., pp. xix-xxvii.

[110]Gates, *Signifying Monkey*, p. xxvi.

[111]Gilbert and Rossing refer to tropes as "rhetorical stores or commonplaces" in Gilbert and Rossing, "Trumping Tropes with Joke(r)s," p. 95.

[112]Robert Rawlins and Eddine Bahha explain the fake book phenomenon in the following way: "Jazz musicians routinely turn to fake books as a source for jazz standards. Typically, these collections present tunes in a concise format including only the melody, chord changes, and some-

music, then, tropes are not so much figures of speech as they are formulae drawn from repositories of speech templates, music templates, or story templates depending on the context.[113] Perhaps the closest parallel we have in classical rhetoric is the commendation of memorizing speech templates or strategies of argumentation, more commonly referred to as "topics" as *topoi*.[114] Although tropes are dissimilar from *topoi* in other ways, one of their points of convergence is template internalization.

In the context of preaching, I understand tropes to be *culturally relevant oral formulas or metaphors that preachers utilize and return to for the purpose of rhetorical effect*. In my definition, I attempt to blend the rhetorical, cultural, and performative connotations of tropes, since all are present in the sermon. One way to think of tropes in a preaching context would be to imagine them as a series of arrows in the preacher's quiver. They can be pulled out at any time and in any sermon. At least two examples of "troping" can be identified in Taylor's preaching.

The first trope can be traced back to Taylor's radio ministry in 1969 and persists until at least 1988, two years before his retirement from Concord Baptist Church in Brooklyn. It is an example of a *culturally*

---

times the lyrics. Unlike collections of sheet music that include formulaic, simplified arguments, fake books allow for stylistic diversity and creative freedom. High-quality fake books from reputable publishers (such as the Hal Leonard *Real Book*) are essential to any jazz musician's library" (p. 211). For a comprehensive list of jazz fake books, see Robert Rawlins and Nor Eddine Bahha, *Jazzology: The Encyclopedia of Jazz Theory for All Musicians*, ed. Barrett Tagliarino (Milwaukee: Hal Leonard, 2005).

[113] According to Dusya Vera and Mary Crossan, "Improvisation does not mean that anything goes; improvisation always occurs within a structure and all improvisers draw on ready-mades" (p. 741). For Vera and Crossan's discussion of "ready-mades," see Vera and Crossan, "Theatrical Improvisation," pp. 727, 739, 741. In *The Jazz of Preaching*, Kirk Byron Jones discusses the phenomenon of "shedding" or "wood-shedding," which are melodies from rehearsal that can be accessed in live performance. See Jones, *Jazz of Preaching*, p. 85. For further discussion on learning story templates like "status reversal" and others, see Johnstone, *Impro: Improvisation and the Theatre*, pp. 39, 72, 131-42.

[114] For an example of one ancient rhetorician's discussion of *topoi*, see book 2, chapter 23, "On Common Topics," in Aristotle, *On Rhetoric*, pp. 190-204. See also George Kennedy's discussion of the ways Cicero and Quintilian revisited Aristotle's theories and topics in George A. Kennedy, *A New History of Classical Rhetoric* (Princeton, NJ: Princeton University Press, 1994), pp. 81-82. One of the few homileticians (if not the only one) who connects the ancient rhetorical category of *topoi* to African American preaching practices is Richard Lischer. In his book *Preacher King*, Lischer claims that Martin Luther King Jr. regularly drew on classic strategies of argument, *topoi*, from past preachers like Phillips Brooks and others. See Richard Lischer, *The Preacher King: Martin Luther King Jr. and the Word That Moved America* (New York: Oxford University Press, 1995), pp. 94-96.

relevant oral formula, one that is used and reused for the purpose of rhetorical effect. In the following series of examples, note the repetition, evolution, and revision of the trope:

> [1969] Do we come here by way of long human memory from some place where life and circumstance are unthreatened? Where "no chilling winds, **no poisonous breath can reach that healthful shore, sickness and sorrow and pain and death are felt and feared no more**"?[115]

> [1979] Press on! This day the noise of battle, tomorrow, the victor's song. Press on, we are "bound of Emmanuel's land, **where no poisonous breath can touch that healthful shore, where sin and sorrow and pain and death are felt and feared no more**."[116]

> [1986] In God's own time, **sickness and sorrow and pain and death we will fear no more**. In God's own time, the clouds will pass away.[117]

> [1996] Life can be very difficult. But, press on! Today the battle shout, tomorrow the victor's song. Press on! We're bound for Emmanuel's land, where **sickness and sorrow and pain and death are felt and feared no more**. Press on![118]

> [1988] Then we who are caught up shall meet him in the sky, caught up where sin and sorrow will last no more. Caught up where trouble cannot come. Caught up where **sickness and sorrow, pain and death are felt and feared no more**. Caught up.[119]

> [1988] But I will say to you who have opened the door [to death], the Lord calls "goodnight," not "goodbye." Good night! We shall meet on that healthy shore **"where sickness and sorrow and pain and death are felt and feared no more"**![120]

---

[115]This radio sermon was titled, "Living with Change" and was delivered on August 14, 1969. See WGT 1:96 (emphasis added).

[116]"The Christian Goal in Life," WGT 2:60. Sermon originally preached at Concord Baptist Church on January 17, 1979.

[117]"The Song of Moses and the Song of the Lamb." Sermon delivered originally at New Light Baptist Church in Baton Rouge, Louisiana, on February 2, 1986. See WGT 3:162 (emphasis added).

[118]"A Christian Plan for Living," WGT 3:80. Sermon delivered at Galilee Baptist Church in Trenton, NJ, on September 8, 1996.

[119]"Philadelphia: The Keepers Are Kept, Part 2," sermon delivered May 1, 1988, at Concord Baptist in Brooklyn, New York, WGT 4:233.

[120]"Laodicea, part III: The Door of the Soul," delivered June 5, 1988, at Concord Baptist in Brooklyn, NY, WGT 4:258.

There are several other tropes in these quotations besides the one I have highlighted. "We're bound for Emmanuel's land," "the victor's song," "the noise of battle," "opened the door," and "meet him in the sky" are all examples of tropes. Also, the phrase "healthful shore" is an example of a trope from the highlighted quotation. In each of these instances, Taylor uses metaphor; the figurative language functions to turn the reader/listener away from the original meaning of the phrase. Although other tropes can be identified, my emphasis in citing this example is on the repetition, emendation, and revision of the phrase over time. Although Taylor is using individual tropes, the repetition and revision of the phrase itself suggests that he is also "troping" in a way much like Gates' description of Signifyin(g).

In the first example, a radio sermon delivered in 1969, we witness the inception of the trope through Taylor's acknowledgment of it as a quotation. In his sermon introduction, Taylor draws the quotation from the fifth verse of a Samuel Stennett hymn published in 1787 titled "On Jordan's Stormy Banks I Stand." He frames it within the larger context of a series of rhetorical questions (four in total) designed to get the listener to ponder the human longing for permanence and stability. He asks: "Do we come here by way of long human memory from some place where life and circumstance are unthreatened?" Then, as the years pass, Taylor redacts the quotation so that the phrase, "sickness and sorrow and pain and death are felt and feared no more" is all that remains. A hymn verse that began as a lengthy quotation is shortened and appropriated for different contexts and situations. Also, when Taylor uses this trope in subsequent years the quotation is no longer in the introduction, but is part of a celebrative conclusion in which he gives his listeners a vision of the future hope of "Emmanuel's land." In other words, the function of the quotation changes; it no longer serves as a reminder of the human longing for permanence and stability as in the first example, but as a reminder to place our hope in a God who has prepared a place for us where "sickness and sorrow and pain and death are felt and feared no more."

The second trope is a *familiar metaphor* as opposed to an oral formula. Recall that my understanding of tropes is not confined to oral formulas alone but extends also to metaphors that are culturally relevant to a preacher's listeners. This time, instead of quoting from a hymn line and then appropriating that hymn line to suit his needs, as we saw in the first trope, Taylor takes the larger theme *of being set free from imprisonment by Jesus Christ*, and he returns to that theme repeatedly throughout his ministry. Once again, the metaphor of being set free from imprisonment is a trope in and of itself. Taylor is not claiming that Jesus *literally* sets us free from prison, but that he does so figuratively and metaphorically. The context and the figure of speech turn us away from the literal meaning. My interest, however, just as in the first example, is in the repetition, evolution, and revision of the metaphor over time. Notice the ways that Taylor draws on this trope at various points in his preaching ministry:

> [1958] We have a God as we have known him in Christ who has come, as the elders of my race used to say, to our dungeon door and has entered there to sit where the **prisoner** sits until **freedom** can be wrought.[121]

> [1970] Standing there at Calvary, musing upon it, bowing the head and opening the heart, we know something has been done for us that nobody but Jesus could do. We reach for figures and metaphors. There the separating veil is torn in two. There the **prisoner's cell** swings wide. There is something about that lonely, lightless hill called Calvary which **delivers** us.[122]

> [1974] Ah, we may wince, but we are never long free of that yearning to become better, that instinctive squirming that to be **let loose** from some **imprisoning** and crippling web in which we are caught.[123]

> [1980s] You and I ought first to believe in our hearts because of Jesus Christ, and we ought to declare to our people that there are no boundaries beyond which God lacks sovereignty. He does give **deliverance** to the **prisoner** in the darkest dungeon. And he does give liberation to the slave in the most dehumanized captivity. That's the heart of the gospel.[124]

> [1988] It belongs to us, a brighter day, a better day, a day when we are

---

[121]"The Elements of Evangelism." Sermon delivered originally before the American Baptist Convention in Cincinnati June 1958. See WGT 4:39.

[122]"Still Another Look at Calvary." Sermon delivered originally as an NBC radio sermon on March 22, 1970. See WGT 1:147.

[123]"Hearts Waiting for What?" Sermon delivered on September 29, 1974. Location unknown. See WGT 6:96.

[124]"The Everywhereness of God." Delivered in the 1980s. Specific date and location unknown. See WGT 3:104.

delivered from all that cripples us and all that shackles us and all that **imprisons** us.[125]

Taylor uses individual tropes in these quotations, such as Jesus coming to our "dungeon door," the "prisoner's cell swings wide," and "the darkest dungeon." But, again, he does more than use individualized tropes. He engages in troping through the invocation, revision, and recasting of a familiar metaphor—deliverance from imprisonment—over the span of several decades. To return to Gates's description of Signifyin(g), "One does not Signify some thing; one Signifies in *some way*."[126] In these examples, Taylor is both using tropes and "troping."

In his lectures on preaching, Taylor also draws on the trope of freedom from imprisonment to describe the preacher's responsibility to facilitate release from captivity:

> [1976] Wherever one's preaching lot is cast, there will be men and women long in **captivity**, their eyes unaccustomed to the light which belongs to those who know the glorious liberty of the sons of God. In **darkened cells** of the spirit, half dead they sit. And then, please God, on the edge of the mountain they see the running feet of the courier and know by his garments that he is the king's messenger. They know also that he bears a welcome and long longed-for word of a mighty battle and a great victory, and that because of that victory soon **their cell doors will swing wide** and they will **stand free** in the sunlight once again.[127]

> [1978] And that **prisoner** knows that a great and crucial battle is being fought. Upon that battle turns the fate of the prisoner, and then on a certain day he looks out and sees on the ledge of the mountain road a courier whose uniform tells him he is the courier of his own government, his own sovereign. You [preachers] will then face your future with confidence, knowing that **you bear to troubled prisoners the tidings of their liberation**—by God's grace come to Earth in the Lord Christ.[128]

---

[125]"Thyatira, Part II: The Great Possibility." Delivered originally at Concord Baptist Church in Brooklyn, New York, on March 27, 1988. See WGT 4:204.

[126]Gates, *Signifying Monkey*, p. 78.

[127]"The Foolishness of Preaching." Lecture delivered in New Haven, Connecticut, as part of Yale's Lyman Beecher Lectures in 1976. See WGT 5:169.

[128]"The Preaching of the Black Patriarchs, Part 2." Lecture delivered in Durham, North Carolina, as part of the Gardner C. Taylor Lectures on Preaching in 1976. See WGT 5:218.

In these excerpts, Taylor adds a twist to the metaphor. In the lectures, he calls on preachers to be "couriers" who spread the word that Christ has set the prisoner free. In both examples cited above, Taylor reflects on Isaiah 52:7, "How beautiful upon the mountains are the feet of the messenger who announces peace, who brings good news." Here is the difference. In the sermons, he uses the trope to appeal to the hope that Christ offers by setting us free from imprisonment, whereas in the lectures he uses the trope as a way to frame the preacher's responsibility as a courier to God's people. The privilege of the preacher is that he bears "a welcome and long longed-for word of a mighty battle and a great victory"; he bears to "troubled prisoners the tidings of their liberation." Once again, Taylor uses individual tropes such as "captivity" and "cell doors" while simultaneously invoking a larger metatrope: release from captivity.

The two tropes I mentioned as examples are part of a large and extensive repertoire from which Taylor draws in his preaching. For instance, another example of a culturally relevant oral formula is his repetition of the hymn line, "There's a bright side somewhere! Don't you rest until you find it!" which he draws on at least seven times in the published sermons found in the six-volume Words of Gardner Taylor series. Another example, this time of the second type of trope, is his appeal to a different metaphor: Christ delivering us from bondage/slavery to sin, a theme he returns to at least twelve times in his sermons and lectures. Examples like these abound.

Taylor's tropological practice has both rhetorical and theological significance. At the rhetorical level, Taylor's troping reveals a fascinating connection to Gates's description of tropes/troping in African American cultural practice. Through "troping," Taylor is Signifyin(g), to use Gates's language. One of the ways African Americans Signify, Gates argues, is through "tropological revision." Tropological revision, he explains, is "the manner in which a specific trope is repeated, with differences, between two or more texts. The revision of specific tropes recurs with surprising frequency in the Afro-American literary tradition."[129]

---

[129]Gates, *Signifying Monkey*, p. xxv.

Both examples, the repetition and revision of a hymn line and the invocation of a familiar metaphor—release from captivity—are arguably examples of tropological revision. The repetition, revision, and changing of a hymn line is an example of tropological revision: a culturally relevant oral formula is repeated, revised, and its function changes over time. A familiar metaphor such as release from captivity is also an example of tropological revision. It is a metaphor that connects listeners to a larger tradition both past and present—recall that Taylor says, "Christ who has come, *as the elders of my race used to say*, to our dungeon door." Taylor draws from a larger tradition in which this trope is historically relevant, and he repeats, revises, and returns to it over an extended period of time.[130] The trope is not uniquely his; it is part of a larger tradition.

For Gates, repetition of oral formulas and refiguration of familiar metaphors are constitutive practices in the African American literary and oral traditions, whether through tropological revision or through the three other forms of Signifyin(g) he mentions: the speakerly text, talking texts, and rewriting the speakerly.[131] He writes, "the originality of so much of the black tradition emphasizes *refiguration*, or repetition and difference, or troping, underscoring the foregrounding of the chain of signifiers, rather than the mimetic representation of novel content."[132] In other words, originality and innovation have less to do with the invention of new content ex nihilo and more to do with the refiguration and reconstitution of content that is culturally familiar. On account of this fact, it is not at all strange to hear Taylor troping on one of his father's sermons, a memorable phrase or stanza from a Martin Luther King Jr. sermon, or on something he heard from another preacher while out on the national preaching circuit. To do this with integrity is not at

---

[130]Another example of a trope that is familiar in African American church contexts would be the trope of the valley of dry bones in Ezekiel 37. African American preachers engage in "tropological revision" of this familiar trope by repeating, revising, and returning to it in their preaching over time. See Luke A. Powery, *Dem Dry Bones: Preaching, Death, and Hope* (Minneapolis: Fortress, 2012), pp. 15-17. For an illuminating article that discusses tropes and signifying in African American preaching, see Tim Sensing, "African American Preaching," *Journal of the American Academy of Ministry* 7 (Winter/Spring 2001): 38-53.

[131]Gates, *Signifying Monkey*, pp. xxv-xxvi.

[132]Ibid., p. 79.

all considered a copyright infringement. It is an homage to one's elders or colleagues in ministry.

Likewise, the theological significance of Taylor's usage of tropes and his practice of troping is at least worth mentioning. Not only does Taylor point toward hope through playing with tropes, but Taylor also *performs* hope through playing with tropes. In addition to Signifying hope in something, he Signifies hope in some way. Hope described is hope performed.

CONCLUSION

Taylor's performative improvisation through practices such as creating free spaces, practicing attunement, and playing with tropes disrupts traditional homiletical classification by revealing the nature of his improvisational-intercultural commitments. His willingness to create free spaces in the sermon-as-prepared makes him neither a conventional manuscript preacher nor a traditional folk preacher. He prepares a manuscript, but he also avails himself of the unforeseen, unplanned moments in the live sermon. While his spontaneity is arguably guided by an attendance to the Spirit of God (my aim is not to bracket out the spiritual dynamics at work in spontaneous speech), when examined from a *performative* vantage point, spontaneity takes place in the context of a wider performative ecology. It is the "outcome of years of practice and training and thousands of experiments," to return to Hauerwas.[133] In some respects, Taylor's willingness to counterbalance advanced preparation with real-time improvisation means that he defies traditional circumscription and classification, at least of the sort that homileticians like to use to classify preachers. Traditional binaries are somewhat problematic.

Taylor's practice of attunement reveals two significant insights about his commitment to performative improvisation. First, it reveals the respect he has for his listeners on account of his desire to read and respond to them. For instance, in African American settings, he displays this willingness in live interaction, through making improvisational changes as a result of call and response with the congregation. Second,

---

[133]Hauerwas, *Against the Nations*, p. 52.

it reveals his commitment to transgressing boundaries of racial, cultural, and ecclesial difference. In a white Presbyterian setting, he makes changes to both the delivery and the content of the sermon in order to attune to a culturally different congregation. In the next two chapters, I explain why transgressing racial, cultural, and ecclesial boundaries or *crossing over* is a feature of Taylor's preaching at the metaphorical and intercultural levels.

Taylor's "troping" shares important family resemblances with improvisational performance artists. Like jazz musicians and *improvisateurs* in the theater, he draws from a repertoire of stored material. In music or theater, artists learn a fake book or use "ready-mades," whereas in preaching tropes are oral formulas and familiar metaphors. Perhaps the most appropriate way to describe this phenomenon would be to return to Gabriele Tomasi's phrase "the *habitus* of the performer," that is, the embodied knowledge an experienced performer accesses through a combination of skill, training, practice, and attentiveness to the tradition and the community.[134] Taylor's troping reveals a distinct performative *habitus*.

From a homiletical-pedagogical vantage point, Taylor's practice of improvisation raises important questions about how homileticians teach preaching. In seminaries where the manuscript tradition is privileged, how might we encourage students to counterbalance their ties to convention with a commitment to being more intuitive and interactive before the sermon and during the sermon? Or, in seminaries or churches where extemporaneity and ad-hoc approaches to preaching are encouraged, how might we emphasize the importance of careful preparation and precision?

In every seminary, those who teach preaching might ask: How do we teach students to conceive of the sermon itself as a site for epistemic insight, a matrix for performative, theological, and spiritual reflection? How do we teach them to see themselves in situ, to use a term that Augusto Boal uses, that is, to see themselves seeing?[135] And how do we

---

[134]Tomasi, "On the Spontaneity of Jazz Improvisation," p. 87.

[135]Augusto Boal writes: "Theatre is born when the human being discovers that it can observe itself; when it discovers that, in this act of seeing, it can see itself-see itself *in situ*: see itself seeing." See Augusto Boal, *The Rainbow of Desire: The Boal Method of Theatre and Therapy* (New York: Routledge, 2003), p. 13.

encourage students to develop a performative habitus that honors their creativity, honors their church traditions, and honors God? Students who are able to bring to consciousness their performative *habitus*, to see themselves seeing, will not only grow spiritually and improve as preachers; they will be on their way to enhanced improvisational proficiency.

3

ROOTED, BUT
NOT RESTRICTED

Metaphorical Improvisation

We are not owned by our culture; it is a secondary identity
over which we rank the demands of God.

Gardner C. Taylor
Words of Gardner Taylor vol. 5

◆

In early December 2012, sports analysts from ESPN's hit show *First Take* engaged in a debate over a professional football player named Robert Griffin III (nicknamed RG3), a talented African American rookie quarterback for the Washington Redskins. When the conversation began, the four analysts—two white and two black—discussed Griffin's athleticism and successful play at the position. Then the conversation shifted quickly to a discussion about race, more specifically Griffin's race.

Rob Parker, one of the African American analysts, began describing his discomfort with Griffin's public performance of blackness. He wasn't sure what to make of the young quarterback and wondered aloud whether Griffin was a "brother or a cornball brother?" When another analyst asked: "What does that mean?" Parker replied: "Well, he's black, he kind of does his thing. But he's not really down with the cause, he's not one of us. He's *kind of black*."[1] Parker went on to question Griffin's

---

[1]Chris Greenberg, "Rob Parker on RG3: ESPN 'First Take' Host Asks If Robert Griffin III Is a

choice of a white fiancée and unconfirmed rumors that Griffin was a Republican. When asked about Griffin's choice of braids as a hairstyle, Parker said: "Now that's different. To me, that's very urban. Wearing braids is . . . you're a brother. You're a brother if you have braids on." When encouraged to join in the discussion about Griffin's blackness, Stephen A. Smith, the other African American sports analyst, stated:

> Well, first of all let me say this: I'm uncomfortable with where we just went. RG3, the ethnicity, the color of his fiancée is none of our business. It's irrelevant. He can live his life any way he chooses. The braids that he has in his hair, that's his business, that's his life. I don't judge someone's blackness based on those kind of things. I just don't do that. I'm not that kind of guy.

In subsequent days, under pressure to respond, Robert Griffin III made the following statement at a team press conference: "For me, you don't ever want to be defined by the color of your skin. You want to be defined by your work ethic, the person that you are, your character, your personality. That's what I've tried to go out and do. I am an African-American in America. That will never change. But I don't have to be defined by that."[2] For obvious reasons, Parker's comments set off a media firestorm, and he was suspended from ESPN for making them. In addition, his open questioning of Griffin's blackness reintroduced a challenging series of ongoing questions in the African American community: What does it mean to be black? Is it based on one's choices—how you speak, whom you marry, how you vote, where you go to college? Also, who gets to decide when someone is not being "black enough" or is "acting white"?

Sadly, the accusation from within the black community that a person is "acting white" has a long and painful history. Whether that means one person calling another an "Uncle Tom," based on the character by that name in Harriet Beecher Stowe's *Uncle Tom's Cabin*, Marcus Garvey questioning W. E. B. Du Bois's white philosophical conversation partners,

'Cornball Brother,'" *Huffington Post*, December 13, 2012, accessed December 19, 2012, www.huffingtonpost.com/2012/12/13/rob-parker-robert-griffin-race-first-take_n_2295726.html (emphasis added).

[2]Jim Corbett, "Robert Griffin III Refuses to Be Defined by Race," *USA Today*, December 12, 2012, www.usatoday.com/story/sports/nfl/redskins/2012/12/12/robert-griffin-iii-washington-redskins-race/1765701/.

Malcolm X going on national television shortly after the March on Washington and accusing Martin Luther King Jr. of "acting white," Jesse Jackson questioning Barack Obama's racial credentials during the 2008 presidential campaign or, in this case, Rob Parker wondering aloud whether Griffin is a "cornball brother," these and many other frank conversations, sometimes in public and more often in private, have challenged and often hurt those involved in them voluntarily or involuntarily.[3]

As a crossover preacher, Gardner Taylor was not spared from these accusations. Sometimes he was criticized for not whooping like other black preachers, other times for not using the language of the urban ghetto, and other times for quoting too often from European preachers. In many and various ways he was told he was not being "black enough." Thus, as a public figure, he had to battle against double prejudice: prejudice from *outside* the African American community for being black and prejudice from *within* the African American community for not being black enough. These criticisms were not only unjust; they also arose from the misunderstanding that blackness in general and black preaching in particular were monolithic and univocal. Instead of a category like race being construed as complex, nuanced structures of meaning in which variation and diversity are present, race was constructed in reductive binaries: authentic blackness versus inauthentic blackness, insider versus outsider, acting black versus acting white.

This chapter problematizes essentialist definitions of blackness, specifically in James H. Cone's theology and in Henry H. Mitchell's homiletic, in order to demonstrate that Taylor's metaphorical-improvisational approach offers an alternative vision. I argue that Taylor's negotiation of race and being racialized is neither essentialist nor reductive; rather, it is improvisational. At the risk of oversimplification, one might say it is much closer to Robert Griffin's or Stephen A. Smith's vision of blackness than Rob Parker's: race forms part of Taylor's identity but does not en-

---

[3]See Harriet Beecher Stowe, *Uncle Tom's Cabin, Or, Life Among the Lowly* (Cambridge, MA: Belknap Press, 1962). Ron Christie has written the definitive book on the painful history of the racial slur "acting white." He covers the genesis of "acting white" and discusses figures such as Garvey and Du Bois, Malcolm X and Martin Luther King Jr., and Barack Obama. He does not include Rob Parker's comments since they are more recent. See Ron Christie, *Acting White: The Curious History of a Racial Slur* (New York: Thomas Dunne Books/St. Martin's Press, 2010).

capsulate or define it. He is rooted but not restricted by this category. To return to Griffin's words, "I am an African-American in America. That will never change. But I don't have to be defined by that."[4]

Later in this chapter, the term we will use to describe Taylor's improvised negotiation of race is *transgressive blackness*. By transgressive blackness is meant the rupturing of reifications of blackness as an ossified or static identity over which nothing can be placed. Instead of dredging up the negative connotations of the word *transgressive* and its associations with sinfulness or moral malfeasance, the choice of the word is designed to bring to the fore its other connotation: *crossing over* a boundary or border. To cross over is to refuse to be circumscribed. The metaphors of transgressing boundaries and border crossing are familiar and accessible in nonmajority biblical-theological scholarship.[5]

Transgressing means that one decides to become a crossover preacher through rupturing rather than reifying narrow classification. To cross a border is to step outside its limits, to relocate its perceived center by expanding it and moving into new terrain. In 1950s sports, transgression is Jackie Robinson desegregating Major League Baseball with the Brooklyn Dodgers. In music, it is Charlie Parker or Louis Armstrong bringing jazz and blues to mainstream society. In the segregated South of the 1950s, it is Rosa Parks refusing to sit in the back of the bus. In preaching, it is Gardner C. Taylor reframing and expanding blackness narrowly defined through improvisation. Taylor performed *transgressive*

---

[4]Corbett, "Robert Griffin III Refuses to Be Defined by Race."

[5]For examples of the border metaphor among Latin@ and Latin American theologians, see Gloria Anzaldúa, *Borderlands=La Frontera* (San Francisco: Aunt Lute Books, 1999); Samuel E. Escobar, *Changing Tides: Latin America and World Mission Today* (Maryknoll, NY: Orbis Books, 2002). For examples in Asian American and Asian theologies, see articles by M. Thomas Thangaraj and Kwok Pui-Lan in D. N. Premnath, ed., *Border Crossings: Cross-Cultural Hermeneutics* (Maryknoll, NY: Orbis Books, 2007). See also Peter C. Phan, *In Our Own Tongues: Perspectives from Asia on Mission and Inculturation* (Maryknoll, NY: Orbis Books, 2003). Also, in *Preaching and the Other*, homiletician Ronald J. Allen observes that transgression and border crossing are common themes among postmodern thinkers such as Michel Foucault. Allen writes: "Many postmodern thinkers elevate the practice of transgression to a philosophical principle and practice. In this context, transgression refers to crossing the boundaries or limits of conventional academic disciplines and other areas of specialization." See Ronald J. Allen, *Preaching and the Other: Studies of Postmodern Insights* (St. Louis: Chalice, 2009), p. 99. Cf. also Michel Foucault, "Preface to Transgression," in *Language, Counter-Memory, Practice: Selected Essays and Interviews* (Ithaca, NY: Cornell University Press, 1977), pp. 29-52.

blackness in this sense: he crossed boundaries of what blackness was and was not supposed to be.

My argument unfolds in an inductive manner. First, I problematize James Cone's vision of blackness by enlisting three African American theologians—Victor Anderson, Brian Bantum, and J. Kameron Carter—as my interlocutors, all of whom criticize Cone's theology of blackness, albeit from different vantage points. Second, I explore an alternative vision of blackness—blackness-as-improvisation. Drawing from Cornel West's concept of protean reflexivity and Michael Eric Dyson's metaphor of bricolage, I claim that improvisation is a constitutive metaphor for constructions of blackness. Third, I critique Henry H. Mitchell's definition of black preaching by suggesting that he (inadvertently) parochializes the same preaching tradition he seeks to honor and celebrate. That is to say, his homiletical project tends to make black preaching a univocal rather than plurivocal tradition in which diversity is minimized and uniformity is maximized. Fourth, I point to different trajectories in African American homiletics that challenge Mitchell's proposal. I lift up four approaches—structuralist, experientialist, hermeneutical, and improvisational—in order to highlight the diversity within the black homiletical tradition. Finally, I discuss Taylor's metaphorical-improvisational negotiation of race—what I call *transgressive blackness*—and point to the ways he transgresses normative black theology and black homiletics.

THE LEGACY OF JAMES H. CONE: CRITIQUES FROM AFRICAN AMERICAN THEOLOGIANS

The focus of James H. Cone's theology is African American survival in the face of oppression for the sake of liberation.[6] Cone himself describes his theology as a "theology of survival" that interprets the "theological significance of the being of a community whose existence is threatened by the power of non-being."[7] Considering the plight of

---

[6] Victor Anderson notes that, two decades later, C. Eric Lincoln and Lawrence Mamiya described African American culture as "the sum of options for creative survival." See C. Eric Lincoln and Lawrence H. Mamiya, *The Black Church in the African American Experience* (Durham, NC: Duke University Press, 1990), p. 3, as cited in Victor Anderson, *Beyond Ontological Blackness: An Essay on African American Religious and Cultural Criticism* (New York: Continuum, 1995), p. 89.
[7] James H. Cone, *A Black Theology of Liberation* (Maryknoll, NY: Orbis Books, 1990), p. 16.

African Americans historically and the racist systems and structures in place at institutions of higher learning during Cone's student days and beyond, is it any wonder why liberation theology seemed so compelling to him? Not only is the threat of nonbeing a powerful motivator for a community facing oppression, but also the possibility of liberation represents a dynamic and compelling goal.

Cone's liberation theology is grounded in this-worldly Christology; his interest is in a Jesus-from-below, not a Jesus-from-above. Jesus comes as a liberator of human captives. He comes so that the voices of the voiceless can be heard and, in Cone's case, the voices of those in the black community. For Cone, Jesus does not save us primarily to grant us entry into heaven; he comes to upend and overturn systems and structures that propagate evil.

Cone's proposal not only challenged otherworldly Christology as inherently escapist; it also posed a significant challenge to so-called traditional systematic theology. It exploded the myth among Cone's white colleagues that their theology somehow came from what Paul Ricoeur refers to as the "nonplace of the transcendental subject."[8] At the root of "nonplace" theologies, Cone argues, we find ideologies, that is, a priori ideologies that "blind us from certain aspects of the truth."[9] Unless theologians understand that *all* theological questions come from a place, that is, a particular social location that shapes the questions asked and answers given, the truth that is sought will remain elusive and unattainable. To deny one's social location or place and to suggest that one's theology is somehow a-contextual is to subscribe to an ideological position that encourages blindness rather than abrogating it, that impedes liberation rather than advancing it. Cone not only sought to benefit the African American community, but he also sought to shake loose theological education from its racist moorings. His project undermined racist ideology through its insistence that Jesus was on the side of the oppressed while *also* seeking to dismantle North American white male bourgeois mainline theology from its hegemony over theological discourse. His theology was designed to assist African Americans in lib-

---

[8]Paul Ricoeur, *From Text to Action* (Evanston, IL: Northwestern University Press, 2007), p. 302.
[9]James H. Cone, *God of the Oppressed* (New York: Seabury, 1975), p. 92.

eration from oppression and to confront white theologians as to the blindness of their racism.

Although Cone's contribution is significant and many of his students have carried on his legacy, a growing number of theologians from within the African American theological community have expressed their discomfort as to the tenability of the project itself, theologians such as Victor Anderson, Brian Bantum, and J. Kameron Carter, among others. None of these theologians questions whether Cone's work raises to consciousness the significance of race and the problem of racism among both white and black Americans. They acknowledge this fact, and they celebrate it. But they also wonder: is it possible that Cone's racial categories and racial reasoning is problematic? What if Cone imagines race to be an idealized, essentialist *stasis* rather than a real-world, nonessentialist *kinesis*, and, if so, does this imagined *stasis* catalyze the problems he seeks to confront? What if his depiction of race, blackness in particular, promotes a reification of race that perpetuates the problem of racism rather than eradicating it? Can Cone's project really lead to liberation if he attacks modern racial reasoning using the broken tools of modern racial reasoning? Do the ends justify the means? We begin with Victor Anderson's critique.

Victor Anderson: "A blackness that whiteness created." In *Beyond Ontological Blackness*, Victor Anderson sharply critiques Cone's proposal. He argues that the wound of racism cannot be healed through invoking the sort of essentialist categories (e.g., blackness and whiteness) that are central to Cone's project. Only by moving away from "ontological blackness" can racial discourse do the constructive work for which it is designed.[10] The main problem with reifying blackness, Anderson argues, is that it becomes bound and beholden to whiteness. That is to say, it finds its ground in a racist binary: blackness *with respect to* whiteness or, to use Anderson's language, a "blackness that whiteness created."[11] Al-

---

[10] Anderson defines ontological blackness as a "covering term that connotes categorical, essentialist, and representational languages depicting black life and experience" (Anderson, *Beyond Ontological Blackness*, p. 11).

[11] Anderson writes: "the cult of European genius, with its essentially heroic, epochal, and culture-advancing qualities, has likewise determined how African Americans represents themselves as the mirror of European genius: *ontological blackness signifies the blackness that whiteness created*" (ibid.,

though one can and should expect a reactionary stance wherever racist systems and structures exist and are in need of reformation, Anderson's concern is that reification makes one beholden to the oppression one seeks to eradicate. The problem with unnuanced catalytic theology is that it is almost always bound to the source of its oppression. It uses racist categories to challenge racist frameworks, thus sawing off the same limb from which it makes its claim.

Anderson takes more specific aim at Cone's theology in chapter three of *Beyond Ontological Blackness*. His first critique pertains to the axiological tenets of the movement. Anderson argues that black liberation theology in general and Cone's theology in particular are based in "struggle, resistance, and survival" rather than "thriving, flourishing, or fulfillment."[12] Because Cone and others opted for the former, they enclosed their ideas in an oppressive rather than liberative system. Oppressive conditions have to remain in place in order for resistance, struggle, and survival to be maintained. In Cone's framework, argues Anderson, "oppression is required for the self-disclosure of the oppressed."[13] In other words, self and communal identity can appear only within structures of oppression. What about the unintended, unforeseen consequences to Cone's proposal?

Cone's theology, Anderson suggests, raises just as many questions as it answers. If an oppressive, racist framework must be in place in order for Cone's axiological tenets to remain tenable, then how can this be liberative? Does a system based in struggle, resistance, and survival actually perpetuate racism? Although an axiom such as resistance is still important in a society such as our own where racism remains a pervasive

---

p. 13). On a parenthetical note, Anderson's critique is also Cornel West's point in his critique of African American protest art. West writes: "The irony of the view of black art as protest—as description of the inhumane circumstances of much of black life and as heartfelt resistance to these circumstances—is that it is still preoccupied with the white normative gaze, and it reduces black people to mere reactors to white power." West's language of the "white normative gaze" and of reactive rather than proactive discourse is simply another way of getting at the problem that Anderson identifies, the problem of ontological blackness. If blackness can only be defined or described as blackness-with-respect-to-whiteness, then it remains bound and beholden to the same system that Cone and others are trying to destroy. See Cornel West, *The Cornel West Reader* (New York: Basic Civitas Books, 1999), p. 455.

[12]Anderson, *Beyond Ontological Blackness*, p. 87.

[13]Ibid.

problem, the "What next?" question is also important. In the post–civil rights era, what about other axioms like thriving, flourishing, and fulfillment? What comes next after liberation is realized, when battles for survival are less salient than opportunities for fulfillment? What then?

Anderson reveals a significant critique: Cone and others made totalizing assumptions about African Americans that are difficult to maintain because some tenets are emphasized over others. He writes: "To make suffering, rebellion, and survival essential marks of black existence, it seems to me, trivializes the nature of oppression many blacks genuinely experience by the absurdity that anyone who is black is also oppressed."[14] One might ask: Do Cone's theological assumptions hold up under scrutiny if not *all* African Americans living in twenty-first-century America are equally oppressed? Do poor African Americans in Ferguson, Baltimore, or New Orleans face the exact same oppression as rich African Americans in Beverly Hills or Manhattan, or are there points of convergence and divergence?

Anderson's second critique challenges Cone's reification of blackness. In *A Black Theology of Liberation*, Cone maintains: "[The black experience] means having natural hair cuts, wearing African dashikis, and dancing to the sound of Johnny Lee Hooker or B. B. King, knowing that no matter how hard whitey tries there can be no real duplication of the black 'soul.'"[15] Although these comments, originally written in 1970, make more sense and sound less archaic in the larger social setting of the black power and the "black is beautiful" movements early in that decade, their essentialist assumptions remain somewhat problematic. Can Cone really speak of the "black experience" or the "black soul" by invoking markers like music and haircuts, or is he being reductionistic? Does Cone imagine an unrealistic, monolithic, and singular black experience that ignores complexity and variation *within* the African American community? Anderson's answer is a definitive *yes*. Whenever one speaks of *a* black experience or *a* black soul without qualification or nuance, the risk is a totalitarian reification of race that is unhelpful and unconstructive. Anderson maintains that such appeals to blackness as a totality

---

[14]Ibid., p. 103.
[15]Cone, *Black Theology of Liberation*, p. 25.

of meaning stunt possibilities for transcendence. He writes:

> In black theology, blackness has become a totality of meaning. It cannot
> point to any transcendent meaning beyond itself without also frag-
> menting. Because black life is fundamentally determined by black suf-
> fering and resistance to whiteness (the power of non-being), black exis-
> tence is without the possibility of transcendence from the blackness that
> whiteness created. Without transcendence from the determinacy of
> whiteness, black theology's promise of liberation remains existentially a
> function of black self-consciousness (to see oneself as black, free, and
> self-determined).[16]

That is to say, unless blackness is able to transcend the blackness that
whiteness created and find its legitimacy outside the narrow confines of
the oppressive system it seeks to overthrow, it cannot be constructive in
any meaningful sense.

Moreover, the reification of race-as-definitive-category is not only
dangerous philosophically; it is also dangerous theologically. "From a
religious point of view," Anderson writes, "when race is made total, then
ontological blackness is idolatrous, approaching racial henotheism."[17]
Since Cone's black liberation theology cannot exist or stand alone
without white racist ideology and because it seems to reify race in a totalitarian (idolatrous?) way, it remains, to use Anderson's phrase, a theology in a "crisis of legitimation."[18] Cone's message might be a pro-
vocative description of blackness but, according to Anderson, it is a
description of "a blackness that whiteness created."

Brian Bantum: Christological constriction. Brian Bantum challenges
Cone's project from a different angle: Christology. In *God of the Oppressed*, Cone famously said, "Jesus is black," meaning that God is unquestionably on the side of the oppressed.[19] In so doing, Cone conveys
the point that African Americans attach both symbolic and literal significance to Jesus as an oppressed Jew. The theological significance of

---

[16]Anderson, *Beyond Ontological Blackness*, p. 92.
[17]Ibid., p. 15.
[18]Ibid., p. 117.
[19]Cone, *God of the Oppressed*, p. 136. Cone was following in the footsteps of Albert B. Cleage, *The
Black Messiah* (New York: Sheed and Ward, 1968).

Jesus, Cone argued, is best discerned and articulated through conceiving of Jesus "primarily within black experience, as a black body."[20]

The problem Bantum sees with Cone's Christology is not one of content but scope. His concern is with the dangers of christological constriction. In principle, he accepts Cone's belief that Jesus came to liberate the oppressed. His concern is with Cone's *limitation* of Jesus' ministry to the *earthly* deliverance of the oppressed. The scope is too narrow, Bantum argues. If Jesus came *only* to deliver the oppressed from earthly domination, this not only makes the scope of Jesus' salvific work too narrow; it also subjects black liberation theology to the "white colonial theo-imagination."[21]

First, Bantum challenges Cone's Christology as reductionistic. When Cone says, "Jesus is black," that is, a black body in the context of a black experience, he mistakenly "distill[s] the totality of Jesus' person and ministry into the negotiation of a politically oppressive reality."[22] Although particularizing Jesus into a political moment and body can be beneficial and constructive theologically in that it points us to a Jesus who is *pro nobis* and not merely *extra nos*, this move also risks removing from the incarnation its cosmic and eschatological significance. Cone's emphasis on Jesus' sociopolitical particularity necessitates an inversion of Jesus' identity to this-worldly reality alone. Instead of Jesus being the "captain of the ship," to use Bantum's language, Jesus is the "chattel" at the bottom of the ship.[23] While metaphorically speaking Jesus is able to be both captain and chattel, when Cone privileges Jesus-as-chattel and ignores Jesus-as-captain, a major tenet of Jesus' identity is obstructed. Bantum writes: "For Cone, Jesus' particularity effectively becomes inverted from Jesus as Jew/oppressed to Jesus as oppressed/Jew. Ultimately, this leaves not only Jesus as fundamentally a body, but also redemption as primarily bodily."[24] Put differently, oppression circumscribes Jesus-as-Jew rather than Jesus-as-Jew circumscribing oppression. In this framework, Jesus'

---

[20]Brian Bantum, *Redeeming Mulatto: A Theology of Race and Christian Hybridity* (Waco, TX: Baylor University Press, 2010), p. 4.

[21]Ibid., p. 5.

[22]Ibid., p. 4.

[23]Ibid.

[24]Ibid.

identity is legitimated *within* the conditions and parameters of oppression, and his work is limited *to* earthly and bodily deliverance of the oppressed. This raises many problems and theological challenges, and at least one important question: Did Jesus come only for the earthly deliverance of the oppressed?

One way to address this question and to make our way out of this theological quagmire is to place Cone's theology in conversation with that of Jürgen Moltmann and Miroslav Volf. Drawing primarily from Moltmann's *The Spirit of Life*, Volf argues that Christ's solidarity with the oppressed should be counterbalanced with his atonement for oppressors. Put simply, Jesus makes room at the cross to embrace both the oppressed and the oppressor. Just as Jesus' sufferings are not his alone, but those of the poor and the weak (à la Cone), so also his sufferings atone for those who oppress the poor and the weak (à la Moltmann/Volf). Jesus' self-giving sacrifice is both an act of solidarity and, in the words of Moltmann, "the divine atonement for sin, for injustice and violence on the earth."[25] Although God acts in solidarity with victims, God also makes space to atone for perpetrators. The self-emptying love of Christ for the other, what Volf refers to as "divine self-donation," is expansive enough to include both victim and victimizer.[26] "At the heart of the cross," argues Volf, is "Christ's stance of not letting the other remain an enemy and of creating space in himself for the offender to come in."[27] Christ's arms open wide enough at the cross to include the victim and the perpetrator, the oppressed and the oppressor. What is present in Volf and Moltmann and absent from Cone is a theology that makes space for the oppressed *and* the oppressor. We find a Jesus who stands in solidarity with victims yet also is unwilling to let victimizers remain enemies of God.

In my judgment, the biblical-theological problem with Cone's argument is that he starts and ends with the oppressed without considering the possibilities of redemption for the oppressors. In this sense he

---

[25]Jürgen Moltmann, *The Spirit of Life: A Universal Affirmation* (Minneapolis: Fortress, 1992), p. 136.

[26]Miroslav Volf, *Exclusion and Embrace: A Theological Exploration of Identity, Otherness, and Reconciliation* (Nashville: Abingdon, 1996), p. 23.

[27]Ibid., p. 126.

is a proponent of limited atonement. The logic of Cone's theology suggests Jesus came only for this-worldly deliverance of the downtrodden, that is, for the oppressed elect. In this framework, not only does salvation lose its cosmic and eschatological significance, but also no room is made at the cross for perpetrators to find divine mercy and grace alongside victims.

Bantum also argues that Cone's Christology keeps black theology from standing on its own apart from white domination. Like Anderson, Bantum suggests that the blackness Cone defends is a blackness that whiteness created. It requires oppression for its voice to be heard. Cone's way of approaching the problem of racism prevents rather than promotes lasting change because it uses the same broken tools of modern racial reasoning that it seeks to subvert. It encloses itself within the system it wants to overturn. Reflecting on Cone's claim that "Jesus is black" and the bearing this claim has on black theology, Bantum writes:

> This enclosure of Christ's redemptive moment into not Jesus' body but black bodies, positions Black Theology as a perpetual space of self-preservation that maintains black reflection within the ever-threatening onslaught of white colonial theo-imagination.... The reflex of a practical embodied self-preservation is a crucial one given the dearth of Christian intellectuals of color within the academy and their struggle for reception within their respective fields. But do not the claims Jesus made about himself seem to suggest a transformation that complicates identities rather than confirms them? Does Jesus' presence among us as God, as a Jew, as oppressed, but also divine and human, born of Spirit *and* flesh, make possible not only a wider set of allegiances, but require it of our lives as disciples?[28]

Although Cone's theology may broaden the extent of "Christ's redemptive moment" in significant ways by pressing theologians to consider Jesus' identity as an oppressed Jew and his physical deliverance of the oppressed as more constitutive to his mission than previously considered, the fallout cannot be overlooked if such a position constrains black theology to a reactive and self-preserving stance.

---

[28]Bantum, *Redeeming Mulatto*, p. 5.

When Cone argues for Jesus' blackness, he risks enclosing Jesus within a reductive category by setting parameters around race as static rather than kinetic, and oppression as universally experienced rather than contextually nuanced. Two ironies emerge from such a position. First, the consequence of a vision of oppression as universally experienced in the same way is that it moves away from place toward nonplace. Although this is no doubt an unintentional consequence, recall one of the central tenets of Cone's argument: at the root of "nonplace" theologies we find ideologies, that is, a priori ideologies that "blind us from certain aspects of the truth."[29] Second, the essentialist assumptions that undergird Cone's reification of blackness-as-category hurt rather than help his argument. Reducing rather than complexifying diverse experiences and variegated cultural practices encloses and constricts the category itself. How can one celebrate all of the richness and fecundity of a tradition if he only celebrates one aspect of it?

J. Kameron Carter: On the dangers of a "black message in a white envelope." The final critique of Cone examined here is in J. Kameron Carter's *Race: A Theological Account.* Like Anderson, Carter is quick to acknowledge Cone's theological contributions. He sees him as a pioneer, a man with immense courage to disrupt modernity's "analytics of race" by challenging status quo white bourgeois race(ist) theology.[30] Carter also believes Cone was a "revolutionary" theologian who, like Irenaeus, insisted on "the significance of Israel for Christian faith."[31] Although he lauds Cone's contributions, at the same time he criticizes Cone (and other black liberation theologians) for reinscribing racist ideology and hermetically sealing black identity.

Carter's first criticism of Cone is that he "unwittingly reinscribes the aberrant theology (or pseudotheology) of modern racial reasoning."[32] Carter's aim in *Race* is to deal with the "theological problem of whiteness" by deconstructing the white racist colonial imagination and forging a new nonracist theological imagination. The problem he has with Cone's

---

[29]Cone, *God of the Oppressed*, p. 92.
[30]J. Kameron Carter writes: "Cone's black liberation theology comes to the threshold of an intellectual program that theologically disrupts modernity's analytics of race." J. Kameron Carter, *Race: A Theological Account* (Oxford: Oxford University Press, 2008), p. 158.
[31]Ibid., p. 170.
[32]Ibid., p. 158.

reified-essentialized blackness is that it tends to perpetuate the white racist imagination instead of providing an alternative and better vision.[33] Although Cone's work challenges racism as an oppressive system in need of liberation, it fails to upend or overturn that system. It deconstructs the framework effectively, but fails to replace it with a more compelling vision. Cone's vision of blackness, to use Carter's phrase, is the "photo negative" of whiteness.[34] Instead of reforming or reimagining the system, Cone reinscribes it. Carter writes: "Black liberation theology's attempt philosophically and theologically to salvage the blackness that modernity has constructed by converting it into a site of cultural power (and thus into a site at which to stage 'the courage to be') is not radical enough. This is because it ironically leaves whiteness in place."[35] Thus the blackness Cone proffers is a blackness-with-reference-to-whiteness. Although it sets out to challenge and even offset whiteness from its pseudo-normativity, unfortunately, it does the reverse: it entrenches whiteness by entrenching itself, the reason it is "not radical enough." In Carter's judgment, it plays by the system's rules in order to try to change the system. The problem with this is obvious: to return to Victor Anderson for a moment, in Cone's framework, "[blackness] requires whiteness, white racism, and white theology for the self-disclosure of its new black being and its legitimacy."[36] Instead of inventing or reimagining new

---

[33]In the prologue to *Race*, Carter writes: "My fundamental contention is that modernity's racial imagination has its genesis in the theological problem of Christianity's quest to sever itself from its Jewish roots. This severance was carried out in two distinct but integrated steps. First, Jews were cast as a race group in contrast to Western Christians. . . . Second, having racialized Jews as a people of the Orient and thus Judaism as a 'religion' of the East, Jews were then deemed inferior to Christians of the Occident or the West. Hence, the racial imagination (the first step) proved as well to be a racist imagination of white supremacy (the second step). Within the gulf enacted by Christianity and the Jews, the *racial*, which proves to be a *racist*, imagination was forged" (ibid., p. 4). For an alternative and contrasting account of the relationship between Israel and early Christians, see Willie James Jennings, *The Christian Imagination: Theology and the Origins of Race* (New Haven, CT: Yale University Press, 2010).

[34]Reflecting on blackness and whiteness and the problems created by both of these categories when they follow the rules of racial modernity, Carter writes: "As a theological problem, whiteness names the refusal to trade against race. It names the refusal to enter into dependent, promiscuous, and, in short, 'contaminated' relations that resist an idolatrously false purity. The blackness that whiteness creates names the same refusal, albeit cast as the photo negative that yet retains the problem" (ibid., p. 192).

[35]Ibid.

[36]Anderson, *Beyond Ontological Blackness*, p. 91.

black identity in a reimagined nonracist framework, Cone reinscribes black identity within an actual racist framework. Again, the metaphor proves useful: what remains is a black message in a white envelope.

Carter's second criticism of Cone pertains to the way liberation theology seals off black identity within a closed system. It frames blackness within a *this-not-that* framework. Carter keeps returning to two terms throughout the book—*enclosure* and *sealing*—to describe how a blackness-whiteness binary oversimplifies and reduces identity rather than complexifying and opening it.[37] The problem with black liberation theology and its impact on black identity is that it imagines race, religion, and culture as "hermetically enclosed, sealed within themselves, and 'opaque' to any exteriority. Black folks can only speak as 'black.' In the parlance of race theory, they become 'reified' or made 'essential.'"[38] In this framework, culture—whether white, black, or otherwise—is oversimplified, cut off from the possibilities of "cultural intimacy and thus reciprocity," and replaced by culture as a site of "closure and containment."[39] Instead of black theologians promoting black identity(ies) as a rich, kinetic, and variegated matrix of cultural and social meanings and perceptions, they risk flattening identity(ies) out to a reductive and narrow categorization. Blackness is not conceived of as a complex matrix of meanings, but as one monolithic, essentialized meaning; not a broad landscape, but a fixed point on a map. The consequences of enclosed identity are twofold: first, the self is cordoned off from its interdependence with the other, and, second, transcendence is disallowed, thus stunting the divine-human covenantal relationship.

The reimagining of identity Carter calls for is one that is interdependent and covenantal. Binaries like blackness-whiteness or even American-foreigner may be useful in some arenas, but when left unchecked, they move Christians away from dependence on God and *in-*

---

[37]For the most compelling instances of "enclosure" or "enclosed," see Carter, *Race*, pp. 132, 166-67, 310, 352. For the most compelling instances of "sealed," see ibid., pp. 126, 230, 279, 351, 366, 439.

[38]Carter, *Race*, p. 126. In fairness, Carter's critique in this quotation pertains to "problematic appropriations and readings" of Albert J. Raboteau's *Slave Religion*, where black religion is understood as some kind of "cultural reflex." However, the same critique can be lodged against Cone as well in that his system emphasizes a monolithic, static kind of blackness that can also be described as "hermetically enclosed."

[39]Ibid., p. 230.

*ter*dependence with one another. Only by departing from racial reification is the self "known in, through, and *as* another."[40] Only in leaving behind colonial and imperial impulses can nations reimagine themselves as "bound to the destinies of other nations and their sense of peoplehood."[41] Rather than relying on the politics of cultural or national identity, Carter invites Christians to reimagine identity as *covenantally* bound to the God of Israel, who is also the God of the nations. When Christians recognize their boundedness to the divine covenant, they are set free to participate in the transcendent love and action of God. By resisting the binaries that seal off identity, they subversively free themselves from enclosed definitions of who they are. Hear again Robert Griffin III's public statement: "I am an African-American in America. That will never change. But I don't have to be defined by that."[42] Through participation and partnership, that is, participating in the "language of divine sonship, the language of God" and partnering with humanity and with creation, one is caught up in "eschatological movement toward the kingdom of God."[43] The result is straightforward and dramatic: closed systems and structures are ruptured rather than reified! As Carter puts it, "Nationalism, or identity as construed in binary terms and therefore as self-enclosure, is broken."[44]

To summarize, Cone's black liberation theology may advance black theology within a racist framework, but it does not sufficiently reimagine

---

[40]Ibid., p. 310. Although he does not acknowledge it, Carter is making a Ricoeurian move in pointing to the dependence on the other. In *Oneself as Another*, Paul Ricoeur argues that the other helps me "gather myself together, strengthen myself, and maintain myself in identity." Not only do I alter the identity of the other, argues Ricoeur, but the other also alters me. In this dialectical relationship, neither the self nor the other-than-self are eclipsed or erased. The presence of the other does not require my annihilation or self-loathing, contra Emmanuel Lévinas. Rather, the other's presence builds self-esteem and facilitates respect for what is foreign. See Paul Ricoeur, *Oneself as Another* (Chicago: University of Chicago Press, 1992), p. 332. By contrast, Emmanuel Lévinas argues for a nonreciprocal relation between the self and the other wherein the other's identity eclipses and ruptures the identity of the self. Lévinas writes: "In the very heart of the relationship with the other that characterizes our social life, alterity appears as a non-reciprocal relationship-that is, as contrasting strongly with contemporaneousness. The Other as Other is not only an alter ego: the Other is what I myself am not." Emmanuel Lévinas, *Time and the Other and Additional Essays* (Pittsburgh: Duquesne University Press, 1987), p. 83.

[41]Carter, *Race*, p. 310.

[42]Corbett, "Robert Griffin III Refuses to Be Defined by Race."

[43]Carter, *Race*, p. 310.

[44]Ibid.

black theology in a nonracist framework. It challenges the system but does not sufficiently overturn or upend it. Instead of repairing the broken system, it reinscribes it. While Anderson, Bantum, and Carter laud Cone for making significant strides in liberating theology from the white racist colonial imagination—which he most certainly does—all three theologians agree that black theology must move *beyond* entrenched depictions of blackness. The essentialist move makes identity into a fixture that is hermetically sealed, and it disallows transcendence. Although Cone's ontological vision of blackness needs to be contextualized to the era of the late 1960s and early 1970s—the time he was writing *A Black Theology of Liberation* and *God of the Oppressed*—its essentialisms are increasingly difficult to maintain beyond the era in which they were written.

Anderson, Bantum, and Carter all make a similar observation: *blackness is far from monolithic.*[45] It is complex, diverse, and protean. As we will see in the next section, a more helpful way to describe this category is not through a vision of blackness vis-à-vis whiteness, but through the metaphor of improvisation. Drawing from the work of Cornel West and Michael Eric Dyson, I argue that metaphorical improvisation is a viable structure by which to frame blackness-as-category. In a later section, I show how metaphorical improvisation connects to Gardner C. Taylor's homiletic and critiques Henry H. Mitchell's homiletic.

IMPROVISATIONAL BLACKNESS: PROTEAN REFLEXIVITY AND CREATIVE BRICOLAGE

Improvisation as a metaphor for blackness is not a twenty-first-century phenomenon; it gained traction in the mid-twentieth century. In *The Shadow and the Act*, Walton M. Muyumba notes the long-standing connection between twentieth-century African American philosophical pragmatism and jazz improvisation. In the mid-twentieth century,

---

[45]For instance, Marvin McMickle has pointed to class disparities among African Americans as evidence that class is a significant factor in lived experience. Specifically, McMickle has this to say about the rise of the black middle class: "The people inside and outside the black churches of inner-city America may look like each other, but in terms of values, vocabulary, worldview, and a vision for the future, the socioeconomic factors that divide them are far more significant than the single racial identification that links them together." See Marvin A. McMickle, *Preaching to the Black Middle Class: Words of Challenge, Words of Hope* (Valley Forge, PA: Judson Press, 2000), p. 2.

public intellectuals such as Ralph Ellison, James Baldwin, and Amiri Baraka paved the way for a new generation of scholars such as Cornel West, Michael Eric Dyson, and others to reimagine African American existence as an *improvisational* way of being and acting.[46] For writers like West, who self-identified with American pragmatic philosophy and connected his thinking back to jazz and blues performance, improvisation represented a rich "pragmatic metaphor for creating more discourse about individual identities and freedoms for shifting the American social mainstream toward a more inclusive form of democracy."[47] According to Muyumba, the connection between jazz performance and African American pragmatic philosophy is as follows: "Jazz performance and musicians provide various models for African American intellectuals to think through the making of racialized, gendered, and American identities. Jazz helps us construct histories, create discourses, and build communities."[48] In other words, improvisation rings true in both communities—jazz music and African American intellectual practice—for in both one sees the juxtaposition of convention and innovation, constriction and volition, tradition and self-actualization, communal and self-construction. Identity is forged *and* reconstituted. Histories are constructed *and* relived, discourses created *and* retold, communities built *and* preserved. Many African Americans and even some members of the global African diaspora identify with improvisation as a descriptive term for existence.[49] For different reasons

[46]In the twentieth anniversary edition of *Prophesy Deliverance!* West discusses the centrality of improvisation as a metaphor not only for blackness, but also for his version of pragmatic philosophy/Christianity, what he refers to elsewhere as "prophetic pragmatism." West writes: "My self-styled allegiance to American pragmatism and American jazz is first and foremost a commitment to polyphonic inquiry and *improvisational* conversation." Shortly thereafter, West also discusses the connection between improvisation and democracy: "If there is a master term in my text—and work—it is democracy. I understand democracy as a mode of being, a way of life, a disposition toward the world that is flexible, protean, and *improvisational* existential practice." See Cornel West, *Prophesy Deliverance! An Afro-American Revolutionary Christianity* (Louisville: Westminster John Knox, 2002), pp. 8-9 (emphases added).

[47]Walton M. Muyumba, *The Shadow and the Act: Black Intellectual Practice, Jazz Improvisation, and Philosophical Pragmatism* (Chicago: University of Chicago Press, 2009), pp. ix-x. For another resource tracing the connection between jazz improvisation and American philosophical pragmatism, see Michael Magee, *Emancipating Pragmatism: Emerson, Jazz, and Experimental Writing* (Tuscaloosa: University of Alabama Press, 2004).

[48]Muyumba, *Shadow and the Act*, p. 18.

[49]Patricia D. Fox argues that improvisation helps us understand and construct descriptions of

and with different philosophical accents, Cornel West and Michael Eric Dyson utilize improvisation as a constitutive metaphor for race. With West, it is his depiction of blackness as protean reflexivity. With Dyson, it is his depiction of blackness as bricolage.

Cornel West: Blackness as protean reflexivity. In *Race Matters*, Cornel West argues for a vision of blackness as protean reflexivity. By protean reflexivity I mean *improvisational aptitude and action across racial and cultural difference.* The "cultural hybrid character of black life," claims West, is best described by providing an analogy with jazz music. Like jazz, blackness represents a *"mode of being* in the world, an improvisational mode of protean, fluid, and flexible dispositions."[50] West's interest in the cultural hybridity of black life and its parallels with jazz music lead him down a different path than Cone. For West, black identity is more fluid and kinetic, whereas for Cone it is monolithic and static. His vision of blackness is hybrid instead of purist.[51] In fact, West's Christian conviction leads him to resist the categorization or commodification of *any* form of essentialized blackness. For him, such a move would be idolatrous. In *Prophesy Deliverance!* West writes: "For me, prophetic Christianity is a deep suspicion of any form of idolatry—of any human effort to evade or deny the contingency and fragility of any human construct (including religious ones). Modern attempts to ossify, petrify, or freeze

---

blackness in Latin America. In describing blackness in the Latin American landscape, Fox writes: "Refashioned by improvisation (permutability and deculturation), the casual and informal patterning of Africana cultural production reflects life strategies: those 'certain specific ways' in which Blackness references a 'certain specific' worldview without, however, denigrating into an essentialist or monolithic Blackness." See Patricia D. Fox, *Being and Blackness in Latin America: Uprootedness and Improvisation* (Gainesville: University Press of Florida, 2006), p. 57.

[50]Cornel West, *Race Matters* (Boston: Beacon Press, 1993), pp. 104-5.

[51]Michael Eric Dyson calls into question the myth of "cultural purity" in the black community with the hope of dispelling the notion that there is authentic blackness out there somewhere. Dyson writes: "Prolonged concentration on a fictitious, romantic black cultural purity obscures the virtues of complex black identity. An edifying impurity infuses black experiments with self-understanding and fires the urge to embrace discarded selves shaped in the liberty of radical *improvisation.* Fiction and jazz, for instance, urge us to savor the outer limits of our imagination as the sacred space of cultural identity. When advocates of particular versions of Afrocentrism and black nationalism claim a common uniqueness for black life, they deny the repertoire of difference that characterizes African culture. Such conflicts teach us to spell black culture and language in the plural, signifying the diversity that continually expands the circumference of black identities." See Michael Eric Dyson, *Between God and Gangsta Rap: Bearing Witness to Black Culture* (New York: Oxford University Press, 1996), pp. 123-24 (emphasis added).

human creations of method, technique, rationality, sexuality, nationality, race, or empire are suspect."[52]

If anything, West's vision of protean reflexivity is a significant departure from Cone's proposal. For West, identities are not fixed; they are fluid and flexible. Instead of stasis and circumscription, one finds kinesis and transgression. An improvisational mode of being requires the dynamic interplay of unity and boundary crossing, established and imagined identity. It produces healthy, creative tension among African Americans, thus mobilizing and empowering them to resist fixed definitions of who they are. Protean reflexivity is both descriptive and prescriptive in that it describes quotidian realities for many African Americans in a racist society while also drawing out their potentially galvanizing implications.

Another way to describe West's argument in *Race Matters* and elsewhere would be to restate his assertion in a more overtly political way: for many African Americans, being black in America necessitates *protean reflexivity*. Again, what I mean by protean reflexivity here, and what I think West means is *improvisational aptitude and action across racial and cultural difference*. This reflexivity is born partly out of necessity and partly from volition. It is arises out of necessity in that many African Americans, as members of a historically oppressed people group, facing daily the realities of racism, must be improvisationally adept as a form of survival. For many, swimming against oppressive currents *requires* a commitment to proteanism. It is volitional in the sense that strategic use of improvisation is an emancipatory act, a constructive action whereby one "create[s] free spaces within the framework," but this time metaphorically.[53] Such an act extends beyond the speech event to existence itself. Although one is beholden to constraints within a framework, one also employs intuition and innovation in order to expand and even transgress these onto-relational constraints. One operates within "given constraints so that individual creativity can unfold."[54] A person chooses protean reflexivity not only as a means of survival but

---

[52]West, *Prophesy Deliverance!*, p. 8.
[53]Malgorzata Bartula, Stefan Schroer, and Roberto Ciulli, *On Improvisation: Nine Conversations with Roberto Ciulli*, trans. Geoffrey V. Davis (New York: Peter Lang, 2003), p. 38.
[54]Ibid.

also as a pathway to freedom, working within the framework to subvert and upend the framework.[55]

Protean reflexivity is also a practice that helps many African Americans advance in a racist society. Although improvisation is not always necessary or expedient for a large segment of whites, for many nonwhites it is practically an imperative for professional advancement. Living in a majority culture, many nonwhites are accustomed to improvisational negotiation and renegotiation in order to go to college, find work, and advance professionally. Intercultural competence, or knowledge acquisition, aptitude, and action across difference, what I refer to in chapter four as the 3A Framework, makes human flourishing possible among nonwhites.

Although West's language of protean reflexivity is an understandable and salient description for African Americans accustomed to navigating majority culture, and his terminology is helpful to other nonwhites for whom proteanism helps to make sense of their experiences, his proposal is not without its limitations. Is *Race Matters* a book about race, or about class, or is it a book about race and class? Perhaps social location is more complex than West seems to imply. Although race is a significant contributing factor, it is not the only contributing factor. One's social location, situatedness, and positionality are composed of a complex matrix of individual and corporate identity markers. No doubt race is significant, perhaps critical, especially in a racialized society, but class, gender, education, and access to opportunity are also significant. As was mentioned earlier in my discussion of Anderson's critique of Cone, the temptation is to slip into totalizing, essentialist, and reductive statements about what all African Americans encounter or what all African Americans face. Sometimes West does this, perhaps unconsciously. It would be more accurate for West to argue that some or many African Americans know how to wield *protean reflexivity*, especially those accustomed to navigating the majority context on a regular basis. Those whose quotidian

---

[55]Theologian Mark Lewis Taylor discusses the significance of nonwhite persons working within structures in order to upend and overturn structures, a phenomenon he refers to as "weighing-in." By weighing-in, Taylor means wielding political disruption *within* an established racist societal framework in order to "haunt, unsettle, or perhaps dissolve" systems and structures of knowledge and power. See Mark L. Taylor, *The Theological and the Political: On the Weight of the World* (Minneapolis: Fortress, 2011), p. 62.

interactions are primarily (if not exclusively?) among members of their own race, for instance, African Americans who interact almost exclusively with other African Americans on a daily basis, may not wield protean reflexivity in the same way or with the same effect as those who navigate racial and cultural difference on a regular basis.

Michael Eric Dyson: Blackness as bricolage. In his book *Open Mike: Reflections on Philosophy, Race, Sex, Culture and Religion*, Michael Eric Dyson refers to improvisation as the "great next" for African American discourse in the twenty-first century.[56] Like West, Dyson appeals to jazz music as a salient metaphor for African American cultural practice.[57] In jazz music, at least historically, one discerns a commitment to "black cosmopolitanism" that, in Dyson's view, can and should be mirrored in black intellectualism.[58] Instead of encouraging nativism and isolationism, jazz music "inspires interracial cultural exchange."[59] Just as jazz musicians can self-identify with the group while also maintaining a commitment to cosmopolitan values, likewise, according to Dyson, African American intellectuals are able to maintain what philosopher Lorenzo Simpson calls "situated cosmopolitanism," that is, cultural rootedness without forsaking one's commitment to being a citizen of the world.[60]

The main image Dyson lifts up for the "great next" of African American improvisation is *bricolage*.[61] Drawing from French anthro-

---

[56] Michael Eric Dyson, *Open Mike: Reflections on Philosophy, Race, Sex, Culture and Religion* (New York: Basic Civitas Books, 2003), p. 206.

[57] Dyson also makes connections between jazz music and hip-hop/rap music. He sees jazz music as the first iteration of black fecundity and possibility, and rap/hip-hop music as the second iteration. For more, see Dyson, *Between God and Gangsta Rap*.

[58] Commenting on the rise of jazz music in New Orleans, Dyson writes: "This explosion of African creativity constituted a veritable Negropolis, a black cosmopolitanism whose influence sprawled beyond its original indigenous borders to capture large segments of American society." See Dyson, *Open Mike*, p. 187.

[59] Ibid.

[60] Lorenzo Charles Simpson, *The Unfinished Project: Towards a Postmetaphysical Humanism* (New York: Routledge, 2001), p. 78.

[61] Princeton sociologist Robert Wuthnow also uses the image of bricolage, but for an entirely different purpose. Wuthnow suggests that being a "tinkerer" or "bricoleur" is a defining characteristic of young adults who are currently in their twenties and thirties, especially as it pertains to religion. The tinkerer sifts through ideas and practices from a variety of places and constructs a unique "bricolage" in order to engage in identity construction. See Robert Wuthnow, *After the Baby Boomers: How Twenty- and Thirty-Somethings Are Shaping the Future of American Religion* (Princeton, NJ: Princeton University Press, 2007), pp. 13-16, 134-36.

pologist Claude Lévi-Strauss, Dyson describes bricoleurs as those who "mak[e] do with what is at hand," while also creating and reinventing themselves.[62] Despite being forced throughout their history to make do with "leftovers" and "fragments" from the dominant culture, according to Dyson, African Americans creatively used what they were handed to forge new identities as a community.[63] Historically, improvisation has been the way by which many African Americans use the materials available to them to innovate within and contribute to society. Improvisation is the way they name and practice "black possibility and fecundity that spawns newer forms of cultural expression."[64] Dyson writes:

> Bricolage is about the possibilities inherent in taking the fragments, the leftovers that are both literally and symbolically at hand, and doing something imaginative and substantive with them.... Black artistic expression often involves taking the sonic fragments and cultural leftovers of dominant culture and making a black cultural product that is desirable, even irresistible, to the margins and the mainstream. The beauty of black culture is its ability to re-create and reinvent itself as the great next thing in the long evolution of creative possibilities, at precisely the moment it's being written off.[65]

Although "sonic fragments" and "cultural leftovers" may be the only materials at hand, they make up the "stuff" of artistic invention and innovation. Much like the assemblage art movement in Europe and the United States from the 1950s through the 1980s, many African Americans know how to "make do" with the leftovers (both literal and symbolic) of the dominant culture in order to create artistic expression.[66]

---

[62]Dyson, *Open Mike*, p. 206. Recall that Dyson appropriates Claude Lévi-Strauss's concept of bricolage as it is found in Lévi-Strauss, *The Savage Mind* (Chicago: University of Chicago Press, 1966), pp. 16-36. According to Lévi-Strauss, the bricoleur is adept at addressing himself or herself to "a collection of oddments left over from human endeavors" (ibid., p. 19). Dyson resonates with Lévi-Strauss's metaphor because, historically speaking, African Americans have had to operate with fragments, oddments, and leftovers from the majority society.

[63]Dyson, *Open Mike*, p. 206.

[64]Ibid.

[65]Ibid.

[66]The term *assemblage art* was first used by the artist Jean Dubuffet in 1953 as a way of describing his own work. British art critic and historian John A. Walker defines assemblage art as "a technique or method similar to montage-constructing a work from various bits and pieces—while Assem-

For many African Americans, being black means being an assemblage artist—a bricoleur.

Unlike Cone's conception of blackness as ontological reality, Dyson conceives of blackness as political-artistic action. Improvisational bricolage is a skill cultivated through practice. Instead of lifting up a "blackness that whiteness created" à la Anderson's critique of Cone, he lifts up a vision of blackness that creates and recreates itself.[67] It does not require a binary for its existence. Bricoleurs do not define themselves vis à vis whiteness; they circumnavigate whiteness through invention and innovation as a form of political subversion. Sometimes the motivation for this is personal human flourishing. Other times it is community advancement. Still other times the aim is to confront racism.[68] Regardless of the motivation, Dyson suggests that being a bricoleur is a skill born out of necessity and cultivated through a commitment to action. Bricolage requires intercultural negotiation. It is action based.

Negotiating race and ethnicity as a minority in the United States involves learning how to be an improvisational bricoleur. This can look a lot of different ways. For African Americans, it might look like Sam Cooke growing up in inner-city Los Angeles, but finding a way to bring black gospel music to mainstream society.[69] Perhaps it is Senator Carol Mosley-Braun outmaneuvering the Chicago political machine to win a Senate seat in Illinois.[70] As we will see later, it is Gardner C. Taylor growing up during Jim Crow–era segregation in Louisiana, but flour-

---

blage Art describes the end results of that process. This form of art marked a departure from traditional art forms. Objects were made from various materials and items of junk; they were mixed-media works or composites and thus they transgressed the purity of medium aesthetic and blurred the difference between painting and sculpture." Put simply, assemblage artists are bricoleurs. They take discarded waste and leftovers and use this refuse to construct meaningful and inspiring art. See John A. Walker, *Glossary of Art, Architecture, and Design Since 1945* (Boston: G. K. Hall, 1992), p. 88.

[67]Anderson, *Beyond Ontological Blackness*, p. 13.

[68]Mark Lewis Taylor refers to this last motivation as a "counterpractice." Taylor writes: "The world is heavy, then, with social practices that generate death and dying. Though this necropolitics consigns more and more people to 'zones of abandonment'... those subordinated to the necropolitics nevertheless rework the agonism, insist on being human, 'weigh-in' with *counterpractices* that are not only agonistic in their own right but also are often motivated by nonagonistic visions and practices." See Mark Lewis Taylor, *The Theological and the Political*, p. 7 (emphasis added).

[69]Dyson discusses Sam Cooke's improvisational abilities in Dyson, *Between God and Gangsta Rap*, p. 61.

[70]Dyson discusses Carol Mosley-Braun's improvisational abilities in ibid., p. 93.

ishing at Oberlin College despite being one of the few African Americans enrolled, or befriending white mainline preachers in Manhattan (e.g., Paul Scherer) during his ministry in Brooklyn. In a sense, Taylor took "leftovers" from the dominant culture and used them to recreate himself. More than most, Taylor knew how to be a "black bricoleur." Before turning to Taylor's negotiation of blackness as a transgression of narrow categorization, however, we turn from systematic theology to homiletics, and to a person whose theology shares significant resemblances with James H. Cone's theology—Henry H. Mitchell.

HENRY H. MITCHELL AND THE PROBLEM WITH
UNIVOCAL AFRICAN AMERICAN PREACHING

Following Cone's lead in systematic theology, Henry H. Mitchell made essentialist claims about African American preaching that circumscribed it within a narrow field and parochialized it as a tradition. Mitchell's project is understandable given that he, like Cone, had to battle against institutionalized racism. But, also like Cone, Mitchell's claims also tend to flatten out complexity by privileging uniformity *across* the tradition over diversity *within* the tradition. Mitchell's vision of black preaching is univocal (one voice) instead of plurivocal (many voices). Not only is the black preaching tradition more plurivocal than Mitchell's account permits; we will see later that Gardner Taylor's improvisational approach defies the circumscription Mitchell's approach propagates.

In fairness, Mitchell's attempt in the 1970s to define and describe black preaching arose partly out of personal frustration and partly out of an accurate assessment that African American students were not receiving adequate resources from white theological seminaries. Much of his frustration came from years of trying to be a bridge person between white and black Christians in the church and leaving those experiences disappointed and disillusioned. In *Black Preaching*, he describes his challenging journey:

> Years of frustration have crushed the hopeful idea that the proof of unity of all varieties of American Christianity is possible in our time. The slings and arrows of outrageous half-integration, experienced at the most promising integrationist vantage points, drove me to the solace and support of

my own Black identity and of my likewise un-integrated Black Brethren. ...Blacks must celebrate the Black contribution as it is before they subject it to the inevitable and subtle twists of translation to another culture.[71]

Mitchell's frustration should not be interpreted as hopelessness. He does believe the dream of a "raceless church" will one day be realized, even if this category is somewhat problematic.[72] In the meantime, he claims, the onus is on the black community to name its tradition on its own terms and to celebrate its contribution without apology.

The other reason Mitchell wrote *Black Preaching* was to provide African American theological students with an aid for preaching in black churches. For decades, seminary students from black churches participated in preaching courses taught by white instructors that were not only peripheral to their experience, but also unhelpful to their training. Mitchell's work aimed to "reduce the Black dependence on the white concept of what preaching is all about or *should* be all about."[73] For those who thought he was swinging the pendulum too far in the other direction, Mitchell begged to differ. Theological education, he argued, was "one-sided for most of its existence."[74] Not only could a resource on black preaching assist students preparing for ministry in the black church; it could also make theological education more balanced, nuanced, and inclusive of all communities.

For the most part, Mitchell fulfills his goals. His book *is* a celebration of black preaching, and it provides a suitable alternative for African American students enrolled at white seminaries. It exposes blind spots in white homiletics by stating that black preaching is a rich and historic tradition, one that can no longer be ignored or cast aside as unworthy of homiletical-theological reflection. Like Cone in systematic theology, Mitchell brought to consciousness white homileticians' veiled assumptions about preaching by shaking loose the discourse from the grip of white hegemony. He did not want to add to the existing discourse; he wanted to change the discourse. *Black Preaching* functions as both a light

---

[71]Henry H. Mitchell, *Black Preaching* (New York: Harper & Row, 1979), p. 12.
[72]Ibid.
[73]Ibid., p. 14.
[74]Ibid., p. 20.

and a mirror: it shines a light on black preaching by celebrating its distinct contribution, and it holds up a mirror to racism in white homiletics by critiquing it for its obliviousness to other traditions.

Few if any would question whether Mitchell's book succeeds at celebrating black preaching or forcing white homiletics to attend to its various blind spots. What has been questioned in recent years is the assumptions Mitchell makes about what makes black preaching distinctive, what it is and isn't, its parameters. For example, Olin Moyd and Cleophus J. LaRue challenge Mitchell's contention that celebration is the most distinctive feature of black preaching. They deny that a celebrative climax must always mark the sermon's conclusion. Mitchell does not see much room for diversity of opinion or disagreement here when he writes: "We in the African American tradition have cultural roots that demand that a sermon end in celebration."[75] By contrast, Moyd argues that if celebration means "ecstatic talking and hearing and involvement in the story, then . . . celebration is interspersed throughout [the sermon], with greater intensity toward the end."[76] Although the climax may be the sermon's highest point of intensity, Moyd argues, it may or may not be its highest point of celebration. In *Power in the Pulpit*, Cleophus J. LaRue adds his voice to the celebration debate. He writes:

> For some the sermon should always end in a joyous celebration, while for others the most important thing is that the sermon end in a manner that is logically consistent with the controlling thought. . . . The closing of the sermon should not be a disjointed distraction or some kind of tacked-on rhetorical flourish . . . rather it should send the listeners away with a clear sense of what the preacher was intending to convey throughout the entire message.[77]

Both LaRue and Moyd agree that celebration does not have to be coterminous with the conclusion. They advocate for more diversity in the tone, emotion, and resolution of the sermon's conclusion.

---

[75]Henry H. Mitchell, *Celebration and Experience in Preaching* (Nashville: Abingdon, 1990), p. 12.

[76]See Olin P. Moyd, *The Sacred Art: Preaching & Theology in the African American Tradition* (Valley Forge, PA: Judson Press, 1995), p. 109, as cited in Richard L. Eslinger, *A New Hearing: Living Options in Homiletic Method* (Nashville: Abingdon, 1987), p. 139.

[77]The preachers interviewed by LaRue suggested that other intended effects beside celebration could include reflection, repentance, action, etc. See Cleophus J. LaRue, *Power in the Pulpit: How America's Most Effective Black Preachers Prepare Their Sermons* (Louisville: Westminster John Knox, 2002), p. 8.

Luke Powery critiques a different essentialist claim of Mitchell's: that the African American community has access to the Holy Spirit in a way other communities do not. According to Mitchell, when one compares and contrasts all the cultures in the United States, African Americans are the "most responsive culture to the movement of the Holy Spirit."[78] Powery takes exception to Mitchell's not so subtle way of overspiritualizing black culture. Powery writes:

> [Mitchell's] stance breathes of cultural arrogance because he seems to suggest that other cultures are not as responsive to the Spirit as African Americans when in fact it may be that other cultures just respond differently to the Spirit. Even within a particular cultural milieu (for example, African American), response to the Spirit is not monolithic.[79]

For obvious reasons, no culture has a monopoly on the Holy Spirit. No culture has privileged access to the Spirit of God as if there were a first-tier cultural spirituality versus a second-tier cultural spirituality. Moreover, diversity exists *within* African American spirituality and not just outside of it. The issue is not whether one culture responds to the Spirit more than another culture responds, as if such metrics were measurable. The issue is how to interpret the different ways that different cultures respond to the Spirit. It borders on pretension to claim that one culture in particular has privileged possession of or access to the Spirit of God. The Spirit will not be circumscribed either.

Kenyatta Gilbert challenges Mitchell's argument from two sides: language and culture. One of the essentialisms he confronts is Mitchell's claim that black preaching requires "Blackese," defined as the "rich rendition of English spoken in the Black ghetto."[80] Mitchell writes: "Neither faith nor culture will be communicated by a preacher whose language sounds to the ghetto resident as if he is putting on airs, for implicit in his posturing is a deprecation for the people he wants to serve. . . . His language must be Black enough to generate confidence in an

---

[78]Henry H. Mitchell, "The Holy Spirit: A Folk Perspective," *The Living Pulpit* 5, no. 1 (March 1996): 40-41, as cited in Luke A. Powery, *Spirit Speech: Celebration and Lament in Preaching* (Nashville: Abingdon, 2009), p. 1.

[79]Powery, *Spirit Speech*, p. 1.

[80]Mitchell, *Black Preaching*, pp. 148, 158.

identity which is clearly Black."[81] Mitchell's claim here is that the intentional mixing of sentence structure, grammar, and syntax are essential to effective ministry by any pastor in the black church. It is through black language identification rather than white language erudition that connection takes place. One of the problems with Mitchell's assertion is that there is a lack of agreement on "Black language"—how to define, describe, or use it. Commenting on the role of urban ghetto language in black preaching, Gilbert writes: "Few would consider [black language] a hallmark since there is no consensus about what constitutes 'Black language.' It is more accurate to say that Black preaching is always responsive to and mindful of the vernacular of the people."[82]

Also, when Mitchell's argument for "Blackese" is placed alongside Gardner C. Taylor's insistence that black preachers should *not* mispronounce words or use incorrect grammar and syntax, a greater weight is added to Gilbert's critique. Although Taylor's church was located in Brooklyn, he refused to use the language of the urban ghetto. Members of the Concord congregation seemed to appreciate Taylor's concern for precise, poetic language. They did not think that correct grammar and syntax meant a "deprecation for the people he want[ed] to serve." Recall from chapter one what one of his church members, Anna Belle, stated after hearing Taylor's first sermon at Concord: "When he came that first Sunday morning, he electrified the congregation with his mastery of the English language. . . . He had us on our feet."[83] It becomes more difficult (rather than less) to defend Mitchell's insistence on preaching "Blackese" in *all* black congregations when Taylor, the "Dean of the nation's black preachers," emphasized correct grammar and syntax over the language of the urban ghetto. Add to this the fact that members of the Concord

---

[81]Ibid., p. 152. In a different book, *Black Belief,* Mitchell makes the following claim about black preachers: "The professionally educated Black preacher who is really effective among the Black majority will translate his most sophisticated insights into the folk idiom and imagery of their culture, not vice versa. Wherever the Black masses have a choice, they choose their own culture, maintaining their own continuous style in everything from food to faith." See Henry H. Mitchell, *Black Belief: Folk Beliefs of Blacks in America and West Africa* (New York: Harper & Row, 1975), p. 13.

[82]Kenyatta R. Gilbert, *The Journey and Promise of African American Preaching* (Minneapolis: Fortress, 2011), p. 25.

[83]"Interview with Anna Belle," in Gerald Lamont Thomas, *African American Preaching: The Contribution of Dr. Gardner C. Taylor* (New York: Peter Lang, 2004), p. 98.

congregation, people like Anna Belle, felt like Taylor's concern for precision and correctness was honoring rather than condescending, and the argument becomes more difficult to maintain.

The other criticism Gilbert lodges against Mitchell is his essentialization of black culture. In fact, he confronts Mitchell's reification of blackness more directly than Moyd, LaRue, or Powery. Gilbert sees Mitchell's work as another example of scholarship that centers itself on critiquing "some normative male-Eurocentric theological view."[84] While no doubt questioning and challenging white normativity has merit, Gilbert points to a lacuna in Mitchell's work: *black normativity is never called into question or challenged in a meaningful way*. Also, because Mitchell focuses too much attention on critique and not enough on construction, Gilbert adds, "what is [mis]communicated is that the genius of Black scholarship and focus on historically marginalized communities is found in criticism."[85] The problem with scholarship from this vantage point is that, whenever theological construction is replaced with theological critique, the community's capacity to be generative rather than reactionary is undermined. As African American theologian Stephen Ray puts it, the message conveyed is an "agnosticism about the capacity of these originating communities to produce works that are generally constructive to the Christian tradition."[86] The message the community sends to other communities—white and nonwhite—is that its voice deserves a hearing only insofar as it reacts to and critiques the false illusion of white normativity. Thus the same problematic identified by Anderson, Bantum, and Carter returns to the fore. Instead of blackness for its own sake as a site of construction, it becomes a "blackness that whiteness created."[87] Instead of a black message on its own terms, it becomes a "black message sealed within a white envelope."[88]

Mitchell's aim is to make a significant departure from his white counterparts in homiletics. Yet is it possible that, like Cone, his tendency

---

[84]Gilbert, *Journey and Promise*, p. 27.

[85]Ibid.

[86]Stephen Ray, "E-Racing While Black," in *Being Black, Teaching Black*, ed. Nancy Lynn Westfield (Nashville: Abingdon, 2008), p. 52, as cited in Gilbert, *Journey and Promise*, p. 28.

[87]Anderson, *Beyond Ontological Blackness*, p. 13.

[88]Carter, *Race*, p. 279.

toward racial reification does more harm than good? How helpful is it over the long haul to challenge unnuanced white normativity with unnuanced black normativity? Does lifting up a univocal black preaching tradition make sense if the tradition is plurivocal?

In my judgment, Mitchell holds too closely to "relatively fixed interpretations of 'blackness' and what constitutes a 'black sermon.'"[89] On account of this, too many questions remain unanswered. For instance, does a sermon count as "black" if James Forbes preaches it at the Riverside Church in Manhattan? When Ella Mitchell (Henry Mitchell's wife) preached a sermon at Amherst College in western Massachusetts, was it still a "black sermon" even if it was delivered outside the black church to a predominantly white audience? When Gardner C. Taylor delivered a sermon at Louisiana Baptist Seminary in New Orleans, a predominantly white, Southern Baptist school, did it still count as black? What about when he preached for NBC's *National Radio Pulpit*? Also, what about contemporary African American preachers who preach in multiethnic church settings, such as Bryan Loritts in New York or Ralph Douglas West in Houston? As Gilbert points out, "Without much effort African American preachers tend to be carriers of culture wherever they preach."[90] If this is true, does it not become more rather than less difficult to ascribe to fixed assessments of what counts and doesn't count as an authentically black sermon?

PLURIVOCITY: THE FOUR-PART CHORUS OF AFRICAN AMERICAN HOMILETICAL THEORY

Let me complicate the category by suggesting that we imagine African American preaching as a four-part chorus. In a requiem or oratorio, sopranos, altos, tenors, and basses participate in a larger musical performance; they are part of a unified chorus despite singing different parts. That being stated, unity should not be confused with uniformity. The chorus does not sing in unison; it sings in harmony. It is not univocal; it is plurivocal. Each member of the choir sings one of (usually) four or more distinctive parts. Even though each part contributes to the melody,

---

[89]Gilbert, *Journey and Promise*, p. 27.
[90]Ibid., p. 28.

it does not constitute the oratorio in and of itself. One way to describe and survey African American preaching and homiletical theory is through the image of a four-part chorus that consists of structural, experiential, hermeneutical, and improvisational approaches. My use of four-part chorus imagery is not an attempt to give an irenic or reductive account of differences and divergences in African American preaching and homiletical theory, but to organize the various strands of thought in juxtaposition with Taylor's homiletical approach.

The first members of the four-part chorus are *structuralists*. The homileticians who represent this approach—James Henry Harris, James Earl Massey, and Olin P. Moyd—contend that there are distinctive structural traits that define a "black sermon." The content and its trajectory within the sermon are central. In *Preaching Liberation*, Harris argues that for a sermon to be recognizably black it must be christocentric, Afrocentric, and liberationist.[91] The sermon is deemed successful if it: proclaims Jesus as liberator (christocentric); encourages the congregation to be socially critical, free from bondage, and celebrative (liberationist); and encourages listeners to be proud of their African heritage (Afrocentric). Harris's work is highly influenced by that of James H. Cone and Gayraud Wilmore.

James Earl Massey's *The Responsible Pulpit* is another example of a structuralist approach.[92] According to Massey, the sermon needs five basic elements: it must be functional, festive, communal, radical, and climactic.[93] By *functional* Massey means a persuasive purpose behind the sermon; by *festive* he means celebrative; by *communal* he means congregationally focused; by *radical* he means prophetic; and by *climactic* he means inspirational, moving conclusions.[94] Massey's later publication

---

[91]Harris touches on each of these three components in different places in this book. For his treatment of the need to be christocentric in preaching, see James Henry Harris, *Preaching Liberation* (Minneapolis: Fortress, 1995), pp. 31-43. For his treatment of the need to be liberationist in preaching, see ibid., pp. ix, 9, 15-16. For his treatment of the need to be Afrocentric, see ibid., pp. 38, 81, 113. L. Susan Bond provides a summary of Harris's threefold description of preaching in Bond, *Contemporary African American Preaching: Diversity in Theory and Style* (St. Louis: Chalice, 2003), p. 2.

[92]James Earl Massey, *The Responsible Pulpit* (Anderson, IN: Warner Press, 1974).

[93]Ibid., p. 101-10.

[94]One of the gaps in the literature is attention to the prophetic elements of black preaching. One finds more attention to the prophetic by studying black liberation theologians like James H. Cone,

Stewards of the Story seems to supplement his earlier work by placing a greater emphasis on narrative and rhetoric.[95] Unlike Harris, who is more sympathetic to liberation theology, Massey is more of a traditionalist.

The final example of the structuralist approach is found in Olin P. Moyd's *The Sacred Art: Preaching and Theology in the African American Tradition.* Moyd's criteria for the sermon are as follows: the sermon must contain rhetoric, repetition, rhythm, rest, spontaneity, tone, chant, cadence, melody, drama, and epic. Although Moyd is aware that these are not used in every sermon, nevertheless, he suggests that these criteria are

---

or Gayraud Wilmore, but it can also be found in the work of pragmatic philosopher Cornel West. Among homileticians, Charles L. Campbell discusses the significance of prophetic preaching. For instance, in *The Word Before the Powers,* Campbell argues that the preacher's responsibility is, first, *to expose* powers and principalities that promote evil and, second, *to envision* their demise through apocalyptic imagery and prophetic statements. Charles L. Campbell, *The Word Before the Powers: An Ethic of Preaching* (Louisville: Westminster John Knox, 2002), pp. 96, 130, 146. Kenyatta R. Gilbert also discusses the importance of the "prophetic voice." In *The Journey and Promise of African American Preaching,* Gilbert frames the prophetic voice as one voice among three that the black preacher invokes in preaching. For Gilbert, "tri-vocal preaching" consists partially of the prophetic voice, but it also includes the priestly and sagely voices, respectively. See Gilbert, *Journey and Promise*, p. 12.

[95] See James Earl Massey, *Stewards of the Story: The Task of Preaching* (Louisville: Westminster John Knox, 2006). Massey emphasizes a structural approach in this book as well. He argues that Christian sermons are influenced by four structural demands or factors: "the recital cast of biblical narratives," "the rhetorical demand" of recasting the biblical message in the modern time, the "ritual setting" of the sermon event, and the daily "realities that inform us for preaching." See ibid., p. xv.

Rhetoric and narrative are discussed not only in Massey's later work, but elsewhere in African American homiletics. LaRue argues that rhetoric is not only important, but has a *sacred* quality. Well-crafted rhetoric, claims LaRue, awakens in black parishioners a "sense of the holy" in much the same way that architecture and classical music do in many Euro-American churches. The "judicious use of rhetorical devices" can facilitate in the community an encounter with God. See Cleophus J. LaRue, *The Heart of Black Preaching* (Louisville: Westminster John Knox, 2000), p. 10. Some of the rhetorical devices that one may find in the sermon are alliteration, anaphora, immediacy, apostrophe, panoramic survey, narrative, repetition, vivid imagery, and metaphor. William L. Hogan lists these devices in the same order in William L. Hogan, "White Guys Can't Preach: What I Have Learned from African American Preachers" (paper presented at the Evangelical Homiletics Society, South Hamilton, Massachusetts, 1996). Since black preaching is primarily an oral tradition and has its historical roots in orality, narrative and story have been given more focus and interest in homiletical literature over the last few decades. Because oral traditions pass on their memories and values primarily through stories, homileticians have shown renewed interest in where these resonances are discernible in black preaching. To learn more about narrative and its import for African American preaching, see Henry H. Mitchell's chapter in Eslinger, *A New Hearing.* Cf. also William B. McClain, "African American Contexts of Narrative Preaching," in *What's the Shape of Narrative Preaching? Essays in Honor of Eugene L. Lowry,* ed. Mike Graves and David J. Schlafer (St. Louis: Chalice, 2008), pp. 55-67. See also Harris's chapter "The Sermon as Story," in James Henry Harris, *The Word Made Plain: The Power and Promise of Preaching* (Minneapolis: Fortress, 2004), pp. 100-126.

"distinguishing elements in the African American preaching style."[96] They function like threads that weave together the content and structure of the sermon.

The next members of the four-part choir of African American preaching are *the experientialists*. For the sake of clarity, we will divide this section into two smaller parts, into first and second altos, if you will. Within the larger category of experientialists, one part focuses on the *dialogical* aspects of black preaching and the other on *celebratory* aspects. One way to think about the dialogical aspects would be to think of the word *duet*. If one person sits down at the piano and is ready to perform a duet, she cannot perform the duet by playing the bass line only. She needs a second person to sit down next to her to play the treble line. Just as there is a necessary interdependence between performers in a duet, so also there is a necessary interdependence between preacher and congregation in the case of a dialogical sermon.

Evans Crawford's *The Hum: Call and Response in African American Preaching* is the clearest example of the dialogical approach.[97] Crawford is a folk-preaching theorist who sees black preaching as a folk tradition rooted in the oral and aural aspects of sermonic discourse. Thus he is less interested in *what* words are said than he is in *how* words are said. He concerns himself with audience cues, oral formulas, performance, musicality, and most importantly, call and response. "Homiletical musicality" is a term Crawford uses to define "the way in which the preacher uses timing, pauses, inflection, pace, and other musical

---

[96]Moyd, *Sacred Art*, p. 89.

[97]Evans Crawford is a good choice as representative of the dialogical approach, but many others have written on this subject as well. Although Troeger cowrote the book with Crawford, the dialogical approach reflects Crawford's concern for the folk aspects to call and response rather than Troeger's concerns. In other words, it would be accurate to refer to Crawford as a folk-preaching theorist, but it would not be accurate to refer to Troeger as a folk-preaching theorist. See Evans E. Crawford with Thomas H. Troeger, *The Hum: Call and Response in African American Preaching* (Nashville: Abingdon, 1995). Cf. also William C. Turner, "The Musicality of Black Preaching," *Journal of Black Sacred Music* 2, no. 1 (Spring 1988): 21-27; Gerald L. Davis, *I Got the Word in Me and I Can Sing It, You Know: A Study of the Performed African American Sermon* (Philadelphia: University of Pennsylvania Press, 1985); Albert J. Raboteau, *A Fire in the Bones: Reflections on African-American Religious History* (Boston: Beacon, 1995), especially the chapter titled "The Chanted Sermon"; Jon Michael Spencer, *Sacred Symphony: The Chanted Sermon of the Black Preacher* (New York: Greenwood, 1987). There are many advocates of this approach, but for the sake of brevity, I only discuss Crawford's book.

qualities of speech to engage all that the listener is in the act of proclamation."[98] He also focuses on the ritualistic behavior between preacher and congregation during the preaching moment. Again, think of the image of the duet, a word Crawford actually uses to describe his approach. One person can only perform properly when the other person is performing too. The preacher and congregation engage in a "duet" of common rituals in which both speak, shout, or sing key phrases and give specific cues.[99] They are necessarily interdependent. The ritual of call and response creates a common bond and intimate connection between them and, if done well, can awaken love, thanksgiving, and praise to God.

In dialogical sermons, the context of the black church is important. Crawford seems to suggest that African American listeners *expect* to hear a word from the Lord during the sermon. Instead of a hermeneutic of suspicion toward the preacher, one often finds support, attention, appreciation, and expectation. The call and response, back-and-forth "duet" between preacher and congregation is mutually encouraging when both parties perform the ritual. If the preacher is doing well, the congregation will support him or her with phrases like, "Thank you, Jesus," "Yes, Lord," "Come on!" and "Preach!" If the preacher gets on the wrong track, the congregation will help him or her get back on the right track with phrases like, "Help him, Jesus!" or "Help her, Holy Ghost!"[100] The preacher does not have to wait until after the sermon for feedback. It comes *during* the sermon.

If dialogue is the key for Crawford, then the key to understanding African American preaching for Henry H. Mitchell is *celebration*, the second subcategory of the experiential approach.[101] As was previously mentioned, Mitchell claims that celebration is not *one* distinctive of the tradition, but *the* distinctive mark of black preaching. The sermon's

---

[98]Crawford and Troeger, *Hum*, p. 16.

[99]The terminology of *duet* is also used by Richard L. Eslinger, *The Web of Preaching: New Options in Homiletic Method* (Nashville: Abingdon, 2002), p. 107.

[100]For more on the phrases used during call and response, see Crawford and Troeger, *Hum*, p. 86.

[101]On a parenthetical note, another person who makes celebration central is Frank A. Thomas, Mitchell's protégé. Furthermore, recall that for Massey, Moyd, and Harris, celebration is one of the distinctive qualities of black preaching. See Frank A. Thomas, *They Like to Never Quit Praisin' God: The Role of Celebration in Preaching* (Cleveland: United Church Press, 1997).

function is that of an emotive/celebrative encounter that leads to and climaxes in celebration.

The benefits of emphasizing celebration are threefold. The first benefit is that celebration provides ecstatic reinforcement that leads to increased retention of the sermon. The second benefit is that celebration leads to changed behavior. Mitchell points out that people are more likely to *do* what they celebrate.[102] The third benefit is that celebration promotes holistic experience in worship. It appeals to the emotive in addition to the cognitive, to *pathos* as well as *logos* and *ethos*. However, Mitchell realizes that celebration also carries with it at least one risk. Sometimes celebrative climaxes are not only disjointed from the biblical text, but they have nothing to do with the biblical text. These are celebrative conclusions with no answer to the question, "What is the scriptural text saying and doing?" Without connection to the Scriptures in some way, he argues, these conclusions risk being manipulative. To use Mitchell's phrase, many preachers fall into the trap of "serving a beef dinner and then drowning the beef in chicken gravy."[103] Failing to stay tethered to the text ruins the "flavor" of the sermon.

As was noted, some homileticians disagree with Mitchell's assertion that celebration is endemic to the sermon itself or coterminous with the sermon's conclusion. Scholars such as Olin P. Moyd and Cleophus J. LaRue contend that celebration can be interspersed throughout a sermon. For many black preachers, the conclusion of a sermon depends entirely on the controlling thought.[104] Some sermons end in celebration, and maybe even the majority, but this does not mean celebration is required or should be a prerequisite to success. It is an important component of African American preaching, but not in the way that Mitchell

---

[102]Mitchell argues that celebration inevitably leads to changed behavior, that people will *do* what they celebrate. The joy they experience not only helps them better recall the content of a sermon, but it also has the power to change their behavior. As evidence, he cites at least one study that demonstrates the increased ability in school children to remember things that they celebrate. When the children would have parties and celebrations, and experience joy over the subject matter, they would be more likely to retain it. Whether it is children at school or Christians in worship, Mitchell argues that "ecstatic reinforcement" leads to increased retention and changed behavior. See Mitchell, *Celebration and Experience in Preaching*, p. 30.

[103]Mitchell, *Black Preaching*, p. 189.

[104]Moyd, *Sacred Art*, p. 109. See also *Power in the Pulpit*, p. 8.

privileges it. Moreover, celebration is often spontaneous rather than formulaic, Holy Spirit–led and not predetermined by the preacher.

The third section of the chorus is the *hermeneutical approach*. Cleophus J. LaRue's *The Heart of Black Preaching* represents a significant departure from Mitchell and Crawford, and from the structuralists as well. LaRue's emphases are on theology, the interpretive process, shared history/setting, and communal interpretation. He locates the raison d'être of African American preaching in a "distinctive, biblical hermeneutic."[105] LaRue adapts the work of David Kelsey, who claims that individual theologians have particular methods or interpretive templates for understanding biblical texts based on what they perceive to be the essence of Christianity, what he refers to as *discrimen*.[106] LaRue takes Kelsey's argument and appropriates it for what he believes is a communal *discrimen* operative in the black church. The historical and social situation of the majority of African Americans, he argues, necessarily shapes their beliefs about God, the Bible, faith, and preaching. Shared history and social standing shape the community's interpretive *discrimen*. Historically, many black preachers have believed in "a sovereign God who acts in concrete and practical ways on behalf of the marginalized and powerless," which LaRue claims is the operative *discrimen* of the black church.[107] Congregations have maintained belief in a God who is unquestionably on their side. The experienced preacher in this tradition knows this intuitively and perhaps subconsciously—sermons are most effective when they point to a God who is *for* God's people. Thus black preaching is distinguished by a prevailing communal hermeneutic through space and time.

In *Yet with a Steady Beat: Afrocentric Biblical Interpretation*, Carolyn M. Jones's chapter, "The Task of African American Biblical Hermeneutics," adds further support to LaRue's emphasis on the hermeneutical concerns of the interpretive community.[108] Jones argues that "traditional

---

[105]LaRue, *Heart of Black Preaching*, p. 9.

[106]LaRue claims that David H. Kelsey's argument in *The Uses of Scripture in Recent Theology* (Philadelphia: Fortress, 1975) can also be transposed and extended to the African American church as a whole, historically and in the present day, in LaRue, *Heart of Black Preaching*, pp. 3-4.

[107]LaRue, *Heart of Black Preaching*, pp. 18-19.

[108]Carolyn M. Jones, "The Task of African American Biblical Hermeneutics," in *Yet with a Steady Beat: Contemporary U.S. Afrocentric Biblical Interpretation*, ed. Randall C. Bailey (Atlanta: Society of Biblical Literature, 2003), pp. 161-62.

hermeneutics" concerns itself primarily with one's individual interpretation, the self apart from others. Since African Americans were not granted "full selfhood" until the late twentieth century, they have interpreted texts socially and in the wider context of community out of necessity rather than luxury.[109] Consequently, the preacher's primary question has *not* been "What does the text say to me?" but "What does the text say to my community?" The point here is *not* that the preacher fails to ask the question "What is the text saying and doing?" The point is that the preacher deploys an interpretive *discrimen* that is more communal rather than individualistic when moving from text to sermon.

The key words to remember for LaRue's work are *theology*, *content*, *interpretive process*, and *community*. For LaRue, these are the true heart of black preaching. Narrative, rhetoric, celebration, and dialogue have a place at the table but are not the legs that hold the table up. These are not the dimensions that make black preaching distinctive. LaRue does not devalue or ignore the importance of form and style; rather, he probes more deeply into the theological interpretive strategies that support them.

Another scholar whose work can be classified as "hermeneutical" is Kenyatta Gilbert. In *The Journey and Promise of African American Preaching*, Gilbert calls on African American preachers to adopt an interpretive strategy and preaching practice that employs three distinct orientations, what he calls "voices." The three voices Gilbert recommends in interpretive and preaching practice are the prophetic voice, the priestly voice, and the sagely voice. Whenever preachers exegete texts, reflect on the practices of the church, or comment on public life, they must do so by invoking all three voices. Gilbert calls on preachers to speak "trivocally" rather than "univocally." The term he uses is *trivocal preaching*.[110] When preachers speak with the prophetic voice, they expose injustice to the light of God's "divine intentionality—what God demands and ex-

---

[109]Ibid., p. 162.

[110]Gilbert, *Journey and Promise*, p. 11. In emphasizing the significance of three-dimensional versus one-dimensional preaching, Gilbert writes: "The need for African American preachers to reconceive vigorously the prophetic, priestly, and sagely voices of the preaching ministry is vitally important, because these voices, in religious practice, have become indiscernible or isolated from one another" (ibid., p. 15).

pects of God's own human creation."[111] Gilbert also describes the prophetic voice as "a mediating voice of God's activity to transform church and society in a present-future sense based on the principle of justice."[112] In other words, those who preach with this voice are also called to direct their listeners' attention and affections to a God of hope and justice, to help their congregants see and comprehend the reign of God. The task is twofold: to preach a word that exposes injustice in all its ugliness and sinfulness while also emphasizing God's power to transform the church and the world. To use Charles L. Campbell's terminology, the prophetic preacher's task requires a commitment to both "exposing" and "envisioning": exposing the powers and principalities and envisioning their demise.[113] However, preaching that only aims at exposing injustice and idolatry is shortsighted.[114]

When preachers speak with the priestly voice, they actualize their commitment to intercession, and they emphasize God's will for individual sanctification and communal solidarity. As functional priests, they bring the people before God and bring God before the people, committing to the work of "intercessory prayer within and for the community at large."[115] In emphasizing individual sanctification, preachers mediate the presence of God for the sake of divine-human encounter, especially in worship. Gilbert writes: "Often through priestly Black preaching the preacher guides individuals into a religious encounter or experience with God."[116]

When preachers speak with the sagely voice, they juxtapose biblical wisdom with the phronetic, embodied wisdom of the local congregation—its history, culture, and dialect. Sagely preachers interpret "the common life of a particular community of worshippers" as a way of

---

[111]Gilbert, *Journey and Promise*, pp. 12, 81.

[112]Ibid.

[113]Campbell, *Word Before the Powers*, pp. 96, 130, 146.

[114]Gilbert writes: "Some preachers are sufficiently radical but insufficiently self-critical. Under the guise of being prophetic, preachers who take delight in detailing the mortal and venial sins of their listeners or, for that matter, bring criticisms to oppressive world systems 'without tears in their own eyes' are preachers who have lost sight of the grace of God in their own life" (*Journey and Promise*, p. 15).

[115]Gilbert, *Journey and Promise*, p. 13.

[116]Ibid.

naming the presence and action of God in *this* congregation in *this* particular time and place.[117] Gilbert compares the use of the sagely voice to the West African *jaili* tradition. The *jaili* was a poet, singer, and storyteller who preserved the community's history through oral tradition by performing its history and culture before the community itself. The poet remembered and recited the community's story not only as a way to preserve corporate identity, but also to energize the community in its vision and mission. Preservation and mobilization went hand in hand. Similarly, preachers who use the sagely preaching voice simultaneously access and preserve the community's residual history while also "keeping vital the congregation's vision and mission."[118] Of the three voices the preacher accesses and uses in the pulpit—prophetic, priestly, and sagely—the sagely voice is most attentive to the particular aspects of community life and the sources of wisdom within the localized community.

The fourth section of the chorus is the *improvisational approach*. Cleophus J. LaRue uses the term "crossover preacher" to describe those who are able to have "broad appeal to as wide and diverse an audience as possible."[119] In white-majority church or seminary contexts, these are preachers who know how to improvise black preaching in nonblack settings. In multicultural evangelical church settings, these are African American preachers like Tony Evans or Bryan Loritts who are able to negotiate racial and cultural difference depending on the setting, occasion, and audience. In black church settings where opportunities exist to cross boundaries into either white church settings or the public square, these are preachers like Gardner C. Taylor, Jim Forbes, and Martin Luther King Jr. Much like the apostle Paul, who changed "for the sake of the gospel" depending on the company he kept—a Jew to the Jew and a Gentile to the Gentile—these preachers adapt their preaching style to the occasion and audience (1 Cor 9:23). If protean reflexivity is defined

---

[117]Ibid., p. 14.

[118]Ibid.

[119]LaRue was referring to James Forbes specifically when he used this designation. See Cleophus J. LaRue, *I Believe I'll Testify: The Art of African American Preaching* (Louisville: Westminster John Knox, 2011), p. 32. Although the language of *crossover preachers* and *crossover preaching* is a theme throughout this book, in chapter four, I use the terminology more concretely to describe Gardner Taylor's adeptness at intercultural competence.

as *improvisational aptitude and action across racial and cultural difference*, then preachers such as these know how to be and act effectively in majority contexts.

Although the improvisational approach has a large number of practitioners among African American preachers and, for that matter, among other white and nonwhite practitioners, this approach has not yet been discussed in depth in African American homiletical literature. The scholar who comes closest to discussing it is Kenyatta Gilbert, who, although he mentions the challenges of circumscribing blackness in multicultural church settings and nonblack church settings (e.g., James Forbes at the Riverside Church in Manhattan), mentions these concerns only in passing.[120]

Although analyzing the various possibilities, trajectories, and figures in improvisational black preaching would be fruitful—no doubt comprehensive work in this area can and should be done—an examination of Taylor's commitment to this approach is more germane to the project itself. Thus, in the final section here, we will discuss the improvisational approach from a micro rather than a macro perspective. I ask: How does Taylor wield blackness and black preaching improvisationally? More importantly, how might Taylor be a transgressor of normativity in black preaching and black theology?

TRANSGRESSIVE BLACKNESS: GARDNER C. TAYLOR AS RACIAL *IMPROVISATEUR*

Transgressing black theology (narrowly defined). Taylor would probably agree in principle with James H. Cone on several important points, such as the need to critique white models of theological education and the importance of Afrocentric resources for black church preachers enrolled in white seminaries. For instance, with respect to the latter, Taylor recently wrote the foreword to a book called *Preaching with Sacred Fire*, a resource on the history of the African American preaching tradition.[121] Although important points of convergence exist between Taylor and

---

[120]Gilbert, *Journey and Promise*, p. 28.

[121]Martha J. Simmons and Frank A. Thomas, eds., *Preaching with Sacred Fire: An Anthology of African American Sermons, 1750 to the Present* (New York: W. W. Norton, 2010).

Cone, Taylor's vision of blackness appears markedly different and distinguishable from Cone's. If anything, Taylor's understanding and performance of blackness is closest to J. Kameron Carter's. He refuses to let the category of race become hermetically sealed or ontologically enclosed, opting to rupture rather than reify it.

In fact, Taylor seems to resist all stratifications and ossifications of identity. One of the reasons he does this is his conviction that racial reification is tantamount to idolatry. Like West, Taylor maintains a "deep suspicion of any form of idolatry—of any human effort to evade or deny the contingency and fragility of any human construct."[122] Although he is proud to be black, he is also wary of any identity marker that might take the place of God or God's Word. For instance, in his farewell sermon at Concord Baptist in 1990, "Parting Words," Taylor talks about this danger. He believes the reification of one category of identity over against other categories, of race or otherwise, is a dangerous pursuit. It endangers the preacher and compromises the gospel. As he reflects on his four-decade-long calling to be pastor at Concord Baptist, he makes the following comment about his life and ministry there: "I have preached up and down the world for forty-two years. I pray God this morning that I have not added anything to this Word because I am male or *because I am black* or because I am a Baptist or because I am American. All that we need is here. . . . A reduced gospel will not save us."[123] In making this statement, he does not wish to imply there is anything wrong with being black or American or Baptist or male. As was stated previously, he is proud to be black. One of his sermons from the 1960s is titled "The Power of Blackness."[124] Moreover, he is not trying to sound overly literalistic and rigid, even if it may seem that way at first. Elsewhere, Taylor makes clear the dangers of two opposite extremes in scriptural interpretation: uncritical rigidity and un-

---

[122]West, *Prophesy Deliverance!*, p. 8. Victor Anderson also warns of racial identity as racial totality in which blackness becomes "idolatrous, approaching radical henotheism." He writes: "As a religious critic whose religious and moral sensibilities are derived from a radical monotheistic faith, I find myself at odds with such a cultural idolatry." See Anderson, *Beyond Ontological Blackness*, p. 15.

[123]WGT 4:111.

[124]WGT 4:16-23.

committed flippancy. When one is uncritically rigid, he writes, "The sermon is likely to take on a quality of 'ex cathedra' pronouncement. This leaves little room for the sermon to muse upon any human traits and insertions that offer an earthly, credible point of association for the lives of those who sit in the pews." By contrast, when one is uncommitted and flippant, the sermon is likely to "ignore the mysteries of God's self-disclosures and people's uneven responses to those disclosures which are the very kernel of biblical material."[125] Both tendencies are unhelpful. What is required is balance.

Rather, his resistance is against a "reduced gospel" in which the preacher and the people have no freedom to reorder and reframe the center of their identity. He does not allow himself to trust too closely in any identity marker that might stand in the way of the gospel. In one of his sermons, he exclaims: "The gospel was meant to surround our minds and carry them captive, and it will if we open ourselves to its searching and its tenderness and accept it."[126] Any cultural identification—even blackness—that dislocates the gospel from its rightful place is deemed idolatrous. One's cultural background is not *in*significant; it is simply *less* significant. Taylor writes: "The gospel calls us to a stance, a position that is beyond immediate cultural background."[127] It is larger than Baptist theology, American exceptionalism, or African American cultural practices. For the gospel Christian, her culture is a part of who she is, but it is not all encompassing; it cannot exhaust the richness of her status as a treasured child of God. Hear what Taylor says about culture and its relation to the gospel: "Our culture is a given; we are all children and products of it. But having said that, culture is not a prison. It does not have to restrict us; it does not have to circumscribe us. . . . We are not owned by our culture; it is a secondary identity over which we rank the demands of God."[128] Note that Taylor says culture does not have to

---

[125]Taylor concludes: "A sermon has the greatest chance of accomplishing its proper hoped-for and prayed-for purpose in human life when it arises out of the preacher's own faith that in the words of Scripture a Word arises." See Gardner C. Taylor, "Shaping Sermons by the Shape of Text and Preacher," in *Preaching Biblically*, ed. Don M. Wardlaw (Philadelphia: Westminster Press, 1983), p. 137, as cited in Thomas, *African American Preaching*, p. 108.

[126]WGT 4:111.

[127]WGT 5:53.

[128]Ibid.

"restrict us" or "circumscribe us." This harkens back to J. Kameron Carter's point: blackness does not have to be hermetically sealed or ontologically closed to be viable and vital.[129] A Christian does not have to be imprisoned within a closed-off and sealed identity that others set. Ultimately, covenantal relationship with God is what makes us who we are. It is not what we possess in terms of cultural signifiers, but who we are in the eyes of God that matters most. As Taylor puts it, "If the gospel is not able to get us beyond our culture, it is no gospel at all."[130]

Taylor transgresses Cone's iteration of black liberation theology by rejecting race as totality through backgrounding his personal and corporate identity markers and foregrounding his identity *sub spatiae eternetatis*: in light of eternity. No doubt he is proud to be black; that much is clear. Nevertheless, he still ranks his pride in being black as a "secondary identity over which we rank the demands of God."[131] Being black does not exclusively define him. His blackness orbits as a planet would around the sun; the sun is fixed, and the planet is what moves. He centers on the one to whom he relates as a child of the covenant: God in Jesus Christ.

Although Taylor claims that we are all "conditioned by our culture," one of the weaknesses of his argument is that he fails to account for how his understanding and expression of *the gospel* is also conditioned. In other words, one can apply the same argument that Taylor makes vis-à-vis culture to describe how our expression and articulation of the gospel are culturally conditioned.

The claim that gospel articulation is governed by cultural parameters is not a new claim. In *Foolishness to the Greeks: The Gospel and Western Culture*, published in 1986, missiologist Lesslie Newbigin writes:

> The idea that one can or could at any time separate out by some process
> of distillation a pure gospel unadulterated by any cultural accretions is an
> illusion. It is in fact, an abandonment of the gospel, for the gospel is about

---

[129]In her book *Theories of Culture*, Kathryn Tanner points out that static, fixed definitions of culture are giving way to a more fluid, kinetic understanding of culture, more of a "postmodern stress on interactive process and negotiation, indeterminacy, fragmentation, conflict, and porosity." See Kathryn Tanner, *Theories of Culture: A New Agenda for Theology* (Minneapolis: Fortress, 1997), p. 38.

[130]WGT 5:53.

[131]WGT 5:52.

the word made flesh. Every statement of the gospel in words is conditioned by the culture of which those words are a part, and every style of life that claims to embody the truth of the gospel is a culturally conditioned style of life. *There can never be a culture-free gospel.*[132]

If Newbigin is correct that there can never be a culture-free gospel, then the next logical question is, *How might our (or Taylor's) expression and articulation of the gospel be culturally conditioned?* Unfortunately, the answer to this question is not sufficiently developed in Taylor's sermons and lectures.

Transgressing black preaching (narrowly defined). Although Taylor gives every indication that he is proud to be black, at the same time he refuses to be circumscribed by narrow definitions of blackness imposed on him from within or without the black community. To use a phrase of Michael Eric Dyson's, Taylor is "rooted in but not restricted by blackness."[133] Metaphorical *improvisateurs* insist on being rooted in but not restricted by categorization. Taylor's negotiation of race is transgressive in the sense that it challenges convention and resists enclosure. Just as his preaching practice is not restricted by narrow visions of ontological blackness in theology, so also it is not restricted by the constraints of black preaching narrowly defined. As was stated earlier, black preaching is a plurivocal, not univocal tradition. It is not myopic but stereoscopic. What we discover in Taylor is a latent transgression of Henry H. Mitchell's vision of black preaching's univocal normativity. Let

---

[132]Although Lesslie Newbigin claims that there is no such thing as a "culture-free gospel," he does not suggest that the gospel is undefinable or lacks definitive parameters. Rather, drawing on Jaroslav Pelikan's *Jesus Through the Centuries,* he simply makes the point that cultures throughout history tend to construct localized theologies with categories, images, terms, and movements that reflect their own cultural situatedness. Newbigin defines the gospel in this way: "In speaking of 'the gospel,' I am, of course, referring to the announcement that in a series of events that have their center in the life, ministry, death, and resurrection of Jesus Christ something has happened that alters the human situation and must therefore call into question every human culture." Lesslie Newbigin, *Foolishness to the Greeks: The Gospel and Western Culture* (Grand Rapids: Eerdmans, 1986), p. 4. Cf. also Amos Yong's discussion of the relationship between the gospel and culture. Yong writes: "An incarnational and Pentecostal approach to culture realizes that while distinct, the gospel always comes through culture and that culture can—and indeed, must!—be redeemed for the purposes of the gospel." See Amos Yong, *The Future of Evangelical Theology: Soundings from the Asian American Diaspora* (Downers Grove, IL: IVP Academic, 2014), p. 224.

[133]Michael Eric Dyson, "Tour(é)ing Blackness," in Touré, *Who's Afraid of Post-Blackness? What It Means to Be Black Now* (New York: Free Press, 2011), pp. xii, xx.

me suggest that Taylor transgresses black preaching narrowly defined in at least four ways.

The currency of language. Contrary to Mitchell, Taylor refuses to use the language of the black urban ghetto in his preaching, what Mitchell refers to as "Blackese." This practice stems from his conviction that correct pronunciation, spelling, grammar, and syntax are imperatives for any preacher who desires to communicate a word from God effectively. In a lecture delivered in 1996 called "Great Preachers Remembered," Taylor makes the following point about the power and possibility of language itself:

> The preacher does not have very much to deal with except the currency of his own integrity or her own integrity and the integrity of language. That's all you've got! And if you debase the currency, if you start using words wrongly, and the currency isn't worth much, then you don't have much to deal with. We ought to be very careful.[134]

For Taylor, language is a currency that can either be utilized effectively or debased through "using words wrongly." Like the poet of a sonnet or the lyricist for a song, Taylor sees great potential in precise wording: which words are used and how they are used. Words not only communicate concepts and convey ideas to those who hear them; when rightly used with the right intention, they have the power to disclose worlds. Using words wrongly, that is, using the language of the black urban ghetto per Mitchell's recommendation, according to Taylor, means debasing the currency of language and stunting the possibility for disclosure of worlds. To use Samuel D. Proctor's metaphor, "the trumpet blows an uncertain sound" when we preach using careless language.[135]

Granted, Taylor's class and educational level arguably shaped his commitment to the currency of language (i.e., correct grammar and syntax). His mother, Selina, was an English schoolteacher, and he received a graduate-level education at Oberlin. Consequently, some black church preachers accused Taylor of being elitist. "Why should one use

---

[134]"Great Preachers Remembered," Gardner C. Taylor, *Essential Taylor Audio CD* (Valley Forge, PA: Judson Press, 2001).

[135]Samuel D. Proctor, *The Certain Sound of the Trumpet: Crafting a Sermon of Authority* (Valley Forge, PA: Judson Press, 1994), p. 134.

the language of the oppressor?" they suggested. Why not use colloquial language more familiar to urban youth? One African American preacher I spoke with provided a more nuanced account. One generation removed from Taylor, and an admirer of Taylor's preaching, he used words like "traditional" and "formal" to describe Taylor's commitment to perfect grammar and syntax. When describing him, he said: "He was old school." In other words, he was a product of his time, class, and educational level.

Perhaps a way to adjudicate the tension between Taylor and Mitchell with respect to language and how it is used would be to suggest that they have two different visions for community uplift. Mitchell believes that when a preacher uses urban vernacular, he or she is using language that is accessible and understandable; he or she is being incarnational. Uplift sounds like identification and solidarity. By contrast, Taylor believes that when a preacher uses correct grammar and syntax he or she is accessing the power and precision of language to inspire, motivate, and challenge the community to seek after a God of power and precision. Uplift sounds like respecting and appreciating God's power to reach people through carefully chosen words—through the currency of language.

"Your words should sing." Another way Taylor transgresses normativity in black preaching is that he never whoops or chants his sermon. In fairness, Mitchell is not a whooper either, and in *Black Preaching* he leaves some room open for diversity and divergence in the tradition. But there are some who believe the whooped or chanted sermon is a prerequisite to effective preaching. If you cannot whoop, you cannot preach, so the argument goes. If that were true, then Taylor and many others would be disqualified from participation.

When Taylor was in his mid- to late twenties in Louisiana, he tried whooping in the style of the traditional folk preacher but was unsuccessful. As his friend C. D. Simmons, a Louisiana pastor who heard him preach in the 1940s, recounts,

> Taylor was not a whooper, it was not him. Whatever arousing he did came from what he said and how he said it. He told J. B. Huey, a down home, old fashion preacher, after a convention sermon, "I wish I had what you got." He attempted it [whooping] a few times, but soon accepted that it

was not for him and he had to go his own way. Taylor was on the intellectual type, logical, and deep as well.[136]

During his years in Louisiana, Taylor abandoned whooping altogether and never returned to it throughout his entire preaching ministry in Brooklyn. He was not embarrassed to be associated with whooping. Otherwise he would not have said to his friend Huey, "I wish I had what you got." Also, notice that he stopped whooping while still living in Louisiana rather than abandoning it after he moved to Brooklyn, so his "decision" had nothing to do with moving to a major urban metropolis. In fact, Taylor spent significant years of the New York phase of his ministry maintaining a personal friendship with another pastor in Brooklyn—C. L. Franklin—who was one of black preaching's most famous chanter-whoopers.[137]

Here is another way to think about it. Taylor's turn from whooping and chanting represented a shift away from folk preaching toward the artful use of language.[138] He chose to trade in (*not* trade up) the tonality of music for the poetics of language. On one occasion, when Cleophus J. LaRue asked him about whooping or singing in a sermon, Taylor answered: "Your words should sing."[139] Put differently, the preacher's words make the music, not the preacher.

Drawing from more than one well. Transgressive *improvisateurs* do not draw from one well exclusively; they draw from more than one. This is true of Taylor. For instance, as was previously mentioned, in his Yale Beecher Lectures, delivered in 1976, Taylor quotes the names of European preachers of the past such as Jean Massillon of France, W. Frederick Robertson of England, and Alexander McLaren of Scotland. These

[136]C. D. Simmons interview as cited in Thomas, *African American Preaching*, p. 97.

[137]C. L. Franklin was the pastor of Lebanon Baptist Church in Brooklyn from 1938 until his death in 1958. Franklin and Taylor were friends and partners in ministry. A picture of Gardner Taylor attending a "mortgage-burning ceremony" celebration at Mount Lebanon in 1955 can be found in Clarence Taylor, *The Black Churches of Brooklyn* (New York: Columbia University Press, 1994), p. 74. Also, Mount Lebanon's history page on its website discusses Taylor's connection. To read more about this event, go to http://mymlbc.org/history.php.

[138]For more on the artful use of language, see LaRue's chapter, "Why Black Preachers Still Love Artful Language," in LaRue, *I Believe I'll Testify*, pp. 81-98.

[139]Personal interview with Cleophus J. LaRue, 2012. See also James Earl Massey, "Composing Sermons That Sing!," in *Our Sufficiency Is of God: Essays on Preaching in Honor of Gardner C. Taylor*, ed. Timothy George, James Earl Massey, and Robert Smith Jr. (Macon, GA: Mercer University Press, 2010), pp. 11-22.

names were more familiar to his predominantly white audience than the names of African American preachers of past generations like Daniel Alexander Payne, Francis J. Grimké, or Theodore Sedgwick Wright. At one level, Taylor did what most preachers do—he adapted his lecture to his audience, an audience of predominantly white listeners at Yale University. At another level, however, Taylor's decision points again to his discomfort with black preaching narrowly defined. The point is not that Taylor displaces black preachers in favor of European preachers or vice versa; rather, it is that he does not confine his vision of preaching to one particular group of people or another. He is strategic about drawing from more than one well.[140]

Appealing to more than one audience. The final act of transgression against black preaching narrowly defined pertains to Taylor's intended audience. Although he preached predominantly to African Americans, he never claimed to preach exclusively to African Americans. He was one among many in his generation, who, according to LaRue, were "hesitant to style their works on preaching as peculiarly or uniquely black."[141] Although Taylor was called the "dean of the nation's black preachers," he did not see himself as preaching exclusively to the black community. Perhaps we might say that his sermons came *from* but were not exclusively *for* the black community. No doubt he had an eye fixed on the black community—its hurts, its challenges, its plight in a racist society—but his reach was always intended to be wider than his own community. Reflecting on the shift that took place in his life generally and in his sermons particularly in the mid- to late 1950s, Taylor states,

> I think my preaching expanded into the realization that there are not only the specifics of a particular circumstance in society, but there are the great universal considerations, our hopes, our fears, the fact that we are born,

---

[140]Samuel D. Proctor takes a similar approach to Taylor's in his belief that preachers should draw from more than one well, but he approaches the matter from a different vantage point. Proctor suggests that preachers should not only "call on" witnesses from Scripture, but also call on witnesses from "history, literature and logic." He describes his commitment to calling on multiple witnesses as "interdisciplinarity" (p. 15). He compares it to adding multiple layers to one's preaching. He writes: "It is like layers of finish on a surface: one layer from Scripture, one from logic, one from another discipline, and a layer from the preacher's own observations" (p. 114). See Proctor, *Certain Sound of the Trumpet.*

[141]LaRue, *I Believe I'll Testify*, p. 32.

we love, we hate, we sicken, we die, we laugh, we cry, all the things among those things. If indeed I was liberated from being a preacher *exclusively to black people*, it was in the mid 1950s, even when I began to broaden my sense of the needs of people.[142]

In a sense, it was a shift away from being black while also being human toward being human while also being black. Although cultural categories are important, remember again that, in Taylor's eyes, they are a "secondary identity over which we rank the demands of God."[143] His move toward the plight and potentiality of humanness with all of its interior fissures and fractures, its frailty and contradictions, its finitude and brokenness, was a form of strategic rupturing. It meant that his intended audience was every human being no matter his or her race, gender, or ethnicity. He preached to general humanity while still having an eye toward the particular experiences of African Americans.

Taylor's shift away from blackness/black preaching narrowly defined, or transgressive blackness, ruptures potential reifications of blackness as an ossified or static identity over which nothing can be placed. It resists enclosure and containment. By appealing to more than one constituency, he broadened his reach across racial, cultural, and ecclesial difference, and he transgressed the false notion that black preaching could only be done *by* African Americans *to* African Americans.

CONCLUSION

To be a transgressor of modern racialized reasoning is to be a border crosser—a crossover preacher—one who defies circumscription through expanding existing boundaries and breaking and remaking norms. In Taylor, we find these characteristics: he refuses to be sealed off by narrow depictions of blackness; he ruptures idolizing, essentialist reifications of race; and he breaks and remakes the homiletical norms definitively set forth by Mitchell. He transgresses the norms of black preaching narrowly defined in four ways specifically: emphasizing the currency of language, claiming that our "words should sing," drawing from more than

---

[142]These comments were recorded in a telephone interview with Gerald Lamont Thomas. See Thomas, *African American Preaching*, p. 100 (emphasis added).
[143]WGT 5:53.

one well (which is also a form of performative pastiche), and appealing to more than one constituency.

Taylor's blackness is neither hermetically sealed nor ontologically enclosed. Nuance is important here. Instead of shunning black identity, he shuns the *ossification* of black identity as potentially idolatrous. Instead of foregrounding ontological blackness as the center, he foregrounds God's covenantal relationship with humanity. Although Taylor understands blackness as a significant category, a gift from God worthy of celebration, he refuses to let blackness define him in an exhaustive, ultimate, or final way. To return to Michael Eric Dyson's phrase, Taylor is "rooted in but not restricted by blackness."[144] Thus we can say that Taylor, at least in a sense, decenters a false center in order to recenter himself on the One who is the true center. (We will discuss the theological rationale for de-centering later in chapter four.) Instead of decentering the gospel so that he might center on being black, he decenters blackness so that he might center on the gospel. To return to Robert Griffin's words one last time, Taylor knows and understands: "I am an African-American in America. That will never change." And like Griffin, he believes: "I don't have to be defined by that."[145]

---

[144]Dyson, "Tour(é)ing Blackness," pp. xii, xx.
[145]Corbett, "Robert Griffin III Refuses to Be Defined by Race."

4

TRANSGRESSING THE DIVIDES

INTERCULTURAL COMPETENCE

*The priority of the other person begins in
this self-effacing gesture, in our ceding our place.
This is the road that can lead to holiness.*

EMMANUEL LÉVINAS
Is It Righteous to Be?: Interviews with Emmanuel Lévinas

*For in the one Spirit we were all baptized
into one body—Jews or Greeks, slaves or free—and
we were all made to drink of one Spirit.*

1 CORINTHIANS 12:13

◆

A popular Chinese fable begins with two men walking along the river. One says to the other, "Look how happy the fish are as they swim in the river!" The other responds: "You are not a fish. How do you know whether the fish are happy?" The man answers back: "Ah! But you are not me! How do you know whether I know what the fish think?"[1]

Fables like these reveal one of many blind spots in human rationality:

---

[1]Story cited in Martha Minnow, *Making All the Difference: Inclusion, Exclusion, and American Law* (Ithaca, NY: Cornell University Press, 1991), p. 227.

the tendency to make false assumptions about others, in particular what they think and feel. In encounters like these, the questioner fails to understand that the questions asked and answers given are conditioned by the context from which the questions come. One's assumptions as to the thoughts and feelings of others may indeed be correct, but they may also be incorrect. "How do you know whether I know . . . ?" the man asks his friend. The tendency to make false assumptions about others is compounded when one's dialogue partners are culturally and racially different others. Communication is already difficult and dynamic, and takes place on more than one channel *without* intercultural exchange. When one adds the additional layer of cultural and ethnic difference to the equation, the results can either be invigorating or disastrous for one or both parties depending on the exchange itself.

In order to account for the challenges and opportunities that intercultural exchange poses, intercultural communication has emerged as a discipline and even come of age in the past fifty years. According to intercultural studies theorists A. Scott Moreau, Evvy Hay Campbell, and Susan Greener, intercultural communication has established itself as both a viable and vital discipline at "hundreds of colleges and universities."[2] Since an analysis of a burgeoning field like intercultural communication is beyond the scope of this chapter and outside the primary subject matter of this book, a narrower subset will be considered: *intercultural competence.* To be interculturally competent means to possess the knowledge, skills, and habits required for negotiating difference effectively.

In this chapter, we will return to Taylor-as-case-study by arguing that his adeptness at metaphorical improvisation is another way of emblemizing what intercultural communication theorists refer to as intercultural competence. Not only did Taylor possess the requisite knowledge, skills, and habits, but he utilized them decades before communication and education theorists were arguing for their indispensability. That is to say, he was a forerunner in intercultural competence (IC). His skill *at* negotiating difference effectively preceded academic discussions *about*

---

[2]A. Scott Moreau, Evvy Hay Campbell, and Susan Greener, *Effective Intercultural Communication: A Christian Perspective* (Grand Rapids: Baker, 2014), p. 1.

negotiating difference effectively. As was the case with Martin Luther King Jr., Taylor's proficiency at intercultural competence won him a hearing in settings where African American voices were often excluded. At a time when traversing racial, cultural, or ecumenical difference was neither easy nor common, he was a "crossover preacher," to return to Cleophus J. LaRue's phrase.[3]

More significant for contemporary homiletics, Taylor's skill at intercultural competence positions him as a forerunner or harbinger from whom homileticians and church pastors alike can benefit. He exhibits the sort of intercultural proficiency that will be required of those trying to minister in an intercultural (or multiethnic) church at present in the United States or who will be ministering in a US church context with an intercultural trajectory in its future.

I begin by surveying literature in IC theory in order to arrive at my own definition, and I recommend approaching the IC conversation through what I call the "3A Model of Intercultural Competence Proficiency"—the three A's being acquisition, aptitude, and action. Then I claim that, in Gardner C. Taylor's life and ministry, we witness the cultivation and actualization of IC proficiency. We will track the development of Taylor's IC by starting with his experiences growing up in the segregated South, moving to his university years at Leland College and Oberlin College, and then observing his commitments to ecumenical partnership across racial difference during his years at Concord. Finally, I establish a biblical and theological rationale for IC in order to demonstrate its significance to theological discussion and Christian discipleship.

In featuring intercultural questions, we will not abandon improvisation as a salient metaphor for understanding Taylor's preaching performatively and metaphorically. Instead, I suggest that his improvisational approach is simultaneously an intercultural approach. In other words, intercultural competence is another way of describing improvisation-in-action with respect to context. Although improvisation as such does not figure prom-

---

[3]See Cleophus J. LaRue, *I Believe I'll Testify: The Art of African American Preaching* (Louisville: Westminster John Knox, 2011), p. 32. Cf. also the discussion of crossover preachers in Kenyatta R. Gilbert, *The Journey and Promise of African American Preaching* (Minneapolis: Fortress, 2011), p. 28.

inently in this chapter, its expression through the categories of the emerging field of intercultural competence remains in view.

WHAT IS INTERCULTURAL COMPETENCE?

Numerous definitions of intercultural competence (IC) have emerged in recent decades.

- Communication theorist Darla K. Deardorff defines it as "effective and appropriate behavior in an intercultural situation."[4]

- Igor Klyukanov defines it as a "system of knowledge and skills enabling us to communicate successfully with people from other cultures."[5]

- Brian H. Spitzberg and Gabrielle Changnon define it as "appropriate and effective management of interaction between people who, to some degree or another, represent different or divergent affective, cognitive and behavioral orientations to the world."[6]

- P. Christopher Earley and Soon Ang define it as "a person's capability for successful adaptation to new cultural settings, that is, for unfamiliar settings attributable to cultural context."[7]

- Missiologists Gary L. McIntosh and Alan McMahan define it as "tolerance and adaptability to varying cultural expressions."[8]

I define intercultural competence as *the cultivation of knowledge, skills, and habits for effectively negotiating cultural, racial, and ecclesial difference.* To cultivate IC, one commits to a combination of knowledge acquisition, behavioral aptitude, and transgressive action. It is not enough to acquire knowledge about other cultures or to have skills as a competent communicator. One must also leverage one's knowledge and skills in real-life

---

[4]Darla K. Deardorff, "Implementing Intercultural Competence Assessment," in *The Sage Handbook of Intercultural Competence*, ed. Darla K. Deardorff (Thousand Oaks, CA: Sage, 2009), p. 480.

[5]Igor Klyukanov, *Principles of Intercultural Communication* (New York: Pearson, 2005), p. 4.

[6]Brian H. Spitzberg and Gabrielle Changnon, "Conceptualizing Intercultural Competence," in Deardorff, ed., *Sage Handbook of Intercultural Competence*, p. 7.

[7]P. Christopher Earley and Soon Ang refer to intercultural competence as CQ, which is shorthand for cultural intelligence. Their primary audience is the business community. P. Christopher Earley and Soon Ang, *Cultural Intelligence: Individual Interactions Across Cultures* (Stanford, CA: Stanford Business Books, 2003), p. 59.

[8]Gary L. McIntosh and Alan McMahan, *Being the Church in a Multi-Ethnic Community: Why It Matters and How It Works* (Indianapolis: Wesleyan Publishing House, 2012), p. 142.

contexts and real-world relationships in order to cross over borders of difference. That is to say, one must be committed to transformative action in addition to knowledge acquisition and behavioral aptitude. My inclusion of the word *habits* signals a commitment to a definition of IC that is not only knowledge and skill based but also action based. An interculturally competent preacher acquires *knowledge* about cultures, draws on *skills* in intercultural communication settings, and *acts* in ways consistent with a commitment to negotiating difference effectively.

Again, real-world interaction across racial, ethnic, and ecumenical difference is crucial to intercultural competence. Although communication theorists put forth various definitions, all agree that it is impossible to acquire IC in a vacuum; it does not exist in intellectual abstraction. In her article "In Search of Intercultural Competence," Deardorff explains why knowledge acquisition represents only one stage of a multistage process of intercultural proficiency: "Nearly all definitions of intercultural competence include more than knowledge of other cultures, since *knowledge alone is not enough to constitute intercultural competence.* Intercultural competence also involves the development of one's skills and attitudes in successfully interacting with persons of diverse backgrounds."[9]

While those who wish to negotiate difference effectively should know about and value other cultures, knowledge alone does not make a person interculturally competent. Actions complement knowledge and skills. Without diminishing the central importance of skillfully exegeting biblical texts and remaining theologically attentive to God at work in the world, interculturally competent preachers go a step further: they possess "skills and attitudes" that translate into successful actions and interactions with persons from different cultural, ethnic, and ecclesial backgrounds.

---

[9] Darla K. Deardorff, "In Search of Intercultural Competence," *International Educator* 13, no. 2 (Spring 2004): 15 (emphasis added). In some respects, Deardorff makes a claim similar to that of the ancient philosopher Aristotle, who argued that *phronesis*, or practical knowledge of how to do the right things in the right ways at the right time, was essential to the pursuit of intellectual virtue. Aristotle argued that intellectual virtue involved acquiring three different forms of knowledge: (1) *sophia*: theoretical knowledge, (2) *techne*: reasoning knowledge, and (3) *phronesis*: practical knowledge. Of the three forms of knowledge, *phronesis* pertains to right human conduct in concrete situations as opposed to abstract knowledge in theoretical situations. For more on Aristotle's understanding of *phronesis*, see John E. Sisko, "Phronesis," in *Encyclopedia of Ethics: P-W*, ed. Lawrence C. Becker and Charlotte B. Becker (New York: Routledge, 2001).

The 3A Model of Intercultural Competence. Intercultural competence means committing oneself to three practices in particular: acquisition, aptitude, and action, what I call the "3A Model of Intercultural Competence Proficiency."[10] This is not a "developmental" or sequential framework in which one commitment precedes the attainment of a second and then a third commitment.[11] In other words, one does not need not to become a master at knowledge acquisition *before* one can attain skill aptitude or transgressive action, and one does not need to master the second or third commitment before one can move on to knowledge acquisition. According to this model, one pursues knowledge acquisition, skill aptitude, and transgressive action simultaneously. If I were to visually portray my model, it would indicate three overlapping characteristics that dynamically constitute intercultural competence:

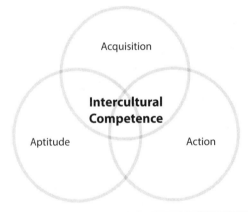

Figure 1. The 3A Model

[10]In intercultural competence theory, the word *model* is used more often than *framework*.
[11]In IC literature, Brian H. Spitzberg and Gabrielle Changnon define developmental models as those that move the learner(s) through "stages of progression that would mark the achievement of more competent levels of interaction." Developmental models are linear and sequential; they involve progression through a series of steps or stages. Two examples of developmental models are Fiora Biagi et al.'s reflective intercultural assessment model (RICA) and Milton J. Bennett's developmental model of intercultural sensitivity (DMIS). See Spitzberg and Changnon, "Conceptualizing Intercultural Competence," p. 21. See also Fiora Biagi et al., "Reflective Intercultural Competence (RIC) and Its Assessment: The RICA Model," in *Intercultural Horizons: Best Practices in Intercultural Competence Development*, ed. Eliza J. Nash, Nevin C. Brown, and Lavinia Bracci (Newcastle upon Tyne, UK: Cambridge Scholars Publishing, 2012), pp. 61-82; and Milton J. Bennett, "Towards Ethnorelativism: A Developmental Model of Intercultural Sensitivity," in *Education for the Intercultural Experience*, ed. R. Michael Paige (Yarmouth, ME: Intercultural Press, 1993), pp. 21-71.

Instead of being sequential and linear, the 3A model is intersectional and interstitial. It is at the interstices of these three dimensions—acquisition, aptitude, and action—that IC proficiency flourishes.

Acquisition. The first dimension of the 3A model is a commitment to *acquisition.* One must be willing to be interculturally reflexive, that is, to acquire knowledge about one's own culture—its beliefs and values—*and* strive to acquire knowledge of another's cultural beliefs and values.[12] At an abstract level, knowledge of another culture involves the acquisition of information about a country's history, literature, stories, processes of interaction, and customs. Flesh-and-blood interlocutors are not required for a person to gain cultural knowledge, at least in the abstract sense. At the concrete level, knowledge of another culture means "procedural knowledge of how to act in specific circumstances" through conversations with an interlocutor, that is, through the process of socialization.[13] In addition to knowledge gained through socialization, procedural knowledge also means knowledge of the socialization process itself. In other words, acquiring knowledge of other cultures does not *just* mean learning stories, customs, and traditions; it also requires learning the appropriate and sensible ways to interact with people in individual, social, and societal situations.

In their book *CQ: Developing Cultural Intelligence at Work*, P. Christopher Earley, Soon Ang, and Joo-Seng Tan suggest that acquiring knowledge about other cultures requires "cultural strategic thinking." They define cultural strategic thinking as "general thinking skills that you use to understand how and why people act as they do in a new culture."[14]

---

[12]The link between culture and beliefs/values is intentional. Although other markers such as food, music, and clothing are still a significant part of national, geographical, and ethnic culture, these are external markers rather than internal markers. Beliefs and values are internal markers; they constitute structures of meaning, the individual and corporate DNA of culture, what can be termed the "software of the mind." See Geert H. Hofstede, Gert Jan Hofstede, and Michael Minkov, *Cultures and Organizations: Software of the Mind: Intercultural Cooperation and Its Importance for Survival* (New York: McGraw-Hill, 2010).

[13]Educational theorist Michael Byram argues that knowledge of other cultures cannot remain in the abstract but must be concretized in social settings. Byram's model, known as intercultural communicative competence (ICC), is designed specifically as a guide for assisting foreign language teachers (FLTs), but the principles that undergird his model have been used more broadly in intercultural communication. Michael Byram, *Teaching and Assessing Intercultural Communicative Competence* (Philadelphia: Multilingual Matters, 1997), p. 23.

[14]Cultural strategic thinking is one of three competencies that Earley, Ang, and Tan set forth in

The primary question one asks is, "How and why do people do what they do here?" It pertains not only to beliefs and values in a culture, but also to the "procedures and routines that people are supposed to use as they work and act."[15] Empathy, observational skills, fast learning, and problem solving in intercultural situations characterize culturally strategic thinkers.

According to Earley, Ang, and Tan, a person who learns to utilize culturally strategic thinking effectively is characterized by the following dispositions: they are "open, alert, and sensitive to new cultures"; "able to draw distinctions and identify similarities between different cultures"; can "develop different strategies for acquiring knowledge relevant to adapting to different cultures"; can "engage in active and dynamic thinking in interacting with people from different cultures"; can "plan, check, and learn from each encounter"; and are "able to resolve cultural dilemmas or problems in the encounter."[16]

One of the gaps in Early, Ang, and Tan's work is the importance of learning about one's own cultural beliefs and values. When it comes to knowledge acquisition, reflexivity is critical to IC attainment. Self-knowledge and knowledge of other cultures are interrelated. In many ways, Earley, Ang, and Tan do not go far enough in their discussion of culturally strategic thinking. They leave out an all-important step: *critical*

---

their CQ model. The other two competencies are motivation and behavior. See P. Christopher Earley, Soon Ang, and Joo-Seng Tan, *CQ: Developing Cultural Intelligence at Work* (Stanford, CA: Stanford Business Books, 2006), p. 5. Their primary interest is in reaching out to the business community rather than the academy. However, their interest in equipping those in the marketplace at a practical level does not preclude them from pursuing a theoretical framework to undergird their argument. The simple truth that some persons are more adept at adapting and improvising across different cultural contexts and frameworks constitutes sufficient if not compelling evidence that many kinds of intelligence exist besides those measured on an IQ test. Their shorthand for cultural intelligence, CQ, is a way of signaling to their readers that cultural intelligence is an important facet of one's overall intelligence. They are reticent to connect CQ too closely to the idea of intelligence quotient (IQ), since IQ scores are mathematical and nonrelational. They use CQ much like psychological or educational theorists use EQ (emotional intelligence), that is, they use it as a measure of relational and interpersonal capability. For Earley and Ang's discussion of CQ, IQ, and EQ, see Earley and Ang, *Cultural Intelligence*, p. 4. For discussions on emotional intelligence (EQ) in psychology, education, and communication, see Daniel Goleman, *Emotional Intelligence* (New York: Bantam Books, 2005); Jerrell C. Cassady and Mourad Ali Eissa, eds., *Emotional Intelligence: Perspectives from Educational and Positive Psychology* (New York: Peter Lang, 2008); Robert J. Emmerling, Vinod K. Shanwal, and Manas K. Mandal, eds., *Emotional Intelligence: Theoretical and Cultural Perspectives* (New York: Nova Science Publishers, 2008).

[15] Earley, Ang, and Tan, *CQ*, p. 5.
[16] Ibid., p. 51.

reflexive thinking about one's own cultural framework. Being a student of other cultures is insufficient. One must also scrutinize and interrogate one's own culture.

In his research, intercultural theorist Michael Harris Bond conducted interviews with eighteen intercultural scholars and uncovered the following: most of these scholars did not engage in reflexive cultural self-study with any rigor or devotion despite being deeply committed to intercultural education.[17] Study of one's own culture is critical! To paraphrase anthropologist Edward T. Hall, one must undergo enculturation (i.e., identifying the beliefs and values of one's own culture) if one also wishes to be proficient at acculturation (i.e., engaging successfully with other cultures).[18] Enculturation and acculturation are dialectically con-

---

[17]See Michael Harris Bond, *Working at the Interface of Culture: Eighteen Lives in Social Science* (New York: Routledge, 1997). Robert C. Weigl draws on the work of Michael Harris Bond in his research as well. Cf. also Robert C. Weigl, "Intercultural Competence Through Cultural Self-Study: A Strategy for Adult Learners," *International Journal of Intercultural Relations* 33 (2009): 348.

[18]See Edward T. Hall, *Beyond Culture* (Garden City, NY: Anchor, 1976), pp. 79-101. See also Gary R. Weaver, "Understanding and Coping with Cross-Cultural Adjustment Stress," in *Culture, Communication, and Conflict*, ed. Gary R. Weaver (Boston: Pearson Learning Solutions, 2000), p. 190. Typically, anthropologists use the word *acculturation* differently from how some theologians use it. In anthropology, *acculturation* usually refers to adaptation to a new, foreign culture through observing and participating in its practices, language, and values. For instance, if someone born in the United States with absolutely no ties to Japan moves to Tokyo for employment, that person would likely undergo a process of acculturation, that is, a period of observing, learning, and participating in the practices, language, and values of the host culture. In this sense, acculturation is neither positive nor negative; it is descriptive. However, the word has more of a negative connotation in some Protestant theological circles. To some theologians, *acculturation* refers to the church's uncritical embrace of culture to the extent that it loses its distinctive witness. In its most profane sense, acculturation is blind capitulation to the powers and principalities of this world through corrupt genuflecting before those in positions of power. In so doing, the church becomes a sycophant of the state rather than its conscience. One example of acculturation according to this definition might be Protestant Christianity at the onset of World War I in Germany. During this period, the German government, led by Kaiser Wilhelm II, made a reductive connection between German *Kultur* (culture) and German Protestant Christianity. Their logic was that being a Christian meant being a patriotic German, and being a patriotic German meant being a Christian. Church leaders also became acculturated to this way of thinking. In August 1914, ninety-three German intellectuals, prominent theologians included, signed a war manifesto in support of Kaiser Wilhelm II. Looking back on this phase of German Protestantism, Barth reflects with horror and despair at these events and describes the realization he had concerning the theology of his teachers: "I suddenly realized that I could not any longer follow either their ethics and dogmatics or their understanding of the Bible and history." See Karl Barth, "Evangelical Theology in the Nineteenth Century," in *The Humanity of God*, trans. Thomas Wieser (Atlanta: John Knox, 1978), p. 14. Other theologians use the term *inculturation* to refer to the same phenomenon of the church capitulating to the culture. For instance, David Bosch suggests that some churches become so inculturated to the state that Christianity becomes "nothing but the religious dimension of the

joined to any process in which intercultural competence is the goal.

Robert C. Weigl is another intercultural theorist who contends that cultural self-study is vital to knowledge acquisition and growth in intercultural education. Weigl teaches at the University of Virginia and is an instructor in the "Semester at Sea" program. In training students to become effective interculturalists, he insists that they become "bidirectional" in their learning. Interculturalists-in-training "benefit enormously from knowing themselves [culturally] before undertaking a range of research and service ventures focused on others."[19] Thus each semester Weigl guides his students through a disciplined program of cultural self-study.[20] After years of teaching and conducting research, Weigl discovered that cultural self-studiers exhibit an "enhanced capacity for inter-subjectivity in relation to cultural others," and across the board they are "warmer, more synchronous, and more attentive in intercultural situations." Weigl also maintains that cultural self-study positively affects students in five concrete ways:

- "Cultural self studiers become more curious about other cultures."

- "Concepts and categories used to describe oneself will be used more sensitively and accurately to describe others."

- "Self-studiers are more likely to anticipate the pervasiveness and authority with which culture operates in others' lives."

- "Cultural self-awareness increases self-studiers' capacity to identify bias."

- "Self-studiers discover an emerging capacity to arrest their automatic enactment of their culture in order to more accurately participate in the experiences of those from another culture."[21]

culture—listening to the church, society hears only the sound of its own music." See David J. Bosch, *Transforming Mission: Paradigm Shifts in Theology of Mission* (Maryknoll, NY: Orbis Books, 1991), p. 455.

[19]See Weigl, "Intercultural Competence Through Cultural Self-Study," pp. 347-48.

[20]Not only do Weigl's students do self-reflective journaling, but they also participate in structured projects like the following: "identify with someone targeted for discrimination, plan support for school teachers in culturally mixed classrooms, or design research to study the impact of social primes on minority student performance." In other words, cultural self-study is not just existential and phenomenological; it is also social and academic. See ibid., p. 350.

[21]Ibid.

Put simply, those who critically study their own culture are more effective at adapting to and learning from people from other cultures. They become interculturally proficient with respect to other cultures and with respect to their own culture. Later, in chapter five, we will return to critical cultural self-study and its importance to IC proficiency.

If we think in terms of imagery, knowledge acquisition involves two reflexive commitments: looking in a mirror and gazing through a window. Both are necessary. Mirror work involves interrogating, scrutinizing, and celebrating what one sees in his or her cultural mirror at both a micro level and a macro level. Window work involves studying, interpreting, and relating to the cultural practices, beliefs, and values of other cultures. To borrow Weigl's term, knowledge acquisition is "bidirectional."[22]

Aptitude. The second dimension of the 3A model is *aptitude.* One must be motivated to learn appropriate skills for enhancing effective communication with people from different cultural, ethnic, and ecclesial backgrounds. Thus aptitude is not a neutral endowment; it is a stance or orientation. It involves personal motivation, interpersonal propriety, and skill acquisition. One displays a high level of motivation to learn. Fiora Biagi and others argue that "personal motivation affects in a considerable way" the attainment of intercultural competence. Several IC theorists have pointed to the importance and even indispensability of motivation in acquiring intercultural competence. Brian H. Spitzberg and William R. Cupach suggest that motivation is one of three main components to what they call communicative competence. Biagi and others argue that personal motivation is integral to "the acquisition of RIC [reflective intercultural competence]." Earley, Ang, and Tan suggest that "motivational CQ" is one of three competencies required for improving one's cultural intelligence.[23]

In addition to motivation, aptitude requires interpersonal propriety. It means discovering what is appropriate and fitting for a given intercul-

---

[22]Ibid., p. 347.
[23]See Brian H. Spitzberg and William R. Cupach, *Interpersonal Communication Competence* (Beverly Hills, CA: Sage, 1984), as cited in William B. Gudykunst, *Bridging Differences: Effective Intergroup Communication* (Newbury Park, CA: Sage, 1991), p. 105. See also Biagi et al., "Reflective Intercultural Competence (RIC) and Its Assessment: The RICA Model," p. 63. See also Earley, Ang, and Tan, *CQ*, pp. 28-32, 61.

tural situation. The word *apt* has its root in the Latin *aptus*, meaning, "fitting, suitable, or appropriate."

Finally, aptitude involves skill acquisition. One obtains the necessary skills for communication across difference. Both learning and acquiring skills are essential. To summarize briefly, a person with high IC aptitude is motivated to learn skills that are fitting, suitable, or appropriate to communication in an intercultural situation.

Unfortunately, the tendency in some pockets of the arts and humanities is to shy away from the attainment of skills in favor of mastery of content. Some professors have a tendency to subject their students to content tyranny without providing any frameworks or skills for thinking and problem solving in the real world.[24] Knowledge and skills are inseparably linked in education, or at least they should be. As John M. Wiemann and Clifford W. Kelly observe, "knowledge without skill is socially useless, and skill cannot be obtained without the cognitive ability to diagnose situational demands and constraints."[25] If one is able to acquire knowledge about Honduran culture, for instance, but does not have the requisite skills to communicate meaningfully with Hondurans, then one cannot be said to be interculturally competent with Hondurans and their culture. To be interculturally competent, one must have more than knowledge about another culture. Knowledge is only one part of the equation. One must also have skills.

What specific skills are necessary for IC aptitude? According to Michael Byram's intercultural communicative competence (ICC) model, at least four skills are required: interpreting, relating, discovery, and interaction.[26] Byram defines interpreting as the ability to interpret the symbols, events, and stories of another culture. By "relating" he means

---

[24]Recall that former Harvard president Derek Bok claims that most of today's undergraduate students do not have the necessary skills required to "think interculturally," a theme we return to in chapter five. See Derek Bok, *Our Underachieving Colleges: A Candid Look at How Much Students Learn and Why They Should Be Learning More* (Princeton, NJ: Princeton University Press, 2008), p. 250.

[25]John M. Wiemann and Clifford W. Kelly, "Pragmatics of Interpersonal Competence," in *Rigor and Imagination: Essays from the Legacy of George Bateson*, ed. C. Wilder-Mott and John H. Weakland (New York: Praeger, 1981), p. 290.

[26]He couples these skills as part of two larger categories: skills of interpreting and relating within the larger category known as *savoir comprendre* (understanding knowledge) and skills of discovery and interaction within the larger category of *savoir faire* (knowing what to do).

an ability to *relate* one's interpretations about another culture's symbols and stories to one's own culture and experience. These two skills do not necessarily require a flesh-and-blood interlocutor. For the skill of interpreting, texts and stories can be one's interlocutors.[27] The skill of relating is monological rather than dialogical.

By contrast, the other two skills, discovery and interaction, are more concrete, interpersonal, and experiential than the skills of interpreting and relating. They require an ability to gain knowledge and to apply it in actual intercultural situations. Byram defines discovery as the ability to acquire new knowledge about the cultural practices of another culture through experience. By interaction he means the ability to use one's discoveries in real-time intercultural communication. At this stage, knowing about a culture and performing with proficiency in a culture are intertwined. Becoming proficient at these two skills requires *both* the "ability to acquire new knowledge of a culture and cultural practices *and* the ability to operate knowledge, attitudes, and skills under the constraints of real-time communication and interaction."[28] One must be able to identify meaningful practices of interaction across cultural differences *and* be able to apply this knowledge in real-time intercultural situations.

Although Byram's four skills are a helpful way of framing IC aptitude, other skills are also necessary in order to communicate what is appropriate and fitting in a given intercultural situation. For example, developing a skill such as *tolerance for ambiguity* helps intercultural learners avoid uncritical prejudgments about culturally different others. Without tolerance for ambiguity, the temptation is to minimize the complexities of cultural difference and make unnecessary totalitarian claims about "all human beings" from an ethnocentric vantage point. Milton J. Bennett describes this temptation as the trivialization of difference through "minimization." A person who minimizes difference across cultures leaves no room for cultural ambiguity. He or she tends to "bury difference under the weight of cultural similarities."[29]

---

[27]Byram understands the skills of interpreting and relating as the "ability to interpret a document or event from another culture, to explain it and relate it to documents from one's own." See Byram, *Teaching and Assessing Intercultural Communicative Competence*, p. 52.

[28]Ibid. (emphasis added).

[29]According to Bennett, those who minimize appeal to two defense mechanisms in particular:

Tolerance for stress is also an important skill in IC aptitude.[30] Any person who dislocates himself or herself from an ethnocentric frame of reference and reorients to a multiperspectival frame of reference is destined to experience psychological stress. The ability to tolerate stress, learn from it, and leverage it for good leads to greater emotional health and intercultural communicative competence.

Finally, *empathy* is integral to improving IC aptitude. It is especially important to intercultural competence because one's ability to act "as if" one is from another culture only helps a person to function in that culture effectively. Ray Leki, former director of the US Peace Corps, goes so far as to say that empathy is the best indicator of success in intercultural situations in overseas contexts.[31] Although empathy comes more naturally to some people than others, intercultural theorists like Robert C. Weigl point out that empathy can also be taught.[32] The goal of empathy development is not to master empathy immediately, but to become incrementally more empathetic.

IC aptitude means one commits to learning skills that enhance effective communication in intercultural situations. A person with IC aptitude is motivated to understand what is appropriate and fitting for a given situation, that is, what is apt in an intercultural context. In addition to commending Byram's four skills—interpreting, relating, discovery, and interaction—I have proposed three additional skills—tolerance for ambiguity, tolerance for stress, and empathy. Although communication theorists commend additional skills besides the ones I have mentioned,

---

physical universalism, which sees human behavior as "mainly innate," and *transcendent universalism*, which appeals to transcultural principles, laws, and imperatives such as, "All of us believe in the same God." See Milton J. Bennett, "A Developmental Approach to Training for Intercultural Sensitivity," *International Journal of Intercultural Relations* 10 (1986): 183, 186.

[30] For two different studies in which the author(s) point(s) to a connection between intercultural competence proficiency and stress tolerance, see Daniel Kealey, "The Challenge of International Personnel Selection," in *Handbook of Intercultural Training*, ed. Dan R. Landis and Rabi S. Bhagat (Thousand Oaks, CA: Sage, 1996), pp. 81-105; and Walter J. Lonner and Susanna A. Hayes, "Understanding the Cognitive and Social Aspects of Intercultural Competence," in *Culture and Competence: Contexts of Life Success*, ed. Robert J. Sternberg and Elena L. Grigorenko (Washington, DC: American Psychological Association, 2004), pp. 89-110.

[31] See Weigl, "Intercultural Competence Through Cultural Self-Study," p. 348. For more on the importance of empathy to intercultural competence, see also Bennett, "A Developmental Approach to Training for Intercultural Sensitivity," p. 185.

[32] Weigl, "Intercultural Competence Through Cultural Self-Study," pp. 347-48, 350.

in my judgment, these seven skills help capture what is involved in IC aptitude attainment.[33]

Action. The third and final dimension of the 3A model is *action*. An IC proficient person performs actions that display an ongoing commitment to negotiating difference effectively. Without a doubt, mistakes happen along the way, and some actions are better and wiser than others. The goal is not perfection but progress. With the understanding that giving and receiving grace and mercy are part of the process, actions are still necessary for the 3A model to be effective. Mindful changes in behavior must take place. Acquisition and aptitude are necessary but not sufficient commitments absent or devoid from accompanying actions.

Action requires a willingness to question and interrogate one's behavior, what William B. Gudykunst calls "behavioral flexibility," as well as initiate respectful behaviors toward those from other cultures.[34] J. Stewart Black, Hal B. Gregersen, and Mark E. Mendenhall also make an important point about behavior modification in intercultural situations. "To be effective in another culture," they write, "people must be interested in other cultures, be sensitive enough to notice cultural differences, and then also be willing to *modify their behavior* as an indication of respect for the people of other cultures."[35] Although curiosity and sensitivity are important, to be effective, one must be willing to alter one's behavior. Changing actions, modifying choices "as an indication of respect" for those who are culturally different, is the expectation.

In their work on cultural intelligence, Earley, Ang, and Tan point out that behavior modification is essential to effective communication in intercultural settings. They see it as a form of intelligence, what they call "behavioral CQ," and they define it as performing the right actions

---

[33]For an overview of the various skills that IC scholars emphasize, see Spitzberg and Changnon, "Conceptualizing Intercultural Competence," pp. 38-41.

[34]Gudykunst maintains that "behavioral flexibility" arises when one is willing to tolerate ambiguity and uncertainty in intercultural interactions. He writes: "The more uncertainty oriented we are, the more likely we are willing to question our own behavior and its appropriateness when communicating with strangers." See Gudykunst, *Bridging Differences*, pp. 116-17.

[35]J. Stewart Black, Hal B. Gregersen, and Mark E. Mendenhall, *Global Assignments: Successfully Expatriating and Repatriating International Managers* (San Francisco: Jossey-Bass, 1992), p. 416 (emphasis added).

in an intercultural situation.[36] The relevant question for this competency is, "Am I able to *do the right thing culturally* in specific situations?"
The focus is on *praxis*: doing the right things in the right ways at the
right times. To develop behavioral CQ, one must be willing to move
from being a curious learner to an active practitioner, especially in
communication. People with high levels of behavioral CQ are able to
observe and adapt: they observe verbal and nonverbal forms of communication that are different from their own culture, and they adapt
their pace, volume, use of silence, pausing, gestures, words, and so on,
in a way that reflects the patterns of the host culture.[37] According to
Early, Ang, and Tan, people with high behavioral CQ are also risk
takers. If they don't know the language of the host culture, they are
willing to try and fail until they succeed at speaking. Biagi and others
use the term "social acting" to describe this sort of behavioral intelligence. Social acting means that one knows how to be a "social actor in
the host culture" in a way in which both parties—the host culture
person and the foreigner acting socially in the host culture—communicate with clarity, ease, and comfort.[38]

Significantly, for Christian preachers, behavior modification out of
respect for different cultures is a recurring theme in Scripture, especially
in the New Testament. For instance, the apostle Paul urges table fellowship between Jews and Gentiles in Galatians 2. According to Luke,
Paul quotes Greek poets on Mars Hill in Acts 17. The quintessential
example of behavior modification for the sake of engagement with other
cultures is Paul's classic statement in 1 Corinthians 9:19-23:

---

[36]They define behavioral CQ as "ability to observe, recognize, regulate, adapt, and act appropriately
in intercultural meetings. A person with high behavioral CQ possesses a wide repertoire of expressions—both verbally and in body language. High behavioral CQ means you are able to pick up
subtle cultural signals from others and adapt to talking with people from other cultures in an easy
and relaxed manner." See Earley, Ang, and Tan, *CQ*, p. 83.

[37]Earley, Ang, and Tan use the word *mimicry* to describe reflecting the host culture. However, they
do not use the word in a pejorative or paternalistic sense. For them, mimicry is much like being a
role-based actor rather than a method actor. A method actor experiences his or her role and tries
to embody the part she's playing with all its emotions, perspectives, and incongruities, whereas a
role-based actor *mimics* the emotions, behaviors, and perspectives of her artistic portrayal without
attempting to embody or live in the role in quite the same way. For the discussion of mimicry and
method acting versus role-based acting, see ibid., p. 36.

[38]Biagi et al., "Reflective Intercultural Competence (RIC) and Its Assessment: The RICA Model,"
p. 62.

> Though I am free and belong to no man, I make myself a slave to everyone, to win as many as possible. To the Jews I became like a Jew, to win the Jews. To those under the law I became like one under the law (though I myself am not under the law), so as to win those under the law. To those not having the law I became like one not having the law (though I am not free from God's law but am under Christ's law), so as to win those not having the law. To the weak I became weak, to win the weak. I have become all things to all men so that by all possible means I might save some. I do all this for the sake of the gospel, that I may share in its blessings. (NIV)

In this passage, Paul arguably indicates his desire to move beyond knowledge acquisition and skill aptitude in order to move toward transgressive action among those who are culturally different. The manner of his behavior is contingent on the company he keeps, whether Jew or Gentile, and his motivation for action is guided by an ongoing commitment to do all things "for the sake of the gospel." Although Paul makes clear that there are some limits vis-à-vis acculturation, such as when he refuses to play the eloquence-and-persuasion game with the Greek rhetoricians (1 Cor 2:1-5), or when he refuses to deny the scandal of the cross itself (1 Cor 1:22-25), he also seems to indicate in 1 Corinthians 9 that he is willing to do anything short of sinning to advance the gospel's cause.

It is important to proceed carefully in regard to this passage of Scripture. Some biblical exegetes misuse 1 Corinthians 9:19-23 as a proof text for radical assimilation into a host culture (e.g., Christians pretending to be Muslims "for the sake of the gospel") or more often as a rationale for pragmatic accommodation. Paul's commentary in 1 Corinthians 9 must be seen in light of its wider context of food sacrificed to idols in the public marketplace. In this chapter, Paul is not so much concerned about custom fitting the gospel itself to the needs of his hearers; he is more concerned about abandoning his personal rights and needs so that the gospel itself will retain its central place among Jew and Gentile alike. He's willing to surrender his rights and decenter himself as an apostle, to become whatever he needs to become, for the sake of the gospel. That's what matters most.[39]

---

[39]Moreau, Campbell, and Greener discuss two common misuses of 1 Corinthians 9:19-23: accom-

Thus Paul's desire to "become all things to all men" is not driven by a gross form of pragmatism in which doing whatever works becomes the be-all and end-all of his apostolic calling and mission. Rather, it his desire to do all things *for the sake of the gospel* that primarily drive his openness to behavior modification.

Such willingness to modify one's behavior for the sake of others and in adherence to a higher goal is a distinctive mark of acting out IC in real-world relationships and situations. Although the reasoning that theorists give for communication across difference may not be as missiologically explicit or gospel-centric as it is in 1 Corinthians 9, it is still laudable. Paul's motivation for action remains instructive for today's Christian preachers, and it is congruent with the tenets of IC theory.

At the micro level, 1 Corinthians 9 is about understanding and reaching people—the desire to understand and reach others on their own terms for their own sake because of Christian love for them and for the gospel. This means that the Christian is called to be the first person to walk across the room and stretch out the hand of friendship to the one who is culturally different. Christian discipleship requires transgressing the borders of difference with those who are other-than-oneself. To appropriate a sentence from the anonymous author of the *Epistle to Diognetus*, a letter written about discipleship, for Christian disciples "every foreign land is to them a fatherland and every fatherland a foreign land."[40]

3A model summary. In summary, the 3A model of intercultural competence involves the dynamic overlap of three essential dimensions or

---

modation (pp. 45-46) and infiltration (p. 265). As to the former, they do not argue against accommodation in mission, but drawing on the wider contextual issues at play in 1 Corinthians 9–11 and Gordon D. Fee's analysis of this passage, they argue against using 1 Corinthians 9:19-23 as the main source of justification for accommodation. On the matter of "infiltration evangelism," they cite the ethical problems with some missionaries who use 1 Corinthians 9 as justification for infiltrating other religious faiths (e.g., Islam) by pretending to espouse them "for the sake of the gospel." For these discussions, see Moreau, Campbell, and Greener, *Effective Intercultural Communication*, pp. 45-46, 265. Cf. also Gordon D. Fee, *The First Epistle to the Corinthians* (Grand Rapids: Zondervan, 1987), pp. 432-33.

[40] *The Epistle to Diognetus*, ed. Lewis Bostock Radford (New York: Society for Promoting Christian Knowledge, 1908), p. 63. See also the appeal to adopting the perspective of the author of *The Epistle to Diognetus* through the social trinitarian development of a "catholic personality" in Judith M. Gundry Volf and Miroslav Volf, *A Spacious Heart: Essays on Identity and Belonging* (Valley Forge, PA: Trinity Press International, 1997), p. 44.

stances: (1) acquiring knowledge through cultural self-study and learning about other cultures (acquisition), (2) developing aptitude through the attainment of specific skills in intercultural communication (aptitude), and (3) interacting meaningfully and respectfully with those who are culturally different (action). Intercultural competence proficiency is born out of the interplay of these dimensions rather than the linear progression from one to another. IC proficiency rises as all three emerge and converge with each other.

Developing intercultural competence is neither fast nor easy. At times, this process can be difficult, especially at the beginning, for it displaces and disrupts a person's unconscious ethnocentrism. Moreover, it requires of the individual a high level of curiosity, motivation, and commitment. It is normal to make mistakes along the way, mistakes that are often painful to oneself and to others. Undoubtedly, mistakes are part of the learning process and are essential to making progress over time. As David Livermore points out, "Nobody behaves flawlessly in cross-cultural interactions. And frankly, the mistakes we make are often the best teachers for improving our CQ [cultural intelligence]."[41] In other words, making mistakes is to be expected; it is part of the process. Learning through trial and error enhances communication effectiveness and cultivates IC proficiency. With that stated, we turn our attention back to Taylor and to the ways he embodied intercultural competence.

GARDNER C. TAYLOR AND THE ACTUALIZATION OF INTERCULTURAL COMPETENCE

In Taylor's life and ministry we witness the actualization of intercultural competence proficiency. His adeptness at intercultural competence can also be traced retrospectively to his early childhood and college influences and can be tracked through observing his commitment to ecumenical partnership during his ministry in New York. His early years growing up in Baton Rouge and later on as a student at Oberlin College

---

[41]David A. Livermore, *The Cultural Intelligence Difference: Master the One Skill You Can't Do Without in Today's Global Economy* (New York: American Management Association, 2011), p. 9. Livermore is a student of the Earley, Ang, and Tan school of intercultural competence. He uses CQ terminology in all his published works on intercultural communication.

in Ohio provided formative training for him to emerge and flourish as an interculturally proficient crossover preacher. He also actualized IC through ecumenical partnership and cooperation during his ministry at Concord in Brooklyn. In addition to showing respect and appreciation for different cultural expressions of Christianity, he built strategic partnerships across racial and cultural divides. After discussing Taylor's childhood influences, college influences, and ecumenical partnerships, I describe the ways in which he demonstrated in his life and ministry all three dimensions of the 3A Model of Intercultural Competence Proficiency—acquisition, aptitude, and action.

Growing up in Baton Rouge. Taylor's childhood in Baton Rouge left an indelible mark on him, and it greatly shaped his openness to people of other races and cultures. Given that he was born only fifty-five years after slavery officially ended and was raised in the Deep South during Jim Crow–era segregation, it is indeed remarkable that Taylor's self-reported earliest interactions with whites were mostly positive. The primary reason: his middle-class neighborhood in Baton Rouge was integrated during a time when southern neighborhoods were almost always segregated. In a 2007 interview, he recounts his family's positive interactions with their nonblack neighbors:

> Now, Baton Rouge was a typically southern city. Though south Louisiana, as you perhaps know, had a shade more openness in race than north Louisiana did. I almost regret saying this, but south Louisiana was mainly Catholic. North Louisiana was mainly Protestant and there was that slight division. I grew up on a street that was really integrated. My family was the only family of color on that block. The Jeromes were Italian on the corner, the Lanes were Cajun on the other corner, Mr. Schwartz was of German background—city surveyor. And it was a good experience. So that *I got early training in race relations*, though it was a southern thing. I wouldn't want to misrepresent that.[42]

In describing his neighborhood, Taylor is neither trying to pretend that every single experience with whites was positive nor implying some sort

---

[42]"Gardner Calvin Taylor: Oral History Memoir, Interview 2," interview by Joel C. Gregory, Baylor University Institute for Oral History, March 17, 2008, p. 2 (emphasis added).

of utopian ideal. During this phase of US history, African Americans were still not allowed to vote, were not given equal pay for equal work, went to segregated schools, and in most cases were not allowed to worship at the same churches as whites. This is why Taylor doesn't want to "misrepresent" the macro-level issues going on in the broader American society, especially in the South. Rather, his self-reported recollections are based on micro-level quotidian interactions between members of his family and their neighbors.

Undoubtedly, his father's public vocation helped their social standing in the community, and it shaped where they were able to live. Recall that Taylor's father, Washington Taylor, was a prominent church pastor in Baton Rouge with both local and state influence. However, after Wash died when Gardner was thirteen years old, his mother became a public school teacher at the segregated school in Baton Rouge. Although they were able to keep their home and remain in the same neighborhood, in Taylor's words, "we were land poor, we had some land but no money and the land was not worth anything back then."[43] Taylor's mother was the family's sole breadwinner. His father's position and influence shaped his growing-up years, but only to a certain extent.

Taylor also had positive recollections of playing with white children in his neighborhood. In a 2007 interview, when Joel C. Gregory asked him whether he had hobbies as a child that contributed to his development and maturation as a person, Taylor offered the following response:

> Well, yes, I played sandlot ball and that kind of thing. . . . And on the commons, we called them, the playground, a vacant lot it was—*there was not discrimination.* I remember white youngsters across the street from my house—I told you about my block—where the Hortons [a white family]— Mr. Horton was a clerk at Welsh and Levy, which was our principal men's store. His boys, Frank, and the other boy, Billy, and I played together. Frank later became a congressman in Rochester, New York, and preaching there, our paths crossed again. I was glad to see him.[44]

---

[43]Gerald Lamont Thomas, *African American Preaching: The Contribution of Dr. Gardner C. Taylor* (New York: Peter Lang, 2004), p. 83.
[44]"Gardner Calvin Taylor: Oral History Memoir, Interview 1," Interview by Joel C. Gregory, Baylor University Institute for Oral History, January 22, 2007, pp. 9-10 (emphasis added).

Later in the same interview, when asked about the attitudes of whites in the South, Taylor answers, "There were always, in the South, people—whites—who had a different attitude about race." Again, he mentions the Hortons as a family that didn't have the "usual attitude about race."[45] They were progressive. Reflecting on the role families like the Hortons had on race relations, Taylor comments, "I don't think blacks . . . could have survived at all—had there not always been some whites who were relatively more open to some sense of justice in the South," a generous account of the conditions in Baton Rouge given the history of oppression in the United States more broadly.[46] From Taylor's vantage point, progressive whites like the Hortons helped to make "life survivable."[47]

It was these personal and familial interactions at the local level that shaped Taylor's perspectives on race and that he casts in a positive light in interviews. Daily interactions were germane to his "early training in race relations." Daily lived experience, what Latin@ theologians refer to as *lo cotidiano*, was integral to shaping the person he became.[48]

Leland College and Oberlin. One experience in particular during Taylor's college years left a lifelong impression on him. We discussed this story briefly in chapter one, but I develop it more fully here. In 1937, when Taylor was nineteen years old, he was hired as a chauffeur for the president of Leland College, the all-black junior college he attended in Baton Rouge. One day, he was driving President Barcoates's car, a 1934 Dodge sedan, along a country road in the town of Baker, thirteen miles outside Baton Rouge. A Ford Model T cut across the highway and caused a massive automobile accident in which his car was included. One man died on the spot. The only two witnesses, Taylor said, were two white men. One was a poor farmer and the other was a man named Jesse Starkey, an oil refinery worker. Here was Taylor, an African American male living in the segregated South in 1937 with one white person dead

---

[45]Ibid., p. 28.
[46]Ibid.
[47]Ibid., p. 29.
[48]Latina *mujerista* theologian Ada María Isasi-Díaz writes: "It is in the lived-experiences of the everyday life of *lo cotidiano* that we relate to God, that we come to know who God is and what God is like." See Ada María Isasi-Díaz, *La Lucha Continues: Mujerista Theology* (Maryknoll, NY: Orbis Books, 2004), p. 51.

and two white witnesses. Taylor recounts: "It was inconceivable then for a white person—we thought, at least—to give accurate, impartial testimony where a black was involved with a white."[49]

To Taylor's surprise and even shock, both men—the farmer and the oil refinery worker—came to the court hearing the next morning and told the exact truth of what happened. They explained to the judge that the fault lay solely with the white driver of the Ford Model T and that Taylor had nothing to do with the accident. If it had happened elsewhere and under different conditions with different witnesses, Taylor recounts, "I would have gone to prison or worse."[50] He was exonerated, and at that moment decided he would no longer pursue his dream of being a lawyer. He opted instead to become a preacher. This life-changing event not only reoriented him toward a different vocational calling; it arguably reshaped his perception of those in the majority culture. We can surmise that it made him more receptive to whites in general. If two white men were willing to advocate for him during a time when such honesty and integrity were rare, perhaps he could become more trusting of those in the majority culture.

From 1937 to 1940, Taylor attended Oberlin School of Theology in Ohio, where he pursued a bachelor of divinity degree. He recounts: "At Oberlin was the first time that I lived in an integrated community without the sharp edges of racism."[51] Only a few African American students attended Oberlin at the time, and most of them were from northern states.[52] Save for one minor incident, Taylor's experiences in race relations were mostly positive.[53]

---

[49]"Gardner Calvin Taylor: Oral History Memoir, Interview 1," pp. 12-13.

[50]Ibid.

[51]"Gardner Calvin Taylor: Oral History Memoir, Interview 2," p. 23. This comment does not discount the positive experiences he had growing up in Baton Rouge. Rather, it is an insight about the majority of students and professors at Oberlin being progressive, open-minded, and integrationist in a way that he had not experienced in the South.

[52]Recall that Taylor was only the third person of African American descent to graduate from the Oberlin School of Theology. See Thomas, *African American Preaching*, p. 89.

[53]Gerald Lamont Thomas describes one incident in which a white friend of Taylor's jokingly raised a question about sacred music and the National Baptist Hymnal after which the professor made a condescending remark. Thomas writes: "But the outspoken Taylor arose and said, 'Class, this comes out of where [we] are; this is [our] background, Professor Johnson!' The instructor did not say it anymore." See ibid.

Because Oberlin had predominantly white students and faculty, its periodicals and books were almost exclusively authored by whites and written for white audiences. Instead of seeing this as an obstacle, Taylor saw it as an opportunity. A voracious reader with a near-photographic memory and an insatiable appetite for growing in the preaching craft, he spent hours in the Oberlin library poring over articles and sermons published in *The Christian Century* and *The Christian Century Pulpit*. In a 2008 interview with Gregory, Taylor recounts:

> I spent a lot of time, Dr. Gregory, a whole lot of time in the Oberlin graduate school theology library, reading sermons. Frederick Norwood, the Australian, Leslie Weatherhead, Joseph Fort Newton, Paul Scherer, Ralph Sockman, Harold Phillips, and so forth, including Howard Thurman and people like that. And I guess, I don't know why I did it, but *I was really interested in their sermons*, it appeared. *The Christian Century* then had the *Christian Century Pulpit*, which was a magazine on homiletics, the sermons from well known preachers, Tunis Garwin in Louisville and people like Clarence Macartney in Pittsburgh and on and on and on. And I read those things, and that didn't do me any harm. I found sometimes in them, something kindred to my own sense of the language and my sense of the gospel. I spent hours and hours in that library during my own leisure time, reading those things, and I got a lot from them.[54]

In an earlier interview with Gregory conducted in 2007, Taylor explains the influences these preachers had on him: "I spent many hours reading the sermons in *The Pulpit*, fascinated by the lives of these preachers. . . . I'm sure a lot of that got in me, and, I'm sure I borrowed a lot." With a touch of good humor, he adds, "Maybe borrowed everything."[55]

Fostering an ecumenical spirit of cooperation in New York. Taylor's years in New York represent another vital step in the actualization of IC proficiency. In a 2008 interview with Gregory, Taylor describes the 1950s and 1960s in New York as a time of great ecumenical cooperation and

---

[54]Emphasis added. Note that the only African American on this list of preachers is Howard Thurman. The rest are white. See "Gardner Calvin Taylor: Oral History Memoir, Interview 2," pp. 23–24.

[55]"Gardner Calvin Taylor: Oral History Memoir, Interview 1," pp. 20–21.

unity. When asked, "What was your role in, or take on, the larger ecumenism of that time?" he answered:

> Well, I was naturally drawn into it—partly because it was a time of broadening. And again, as president of the Council of Churches in Brooklyn, and then president of the Council of Churches of New York. Widely because it was needed. It was time for some black presence at that point, at that level of leadership. And it was a great time . . . there was this widening sense of the unity of the faith. And a favorite saying was, "We can do so much more for the kingdom together than we can separate." That was a favorite saying. It was a good time.[56]

As was mentioned in chapter one, Taylor, throughout his years at Concord, made a habit of building strategic partnerships with nonblack pastors and church leaders in New York and elsewhere.

In 1948, when Taylor came to Concord, it already had five thousand members. The church had a large facility, a proud history, an array of ministry programs, and a track record of progressivism concerning civil rights issues. Concord also had an established tradition of excellent preaching pastors, and Taylor was stepping into "one of the most prestigious pulpits in the country."[57] Early in his ministry there, Taylor established himself as both a prominent preacher and a dedicated political activist. Throughout the second half of the 1950s, Taylor was arrested several times (as were so many) for his participation in civil rights demonstrations that involved picket lines and protests. Ironically, one of his earliest arrests came in a protest against the New York City School Board, the same governing body that he would join a few years later.[58]

At Concord, Taylor also developed a reputation as a pastor committed to ecumenical cooperation. To return to a few examples mentioned in chapter one, there was his invitation to Dr. F. Townley Lord to come be

---

[56]"Gardner Calvin Taylor: Oral History Memoir, Interview 3," interview by Joel C. Gregory, Baylor University Institute for Oral History, March 17, 2008, p. 19.

[57]Timothy George, "Introduction: Honor to Whom Honor Is Due," in *Our Sufficiency Is of God: Essays on Preaching in Honor of Gardner C. Taylor*, ed. Timothy George, James Earl Massey, and Robert Smith Jr. (Macon, GA: Mercer University Press, 2010), p. xiv.

[58]For a description of Taylor's involvement with the Democratic Party of King's County, see WGT 1:5. For the final two quotations, Laura Scott Taylor's assessment and Taylor's commitment to a ministry of influence in the pastorate, see George, "Introduction: Honor to Whom Honor Is Due," p. xv.

the *featured* preacher at Concord's 110th anniversary celebration.[59] He cohosted an outdoor event at Cornerstone Baptist Church, an event that was very important to his friend Sandy Ray, in which Billy Graham was the featured speaker.[60] In the early 1950s, he became the president of the local chapter of the Protestant Council of Churches in Brooklyn and later for the entire New York metropolitan area. In these and other ways, Taylor placed himself at the center of ecumenical cooperation in New York. In many ways, "We can do so much more for the kingdom together than we can separate" was *his* slogan.

   Taylor's approach to ministry and the 3A model. In Taylor's accounts of his childhood experiences, college influences, and ecumenical participation, we see evidence of all three aspects of the 3A Model of Intercultural Competence Proficiency—acquisition, aptitude, and action. Taylor displays knowledge *acquisition* not only during his growing-up years but also as an adult doing ministry in New York. Knowledge acquisition is both abstract and concrete. Taylor acquired abstract knowledge through reading texts like *The Christian Century* and *The Christian Century Pulpit.* In doing so, he developed both a critical and appreciative understanding of preaching traditions outside his own. "I got a lot from them," and "I'm sure a lot of that got in me," were statements he used to describe their influence on his preaching. He also acquired "concrete knowledge" through maintaining healthy, mutually beneficial, reciprocal relationships with whites. Michael Byram refers to concrete knowledge as "procedural knowledge of how to act in specific circumstances."[61] His family maintained strong ties to their nonblack neighbors. He played with white kids like the Hortons on the playground and in the sandlot. He attended Oberlin College, where he was only the third African American to graduate from the School of Divinity. In these settings and others Taylor acquired concrete knowledge about how to act and interact with those in the majority culture. In many respects, he was what Earley, Ang, and Tan call a "cultural strategic thinker."[62] He was open to learning

---

[59]"Concord to Mark 110th Anniversary," *NYAN*, May 4, 1957, p. 20.
[60]For more on this significant event in the history of Brooklyn, see "Billy Graham: Heaven Won't Let Racists In," *NYAN*, July 20, 1957, p. 9.
[61]See Byram, *Teaching and Assessing Intercultural Communicative Competence*, p. 23.
[62]Earley, Ang, and Tan, *CQ*, p. 51.

from different cultures and could learn quickly, he developed effective strategies for acquiring knowledge, and he was able to problem solve in intercultural situations.

We have less evidence in Taylor's childhood and college years of cultural self-study, but this does not mean he was unreflective concerning his own cultural biases. We simply don't have the documentation to prove it. What can be demonstrated is that Taylor was at one and the same time proud to be black and reticent to let narrow definitions of blackness circumscribe him. On the one hand, he displayed his commitment to black preaching and to its history through giving lectures at Duke University like "The Preaching of the Black Patriarchs" (1978) and writing the foreword for *Preaching with Sacred Fire*, a resource on the history of African American preaching.[63] On the other hand, he resisted any depictions of blackness narrowly defined. As Taylor himself states, "Our culture is a given; we are all children and products of it. But having said that, culture is not a prison. It does not have to restrict us. It does not have to circumscribe us."[64]

In addition to knowledge acquisition, Taylor also displayed IC *aptitude*. He was motivated to learn the appropriate skills for enhancing communication in intercultural situations. Clearly, Taylor was motivated to learn from preaching traditions that were unfamiliar to him. He went to Oberlin College instead of Morehouse or Howard, two historically black colleges. While at Oberlin, he spent long hours in the library poring over sermons by white preachers. Before delivering the prestigious centennial anniversary Beecher lectures at Yale, Taylor both read and studied the previous ninety-nine lectures. Then, he presented *his* lectures completely from memory. One would be hard pressed to question Taylor's motivation to learn from traditions outside his own.

Aptitude involves obtaining skills that are fitting, suitable, and appropriate to the given situation. Instead of focusing on whether or not Taylor displayed the seven specific skills I listed in my section on ap-

---

[63]For the 1978 lectures at Duke titled, "The Preaching of the Black Patriarchs," see WGT 5:197-218. See also Taylor's foreword in Martha J. Simmons and Frank A. Thomas, eds., *Preaching with Sacred Fire: An Anthology of African American Sermons, 1750 to the Present* (New York: W. W. Norton, 2010).

[64]WGT 5:53.

titude—a list that is meant to be suggestive rather than exhaustive—I will focus on the ways that his study habits and preaching practices demonstrate that he obtained skills in intercultural communication. Recall that Taylor's multicultural neighborhood in Baton Rouge was the place where, he says, "I got early training in race relations."[65] Although some of his skills in IC aptitude go back to his childhood in Baton Rouge, in many ways his days at Oberlin were a turning point.

In his book *African American Preaching: The Contribution of Gardner C. Taylor*, Gerald Lamont Thomas suggests that Taylor's student days at Oberlin were critical to his obtainment of IC aptitude. Thomas doesn't use the language of intercultural competence or aptitude. He opts rather for the language of translation:

> Throughout his theological training, Taylor demonstrated an uncanny ability to "translate" and adapt each professor's lectures into his own context as a black person. Taylor posited [in a telephone interview], "I do not know how I did it, but I did, and it served me well." Thus, in later years, he was able to take European religious thought and see it in its context almost without thinking about it.[66]

According to Thomas, Taylor was able to absorb, appropriate, and translate what he learned from white professors. At one and the same time, he could function effectively in the majority context while adapting what he learned for his own context. Thomas calls this skill "translation," and he suggests that at Oberlin Taylor exhibited this protean capacity across different contexts.

If we use intercultural competence terminology, Milton J. Bennett refers to this level of IC aptitude as "integration." An integrated person is "one who can construe differences as processes, who can adapt to those differences, and who can additionally construe him or herself in various cultural ways."[67] Those who excel at integration can "construe their identities at the margins of two or more cultures and central to none."[68] As early as his student days at Oberlin, Taylor

---

[65]"Gardner Calvin Taylor: Oral History Memoir, Interview 2," p. 2.
[66]Thomas, *African American Preaching*, p. 89.
[67]Bennett, "A Developmental Approach to Training for Intercultural Sensitivity," p. 186.
[68]Mitchell R. Hammer, Milton J. Bennett, and Richard Wiseman, "Measuring Intercultural Sen-

shows an ability to obtain skills for communicating what is fitting, appropriate, and suitable to his own context and to white majority contexts. He knows how to communicate what is apt for a given intercultural situation.

Finally, Taylor demonstrates transgressive *action*, the third dimension of the 3A Model of Intercultural Competence Proficiency. In chapter one, we observed the various ways that Taylor committed himself to action by crossing over borders of difference. A person who is committed to action has an ongoing commitment to negotiating difference effectively and is willing to transgress boundaries, to show respect for and engagement with people from other cultures. A person who can modify behavior knows how to perform "social acting in the host culture."[69] A social actor functions improvisationally with respect to contextual and cultural difference: he or she knows how to act effectively in his or her own context and in the majority culture context, what Biagi and others refer to as C2 (the host culture).[70]

Taylor was an effective "social actor in the host culture" as far back as his childhood days in Baton Rouge, and he displayed an ongoing commitment to transgressing the borders of difference throughout his lifetime. This commitment continued through his days at Oberlin College and matured through his days as a pastor in Brooklyn. Like the apostle Paul, Taylor modified his behavior for the sake of those who were culturally different and for the sake of those in his own context, in a sense becoming a Jew to win the Jews and becoming a Gentile to win the Gentiles. To use Gudykunst's term, Taylor was adept at "behavioral flexibility."[71]

The signs that Taylor committed himself to transgressive action during the New York phase of his ministry are many. In addition to the examples I have mentioned, recall that Taylor also preached radio sermons

---

sitivity: The Intercultural Development Inventory," *International Journal of Intercultural Relations* 27 (2003): 425.

[69]Biagi et al., "Reflective Intercultural Competence (RIC) and Its Assessment: The RICA Model," p. 62.

[70]Ibid. For an account of how C2 functions in the leadership of Christian organizations, see Bryan Loritts, *Right Color, Wrong Culture: The Type of Leader Your Organization Needs to Become Multiethnic* (Chicago: Moody Press, 2014).

[71]Gudykunst, *Bridging Differences*, pp. 116-17.

for NBC. Through radio preaching, he befriended the likes of Paul Scherer, Ralph Sockman, and George Buttrick. Moreover, he was ecumenically minded. Ecumenical cooperation remained at the forefront of his approach to ministry in New York, and his reputation and influence expanded on account of it.

To summarize, Taylor's childhood experiences, college years, and ministry in New York reveal a commitment to all three dynamics of the 3A model of acquisition, aptitude, and action. Taylor displays a significant commitment to acquiring knowledge of other cultures, in this instance the dominant majority culture. He demonstrates aptitude, first on account of his high level of motivation and second by learning the skills required for fitting and appropriate crosscultural communication in a given situation. Finally, he *acts* improvisationally in C2, the host culture. By modifying his behavior, he consistently demonstrates an ability to be improvisationally and interculturally proficient when interacting in majority-culture settings. Taylor's ability to acquire knowledge, demonstrate aptitude, and modify his actions starts in Baton Rouge, develops significantly at Oberlin, and comes to maturation through his commitment to ecumenism in New York.

INTERCULTURAL COMPETENCE: BIBLICAL AND THEOLOGICAL RATIONALE

Now that it has been established that Taylor was IC proficient, in this section, I provide a biblical and theological rationale for intercultural competence as a theologically authorized proficiency. As an evangelical, it is natural for me to start by offering the reader a biblical rationale, although it will become apparent that there is significant overlap between my biblical and theological arguments.

Biblical and theological rationale. The biblical rationale for intercultural proficiency is somewhat straightforward. The gospel is inherently intercultural and inclusive. Although it would not be difficult to uncover instances of ethnocentrism in the Old Testament and New Testament that seem to counteract God's commitment to ethno-inclusivity, there are also strands of the tradition that are more prevalent than these, ones that emphasize God's larger vision of shalom as not only intrarelational but interrelational.[72] My broader concern is not with specific instances of human sinfulness and exclusion but with larger patterns of belief and action.

Throughout the Old Testament, God demonstrates a commitment to helping the people of God move toward cultural others while still maintaining their distinctiveness. One of the reasons Israel is forbidden from mistreating or oppressing aliens and strangers who live among them is that they were once "aliens in the land of Egypt" (Ex 22:21). In other words, by remembering their own foreignness, they remember how to treat foreigners among them.[73] In the book of Jonah, God confronts the prophet's sinful, racist, and ethnocentric antagonism toward the Ninevites and compels him to transgress these boundaries by reminding him

---

[72]For instance, Old Testament scholar Bruce C. Birch acknowledges, "In the modern church there are particular moral objections to the pervasive patriarchy and acceptance of slavery, as well as to frequent expression of ethnocentrism in the Old Testament. None of these are without contrary moral witness in the Old Testament, but the presence of such objectionable perspectives must be acknowledged rather than avoided." See Bruce C. Birch, *Let Justice Roll Down: The Old Testament, Ethics, and Christian Life* (Louisville: Westminster John Knox, 1991), p. 43. For more on ethnocentrism and the challenges associated with it in ancient Israel and in the Hebrew Bible, see Kenton L. Sparks, *Ethnicity and Identity: Prolegomena to the Study of Ethnic Sentiments and Their Expression in the Hebrew Bible* (Winona Lake, IN: Eisenbrauns, 1998); Lawrence M. Wills, *Not God's People: Insiders and Outsiders in the Biblical World* (Lanham, MD: Rowman & Littlefield, 2008); and Brian P. Rainey, "Non-Peoples and Foolish Nations: Xenophobia and Ethnic Foreigners in the Hebrew Bible and Mesopotamia" (PhD diss., Brown University, 2014). For general treatments of race and ethnicity in the Bible, see Mark Brett, ed., *Ethnicity in the Bible* (Leiden, Brill, 1996); and J. Daniel Hays, *From Every People and Nation: A Biblical Theology of Race* (Downers Grove, IL: InterVarsity Press, 2003).

[73]Coming to terms with the self-as-foreigner à la Ricoeur or (J. Kameron) Carter has many benefits, such as the repudiation of racial reification, the recognition of one's interdependence with others, and the renewal of compassion toward those who are seen as culturally foreign others. That stated, not every situation demands perennial reflection as to the foreignness in one's own constitution. For instance, Frank H. Wu points out that the challenge for many Asian Americans is that they are perceived as "perpetual foreigners" even if they are second-, third-, or fourth-generation Americans. In this instance, dwelling on the foreignness of one's own constitution may in fact accomplish the opposite result. Instead of repudiating reification, recognizing interdependence, and renewing compassion, it subjects the person or persons to a form of what Rey Chow calls "coercive mimeticism." Gale E. Yee describes Chow's understanding of coercive mimeticism as follows: a form of oppression in which "racial/ethnic persons are expected to resemble and replicate certain socially endorsed preconceptions about them, and in doing so, authenticate the familiar descriptions of them as ethnics." For Wu's discussion of the label "perpetual foreigner" and its problematic implications when applied to Asian Americans, see Frank H. Wu, *Yellow: Race in America Beyond Black and White* (New York: Basic Books, 2002), pp. 17-18, 79-129. For Yee's discussion of coercive mimeticism, see Gale A. Yee, "Yin/Yang Is Not Me: An Exploration into an Asian American Biblical Hermeneutics," in *Ways of Being, Ways of Reading: Asian American Biblical Interpretation*, ed. Mary F. Foskett and Jeffrey K. Kuan (St. Louis: Chalice, 2006), p. 154. For Chow's discussion of "coercive mimeticism," see Rey Chow, *The Protestant Ethnic & the Spirit of Capitalism* (New York: Columbia University Press, 2002), pp. 95-127.

of God's compassionate concern for the irreligious. "Should I not be concerned about Nineveh, that great city . . . ?" the Lord asks Jonah (Jon 4:11). Another way to ask the same question might be, "Are the Ninevites not also image-bearing creatures whom I also made, Jonah?" In several ways, the book of Jonah is a satirical and prophetic commentary against an ethnocentric vantage point. Why would God's prophet be more concerned about a plant than he was about a whole city whose inhabitants do not know Yahweh? Further, in the book of Amos, the Lord rebukes Israel for feigning cultural superiority or being isolationist by saying: "Are you not like the Ethiopians to me? . . . Did I not bring Israel up from the land of Egypt, and the Philistines from Caphtor and the Arameans from Kir?" (Amos 9:7).

Another significant pattern in the Old Testament takes place in the Psalms. The Lord makes a persistent call to Israel to extend God's praises to the nations. The Psalms show us that divine praise is not for Israel alone but for all who come to Yahweh in faith. The good news of God's reign is offered to all. Here are three concrete examples:

> Declare his glory among the nations,
>   his marvelous deeds among all the peoples. (Ps 96:3)

> Say among the nations, "The LORD is king!
>   The world is firmly established, it shall never be moved.
> He will judge the peoples with equity." (Ps 96:10)

> Praise the LORD, all you nations!
>   Extol him, all you peoples!
> For great is his love toward us,
>   and the faithfulness of the LORD endures forever.
> Praise the LORD! (Ps 117)

In the first two examples, God summons Israel to extend divine praise to the nations around them. Notice that, in the third example, however, the *nations* are summoned to praise Yahweh, and Israel is charged to offer witness to God's חֶסֶד, that is, to God's "steadfast love." Commenting on the connection in Psalm 117 between the command for the nations to praise Yahweh and Israel's testimony to God's חֶסֶד, Old Testament scholar Walter Brueggemann writes: "Israel is able to notice, even in its doxological intensity, that the reality of Yahweh's *hesed* is not an Israelite possession, but it is a gift of Yahweh for all of Yahweh's creatures."[74]

A third pattern in the Old Testament is that God's vision for shalom is not offered solely to those within Israel's borders. At various points, the offer of shalom (present or future) is extended to the other nations with whom Israel comes into contact. God is not just the God of Israel; God is the God of everyone else. Although God makes a particular commitment to a particular people, the nation of Israel, and calls this people to a radical adherence to monotheism and a perennial rejection of syncretism, God's vision is also for Israel to engage the nations rather than escape from them.[75] In the eschatological visions of the prophets, it is not just Israel but also "the peoples" who gather around the mountain of the Lord (Mic 4:1) and worship the Son of Man (Dan 7:14).

While the Old Testament bears witness to Israel's struggles and failures to be ethno-inclusive rather than ethnocentric, it also bears witness to God's commitment to shalom for all peoples and for the nations to join in praise of Yahweh. The point here is simple: crossing borders comes naturally to those who, like God, have a heart for shalom to come to all peoples. To quote again from Brueggemann, "The horizon of 'the gospel' in the Old Testament is not confined to Israel, but looks well beyond Israel to the larger horizon of Yahweh's rule."[76] God calls a particular people to a peculiar monotheism in a pagan world so that they can bring divine praise to all people.

The New Testament also provides a vision of intercultural border crossing. In many ways, it is more radical in its inclusivity than the Old Testament, though, like the Old Testament tradition, there are ethnocentric strands within the New Testament tradition that should not be ignored. In his hometown of Nazareth, Jesus warns against the dangers

---

[74]Walter Brueggemann, *Cadences of Home: Preaching Among Exiles* (Louisville: Westminster John Knox, 1997), p. 83.

[75]Commenting on the charge from God in Jeremiah 29:7 for Israel to "seek the welfare of the city" of Babylon even during its exilic captivity, Brueggemann writes: "There is for Israel no 'separate peace,' no 'private welfare' by withdrawal from the world of international reality. . . . [Jeremiah 29:7] is an insistence that Israel is a member of a larger community of nations over which Yahweh rules. Israel's future is in the midst of a Yahweh-practicing world community and not apart from it" (ibid., p. 90).

[76]Ibid.

of ethnic exceptionalism when he reminds those listening to him in the synagogue that Elijah was sent to a widow in Zarephath and Elisha healed Naaman the Syrian (Lk 4:25-27). This was a vision for transgressing cultural difference that his listeners were unwilling to accept at the time. As a consequence of this, when Jesus' public ministry unfolds, many of his social decisions bear witness to his commitment to a refusal to let the so-called ethnic or social other remain an outsider: dinner at Zacchaeus's house, drawing water alongside a Samaritan woman, healing the sick in the synagogue, and welcoming children. As Peter C. Phan observes, Jesus demonstrates through his choices that he is the quintessential border crosser.[77]

Even the crucifixion scene in the Gospels shows us the ways that Jesus opens wide his arms to people as different as male *and* female disciples who follow him, Roman soldiers who confess him, religious priests who reject him, and common criminals beside him. Even more significant, by opening wide his arms of welcome to include all people who confess faith in him, Jesus compels Christians to open wide our arms to those who are other-than-us. As Miroslav Volf puts it, "We who have been embraced by the outstretched arms of the crucified God open our arms even for the enemies—to make space in ourselves for them and invite them in."[78]

Eschatological visions are also significant to the New Testament witness to ethno-inclusivity. Unity in diversity is found in the heavenly vision of Revelation 7:9, which reads: "After this I looked, and there was a great multitude that no one could count, from every nation, from *all tribes and peoples and languages*, standing before the throne and before

---

[77]Phan writes: "A border crosser at the very roots of his being, Jesus performed his ministry of announcing and ushering in the kingdom of God always at the places where borders meet and hence at the margins of the two worlds separated by their borders. . . . He crossed these borders back and forth, repeatedly and freely, whether geographical, racial, sexual, social, economic, political, cultural, or religious. What is new about his message about the kingdom of God, which is good news to some and a scandal to others, is that for him it removes all borders, both natural and manmade, as barriers and is absolutely all-inclusive. Jews and non-Jews, men and women, the old and the young, the rich and the poor, the powerful and the weak, the healthy and the sick, the clean and the impure, the righteous and the sinners, and any other imaginable categories of peoples and groups—Jesus invited them all to enter into the house of his merciful and forgiving Father." See Peter C. Phan, *In Our Own Tongues: Perspectives from Asia on Mission and Inculturation* (Maryknoll, NY: Orbis Books, 2003), p. 148.

[78]Miroslav Volf, *Exclusion and Embrace: A Theological Exploration of Identity, Otherness, and Reconciliation* (Nashville: Abingdon, 1996), p. 131.

the Lamb, robed in white, with palm branches in their hands" (cf. also Acts 2:5; Rev 5:9).

Finally, recount Paul's commitment to what Gudykunst describes as "behavioral flexibility." His *behavior* is contingent on the company he keeps, Jew or Gentile, and his motivation for action is guided by a commitment to do all things "for the sake of the gospel" (1 Cor 9:19-23). The gospel is the driving force behind Paul's insistence on behavior modification, a gospel that is inherently intercultural and inclusivist. Everything Paul does is centered on and "for the sake of" gospel fidelity.

In addition to the resources available in Scripture, systematic theology also provides spaces for intercultural proficiency to find support. These spaces are better understood as theological stances, and they are the stances of decentering and gospel-centricity.

Decentering the center. Decentering the self is a concept with broad currency in a number of academic disciplines. In psychology, Lawrence Kohlberg and others argue that decentering is a sign that one is moving toward advanced stages of mental development.[79] In communication theory, Wilma Melde contends that decentering is critical to understanding and engaging with other cultures.[80] In intercultural competence theory, Hammer, Bennett, and Wiseman depict decentering as a steady movement from ethnocentrism to ethno-relativism.[81] For Bennett in particular, decentering means becoming ethno-relative in one's orientation.[82] In philosophy, the language of decentering figures

---

[79]Lawrence Kohlberg, Charles Levine, and Alexandra Hewer, *Moral Stages: A Current Formulation and a Response to Critics: Contributions to Human Development* (Basel, Switzerland: Karger, 1983), as cited in Byram, *Teaching and Assessing Intercultural Communicative Competence*, p. 34.

[80]Wilma Melde, *Zur Integration von Landeskunde und Kommunikation im Fremdsprachenunterricht* (Tübingen: Gunter Narr Verlag, 1987), as cited in Byram, *Teaching and Assessing Intercultural Communicative Competence*, p. 34.

[81]Hammer, Bennett, and Wiseman, "Measuring Intercultural Sensitivity: The Intercultural Development Inventory," p. 424.

[82]Bennett gets more specific as to what he means by both terms, *ethnocentrism* and *ethnorelativism*. He defines *ethnocentrism* as referring to "the experience of one's own culture as 'central to reality' . . . the beliefs and behaviors that people receive in their primary socialization are unquestioned; they are experienced as 'just the way things are.'" He defines the opposite extreme, *ethnorelativism*, as "the experience of one's own beliefs and behaviors as just one organization of reality among many viable possibilities." See Milton J. Bennett, "Becoming Interculturally Competent," in *Toward Multiculturalism: A Reader in Multicultural Education*, ed. Jaime S. Wurzel (Newton, MA: Intercultural Resource Corporation, 2004), pp. 62-77.

prominently in the work of Emmanuel Lévinas, especially in his emphasis on "ceding our place."[83] Lévinas calls for an abrogation of egocentricity. The French phrase he uses to describe this abrogation is *après-vous* ("after you"). He writes:

> But in sum, the true, incontestable value, about which it is not ridiculous to think, is holiness. This is not a matter of privations, but it is in the certitude that one must yield to the other the first place in everything, from the *après vous* before an open door right up to the disposition—hardly possible, but holiness demands it—to die for the other.[84]

Lévinas's argument here (and in other publications) is that encounter with others necessarily involves "ceding our place," the precursor to holiness. In a Lévinasian framework, one's relationship to the other is asymmetrical in favor of the other. To use Hans-Georg Gadamer's language, but to appropriate it for the Lévinasian framework, the other's horizon eclipses one's own.[85] For Lévinas as opposed to Gadamer, however, the "horizon" of the self remains constant, whereas the horizon of the other breaks in and disrupts it—it eclipses it.[86] Just as the polite person invites the other to walk through the door first by invoking the phrase *après-vous*, likewise, any human being—philosopher or otherwise—cedes his or her place by inviting the other to occupy the central place. One "yield[s] to the other the first place in everything." In this act, the self is "erased" or abrogated. Although the language of erasure is somewhat problematic, a theme Paul Ricoeur discusses in his critique of Lévinas, the overall point remains salient to the discussion at hand.[87] To

---

[83]Lévinas, *Is It Righteous to Be?*, p. 19.

[84]See ibid., p. 47. The language of decentering the center is also used in Uma Narayan and Sandra Harding, eds., *Decentering the Center: Philosophy for a Multicultural, Postcolonial, and Feminist World* (Bloomington: Indiana University Press, 2000).

[85]Hans-Georg Gadamer writes: "A horizon is not a rigid boundary but something that moves with one and invites one to advance further.... For everything that is given as existent is given in terms of a world and hence brings the world horizon." See Hans-Georg Gadamer, *Truth and Method* (New York: Continuum, 2006), p. 239.

[86]In this regard, Lévinas marks himself out from Gadamer, Paul Ricoeur, and Gabriel Marcel in that he foregrounds exteriority over interiority.

[87]In *Oneself as Another*, Paul Ricoeur challenges the foregrounding of exteriority in Lévinas's work, whether it comes through the language of erasure, self-abrogation, or exteriority over interiority. Ricoeur asks the all-important philosophical question, "If my identity were to lose all importance in every respect, would not the question of others also cease to matter?" Ricoeur's main concern

make a relational-intercultural commitment, that is, to cultivate inter-cultural competence proficiency in relationship, one also makes a philosophical-theological commitment to cede one's place to the other. *Après-vous* is the theological orientation, attitudinal posture, and behav-ioral commitment of the one who cedes his place so that the other might have "the first place in everything."

In systematic theology, decentering figures prominently in Miroslav Volf's discussion of Christology. In *Exclusion and Embrace*, Volf empha-sizes decentering the self-as-center in order to move toward Jesus-Christ-as-center. In so doing, the self is released from its imprisonment as the primary point of reference. As *mujerista* theologian Ada María Isasi-Díaz reminds us, "we must stop making ourselves the point of reference."[88] Volf agrees. When one chooses to "decenter the center," one is set free to allow Christ to occupy his rightful place: the central place. Volf writes:

> The self is both "de-centered" and "re-centered" by one and the same process, by participating in the death and resurrection of Christ through faith and baptism. . . . The center of the self—a center that is both inside and outside—is the story of Jesus Christ, which has become the story of the self. More precisely, *the center is Jesus Christ* crucified and resurrected who has become part and parcel of the very structure itself.[89]

"Without such centeredness," Volf argues, "it would be impossible either to denounce the practice of exclusion or demand the practice of embrace."[90] Through decentering the self-as-center and moving toward Christ-as-center, one creates space for Christ to occupy the central place; moreover, one creates space to acknowledge the other's presence and heed the other's call. *Imitatio Christi* demands the exercise of one's kenotic, self-donating responsibility through ceding the place of honor

---

here is that Lévinas's logic of self-abrogation leads to a distortion of the self and a distortion of the other. When the self is erased or abrogated, Ricoeur asks, how can the other be maintained? If there is no longer a self to receive the other, how can the other be received? In short, Ricoeur fears that Lévinas is advocating for a sort of self-humiliation through abrogation. For this critique, see Paul Ricoeur, *Oneself as Another* (Chicago: University of Chicago Press, 1992), pp. 16, 139.

[88] For an overview of *mujerista* theology, see Isasi-Díaz, *La Lucha Continues*, p. 80.

[89] See Volf, *Exclusion and Embrace*, p. 70. Emphasis added.

[90] Ibid., p. 47.

and permitting the other (rather than the self) to occupy a place of distinction. Such a move leads to dependence and interdependence: confessing one's dependence on Christ-as-center and recognizing one's interdependence with the other. As to the latter necessity, Gardner Taylor reminds us: "We are not here to be merely self-reliant people. . . . Too much emphasis on self-reliance is foolishness, for we are meant to be interdependent, not independent. We are members one of another."[91]

In a 2006 interview with Joel C. Gregory, Taylor talks about decentering, though he does not use the same language. Rather, he discusses the importance of escaping what he describes as the "boundaries of culture." In this interview, Taylor states that he was glad to go to New York when he did (in 1948) because "the whole society was beginning to escape the confinements of culture, of color."[92] He also describes his affinity for crossover preachers: "I've known preachers . . . who have escaped the boundaries of habitation, who are able to address people with the gospel that does not belong to an ethnic dimension." He continues:

> But, it's difficult to get out of the confines of culture. And, of course, the Christian faith has always been a struggle of the faith baptized in the culture or the culture baptized in the faith from the very beginning. I think it comes out in preaching. I mentioned Scherer. I think Scherer had escaped the boundaries of culture. I think on the other side, Howard Thurman to some extent, Martin King, surely, had escaped the boundaries of their culture because many of us cannot preach outside the box.[93]

Note that Taylor describes improvisational-intercultural proficiency as an escape from "the boundaries of habitation," a transgression of boundaries in one's own culture in order to reach those in another culture. In many ways, this is what it means to move from ethnocentrism to ethnorelativism per Bennett, to cede one's place per Lévinas, and to decenter-to-recenter per Volf. While no one is truly able to escape culture-as-ecology, culture-as-enclosure is a different species. Taylor is committed to the rupture of enclosure, a theme we touched on in chapter three, what he describes here as the "boundaries" and "confinement" of culture. De-

---

[91]WGT 1:58.
[92]Gardner C. Taylor, personal interview by Joel C. Gregory, September 2006.
[93]See ibid.

centering displaces culture-as-enclosure and replaces it with culture-as-negotiation-and-transgression.

Notice also that Taylor lifts up the names of preachers who have influenced him: Paul Scherer, a white Lutheran preacher who was able to "escape," a person whom he describes earlier in the interview as his "preaching idol."[94] This means that one does not need to be a member of a minoritzed or racialized community to be a crossover preacher. A majority-culture preacher can be a crossover preacher as well. Taylor also mentions Martin Luther King Jr. and Howard Thurman, two African American preachers who were also able to "escape" the boundaries and confinements of their own culture. Both of these preachers negotiated difference through performative, metaphorical, improvisation-as-intercultural-negotiation. Taylor is too modest to include himself. However, the data throughout this book, in chapter one especially, support the claim that he belongs just as much on this list as the names that he mentions.

Gospel-centricity. The second theological stance is gospel-centricity, that is, a refusal to background the gospel so as to foreground a cultural identity marker. We saw in chapter three that Taylor believes cultural markers such as blackness can be either helpful or harmful depending on their function in relation to the gospel. Taylor's litmus test for whether a cultural marker is helpful or hurtful can be stated in the form of a question: *Does the cultural marker (e.g., blackness) situate itself around the gospel-as-center, or does it enclose the gospel and dislocate it from its central place—a move that risks being idolatrous?* Another way to state the same question might be, *Does the cultural marker orbit around the gospel or does the gospel orbit around the cultural marker, even if one's understanding and*

---

[94] In reflecting on Scherer's influence on him as a preaching idol, mentor, and personal friend, Taylor comments: "I sometimes find it hard to confess this, but I will here. I came out of my own background with that peculiar angle of vision which belongs to minorities born sometimes out of a twisting, a distortion of the gospel—let us face it—but also an authentic angle of vision growing out of experience, out of inherited experience. And with that goes, and with any minority people, a certain imaginativeness. The Irish have it, blacks have it, sometimes, my God, warped and distorted and bent out of shape. I was embarrassed, that would not be too strong a word, at what was natural to me. Paul Scherer, who came out of a Lutheran background (I do not know how he came by it), but I heard in his preaching something of what was native to me. And, it was a great release for me because when I went to Oberlin—and there was great, reverent scholarship, no question about it—but it was all a bleaching out of my background" (ibid.).

articulation of the gospel is culturally conditioned per Newbigin? Of course, Taylor's answer is the former rather than the latter, and I believe his theological commitment to *gospel-centricity* is one of the key reasons he excels at intercultural competence.

In being gospel-centric, I do not believe Taylor is employing a kernel-husk hermeneutic in which the timeless truths of the gospel (kernels) are somehow extracted out from culturally conditioned texts (husks). To say that Taylor is gospel-centric *does not* mean that he is beholden to a binary understanding of gospel and culture in which one's articulation of the gospel is somehow atemporal or unsituated. Rather, for Taylor, the gospel's significance extends beyond the historic first-century formulation of the confession that Jesus is Lord to the event of gospel proclamation. The question *Does the gospel revolve around the cultural marker or the cultural marker revolve around the Gospel?* is not a kernel-husk question designed to differentiate the culture-bound from the cultureless; instead, it is a question of foregrounding versus backgrounding. A more nuanced way to ask the same question might be, *Which of these two commitments should be foregrounded rather than backgrounded: identification with a contemporary cultural marker, or participation in the historic confession, ecclesial experience, and contemporary expression of the gospel tradition in all of its expansiveness?* For Taylor, the obvious answer is the latter.

Taylor's commitment to gospel-centricity is guided both by his interpretation of Scripture and by his doctrinal convictions concerning the incarnation and its implications for preaching. The main passage of Scripture that guides him is 1 Corinthians 9:19-23. Recall that the apostle Paul states in this text that he is willing to become a Jew to the Jew, a Gentile to the Gentile, one under the law to those under the law, and weak to the weak if, by his actions and by God's grace, people will come to salvation in Jesus Christ. In fact, Paul goes so far as to say "I have become all things to all people, that I might by all means save some" (1 Cor 9:22). The word *become* is repeated five times in this passage. Paul is up front about his willingness to *become* X or Y so that the gospel might go forth and the people of Corinth might come to know the God of the gospel.

In his opening lecture at the 1976 Beecher Lectures at Yale, Taylor draws on 1 Corinthians 9 as a passage that calls on the preacher to *become* those to whom she preaches. Take note especially of the example Taylor gives from the theater as well as the connection he makes between preaching and 1 Corinthians 9:23-24:

> When José Ferrer played Iago to Paul Robeson's Othello and Uta Hagen's Desdemona, the gifted Puerto Rican actor said that he found an acting method by which he could move easily and effectively from [the] role of one posing as Othello's friend to the role of one posing as Othello's enemy. Ferrer said that when his part called for him to appear to be Othello's friend, he actually became Othello's friend. When he was to appear as enemy, he actually became an enemy. This is empathy, and for the preacher, empathy must occur at a deeper level, since he or she is truly and crucially participant in the grandeur and sordidness of human experience. *Such a one must become those to whom he or she preaches.* It was not empty rhetoric but a part of the basic formula for his enduring immortality as a preacher which made Paul cry, "To the weak became I as weak, that I might gain the weak: I am made all things to all men, that I might by all means save some. And this I do for the gospel's sake, that I might be partaker thereof with you."[95]

Preaching that is empathetic "enters, actually or vicariously, into the plight and circumstances of human hope and heartbreak."[96] Empathy at a deeper level involves becoming like "those to whom he or she preaches." The preacher who enters into the hope and heartbreak of the human condition does not do so in a manipulative sense. Becoming all things to all people is not another way of advocating a crude form of pragmatism. Preachers are not called to "do whatever works" in order to get the results desired, as is often the case with some megachurch movements in evangelicalism. Rather, Taylor's two main motivations for becoming all things to all people are grounded in love for people and commitment to the gospel.

---

[95] This quotation is originally from the lecture "Recognizing and Removing the Presumptuousness of Preaching," the first of the Beecher Lectures delivered at Yale in 1976. The lectures were published originally in Gardner C. Taylor, *How Shall They Preach? The Lyman Beecher Lectures and Five Lenten Sermons* (Elgin, IL: Progressive Baptist Publishing House, 1977). They were republished in WGT. For the above quotation, see WGT 5:155-56 (emphasis added).

[96] WGT 5:155.

The first motivation, love for people, arises out of Taylor's concern for pastoral care. He believes the preacher is called to actual and vicarious identification with human frailty and brokenness. In the same lecture, Taylor reminds preachers that they must come to terms with this irony in proclamation: "the person who preaches is in need himself or herself of the message which the preacher believes he or she is ordained to utter."[97] Both clergy and laity stand under the same judgment and receive the same mercy from God. That is to say, the preacher is a cotraveler, a fellow pilgrim; like everyone else, a beggar telling other beggars where to find a loaf of bread. He or she makes claims for God to others while also being claimed by God with others. In entering into the frailty of the human condition and through empathetically "becoming" like those to whom one is called to serve, the preacher demonstrates love and pastoral care; concurrently, he or she identifies with God's people in solidarity as fellow human beings, as coparticipants in the human journey.

The second motivation, commitment to the gospel, is an even stronger impetus for becoming all things to all people. The apostle Paul's primary concern in 1 Corinthians 9 is not with getting results or finding the right gimmicks, some sort of crude form of pragmatism; rather, it is rooted in his concern to privilege the gospel as superseding individual rights and self-centered behaviors. Paul is willing to surrender his rights as an apostle, becoming like a Jew to the Jews and a Greek to the Greeks, if it means that the gospel will go forth in power. So also the "stronger brothers" must be willing to surrender their so-called rights to eat meat sacrificed to idols in favor of the "weaker brothers" if it means that, in doing so, the gospel will go forth in power. In 1 Corinthians 9:23, Paul is straightforward and unapologetic about why he modifies his behavior: "I do it all *for the sake of the gospel*, so that I may share in its blessings."

Once again, this brings us back to Taylor's concern for gospel-centricity, that is, for cultural markers orbiting around the gospel instead of the gospel orbiting around cultural markers. Taylor's improvisational-intercultural approach authorizes a "contextualization of proclamation" that is person- and context-specific.[98] Thus preachers do not surrender

---

[97]WGT 5:150.
[98]Gardner C. Taylor, personal interview, March 5, 2012.

fidelity to the gospel for their own sake; they surrender themselves for the gospel's sake. They *become* in order to cross over from the domain of comfort to the domain of engagement with racial, ethnic, and ecclesial others. Again, the issue is not a kernel-husk issue; it is a foregrounding-backgrounding issue. In Christian discipleship and gospel proclamation, whose rights needs to be surrendered, and which identity markers need to be foregrounded? When pressed to make a choice, is one's preaching and one's life cruciform or ethno-form in its orientation?

Taylor's gospel-centricity is also guided by a second conviction concerning the doctrine of the incarnation. He notes that when the Word became flesh, God risked *becoming* those to whom God was trying to reach. As Taylor puts it, "There is a recognition in the gospel, and foreshadowed in the long centuries that the Old Testament chronicles, that not even God could get to us without getting with us. Indeed, this is the gospel of Immanuel—God with us."[99] Drawing on a theological construction employed previously by Martin Luther King Jr., Taylor suggests that, in the incarnation, God undertakes the risk of "specificity." It is one thing to claim that God is a far-off, distant deity who rules over the universe from beyond time and without limitation. It is another thing altogether to claim that God is willing to enter into human specificity through Jesus Christ, to subject the divine Godhead to time and space through human frailty, to *become* those God desires to reach.

Through Jesus Christ, God speaks a *specific* language and embraces a *specific* culture. God condescends through risking specificity. By tabernacling with a specific people in a specific time and place, God demonstrates a divine willingness to take on humanness, to embrace creatureliness, with its requisite restrictions of language and culture. Thus in Christ God shapes God's grace to humanity in ways that are tailor-made and custom-fit to the human situation. As systematic theologian Christopher Morse puts it, "God's providing is always custom made to fit the creaturely recipient so that the creature's freedom is never abrogated but activated."[100] Put simply, God in Christ becomes like us to reach us.

---

[99] WGT 5:156.

[100] Christopher Morse argues that God's grace comes to us in ways that are tailor-made and custom-fit to our unique situatedness. In so doing, God does not deny our freedom as human creatures,

The incarnation grounds Taylor's commitment to proclamation that is gospel-centric while also being contextualized, uncompromising while also being intercultural and protean. In laying out the implications of the incarnation for preaching, Taylor draws attention to God's willingness to risk everything in Christ. Note what Taylor says about specificity here and the way he connects it to the task of preaching:

> God knowingly took some risk. One was the risk of what Dr. Martin Luther King Jr. called "specificity." For the divine Presence to be far off in the heavens, "high and lifted up," is one thing, inspiring awe and reverence and a sense of grand separation from the mean and often ugly things of earth. For the divine Presence to be "geography bound" and "time encapsulated" is something else, for this specificity risks that contempt which is born of familiarity and that suspicion which is associated with what is "merely" flesh and blood.
>
> The preacher, then, bears tidings of another world impinging on this sphere of flesh and blood. He comes declaring that the eternal God has chosen, and supremely in Jesus Christ, this world to be the scene of His saving work and the arena in which he wages his campaign to put down the rebellious places among us and to set the word singing through the whole creation, "The kingdoms of this world have become the kingdoms of our Lord and of His Christ; and he shall reign forever and ever.[101]

The logic of Taylor's argument seems to be as follows: if God is willing to risk much, to embrace specificity by taking on the vulnerability and frailty of the human condition in Jesus Christ, then how much of a risk is it really for preachers to become all things to all people for the gospel's sake? If God risks everything to become, then preachers should be willing to risk something to become. For the sake of the gospel and as ones called to *imitatio Christi*, preachers must be willing to risk becoming like those to whom they preach, to get *to* God's people by getting *with* God's people.

For crossover preachers, commitment to gospel-centricity means foregrounding proclamation—contextually *becoming* for the sake of the

---

but respects our freedom. See Christopher Morse, *Not Every Spirit: A Dogmatics of Christian Disbelief* (New York: Continuum, 2009), p. 219.
[101]WGT 5:157-58.

gospel—and backgrounding any and all identity markers that lead to enclosure or reification. In a sense, preachers say *après-vous* to the gospel itself as the sun around which identity markers orbit. To be clear, saying *après-vous* to the gospel does not require abandoning cultural classification (as if that were possible in a racialized context), but requires de-centering them from this-worldly essentialized centrality. As Amos Yong reminds us, "The gospel is good news only within culture, even as the gospel is never captive to culture."[102] Thus it is not cultural identity classification that needs to be jettisoned, but hermetically sealed cultural captivity. Being an "evangelical" preacher in the best sense of the word involves reorientation and commitment: to reorient one's life *around* the good news that has come, is here, and is coming, and to commit one's life *to* a gospel-centric vision and cruciform disposition.

CONCLUSION

Taylor's life experiences taught him how to become "a social actor in the host culture (C2)."[103] His background taught him how to *think* and *act* interculturally. Yet competence extended beyond the realm of thinking and knowledge. He acquired knowledge, gained skill aptitude, and deployed transgressive action. In engaging with Taylor's life and ministry, we encounter a person with intercultural competence, a proficiency that preachers now and in the future will need more of in the intercultural church that has emerged and is emerging.

In important ways, Taylor's intercultural competence proficiency uniquely positions him as a harbinger whose commitments to intercultural engagement and communication are antecedent to later discussions about these same phenomena in communication theory and education theory. As the church in the United States becomes more intercultural and moves with greater speed toward its intercultural future, the onus for new and effective strategies to account for this change will not only be on preachers, but on those who prepare them to preach. Homileti-

---

[102]Amos Yong, *The Future of Evangelical Theology: Soundings from the Asian American Diaspora* (Downers Grove, IL: IVP Academic, 2014), p. 225.

[103]Biagi et al., "Reflective Intercultural Competence (RIC) and Its Assessment: The RICA Model." Bennett uses the term "Level 6 integration." See Bennett, "A Developmental Approach to Training for Intercultural Sensitivity," p. 186.

cians need to ask, *How should our preaching and teaching strategies change in light of our analysis of Taylor's improvisational and intercultural proficiency, and how do recent developments in improvisational and intercultural theory help us to chart a way forward for the future?* These will be the basic questions we ask in the next chapter as we consider the implications of crossover preaching. As Taylor learned, preachers and homileticians must also learn: it is not sufficient to think *about* interculturality; one must also learn to think and act interculturally.

5

PUTTING FLESH TO BONES

HOMILETICAL STRATEGIES

When the work is almost finished, he stops and says . . .
"Now I can begin. All the mistakes I have made up
to now are teaching me the picture I must paint."

PABLO PICASSO
as quoted by Eugenio Barba

◆

In Taylor's study at Concord Baptist Church in Brooklyn there hung a painting by Australian landscape artist Sir Hans Heysen. Many years earlier, when Taylor was itinerant preaching in Australia, he had the chance to meet Heysen. While in Heysen's studio, Taylor noticed a painting with a right corner that was unfinished, and he asked him about it. Heysen replied with a mix of "pensiveness and wistfulness." "I have never been able to finish it," he said.[1] In some ways, the Heysen painting is a parable for doing constructive homiletical work based on Taylor's improvisational-intercultural approach. One can try to paint a landscape, but can't complete the work.

This chapter provides the reader with concrete strategies for crossover preaching and teaching as an act of (provisional) homiletical-theoretical construction. The central question posed is, *What does improvisational-intercultural preaching and teaching look and sound like?* In answering this

---

[1]WGT 6:120.

question, Taylor's preaching, improvisational theory, and intercultural competence theory are my primary interlocutors. Again, my purpose here is not to provide the reader with a biblical or systematic theology of preaching, and it is not to claim that *all* of preaching hinges on these strategies. Rather, my aim is to ask, *What can we learn from Taylor specifically?* To paraphrase my thesis, Taylor's improvisational-intercultural approach in conversation with improvisational and intercultural theory reveals his contemporary significance in the twenty-first century. Most homileticians already know that biblical, theological, and spiritual proficiency are also required in order for a preacher to thrive in the task of preaching. These are the proficiencies that many of us already know how to teach. My purpose in this chapter is not to discuss the necessity of these other proficiencies; it is to reflect on Taylor-as-case-study, to place these reflections in conversation with the disciplines studied, and to offer concrete ideas that can put "flesh to bones" in the cultivation of *improvisational and intercultural proficiency* in the pulpits and classrooms of today and tomorrow.

In the first part of this chapter, I recommend four strategies for improvisationally competent preaching: play, attune, collaborate, and experiment (PACE). The acronym serves as both an aid for memorization and as a descriptor of forward-thinking improvisational pedagogy, for example, "setting the *PACE* for homiletical teaching in the future." In the second part, I recommend four strategies for interculturally competent preaching and teaching: listen, engage, assess, and decenter (LEAD). Like PACE, this acronym serves as both an aid for memorization and as generative language for forward-thinking intercultural pedagogy, as in "taking the *LEAD* in intercultural homiletics."

No doubt a wide array of other underexplored resources are available that could also enhance preaching and teaching practice.[2] In the area of

---

[2]See Howard Gardner, *Multiple Intelligences: New Horizons* (New York: BasicBooks, 2006). Cf. also Troeger and Tisdale's book chapter drawing on Gardner's work in Thomas H. Troeger and Leonora Tubbs Tisdale, *A Sermon Workbook: Exercises in the Art and Craft of Preaching* (Nashville: Abingdon, 2013), pp. 66-70. For Giroux's work, see Henry A. Giroux, "The Hope of Radical Education: A Conversation with Henry A. Giroux," in *What Schools Can Do: Critical Pedagogy and Practice*, ed. Kathleen Weiler and Candace Mitchell (Albany: SUNY Press, 1992), pp. 13-26. For Freire's work, see Paulo Freire, *Pedagogy of the Oppressed* (New York: Continuum, 1993). Cf. also Paulo Freire, *Learning to Question: A Pedagogy of Liberation* (Geneva: WCC Publications, 1989). Gary Howard

homiletics, Ronald J. Allen, John S. McClure, and others have already done important qualitative research on listening styles in congregations.[3] These publications help to shape, deepen, and expand preaching and teaching practice. Thus, in engaging with improvisational and intercultural theory, my underlying assumption is that thoughtful theological educators will *also* take into account various learning styles, listening styles, power dynamics, and histories of oppression that affect classroom ecology.

We begin with a description of the first four strategies drawn from performance theory—play, attunement, collaboration, and experimentation—or PACE. These strategies are intended to be suggestive proposals rather than exhaustive summations, and are designed to expand rather than delimit our thinking about improvisational proficiency.

PACE: IMPROVISATIONALLY COMPETENT STRATEGIES FOR PREACHING AND TEACHING

Play. The first improvisational strategy is to *play*. Whether in reading, preaching, pedagogy, or life, the possibilities for play are many.[4] In *Free*

is the president and founder of REACH Center for Multicultural Education in Seattle. The mission of REACH is "helping people understand and value diversity" (www.reachctr.org). Howard has published numerous articles and books and is well known for his work educating white Americans about cultural awareness and racism. See Gary Howard, "Whites in Multicultural Education: Rethinking Our Role," in *Multicultural Education, Transformative Knowledge, and Action: Historical and Contemporary Perspectives*, ed. James A. Banks (New York: Teachers College Press, 1996), pp. 323-34.

[3] For Allen's work, see Ronald J. Allen, *Hearing the Sermon: Relationship, Content, Feeling* (St. Louis: Chalice, 2004). For another congregational study of listening styles, see John S. McClure et al., eds., *Listening to Listeners: Homiletical Case Studies* (St. Louis: Chalice, 2004).

[4] Some argue that play is a distinctive part of what it means to be human and that it is definitely more than something children do. Robert Poynton writes: "Play is more than just fun. Play is important, because it opens doors to new possibilities. New ideas are, by definition, strange at first. Through play we explore what they might have to offer. We flirt with the unknown." See Robert Poynton, *Do Improvise: Less Push. More Pause. Better Results. A New Approach to Work (and Life)* (Wales: Do Book Company, 2013), p. 70. In the mid-1950s, cultural historian Johan Huizinga characterized human beings as *homo ludens*, that is, as playful creatures; see Johan Huizinga, *Homo Ludens: A Study of the Play Element in Culture* (Boston: Beacon, 1970). German poet and playwright Friedrich Schiller argues that the will to play is integral to one's desire to be "fully human." He writes: "Man is only fully human when he plays, that is, the 'will to play' (*Spieltrieb*) produces new combinations of matter and form" (original quotation from Schiller's *Aesthetic Letters* and cited in Anthony Frost and Ralph Yarrow, *Improvisation in Drama* [New York: St. Martin's Press, 1990], p. 180). Cf. also Stuart Brown's writing on play from a medical and neuroscience perspective. Brown writes: "Of all animals, humans are the biggest players of all. . . . In an individual who is well ad-

Play: Improvisation in Life and Art, Stephen Nachmanovitch notes the connection between play and creativity. He writes: "To play is to free ourselves from arbitrary restrictions and expand our field of action . . . [it] makes us flexible. By reinterpreting reality and begetting novelty we keep from becoming rigid."[5]

Recall from chapter two that American improvisation's history has its roots in play, in particular Neva L. Boyd's pioneering work in creative group play as a form of problem solving.[6] Play is a common metaphor for improvisational performance and is part of its theoretical parlance. One of American improvisation's matriarchs, Viola Spolin, referred to her performers as "players" rather than actors and used phrases like, "playing the game" or "setting objects in motion between players as in a game" in her descriptions of group performance.[7] Keith Johnstone, also considered a pioneer in American improvisation, made game playing central to his philosophy when he founded *Theatresports*, an organization that brings play and theater together. Describing his commitment to play, Johnstone writes: "*Theatresports* can take jealous and

---

justed and safe, play very likely continues to prompt continued neurogenesis throughout our long lives." See Stuart Brown, *Play: How It Shapes the Brain, Opens the Imagination, and Invigorates the Soul* (New York: Penguin, 2009), p. 58.

[5]Stephen Nachmanovitch, *Free Play: Improvisation in Life and Art* (New York: Jeremy P. Tarcher/ Putnam, 1990), p. 43. In *Theater Games for the Classroom*, Spolin writes: "Play touches and stimulates vitality, awakening the whole person—mind and body, intelligence and creativity, spontaneity and intuition—when all, teacher and students together, are attentive to the moment." See Viola Spolin, *Theater Games for the Classroom: A Teacher's Handbook* (Evanston, IL: Northwestern University Press, 1986), p. 3.

[6]Recall that Spolin's work is the progeny of educational theorist Neva L. Boyd, the Chicago teacher, sociologist, and educational theorist who did pioneering work in creative group play primarily with nonliterate immigrant children. In her work with immigrants, Boyd was successful at producing nonverbal improvisations that were both purposeful and educational. For more on this connection, see Viola Spolin, *Improvisation for the Theater* (Evanston, IL: Northwestern University Press, 1999), p. xlvii; and Frost and Yarrow, *Improvisation in Drama*, p. 50. See also Margaret M. Duffy, "The Roots of American Improvisation: Play, Process, and Pedagogy" (PhD diss., City University of New York, 2011).

[7]Spolin, *Improvisation for the Theater*, pp. 361, 365. Like Spolin, Louis Martin-Guay also privileges the language of players instead of actors. Describing his work in interactive theater, Martin-Guay privileges the term *player* over *actor* because it is "more neutral and all embracing. It describes a state rather than a function. In interactive theatre, no one has a predetermined role" (p. 8). Drawing on the work of Umberto Eco and Réjean Dumouchel, Martin-Guay claims that interactive theater invites audience to "play in and play with drama" (p. 7). See Louis-Martin Guay, "Theatre of the Unexpected: When the Spectator Becomes Actor," trans. Jacqueline Dinsmore, *Canadian Theatre Review* 143 (Summer 2010): 7-8.

self-obsessed beginners and teach them to play games with good nature, and to fail gracefully."[8]

While play as a metaphor (and strategy) is common in discussions about improvisational performance theory, it is surprisingly under-developed in homiletical-theoretical discussion. In *Preaching Jesus*, Charles L. Campbell does not use the language of play per se but does intimate that play is an essential part of preparing and delivering sermons. Preachers, like jazz musicians, do not translate the biblical text literally, Campbell argues, but they "go on" with the text in an improvisational manner in order to speak a fresh, innovative, and relevant word to their communities. In *Discovering the Sermon*, Robert C. Dykstra, a pastoral theologian, calls on preachers to "reclaim their childlike heritage of play and desire" through adopting a spirit of playfulness in their preaching. The way to do this, he argues, is by learning how to play with the text, play witness to life, play with strangers, and play with fire (take risks).[9] In *The Jazz of Preaching*, Kirk Byron Jones claims that *playfulness* is one among four distinct features of jazz music that resonate with the task of preaching.[10] Preachers who "cultivate playfulness in preaching" observe God at work in what seems like the mundane, and they discover humor in the things that people take too seriously.[11] Playfulness is a necessary element to sermon preparation and delivery, Jones suggests. He writes: "the spirit of improvisation *is* the spirit of playfulness." Although each of these writers discusses the importance of play, they only do so in passing. They discuss the phenomenon without discussing the dimensions of it.

How might preachers cultivate playfulness in preaching and teaching without forsaking biblical-exegetical faithfulness or compromising theo-logical integrity? Here I suggest a few possibilities drawn from the re-search developed in chapters one through four.

Play with "free spaces in the framework" through internalization. One

---

[8]Keith Johnstone, *Impro for Storytellers* (New York: Routledge, 1999), p. 23.

[9]Robert Dykstra also notes that "certain social and ecclesial pressures inevitably diminish or deaden that capacity for play and desire." See Robert C. Dykstra, *Discovering a Sermon: Personal Pastoral Preaching* (St. Louis: Chalice, 2001), p. 129.

[10]The other three features are variety, daring, and mastery. See Kirk Byron Jones, *The Jazz of Preaching: How to Preach with Great Freedom and Joy* (Nashville: Abingdon, 2004), pp. 86-95.

[11]Ibid., p. 88.

idea for teachers is to challenge students to preach without manuscripts even if they use a manuscript to prepare. At the basic level, this allows students to attend more to their delivery (e.g., eye contact, gestures, and nonverbals). At a deeper level, it challenges them to follow Robert Smith Jr.'s admonition to prepare notes *on* the page *before* the sermon in order to play notes *off* the page *during* the sermon. Such internalization encourages students to let the Holy Spirit "turn the ink of the manuscript into the blood of spiritual passion."[12] To return to Roberto Ciulli's phrase, it encourages students to "create free spaces within the framework."[13] Free spaces are more likely to emerge in the sermon-as-preached when one internalizes the sermon-as-prepared.

Internalization also grants students an opportunity to connect more with their audience in preaching. In improvisational performance, Robert Poynton notes, "forgetting the audience is lethal."[14] Reading manuscript sermons verbatim makes it more (rather than less) challenging to attend to one's listeners. Cleophus J. LaRue suggests that internalizing the manuscript helps preachers to "experience the powerful effect of learning to look at [our] congregation instead of [our] notes."[15] For students who improvise on the sermon-as-prepared, Kirk Byron Jones suggests ongoing reflection on the sermon-as-preached through asking students questions such as, "Did you add something? Did you refine something? Did you say something in a different way?"[16] Jones claims that analysis and evaluation of improvisational preaching enhances skill and improves preaching performance.

What might happen if Sunday morning pastor-preachers also considered internalizing the manuscript, if they don't do so already? To those who learned how to preach as manuscript preachers, the prospect of abandoning it might seem terrifying. My proposal is not to abandon

---

[12]Robert C. Smith Jr., *Doctrine That Dances: Bringing Doctrinal Preaching and Teaching to Life* (Nashville: B & H Academic, 2008), p. 153.

[13]Malgorzata Bartula, Stefan Schroer, and Roberto Ciulli, *On Improvisation: Nine Conversations with Roberto Ciulli*, trans. Geoffrey V. Davis (New York: Peter Lang, 2003), p. 38.

[14]Poynton, *Do Improvise*, p. 45.

[15]See Cleophus J. LaRue, *I Believe I'll Testify: The Art of African American Preaching* (Louisville: Westminster John Knox, 2011), p. 119. LaRue does suggest that *all* preachers *have to* learn to preach without notes. See ibid., pp. 118-19.

[16]Jones, *Jazz of Preaching*, p. 96.

it but to abandon *using* it in the pulpit. It is more difficult for spontaneous improvisation to emerge if the preacher always reads from a manuscript verbatim. Improvisation means meticulous preparation of the planned sermon for the sake of contingent spontaneity during the preached sermon.

One concrete lesson we learn from Gardner C. Taylor is that internalizing the manuscript can lead to homiletical freedom within the established framework of what one has planned, and can produce more meaningful connection with one's listeners. Taylor internalized his sermons, riffed on what he prepared, and made changes in order to remain connected to his congregation.[17]

Play with time. Another way to encourage improvisational play in preaching is to encourage students to blur the lines between past and present, between ancient text and modern world, in playful but responsible ways. The term that is sometimes used in modern rhetoric is *immediacy*, which I define as *strategic play between the world of the text, the world of the listener, and the future world.*[18] Preachers who use immediacy do not necessarily treat biblical characters like historical figures from the past. In some sermons in black Baptist settings, I have heard Jehoshaphat

---

[17]Recall from his interview with Terry Muck and Paul Robbins of *Leadership* magazine in 1981 that he talks about going beyond the material he prepared when he preached sermons on a weekly basis at Concord Baptist. See Taylor, "The Sweet Torture of Sunday Morning (Interview)," *Leadership* 2, no. 3 (Summer 1981): 16-29.

[18]Classical historian Emmanuel Bourbouhakis claims that early Byzantine Christian preachers used immediacy as a rhetorical device in order to dramatize their sermons. Literary critic George Steiner describes immediacy as a "superposition of past and present" in which readers experience a "slippage in our time sense." Scholars of black slave religion in the United States argue that immediacy was demonstrable in slave preaching and singing. Albert J. Raboteau observes: "The slaves' religious community reached out through space and time to include Jacob, Moses, Joshua, Noah, Daniel, the heroes whose faith had been tested of old." Christa K. Dixon and Russell Ames discuss immediacy with respect to Negro spirituals. Dixon writes, "There was an immediacy about their relationship to biblical persons which allowed for intimacy in the midst of estrangement." She also gives a helpful example: "Slaves didn't sing about David, they sang to David: 'Lil David, play on yo' harp, Hellelu, hallelu." Russell Ames notes the presence of immediacy in Negro spirituals. He writes. "Another remarkable quality of Negro spirituals that distinguishes them rather sharply from white spirituals is their immediacy—the sense that biblical history is taking place right before your eyes or even that you are included in the action." See Emmanuel C. Bourbouhakis, "Rhetoric and Performance," in *The Byzantine World*, ed. Paul Stephenson (New York: Routledge, 2010), pp. 183-84; Albert J. Raboteau, *Slave Religion: The "Invisible Institution" in the Antebellum South* (Oxford: Oxford University Press, 2004), p. 250; Christa Klingbeil Dixon, *Negro Spirituals: From Bible to Folk Song* (Philadelphia: Fortress, 1976), pp. 2-3, 45-46; Russell Ames, *The Story of American Folk Song* (New York: Grosset & Dunlap, 1960), p. 135.

referred to colloquially as "J" and Jesus' disciples described as "my Negroes."[19] Other forms of immediacy are also observable in African American preaching. One might hear the preacher say, "I can see John on the island of Patmos" or "I can hear Paul saying . . ." Other times, the preacher might use intentional anachronism: "Jesus took off his sneakers" or "The disciples went into town to buy a pizza"; enroll listeners in the biblical world: "This church has dry bones, too"; project a future world: "I can see Jesus on his lily-white throne"; or discern typological resonances between the present and the past such as when Martin Luther King Jr. called southern white governors the "pharaohs of the South."[20] Taylor also performs immediacy. In a 1972 sermon delivered at Harvard University on the anniversary of King's death, Taylor used immediacy to conflate the story of John the Baptist in the wilderness with the story of King's humble beginnings in the segregated South.[21]

In each example mentioned, the preacher moves freely between the world of the text, the world of the listener, and the world of the future. The preacher plays with time as something malleable rather than fixed. Perhaps this is what Taylor meant when, in 1983, he stated, "A wise preacher of a generation ago suggested that one ought to 'walk up and down the street where a text lives.'"[22]

Sunday morning preachers can also stretch themselves to play with time through using immediacy. Preachers from traditions outside the African American preaching tradition also blur lines of past, present, and

---

[19]In 1936, American sociologist Arthur Raper observed the following about a black folk preacher he listened to in rural Georgia: "[he] talks to his congregation about Daniel and Moses at mid-day as though he had eaten breakfast with them" (Arthur F. Raper, *Preface to Peasantry; a Tale of Two Black Belt Counties* [Chapel Hill: University of North Carolina Press, 1936], p. 10, as cited in William H. Pipes, *Say Amen, Brother!: Old-Time Negro Preaching, a Study in American Frustration* [Detroit: Wayne State University Press, 1992], p. 141).

[20]"The Death of Evil upon the Seashore," in Martin Luther King Jr., *The Papers of Martin Luther King, Jr.*, ed. Clayborne Carson (Berkeley: University of California Press, 1992), 3:258-62.

[21]After naming all of the important rulers mentioned in Luke 3, Taylor used immediacy to make direct parallels between the rulers of ancient Palestine and current American leaders. Following the exact same pattern as Luke 3, Taylor stated: "Dwight D. Eisenhower being president of the United States, John Patterson, the governor of Alabama, J. Edgar Hoover, the omnipotent autocrat of the FBI, and Billy Graham and Norman Peale, the high priests of Middle America, the word of God came to Martin King in the wilderness of America." This sermon was delivered at a memorial service honoring King in January 1972 at Harvard University in Cambridge, Massachusetts. See Gardner C. Taylor, "The Strange Ways of God," WGT 4:100-108.

[22]"Shaping Sermons by the Shape of Text and Preacher," WGT 5:45-46.

future. For instance, in *Telling the Truth*, Frederick Buechner uses intentional anachronism in his description of Pilate's first encounter with Jesus. He writes:

> He (Pilate) pushes back from his desk and crosses his legs. There is the papery rustle of wings as the pigeon flutters off the sill and floats down toward the cobbles. Standing by the door, the guards aren't paying much attention. One is picking his nose, the other staring up at the ceiling. Cigarette smoke drifts over the surface of the desk—the picture of his wife when she still had her looks, the onyx box from Caesar, the clay plaque with the imprint of his first son's hand on it, made while he was still a child in nursery school. Pilate squints at the man (Jesus) through the smoke and asks his question.[23]

If preachers are willing to use imagination, there is no reason to think they cannot also play with time in their preaching in the same way Buechner plays with time in his writing.

Play in the classroom. The final proposal is directed toward homiletical educators: incorporate play into one's classroom activities, exercises, and assignments. One possibility is to invite students to study the biblical text in a new way as part of their exegetical work prior to the sermon. In *Preaching as Testimony*, Anna Carter Florence recommends exercises to help the preacher break free from flat, unimaginative readings, such as dislocating the text (i.e., taking it to an unfamiliar place), running with it, "blocking" it as one would in a staged play, memorizing it, journaling it, standing it, and reading it with a partner.[24] Alternatively, she asks students to "live with the biblical text" as they go through their everyday lives, keep a journal, or share with the class what they observe. Carter Florence makes it clear that none of these ideas is meant to overtake or displace the hard work of research and in-depth study, but to force the preacher to hear and respond to the text in new ways.

Still another idea is to integrate game playing into one's lesson plans, especially through games that assist memorization, improve sensory

---

[23]Frederick Buechner, *Telling the Truth: The Gospel as Tragedy, Comedy, and Fairy Tale* (San Francisco: Harper & Row, 1977), p. 13.
[24]See Anna Carter Florence, *Preaching as Testimony* (Louisville: Westminster John Knox, 2007), pp. 134-55.

awareness, benefit delivery, and enhance class collaboration. In Spolin's *Improvisation for the Theater* and Johnstone's *Impro* alone we find close to one hundred games and exercises, some of which are transferrable to the preaching classroom. Spolin and Johnstone's games are designed to build trust and rapport in the group and to set students free to respond intuitively. The point, then, is not to string together game after game in order to have fun for fun's sake, but for educators to be strategic about incorporating play into the preaching classroom for the sake of their students' educational formation.

Attune. In *The Jazz of Preaching*, Kirk Byron Jones tells a story about jazz great Wynton Marsalis that helps to introduce the second strategy: *attune.* On a summer night in August 2001, Marsalis was playing "I Don't Stand a Ghost of a Chance with You" at the Village Vanguard, a famous jazz club in New York City. David Hajdu, a journalist for *The Atlantic Monthly*, was there on assignment for the magazine. At the exact moment that Marsalis was coming to the most dramatic point of the song's conclusion, an audience member's cell phone rang. When the phone went off, Marsalis sat on the stage motionless with his "eyebrows arched" while Hajdu scribbled on a sheet of notepaper, "MAGIC, RUINED." After the "cell phone offender" ran into the hallway to take the call,

> Marsalis replayed the silly cell phone melody note for note. Then he repeated it, and began improvising variations on the tune. The audience slowly came back to him. In a few minutes he resolved the improvisation—which had changed keys once or twice and throttled down to a ballad tempo—and ended exactly where he had left off: "With you . . ." The ovation was tremendous.[25]

In this instance, Marsalis did more than turn a problem into a solution. He *attuned* himself to the dynamics of the space through incorporating them into his performance.

I define attunement as *congruity with the space in which one preaches*, and mean by it the skill of reading and responding to the social, phenomenological, and locally contingent dynamics of the space where one

---

[25]See David Hajdu, "Wynton's Blues," *The Atlantic Monthly* (March 2003): 44, as cited in Jones, *Jazz of Preaching*, p. 80.

performs though some definitions of the term are broader.[26] I believe that attunement is an ability that can be learned over time through rehearsal and performance. Marsalis's ability to improvise a cell phone melody in the live moment had less to do with his innate ability than with time spent in hours of rehearsal, experimentation, and performance. Also, though I do not emphasize geographical space in attunement, many preachers recognize that geographical space is significant as well. Preaching in a country church is different from preaching in a large venue like a university chapel or, for someone preaching in a seminary homiletics course, delivering a sermon in a seminar room is different from delivering a sermon in a lecture hall. My emphasis, however, is on attuning to the *dynamics* of the space, that is, the interpersonal, spiritual, and locally contingent dimensions of one's environment.

The study of spatial dynamics is known in sociological circles as proxemics. Only in the last fifty years have performance theorists paid greater attention to the ways that space is used, and not just to the performer, the audience, and the text. The study of space and its use has also made important inroads in philosophy. In his book *The Production of Space*, French philosopher Henri Lefebvre argues that space is more phenomenologically and socially significant than one might initially assume.[27] For Lefebvre, space consists of psychological and social dynamics that either serve as a "tool of thought and action" or as a "means of control, and hence of domination, of power."[28]

---

[26]In a 2011 dissertation on attunement in musical improvisation and its connections to philosophy and theology, Nathan Crawford provides a broader definition. He uses the phrase "triple attunement"—the attunement of "the musician to the tradition (including the composer and the piece), the musician to other musicians, and the musician to the audience." See Nathan Crawford, "Theology as Improvisation: Using the Metaphor of Attunement to Think Theologically" (PhD diss., Loyola University Chicago, 2011), p. 166. Recently, Crawford turned this dissertation into a book. See also Nathan Crawford, *Theology as Improvisation: A Study in the Musical Nature of Theological Thinking* (Boston: Brill, 2013), pp. 101-14.

[27]Lefebvre suggests that space is really a play of three fields: the physical, the mental, and the social. He suggests that his concern with space is about more than the physical, although physicality should not be overlooked. His concern is also with the "logico-epistemological space, the space of social practice, the space occupied by social phenomena, including the projects of the imagination such as projects and projections, symbols and utopias." See Henri Lefebvre, *The Production of Space*, trans. Donald Nicholson-Smith (Malden, MA: Blackwell, 1991), pp. 11-12.

[28]See ibid., p. 26. For Lefebvre, space is more of a sociopolitical construction made up of values, embedded practices, and social perceptions. He applies his philosophical concerns to urban spaces in particular. I would also add the spiritual dimensions of space to Lefebvre's list.

Not surprisingly, improvisational performance theorists also discuss the importance of spatial dynamics. In *Improvisation for the Theater*, Spolin argues that establishing congruity with the space—what I call attunement—helps ensemble performers learn to interact collaboratively in ensemble improvisation.[29] Spolin wanted actors to learn to read and react to the dynamics of the space, to focus more on knowing and using space in performance. Her goal was to free them up to listen, respond, and react, instead of to control, direct, and decide.[30] Notice how she emphasizes attunement:

> The need [is] for players to get out of the head and into the space, free of the restricted response of established behavior, which inhibits spontaneity, and to focus on the actual field—SPACE—upon which the playing (energy exchange) takes place between players. Getting out of the head and into the space strengthens the player's ability to perceive and sense the new with the full body.[31]

In some ways, Spolin makes a claim similar to Lefebvre's, but she uses performative rather than philosophical language. The players (actors) are challenged to conceive of space as multilayered and multivalent. The "actual field" is more than physical dimensions of a given environment; it is social and phenomenological. She writes: "Space can be used to shape the realities we create: an area of no boundaries; without limits; the players use space to bring reality into the phenomenal world; to make space for the object; the larger environment; the space beyond; a place to perceive or receive a communication."[32] The actual field is not the

---

[29]Spolin, *Improvisation for the Theater*. Paul Sills, Spolin's son, drew from her core ideas and exercises first at the University of Chicago with the *Compass Players*, and later as the cofounder/director of the first generation of actors at *The Second City*, the renowned improv club in Chicago. See ibid., p. xlvii.

[30]In addition to Spolin, but to a lesser degree, Frost and Yarrow argue that a key discipline in improvisation is "to avoid the reflex of trying to make it [the performance] into something you think it *ought* to be, rather than letting it become what it *can* be." See Anthony Frost and Ralph Yarrow, *Improvisation in Drama* (New York: St. Martin's Press, 1990), p. 3.

[31]Spolin, *Improvisation for the Theater*, p. liii. Frost and Yarrow also include space as an important element in improvisational theater, though it does not play as central a role in their definition of improvisation: "the skill of using bodies, space, all human resources, to generate a coherent physical expression of an idea, a situation, a character (even perhaps, a text); to do this spontaneously, in response to the immediate stimuli of one's environment, and to do it *à l'improviste*: as though taken by surprise, without preconceptions." Frost and Yarrow, *Improvisation in Drama*, p. 1.

[32]Spolin, *Improvisation for the Theater*, p. 370.

location where a performance takes place, such as the improv club for the actor or the pulpit for the preacher; it is the "realities we create."

The language that performance theorists use to discuss spatial dynamics, terms like attunement, congruity, and getting "into the space," provide us with descriptive terminology to surmise at least one aspect of Taylor's latent improvisational proficiency. Certain nuances in Taylor's approach make it broader and deeper than categories such as attention to context and occasion or audience analysis. Recall from chapter two that Taylor attuned his sermons to the dynamics of the spaces where he preached by making changes both to content and to delivery. He preached three sermons on the same subject, the same passage of Scripture, and with the same core elements, but each sermon sounded different. One was delivered in a black Baptist church in Trenton, New Jersey, another at a black Baptist church in Fort Worth, Texas, and another at a white Presbyterian church in Princeton, New Jersey. When the space changed, Taylor's sermon changed. If Taylor attuned to the spaces in which he preached in a way similar to what Spolin describes, which I believe that he did, this complexifies traditional categories such as adaptation, audience, and context. Space is geographical, architectural, acoustical, interpersonal, phenomenological, and spiritual. In many ways, performance theory deepens and refines Taylor's adeptness at attunement. Not only did the content and delivery change, but the sound changed as well.

Moreover, there are some clues in Taylor's sermons that demonstrate his concern for the geographical space in which he preached. Think physical architecture in addition to social dynamics. For instance, in a 1970s sermon at Concord, he reminds his congregation that when the "pulpit was put in this place in this great cathedral," he told the workman: "paint on this floor before the preacher the words that any of you may read who stand where I stand: 'Sir, we would see Jesus.'"[33] At the prayer service for the inauguration of President Clinton in 1992, Taylor said in his introductory comments: "It seems thoroughly in order that we should come together in this shrine of African Methodism which stands as

---

[33]"Prayer for Spiritual Vision," WGT 2:48.

testament to one stream of determination in this country which found its fount in Richard Allen."[34] Though he mentions physical space in passing in each of these examples, it is still significant that he mentions it. Interestingly, if one visits Concord at some point and walks into the church's Fireside Room, framed and hanging on the wall is the patch of carpet Taylor stood on while preaching for over four decades. Presumably, the space *where* he preached mattered to Taylor.

Perhaps quotations and stories like these are clues that latent in Taylor's homiletical approach there resides a spatial dimension. While it is nearly impossible to prove that Taylor attuned to the space in the same way that performance theorists attune to spaces, we can surmise the following: clues like these at least point to Taylor's interest in geographical space, and the evidence from his sermons that he altered content, delivery, and sound make categories such as audience analysis and attention to occasion insufficient as descriptive terms. Though Taylor was no doubt aware of his audience and mindful of his context, perhaps another layer exists, namely, an acute awareness of the spatial dynamics of the sermon.

Though the study of space has not yet reached the mainstream of contemporary homiletical discussion, Kristin Saldine's PhD dissertation on geo-rhetoric in Jonathan Edwards's preaching and Adam W. Hearlson's study on Martin Heidegger's notions of place are both recent forays into what could be termed "homiletical proxemics."[35] Yet no one has

---

[34]"Facing Facts with Faith," WGT 4:114.

[35]In a recent publication, Michael Brothers briefly discusses proxemics, which he defines as "the relationship of the body to other bodies and objects in space." See Michael Brothers, *Distance in Preaching: Room to Speak, Space to Listen* (Grand Rapids: Eerdmans, 2014), p. 83. For the two dissertations mentioned, see Kristin Emery Saldine, "Preaching God Visible: Geo-Rhetoric and the Theological Appropriation of Landscape Imagery in the Sermons of Jonathan Edwards" (PhD diss., Princeton Theological Seminary, 2004). See also Adam W. Hearlson, "Finding Ourselves There: Martin Heidegger's Notions of Place and What They Might Mean for Preaching" (paper presented at the Annual Academy of Homiletics Conference, Washington, DC, 2009). In his dissertation, Hearlson, drawing primarily on the work of Pierre Bourdieu, makes a fascinating link between the congregations where we preach and the power dynamics that operate among the people to whom we preach. However, Hearlson focuses less on space and place and more on power configurations in communities. See Adam W. Hearlson, "Preaching as Sabotage: Power, Practice, and Proclamation" (PhD diss., Princeton Theological Seminary, 2013). Interestingly, in his book *The Production of Space*, one of Lefebvre's points is that space and power are symbiotically related. See Lefebvre, *Production of Space*, p. 26.

continued the dialogue about spatial dynamics and preaching. My interest in it pertains to *attunement with the dynamics of the space*, which is the language performance theorists use and part of the lexicons of jazz music and improvisational theater.

What might it look like for preachers to get "out of the head and into the space," per Spolin's recommendation? What would happen if preachers became more attuned to spatial-contextual dynamics in preaching? Undoubtedly, those who listen to sermons would benefit. The congregation is not a "javelin catcher."[36] Although listeners are recipients of a proclaimed Word in a sense, they are also coparticipants and collaborators in the sermon in another sense. In the context of Christian worship, one might return to Augusto Boal's phrase by referring to listeners as "spect-actors."[37] They receive *and* they give; they listen *and* they participate.

One of Spolin's famous dictums was "Involve the audience as a fellow player, hand in hand (one body)."[38] Perhaps one of the benefits of attending to space is that it can lead to improved connection with the congregation. Yet how *specifically* might homileticians teach preachers to become more attuned to the space? Here are a few concrete suggestions.

Teach students to listen to verbal and nonverbal cues. Attuned preachers "seek somatic signs, follow hunches, and trust impulses."[39] When listeners communicate that they are tracking with the sermon, attuned preachers consider expanding and elaborating. If listeners fall into inattention, these preachers move on quickly or inject something unforeseen. If listeners are confused, they clarify and restate. The truth is, listeners provide preachers with plenty of insights about their preaching *during* the sermon and not just after they preach. The live sermon is a locus for epistemic insight, that is, for new knowledge to emerge. Attuned preachers attend to these insights. They listen to listeners listening.

For some students listening to cues is easier than for others. In tradi-

[36]Fred B. Craddock, *As One Without Authority* (St. Louis: Chalice, 2001), p. 55.

[37]Augusto Boal, *Games for Actors and Non-Actors* (New York: Routledge, 2002), p. 244.

[38]Spolin, *Improvisation for the Theater*, p. xiv.

[39]Amy Seham, "Play Fair: Feminist Tools for Teaching Improv," in *Radical Acts: Theatre and Feminist Pedagogies of Change*, ed. Ann Elizabeth Armstrong and Kathleen Juhl (San Francisco: Aunt Lute Books, 2007), p. 437.

tions where verbal cues are common, such as in many African American churches, preachers respond based on what parishioners say back to them. If members of an African American congregation say, "Take your time!" then it is time to slow down. If congregants say, "Help him, Jesus," then it is time to either clarify what is being said or to move on to the next point—and quickly. If congregants use phrases like, "Say it!" "Come on!" or "Preach!" then they hear, understand, and like what is being said, and they want to hear more.[40]

But, in congregations where verbal cues are uncommon, nonverbal cues are also possible data from which to draw. Preachers in these contexts must decide whether they are being heard and understood based on eye contact, the position of congregants' bodies, and listener reactions to what is being said. Manuscript preachers tend toward strict adherence to the word on the page, but what if it becomes clear that the congregation does not understand or relate to what is being said? What if a negative sermon illustration is received as a positive illustration? Attuned preachers gauge whether they need to clarify, correct, shift, or continue what they are saying. The data they collect while preaching helps them to "listen, respond, and react" instead of "control, direct, and decide."

Add a proxemics unit. Teachers of preaching could add a learning unit on proxemics to the units on exegesis, hermeneutics, and delivery in their preaching courses. Professors could take a more abstract, philosophical approach through engaging students with Lefebvre's work, or they could take a more explicitly performative approach by engaging students with Spolin's work. My preference is for the latter because the cultivation of concrete skills is probably more beneficial to them.

In *Improvisation for the Theater*, Spolin provides her readers with several activities and exercises designed to help improve spatial attentiveness. In *Theater Games for Rehearsal*, Spolin states that the goal of the director is to help students learn to "see" rather than "stare." She writes: "Actors who stare but do not see prevent themselves from directly experiencing their

---

[40]For a fuller description of verbal cues in black preaching among African American congregations, see Evans E. Crawford with Thomas H. Troeger, *The Hum: Call and Response in African American Preaching* (Nashville: Abingdon, 1995).

environment and from entering into relation with the onstage world."[41] Likewise, she recommends several activities and exercises that can improve one's ability to see the space in which one acts (preaches) and thus become more conscious of how space shapes communication.

Dislocate students from the conventional physical space for preaching. The typical preaching classroom could be one possible space for a sermon, but why not choose a variety of spaces over the course of the semester or year? How about trying a large lecture classroom and a small seminar room, the school chapel and a local church, or perhaps a so-called secular space such as a warehouse or a bowling alley? Perhaps students could study the physical space of their field education site or home church and reflect on the dynamics of that space, or perhaps they could write reflection assignments on the different spaces in which they preach during the semester and how the spaces shape their delivery of the sermon.

Collaborate. The third strategy is to *collaborate*, as Taylor did. It is not overstating to claim that Taylor was a collaborative preacher. He read the sermons of preachers from diverse backgrounds while at Oberlin. He built friendships in the NBC and PNBC as well as across racial and ecclesial difference among leaders of the ABC, the Baptist World Congress, and white mainline preachers in New York. He was consciously ecumenical as president of the Council of Churches in Brooklyn and then in the wider New York area. Recall from chapter four that one of the favorite sayings among church leaders of that time was "We can do so much more for the kingdom together than we can separate."[42]

While collaboration is not a new concept in education, and it certainly does not originate in performance studies, it *does* receive significant attention in improvisational performance literature.[43] American improvi-

---

[41]See Viola Spolin, *Theater Games for Rehearsal: A Director's Handbook* (Evanston, IL: Northwestern University Press, 1985), p. 16.

[42]"Gardner Calvin Taylor: Oral History Memoir, Interview 3," interview by Joel C. Gregory, Baylor University Institute for Oral History, March 17, 2008, p. 19.

[43]For instance, in his 1916 book *Democracy and Education: An Introduction to the Philosophy of Education*, educational theorist John Dewey suggests that collaborative group process through playing games is a valuable educational tool. Using an example of tug-of-war, Dewey describes the necessity of working together at a collaborative level. He writes: "To pull at a rope at which others happen to be pulling is not a shared activity, unless the pulling is done with knowledge that oth-

sation's roots are in collaboration, specifically, problem solving through group process and play.[44] In *Improvisation for the Theater*, Spolin observes: "A healthy group relationship demands a number of individuals working interdependently to complete a given project with full individual participation and personal contribution."[45] For Spolin, actors/ players reach their potential when they learn to work interdependently without any one person dominating the others in the group. When actors learn to work interdependently (not independently), then "Individual energy is released, trust is generated, inspiration and creativity appear. . . . 'Sparks' fly between people when this happens."[46]

In improvisation, the point is to collaborate not to compete, to shift the focus to interdependence instead of independence, to intersubjectivity rather than individuality. Paul Sills, Spolin's son and the cofounder of the famous Chicago improv club *The Second City*, observes:

> True improvisation is a dialogue between people. Not just on the level of what the scene is about, but also a dialogue from the being—something that has never been said before that now comes up, some statement of reality between people. In a dialogue, something happens to the participants. It's not what I know and what you know; it's something that

---

ers are pulling and for the sake of either helping or hindering what they are doing." See John Dewey, *Democracy and Education: An Introduction to the Philosophy of Education* (New York: Macmillan, 1916), p. 36, as cited in Margaret M. Duffy, "The Roots of American Improvisation: Play, Process, and Pedagogy" (PhD diss., City University of New York, 2011), p. 50. Also, Dwight Conquergood, a performance theorist who does not focus on improvisation but ethnography, argues that ethnography must also be collaborative. See Dwight Conquergood, "Rethinking Ethnography: Towards a Critical Cultural Politics," *Communication Monographs* 58 (June 1991): 190.

[44]Recall that Viola Spolin learned about improvisation from Neva L. Boyd, a pioneer in improvisational group play. In 1939, Boyd directed Spolin to one of her first full-time jobs: teaching drama in poor, inner-city neighborhoods for the Chicago Works Progress Administration (WPA), specifically, the WPA's Recreational Project at Hull House. In this job, Spolin developed collaborative games and taught these games to her racially, ethnically, socioeconomically diverse students. The games functioned as a form of creative group problem solving. In a 1974 interview, Spolin recollects: "The games emerged out of necessity. I didn't sit at home and dream them up. When I had a problem, I made up a game. When another problem came up, I just made up a new game" (p. 43). Spolin used these games as a pedagogical tool and later codified them in her 1963 classic *Improvisation for the Theater*. For more on Spolin's job at the WPA and the influence of Boyd on her personally and professionally, see Duffy, "Roots of American Improvisation," esp. pp. 41-44, 66. For Spolin's original interview, see Barry Hyams, "Spolin Game Plan for Improvisational Theater," *Los Angeles Times*, May 26, 1974.

[45]Spolin, *Improvisation for the Theater*, p. 9.

[46]Ibid., p. 24.

happens between us that's a discovery. As I say, you can't make this discovery alone. There is always the other.[47]

According to Sills, performance is not a final product *in which* one actor outperforms the other; it is an ongoing process *by which* mutual, intersubjective, and collaborative dialogue emerges. In *Games for Actors and Non-Actors*, Boal makes a similar statement when he writes: "Nothing should ever be done in a competitive manner—we try to be better than ourselves, not better than others."[48] Elsewhere, he states: "The aim . . . is not to win, but to learn and to train."[49]

As in the actual performance itself, collaboration is also integral to improvisational performance pedagogy. Lynn M. Thomson, who teaches at the Brooklyn College of the City University of New York (CUNY) and is a freelance dramaturgist, argues that collaborative improvisation is indispensible to classroom pedagogy. Thomson believes that classrooms should be radically open spaces in which students practice creative group collaboration because, "Collaboration is a verb not a noun, a process of engagement, a map more than a destination. The process fosters a community of makers, who engender a shared vision, which in turn fuels individual creation."[50] Performance teacher Christie Logan also claims that performance educators should be collaborative teachers. Those who feature teacher-student collaboration, Logan suggests, are "uniquely suited to teaching improvisation and teaching improvisationally."[51]

In homiletics, Lucy Atkinson Rose and John S. McClure both discuss the importance of collaboration with a special focus on how preachers can collaborate with their parishioners. In *Sharing the Word: Preaching in the Roundtable Church*, Rose contends that preaching is at its best when

---

[47]Paul Sills, quoted in Jeffrey Sweet, *Something Wonderful Right Away* (New York: Hal Leonard, 2000), p. 19, as cited in Duffy, "Roots of American Improvisation," p. 58.

[48]Boal, *Games for Actors and Non-Actors*, p. xxx.

[49]Ibid., p. 20. Performance teacher Christie Logan makes a similar claim to Boal's when she writes: "The group itself is a subject of study, as we develop our own processes of improvisation and reflection. We can explore dynamics of our social systems, and rehearse alternative strategies for coping with these. . . . We can decide to collaborate rather than compete." See Christie Logan, "Improvisational Pedagogy," in *The Future of Performance Studies: Visions and Revisions*, ed. Sheron J. Dailey (Annandale, VA: National Communication Association, 1998), p. 183.

[50]Lynn M. Thomson, "Teaching and Rehearsing Collaboration," *Theatre Topics* 13, no. 1 (March 2003): 118.

[51]Logan, "Improvisational Pedagogy," p. 184.

it is conversational and spurs further dialogue.[52] The aim of the sermon, she argues, is not to tell but to share. Instead of being at the head of a rectangular table and in charge, the preacher sees himself as a member at the roundtable, more specifically, the "roundtable church." Preachers don't preach *for* their listeners; they collaborate *with* their listeners. To use imagery, they bridge and carve: they bridge the gap between pulpit and pew and carve out nonthreatening, open spaces in which open dialogue can emerge.[53]

McClure also advocates a collaborative approach to sermon preparation in which preachers and laypeople from both center and margins meet together for roundtable discussions.[54] He suggests rotating people in and out of the roundtable experience in order to hear from many voices and experiences and to avoid creating an in-group. Preachers should hold these meetings outside the church, he argues, in order to maximize effectiveness, spark creativity, and develop public theologies that touch down in the real-world neighborhoods where people live.[55] Taking a page out of McClure and Rose's book, Kirk Byron Jones offers this advice to pastors in *The Jazz of Preaching:* "Meet with area preachers and congregants to work on a sermon together. Evaluate your experience and compare it to working on a sermon alone."[56]

Yet there is still work to do beyond Rose and McClure's contributions, particularly in the area of pedagogy for preaching. *What would it mean for a homiletics teacher to see herself as an improvisational facilitator of a student's education?* Here are a few basic recommendations for becoming more collaborative in our teaching.

Re-conceive the role of the instructor. Christie Logan contends that collaborative instructors conceive of their role as that of nontraditional, nonauthoritarian, democratic facilitators whose "identity is as provi-

[52]Lucy Atkinson Rose, *Sharing the Word: Preaching in the Roundtable Church* (Louisville: Westminster John Knox, 1997).

[53]Ibid., pp. 93-94.

[54]John S. McClure, *The Roundtable Pulpit: Where Leadership and Preaching Meet* (Nashville: Abingdon, 1995).

[55]Ibid. See also McClure's discussion of *The Roundtable Pulpit* in John S. McClure, "Preaching Theology" (paper presented at the Annual Academy of Homiletics Conference, Memphis, 2004), p. 266.

[56]Jones, *Jazz of Preaching*, p. 109.

sional as anyone else's" in the class.[57] Instead of touting their authority over students, they emphasize their responsibility to students.[58] Rather than seeing themselves as "sages on a stage," as experts with credentials, they see themselves as colearners with students.

Like Logan, Lynn M. Thomson pushes back against understandings of the teacher as an omniscient imparter of knowledge.[59] Drawing on the work of Johnstone, Thomson casts the teacher as a collaborative facilitator.[60] She writes, "True collaboration is non-hierarchical. The skilled collaborator, seeking the absence of hierarchy, is sensitive to status and understands how to alter it, in order to remove blocks to communication. Observations about status pervade all classroom discussions about process and a dramaturg's identity."[61] Later Thomson states that expert teachers are not only able to observe and teach status reversal, but they also know how to *do* status reversal. They lower their status and elevate

---

[57]Quoting from Mary Catherine Bateson, Logan writes: "In the collaborative classroom my identity is as provisional as anyone else's; in Bateson's words, ' ... all those others present with me now are a source of identity and partners in my survival' (75). In this sense, the personal is pedagogical." See Logan, "Improvisational Pedagogy," p. 183. See also Mary Catherine Bateson, *Peripheral Visions: Learning Along the Way* (New York: HarperCollins, 1994), p. 75.

[58]Logan writes: "I'm responsible for students' education in this course, certainly; but why does responsibility equate with authority? As professor I'm presumably more expert in the subject matter than the students; but why does expertise equate with authority? And what IS the expertise I'm providing? With each successive reworking of a course, despite my innovations, I'm communicating the same thing: 'This is how you learn; I know because this has worked for me.'" See Logan, "Improvisational Pedagogy," p. 182.

[59]In his book *Group Genius*, psychologist R. Keith Sawyer claims that Western businesses that are known for their innovative products tend to have nonhierarchical structures, or "flat hierarchy." In these companies, Sawyer writes, "Innovation emerges from the bottom up." See R. Keith Sawyer, *Group Genius: The Creative Power of Collaboration* (New York: Basic Books, 2007), p. 16.

[60]Keith Johnstone claimed that "status reversal" was a distinctive component of improvisation, For Johnstone's discussion of "status reversal" and the "see-saw principle" of higher and lower status, see Keith Johnstone, *Impro: Improvisation and the Theatre* (New York: Routledge, 1992), p. 39. Louis-Martin Guay is another improvisational performance theorist who discusses status reversal. In a 2010 article, Guay argues for a shift in our thinking about improvisational theater so that the actor is conceived of as a spectator and the audience is conceived of as an actor. Concerning the role of status, Guay claims that authors who learn how to become spectators can no longer "claim their status as skilled specialists." They must forsake their high status for a lower status, which Guay believes is both necessary and healthy. See Guay, "Theatre of the Unexpected: When the Spectator Becomes Actor," p. 8.

[61]Thomson, "Teaching and Rehearsing Collaboration," p. 126. Another pedagogist (who isn't focused on improvisation specifically) named Maryellen Weimer also focuses on the teacher as a nonauthoritarian, learner-centered guide or midwife. See Weimer's discussion of the role of the teacher in Maryellen Weimer, *Learner-Centered Teaching: Five Key Changes to Practice* (San Francisco: Jossey-Bass, 2002), pp. 72-94.

the status of their students.[62] In my judgment, teachers must decide to be fellow travelers on a journey of discovery; that is, they must be willing to take the same risks they ask their students to take, to lower rather than elevate their status, and to embrace the challenges and opportunities found in a more collaborative approach.

Collaborate to create. Thomson discusses the connection between collaboration and the cultivation of creativity. She writes: "Teaching collaboration demands demystifying creativity."[63] Creativity is neither innate, fixed, and mystical, nor is it the exclusive provenance of the individual. As Robert Poynton notes, "In a sense, *all creativity is co-creativity*. While this is a generalization, it is nonetheless a useful counterpoint to the prevailing impression that creativity depends upon the possession of a special talent that you have, or lack, from birth."[64] Thomson uses the metaphor of discovery—"a persistent relish for the unknown"—to describe how creativity works itself out in a classroom.[65] Creativity is a *desire* more than a *gift*. Creative group collaboration is characterized by "high tolerance for open spaces, advanced skills in uncertainty, a hunger for the question, and a commitment to surpass what is routine."[66] Students thrive in collaborative environments where they can pursue openness, embrace ambiguity, and practice curiosity. As educational theorist Parker J. Palmer reminds us, expert teachers discover "generativity" in their academic lives when they cultivate creativity and imagination in their students' lives.[67]

---

[62]Robert Poynton claims that understanding status and lowering or elevating it depending on context is one of the ways that improvisational performance can benefit understandings of leadership in the workplace. See Poynton, *Do Improvise*, p. 104.

[63]Thomson, "Teaching and Rehearsing Collaboration," p. 120. In *Group Genius*, R. Keith Sawyer also notes the connection between science, improvisation, creativity, and collaboration when he writes: "Using clever research designs, scientists have demonstrated how moments of insight can be traced back to previous dedication, hard work, and collaboration. And they've shown how we all can tap into the creative power of collaboration to make our own insights more frequent and more successful" (Sawyer, *Group Genius*, p. xiii).

[64]Poynton, *Do Improvise*, pp. 85-86 (emphasis added).

[65]Thomson, "Teaching and Rehearsing Collaboration," p. 120.

[66]Ibid.

[67]Drawing on Erik Erikson's work on generativity as a sign of healthy adult identity, Palmer claims that stagnation on the part of teachers leads to cynicism, whereas generativity arising from creative partnership with students results in creative pedagogical renewal. Rather than perpetuating a culture of fear, suggests Palmer, "teachers must turn to students, not away from them," in order for generativity to take place. See Parker J. Palmer, *The Courage to Teach: Exploring the Inner Landscape of a Teacher's Life* (Hoboken, NJ: Wiley, 2010), p. 74.

Psychologist and educational theorist R. Keith Sawyer studied collaborative improvisation in the theater as a way to fund new insights into how creativity works. His analysis of improvised dialogues in improvisational theater led him to develop a framework he called "collaborative emergence."[68] According to Sawyer, the spontaneous and innovative creativity that arises from collaborative group improvisational performance challenges creativity researchers to rethink long-held assumptions about how individual creativity works by forcing them to shift their focus from individual phenomena to "collaborative creative systems."[69] Sawyer believes the same systems that exist in improvisational performance settings also exist in conventional classrooms where informal improvised dialogues take place all the time or in business settings where collaborative decision making fuels innovation.[70]

In his study of classrooms, for example, Sawyer discovered that creative teachers knew how to assume a role less like that of a stage actor reciting lines from a prepared script and more like that of an improvisational actor performing in a troupe.[71] Like improvisational actors, these teachers knew

---

[68]Sawyer suggests that, in improvised dialogues in the theater, collaborative emergence is characterized by the following five elements: "1) unpredictability, 2) non-reducibility to models of participating agents, 3) processual intersubjectivity, 4) a communication that can refer reflexively to itself, and within which the processes of communication themselves can be discussed, and, 5) individual agency and creative potential on the part of individual agents." See R. Keith Sawyer, "The Emergence of Creativity," *Philosophical Psychology* 12, no. 4 (1999): 453. See also Sawyer's book-length account of collaborative emergence in groups in R. Keith Sawyer, *Improvised Dialogues: Emergence and Creativity in Conversation* (Westport, CT: Ablex, 2003).

[69]Sawyer, "Emergence of Creativity," p. 467.

[70]See R. Keith Sawyer, "Improvised Lessons: Collaborative Discussion in the Constructivist Classroom," *Teaching Education* 15, no. 2 (June 2004): 189-201. In *Group Genius*, Sawyer notes: "Collaboration makes the mind more creative because working with others gives you new and unexpected concepts and makes it more likely that your mind will engage in the most creative types of conceptual creativity—combining distant concepts, elaborating concepts by modifying their core features, and creating new concepts. Many new ideas are bad ones; collaboration over time is the best way to select the good ones. And although each spark of insight is small, collaboration brings them all together and results in breakthrough innovation." See Sawyer, *Group Genius*, p. 124.

[71]In a March 2004 journal article, Sawyer claims that the conventional image of the teacher as an actor in a performance (with a script) is overly simplistic and even problematic. He writes: "This metaphor emphasizes important skills for teachers, such as presentation, delivery, voice, movement, and timing. Yet the metaphor of teaching as performance is problematic, because it suggests a solo performer reading from a script, with the students as the passive observing audience." Sawyer argues that "creative teaching is better conceived of as *improvisational performance*." See R. Keith Sawyer, "Creative Teaching: Collaborative Discussion as Disciplined Improvisation," *Educational Researcher* 33, no. 2 (March 2004): 12 (emphasis original).

how to facilitate improvised dialogues in class, dialogues from which spontaneity, freedom, and creativity could emerge. They initiated discussions that were *collaboratively emergent*: collaborative in the sense that "no single participant [including the teacher] can control what emerges; the outcome is collectively determined by all participants," and emergent in the sense that unpredictable outcomes are accepted as normative.[72]

Encourage students to be co-constructors of homiletical knowledge. Collaborative, improvisational teachers believe knowledge is a "shared social activity" rather than a data transaction.[73] They do not see themselves as the chief architects of knowledge construction, but as those who work alongside their students in knowledge *co-construction*.[74] To use a different image, this time from Spolin, they excel at "side-coaching" their students rather than head-coaching them.[75] Professors side-coach their students into becoming co-constructors of classroom learning when they create spaces for them to share their academic, ministry, or preaching knowledge with their peers. It might be a simple assignment such as asking every student to bring in their ten favorite illustrations to share with everyone else in the class. Perhaps the professor creates opportunities for experienced preaching students to share their stories of success and failure or for inexperienced preaching students to share about the

---

[72]Ibid., p. 13.

[73]Ibid., p. 14.

[74]Constructivist educators like Jean Piaget and Lev Vygotsky claim that group process and collaboration are essential to constructivist learning and that knowledge *co-construction* is more effective than knowledge construction. Commenting on the neo-Piagetian social constructivist theory and the Vygotskian-inspired sociocultural theory of education, Sawyer writes: "In sociocultural and social constructivist theory, effective teaching *must be* improvisational, because if the classroom is scripted and directed by the teacher, the students cannot co-construct their own knowledge" (ibid. [emphasis added]). David S. Knowlton observes that not all Christian educators embrace a constructivist theory of learning because of the tendency among secular constructivists to maintain the view that "knowledge and truth do not exist—or, at least, are not relevant—beyond a person's perception of that knowledge and truth" (p. 35). The rationale for using co-constructivist language here is neither to propagate this secular view, as it is problematic theologically, nor is it to enter into debates on the merits and liabilities of constructivism. Rather, it is advocate for a position that students also bring into the classroom knowledge, wisdom, and expertise that homiletics professors tend to miss when they see themselves as the only experts in the room. For an overview of constructivism from a Christian education perspective, see Dave S. Knowlton, "A Constructivist Pedagogue's Personal Narrative of Integrating Faith with Learning: Epistemological and Pedagogical Challenges," *Journal of Research on Christian Education* 11, no. 1 (Spring 2002): 35-36.

[75]See Spolin's "Glossary of Side-Coaching Phrases," in Spolin, *Improvisation for the Theater*, pp. 374-76.

preachers who have influenced them so that a level of parity exists between the experienced and inexperienced preachers. Students who listen to sermons recreationally might bring in audio or video clips from their favorite preachers and talk about why they like a particular preacher or why they chose a particular clip. Students with a passion for preachers from the past might memorize an excerpt from a sermon and perform it for the class or do a presentation.

In a January 2014 article on collaborative improvisation in teaching college writing, Chris Kreiser recommends incorporating an "interview with the author" component to courses.[76] Instead of writing workshops where students edit and fix their papers, Kreiser facilitates interviews in which student-authors circulate their work, and the class interacts with them. Perhaps homiletics professors could institute an "interview with the preacher" element to courses. Students could interact on written or performed drafts of the sermon.

Experiment. The fourth improvisational strategy is to *experiment*. In many ways, Stanley Hauerwas's adage "Spontaneity . . . is but the outcome of years of training and practice and thousands of *experiments*" fits Taylor to a T.[77] His (Taylor's) spontaneity arose from years of training and thousands of experiments. To claim he was experimental does not mean he was an ad-hoc, extemporaneous preacher, and it does not mean that he departed in significant ways from what he rehearsed in sermon planning and preparation. He experimented in different ways. For instance, chapter two showed that he injected unforeseen illustrations and anecdotes and engaged listeners improvisationally through call and response. He also repreached his sermons. These sermons would often start

---

[76]Commenting on the shift from workshops to interviews, Kreiser writes: "An interview is an improvised performance, with a student-author and classmates exchanging writing ideas in a dynamic, fluid conversation. For this activity, the whole class reads a copy of the student author's work and then interviews, that is, asks questions, about the improvisational process used to create this particular product. So two improvisations are being studied—the group improvisation of the actual interview and the improvisation inherent in the author's writing process, which is undertaken in response to a current class writing assignment." See Chris Kreiser, "'I'm Not Just Making This Up as I Go Along': Reclaiming Theories of Improvisation for Discussions of College Writing," *Pedagogy* 14, no. 1 (Winter 2014): 94.

[77]Stanley Hauerwas, *Against the Nations: War and Survival in a Liberal Society* (Minneapolis: Winston, 1985), p. 52, as cited in Jeremy Begbie, *Theology, Music, and Time* (Cambridge: Cambridge University Press, 2000), p. 179 (emphasis added).

at Concord, but then he would tinker with them, developing and transforming them on the road. The core ideas were the same, but the riffs
were different. Instead of refusing to preach the same sermon, Taylor
followed African American preacher Caesar Clark's dictum: "Something
that is worth preaching once is worth preaching more than once."[78]
There were always opportunities to continue experimenting. In these
next paragraphs, I recommend various ways that preachers and homileticians might practice experimentation.

Experiment through risk taking and rehearsal. Experimentation involves
taking risks, and thus involves making mistakes. Improvisational unpredictability necessitates a high tolerance for failure. Whenever unpredictable outcomes exist, it is inevitable that some outcomes will not be as
good as others. In improvisational performance, mistakes are not peculiar
but are a natural part of the process. Dizzy Gillespie was fond of saying:
"There's no such thing as a bad note, it's where you take the note."[79]

Improvisational performers emphasize process over outcomes. It is
not as much about the final product as it is about the process of creating
it. One of the problems with homiletical classrooms is that values like
these, namely, high tolerance for failure and process over outcome, are
not incorporated into classroom ecology. Often students are so worried
about getting the sermon "right," having right theology, right exegetical
methods, and right delivery before their professor and their peers—all
of which is still important. Bad exegesis can do a lot of harm to God's
people. That stated, student tolerance for failure is usually low because
they privilege outcomes over process.

How might professors alter this expectation? One way is to cultivate
an ecology in which risk taking and rehearsal are normative. As was
mentioned, both of these features—risk taking and rehearsal—are integral to improvisational performance. Why couldn't they also be integral to our pedagogy? To experiment, one must welcome the process
of trying and failing and be willing to take risks. Encouraging students
to take risks can look a lot of different ways. Professors might ask stu-

---

[78]Taylor quoting Clark in "Gardner Calvin Taylor: Oral History Memoir, Interview 3," p. 14.
[79]As cited in Frank J. Barrett and Ken Poplowski, "Minimal Structures Within a Song: An Analysis of 'All of Me,'" *Organization Science* 9, no. 5 (October 1998): 559.

dents to pick a challenging biblical text that they think is difficult to preach, to preach on a topic they wish they could preach on but don't feel free to on account of the political environment at their church, or to experiment with their voice and body in delivery. It is far better for them to try and to fail in preaching class than in their local church. What is preaching if not a form of risk taking?

Sunday morning preachers take note: constant rehearsal is a productive way to build up a high tolerance for failure. Robert Poynton observes: "The best way to make sure you have good ideas is to have lots of (good and bad) ideas."[80] The common saying at Pixar Animation Studios is moving "from suck to unsuck."[81] In embracing this posture, one acknowledges that one's first ideas can and should be tested over time through experimentation and revision. Perhaps professors could invite students to write and to preach shorter sermons, and to do so more often. Thomas H. Troeger and Leonora Tubbs Tisdale, who teach at Yale, have their students write thirteen one-page minisermons over the semester (one every week) so that they develop the habit of preaching for the ear.[82]

Another option is for professors to divide students into preaching triads. This often happens in pastoral care courses at seminaries. In pastoral care triads, students have opportunities to "practice" providing counseling to a parishioner. One student role-plays as the parishioner and the other is an observer. Why not develop preaching triads, spaces where students have opportunities to *practice* preaching in smaller groups before preaching to the larger class? That way they experiment at least once with the sermon *before* they preach it in front of their professor and a larger group of their peers. The chances are good that their sermons will be better than they would have been without experimentation through rehearsal.

Experiment with forms. Imagine this practice as the gathering of diverse arrows in one quiver. The preacher who has many arrows in her quiver is more adept at improvising across different contexts and situations.

---

[80]Poynton, *Do Improvise*, p. 78.
[81]As cited in ibid., p. 77.
[82]See Troeger and Tisdale, *Sermon Workbook*, p. 4. Thomas H. Troeger retired in 2015.

Too often, homiletics professors tend to risk imposing their own convictions as to what constitutes a "good" sermon form based on their
unnamed cultural and denominational assumptions. This way of approaching the preaching task may work better in seminaries with students from only one denomination. But, even then, at a Baptist seminary
composed entirely of Baptists, for instance, the professor should ask,
*What kinds of Baptists are represented in my classroom? How are their expec-
tations different?* Professorial bias for or against certain preaching forms
can display itself in a variety of ways. For instance, in the last three
decades, some seminaries have done away with the traditional deductive
three-point sermon in favor of Fred Craddock's inductive approach or
Eugene Lowry's narrative approach. In the name of enriching homiletics
they have narrowed the possibilities and ignored the ongoing variety of
practices in broad segments of the church.

Cleophus J. LaRue notes that sermonic practices in black preaching
seem to support a three-point deductive approach over Craddock's inductive approach, but suggests that in reality "It is not the three-point
sermon that is out, but rather it is the *boring* three-point sermon that
must go."[83] In a book chapter titled "Out of the Loop," Thomas G. Long
describes studying weekly preaching practices in churches, conservative
churches in particular. He claims that these practices reveal the con-
spicuous *absence* of the Lowry method (and Craddock's inductive
method by way of implication).[84] Perhaps the most memorable line of

---

[83]LaRue complains that Craddock takes a dismissive approach to deductive preaching by claiming
it is "outdated, out of touch with the pew, and ill-suited to address modern-day listeners with its
deductive approach, authoritarian stance, and deliberate naming of what the listener should take
away from the sermon." The problem LaRue identifies is straightforward: some of the strongest
torchbearers for the promise and power of preaching can be found among black preachers who
practice three-point preaching on a regular basis. Many black preachers state their main idea up
front without apology and make deductive insights and propositions that expound on it, a practice
in direct opposition to Craddock's method. LaRue notes: "The three-point sermon in the black
church is clothed in imagination, humor, playful engagement, running narrative, picturesque
speech, and audible participation on the part of the congregation." How do we explain three-point
sermons in black preaching if they break Craddock's rules on a regular basis? Has this tradition
not evolved from a deductive to an inductive approach? See Cleophus J. LaRue, "Two Ships Passing in the Night," in *What's the Matter with Preaching Today?*, ed. Mike Graves (Louisville: Westminster John Knox, 2004), p. 131.

[84]Thomas G. Long, "Out of the Loop," in *What's the Shape of Narrative Preaching? Essays in Honor
of Eugene L. Lowry*, ed. Mike Graves and David J. Schlafer (St. Louis: Chalice, 2008), pp. 115-30.

Long's essay is when he states what weekly practices in the church seem to indicate: "Instead of three points and a poem, [now] it's six points and a video clip."[85] LaRue and Long's points are simple: the narratival approach has its merits, but it also has its limits.

Why not experiment with sermon forms and equip students to preach in diverse church settings? Homiletician Leonora Tubbs Tisdale argues that experimentation with sermon form is important for students training to be pastors. It helps them be more imaginative in preparation and more flexible when they get into churches. Tisdale writes:

> The contextual preacher opens himself or herself to the imaginative possibilities such an encounter [with sermon form] can afford. Rather than taking a tried and true sermon form and using it—like a mold—to give shape and form to proclamation, preaching as folk art allows form itself to emerge out of the unique meeting of text and context. There is "play" in the process, as the preacher seeks to craft a form that is both fitting and transformative.[86]

Sometimes preachers get stuck preaching the same sermonic form over and over again, hoping something will change. Far better to learn to use several sermon forms. This is also true in pedagogy. Students can only benefit from learning multiple sermon forms. The point is not for them to learn deductive *or* inductive, but to learn deductive *and* inductive, as well as several other sermon forms.

Not that multiple sermon forms are a general panacea for all that ails contemporary preaching. LaRue reminds us that three-point sermons are useless if they are boring three-point sermons. Tisdale reminds us that sermon form experimentation is taken "toward the end of crafting sermons, the form of whose content is also 'fitting' for a local community of faith."[87] In other words, interest in form does not imply ambivalence toward content. Preoccupation with form is just as risky as ignoring it. Augustine reminds us: "There is a danger of forgetting what one has to say while working out a clever way to say it."[88] As Fred Craddock once

---

85Ibid., p. 128.
86Leonora Tubbs Tisdale, *Preaching as Local Theology and Folk Art* (Minneapolis: Fortress, 1997), p. 141.
87Ibid., p. 142.
88Book IV, sections 11-12, in Augustine, *On Christian Teaching*, trans. R. P. H. Green (New York: Oxford University Press, 2008), p. 103.

said in an audio workshop for *Preaching Today*, "You cannot carve beautiful shapes out of nothing."[89] Certainly more is required of preachers than learning forms.

My interest is in the improvisational skills students gain through experimenting with forms, skills such as multiplicity, transferability, and respect. They learn to preach different sermon forms for *multiple* preaching settings, to *transfer* the knowledge they gain to the specific setting where they are called to pastor, and to *respect* the diverse forms in which sermons come to different congregations in different traditions. In other words, they are dispositionally improvisational.

If the student preaches in class three times, perhaps the professor could challenge him or her to experiment with different forms each time. Another idea is to diversify the genres of texts from which students preach. Jeffrey D. Arthurs's homiletical textbook *Preaching with Variety* helps students experiment with different genres.

Experiment with the "idea bank." Like jazz musicians and improvisational performers in the theater, improvisationally proficient preachers commit themselves to building up a reservoir of stored material. In music or theater, artists learn a fake book or use ready-mades. Some jazz musicians describe this reservoir as an "idea bank."[90] In preaching, one might learn a series of tropes, as Taylor did. There is nothing kitschy or hokey about drawing from stored material. Recall Henry Louis Gates Jr.'s claim that troping is a form of Signifyin(g).[91] African American writers Signify on other writers through practices such as tropological

---

[89]See audio workshops on the following paid-subscription site: www.preachingtoday.com.

[90]Musicologist Martin Norgaard, in a series of interviews with jazz musicians about their solo performances, discovered that one of the "generative strategies" these musicians employed in live performances was drawing from an "idea bank" that they developed in rehearsal. Describing the musicians' rationale for this practice, Norgaard writes: "Using material from an idea bank is a flexible way of incorporating practiced musical elements into a solo. I define the idea bank as the collection of procedural and auditory memories of coherent musical structures, which may vary in explicitness and extent. I found 76 instances in which participants described drawing material from an idea bank. Some ideas from the idea bank are inserted as they are recalled, with no modifications from the memory stored" (Martin Norgaard, "Descriptions of Improvisational Thinking by Artist-Level Jazz Musicians," *Journal of Research in Music Education* 59, no. 2 [2008]: 118).

[91]Gates writes: "Signifyin(g) is troping." See Henry Louis Gates Jr., *The Signifying Monkey: A Theory of Afro-American Literary Criticism* (New York: Oxford University Press, 1988), p. 81.

revision, pastiche, and intertextual conversation.[92] Just as Signifyin(g) on other writers honors them and accesses corporate memory, likewise, Signifyin(g) on tropes accomplishes similar aims.

What preachers probably don't realize is how much they already draw from stored material and practice troping. Perhaps a more theoretical way to describe knowledge of one's idea bank would be to return to a theme in Gabriele Tomasi's writing: "the *habitus* of the performer," the embodied knowledge an experienced performer accesses through a combination of skill, training, practice, and attentiveness to the tradition and the community.[93] Building an idea bank is one of the ways a preacher accesses embodied knowledge. To learn about one's idea bank, one might ask simple questions like, *What key phrases do I return to over and over again in my preaching? What themes keep popping up in my sermons? What stories and illustrations am I drawn to use and reuse? What phrases do I repeat in my public prayers?* The answers to these questions and others bring the content of the preacher's idea bank to consciousness, and they make the preacher more open to drawing from it. Knowing what is stored in the idea bank helps one to develop a more sophisticated performative *habitus*.

Now we turn our attention to four interculturally proficient strategies for preachers and homileticians—listen, engage, assess, and decenter—or LEAD.

LEAD: INTERCULTURALLY COMPETENT STRATEGIES FOR PREACHING AND TEACHING

Listen. The first interculturally competent strategy is to *listen*. One of the recurring themes in Taylor's preaching and lecturing is that he calls preachers to careful, reflective listening. In his 1968 address "The Power of Blackness," delivered to the denominational leaders of the PNBC, Taylor exhorts his colleagues in ministry:

> We who minister to people must *listen carefully* to hear what is being said, to catch the words of truth being uttered in the excessive rhetoric of vio-

---

[92]Ibid., p. xxvi.
[93]Gabriele Tomasi, "On the Spontaneity of Jazz Improvisation," in *Improvisation: Between Technique and Spontaneity*, ed. Marina Santi (Newcastle upon Tyne, UK: Cambridge Scholars Press, 2010), p. 87.

lence of so many of our best young minds. Those of us who are thirty-five and over came forward in an integrationist generation. We are startled and sometimes angered by younger people as they talk about separatism. Much of this talk is angry, petulant, pointless. We need not abandon the dream of an integrated society, but *we need to hear* what is real in much current comment.[94]

In the Beecher Lectures, Taylor makes a more general charge to preachers, claiming that our task is to "*to hear* and suffer deeply" with suffering humanity, to "*listen* and to identify the tread of the eternal God's sovereign purpose marching in the private and public affairs of men," and "*hearing* that approaching, fateful footfall . . . to summon men and women" to do the work of God in the world.[95]

In his sermons, Taylor also explains how deep listening leads people back to God. He states: "Listening ears can hear God in a little baby's cry. . . . But so often we fail to see and hear."[96] In a different sermon, he focuses on God's presence within us, stating, "There is a part of us we cannot understand, something within us, if only we would listen, that raises up our heads and lifts up our hearts."[97] In still another sermon, he describes the beautiful listening made possible for one who knows God intimately; one is able to "listen to the songs the angels sing, and know still that there is more beyond."[98]

Homiletics professors who practice careful listening know how to exercise respect and responsibility, and they encourage openness in the classroom. A homiletics professor's willingness to listen is attitudinal; it involves an "orientation toward openness," to use Hans-Georg Gadamer's phrase: a pedagogical stance in which dialogue, mutuality, and humility shape one's convictions as an educator.[99] An ability to listen to

---

[94]"The Power of Blackness," presidential address at the Progressive National Baptist Convention, Washington, D.C., September 1968, WGT 4:20 (emphasis added).

[95]"Recognizing and Removing the Presumptuousness of Preaching," WGT 5:158.

[96]"The Time of Thy Visitation," delivered on July 5, 1959, for *NBC National Radio Pulpit*. See WGT 1:14.

[97]"The God in Us," delivered on July 19, 1959, for *NBC National Radio Pulpit*. See WGT 1:24.

[98]"What 'Born Again' Really Means," WGT 3:208.

[99]Hans-Georg Gadamer writes: "Only the person who knows how to ask questions is able to persist in his questioning, which involves being able to preserve his orientation toward openness." See Hans-Georg Gadamer, *Truth and Method* (New York: Continuum, 2006), p. 360.

and participate in dialogue is predicated on one's orientation toward openness. Unless one is open, Gadamer says, meaningful dialogue is not possible.[100] Moreover, openness is a key way to acquire knowledge and gain aptitude, the first two A's of the 3A Model of Intercultural Competence Proficiency.

In *Teaching Community*, bell hooks uses the phrase "radical openness" through listening to refer to the "will to explore perspectives different than one's own and change one's mind as new information is presented."[101] Notice hooks's verb choices: explore and change. The focus is not on who we are as teachers, but on who we are becoming as learners. In *Teaching to Transgress*, hooks contends that we should "demand of ourselves and our comrades an *openness* of mind and heart that allows us to face reality even as we collectively imagine ways to move beyond boundaries, to transgress."[102] Notice here hooks's emphasis on demanding, imagining, and transgressing. Educators exercise their responsibility as teachers to shape inclusive classroom ecologies (demanding); they envision alternative possibilities that diverge from the conventional (imagining); and they cross over imagined or actual boundaries in order to discover what is new with their students (transgressing). At its core, interculturally proficient listening is about "openness of mind and heart" toward one's students; it requires radical respect *and* radical responsibility.

---

[100]Gadamer writes: "The truth of experience always implies an orientation toward new experience. That is why a person who is called experienced has become so not only *through* experiences but is also open *to* new experiences. . . . The dialectic of experience has its proper fulfillment not in definitive knowledge but in the openness to experience that is made possible by experience itself" (ibid., p. 350). Commenting on the centrality of *Offenheit* to Gadamer's thinking on alterity, Charles Taylor writes: "The crucial moment is the one where we allow ourselves to be interpolated by the other; where the difference escapes from its categorization as an error, a fault, or a lesser, undeveloped version of what we are, and challenges us to see it as a viable human alternative. This unavoidably calls our own self-understanding into question. This is the stance Gadamer calls 'openness.'" See Charles Taylor, "Understanding the Other: A Gadamerian View on Conceptual Schemes," in *Gadamer's Century: Essays in Honor of Hans-Georg Gadamer*, ed. Jeff Malpas, Ulrich von Arnswald, and Jens Kertscher (Cambridge, MA: MIT Press, 2002), p. 296.

[101]bell hooks, *Teaching Community: A Pedagogy of Hope* (New York: Routledge, 2003), p. 48. The phrase "radical openness" is also one that theologian Beverly J. Lanzetta uses frequently. She writes: "Radical openness implies an openness in principle that faces the untidiness of life, and bears this encounter (whether of happiness or sorrow) without imposing judgments and dogmatic truths." See Beverly J. Lanzetta, *The Other Side of Nothingness: Toward a Theology of Radical Openness* (Albany: SUNY Press, 2001), p. 118.

[102]bell hooks, *Teaching to Transgress: Education as the Practice of Freedom* (New York: Routledge, 1994), p. 207 (emphasis added).

How do we do this, that is, how do we incorporate listening to diverse students in ways that are open, respectful, and responsible? Put differently, how do we practice listening to our students in ways that are interculturally proficient? Here I suggest a few proposals.

Listen to diverse reading strategies. Homiletics professors already know that their students read texts from multiple vantage points.[103] They have diverse life experiences, and they interpret Scripture in a variety of ways. Although part of the instructor's responsibility is to correct faulty readings in favor of better readings, the pedagogical challenge remains as follows: these readings are still real to those who read these texts and experience life in these ways. Critical pedagogist Henry A. Giroux reminds us:

> You can't deny that students have experiences and you can't deny that these experiences are relevant to the learning process even though you might say that these experiences are limited, raw, unfruitful, or whatever. Students have memories, families, religions, feelings, and cultures that give them a distinctive voice. We can critically engage that experience and we can move beyond it. But we can't deny it.[104]

In interculturally proficient classroom settings, students do not have their voices shut down or their life experiences invalidated even if their readings of biblical texts require revision. Some of them have already been shut down on multiple occasions prior to entering seminary. Acknowledging students' vantage points and recognizing their reading strategies as real to them are actually forms of respect. Yet respect is only one part of the educator's task.

Responsibility means we "critically engage" students' experiences and help them move from uncritical, unreflective strategies to critical, reflective strategies. While readings may be real to them, this does not mean that there are not better and worse readings. Interpretive readings that turn grace into a work, blessing into health and wealth, or the gospel

---

[103]Feminist theologian Elaine L. Graham uses the language of "vantage-point" in order to emphasize positionality and locality. See Elaine L. Graham, *Transforming Practice: Pastoral Theology in an Age of Uncertainty* (London: Mowbray, 1996), p. 157.

[104]Giroux, "The Hope of Radical Education," p. 23. Original article appears four years earlier than Weiler and Mitchell's book. See Henry A. Giroux, "The Hope of Radical Education: A Conversation with Henry A. Giroux," *Journal of Education* 170, no. 2 (January 1, 1988): 91-101.

into a form of legalism are readings that need to be critically challenged and even confronted. Being respectful means affirming the authenticity of students' experiences and reading strategies, and being responsible means critically engaging these experiences and reading strategies in order to enhance students' educational and spiritual formation.

One concrete idea for the classroom is to try an exercise recommended by homiletician Mark Allan Powell in *What Do They Hear? Bridging the Gap Between Pulpit and Pew.* Powell conducted case studies among preachers of different nationalities as to their reading strategies for the parable of the prodigal son. He surveyed three nationalities: Americans, Russians from the St. Petersburg region, and Tanzanians. The purpose of the study was to demonstrate divergences across national groups. Taking the parable of the prodigal son in Luke 15 as the main passage, Powell's case studies were designed to promote dialogue about the nuances of the passage, and also to spark meaningful conversations about the ethnic and national templates we use in our reading strategies. Powell uncovered differences among the three groups concerning what the prodigal son's "sin" was and divergences in the connections the commentaries made or failed to make, as well as disparities in the emphasis placed on individual versus corporate sin.[105] Homileticians might try conducting Powell's case

---

[105]Powell was especially interested in the details that were remembered and the details that were omitted, added, or changed in the story when the students were asked to recount it from memory. One hundred percent of the Americans polled remembered that the boy had squandered his inheritance. Only 6 percent remembered that there had been a famine in the land. Thirty-four percent of the Russian group mentioned squandering, but 84 percent remembered that there had been a famine. Powell's hypothesis is that, in 1941, the German army invaded St. Petersburg and subjected the people there to about a nine-hundred-day famine. For this group of Russian pastors, the fact that there was a famine was not an extraneous detail in the story. It was part of their lived experience. In discussions about how the boy had erred, Powell asked the groups: What was the boy's sin? The Americans returned to the fact that he had squandered his inheritance in licentious living. The Russians said in effect: "How revealing is it that Americans think the great sin was wasting money. They think this because money is very important to them" (p. 18). For the Russian test group, the sin was self-sufficiency and forsaking one's family. The Americans tended to construe the boy as wicked for losing his inheritance, whereas the Russians construed the boy as foolish for going out on his own. Powell also found that Eastern commentators highlighted intertextual connections with the Joseph story in Genesis, whereas most Western commentaries did not observe this connection. In the last group, the Tanzanian pastors and seminary students, some remembered the famine and some remembered that he squandered his inheritance, but about 80 percent remembered a detail that neither the Americans nor the Russians remembered: "No one gave him anything to eat." "Why should people give him something to eat?" Powell asked. "He squandered his inheritance." The Tanzanians thought this was a callous perspective.

study approach with students, and then compare and contrast the students' results with those from Russia and Tanzania.

Listen to how we use illustrations and anecdotes. This strategy is especially important for people who already preach on a regular basis, though it also applies to students and educators as well. How one uses illustrations is important not just because of what one says when using illustrative material, but also because of what one does not say. Both the said and the unsaid are important, especially in intercultural settings. Does one's illustrative material reflect listening to diverse voices rather than a single voice? Do one's illustrations communicate univocity or "plurivocity," to appropriate a term from the French philosopher Paul Ricoeur?[106]

As far back as 1988, Ronald J. Allen warned that a preacher's use of illustrations must be accompanied by practical theological reflection. Illustrations indirectly "signal" to the listener what matters and doesn't matter because of what is said and what is left unsaid. Allen writes:

> The illustrations and references to people and groups in the sermon have a particularly important social function as well. Those who appear, and do not appear, signal to the listeners who is important, who is not, who is valued, and who is ignored. The manner in which people and groups are pictured sends a clear message as to which social behaviors are approved and which are not.[107]

Although listening to and learning from diverse voices is probably more important in an intercultural congregation, it is not *un*important in monocultural congregations. In both settings, the said and the

---

The boy was an immigrant in a far-off country. Famines happen, and people lose their money all the time. This is just a part of life. The sin was less of an individual problem and more of a societal problem. In other words, they took a more allegorical approach. The father's house represented the way things should be in the kingdom of God. The far-off country represented life in "a society without honor," a culture that "shows no hospitality to the stranger in its midst" (p. 27). The sin in the parable was both individual and social. See Mark Allan Powell, *What Do They Hear? Bridging the Gap Between Pulpit and Pew* (Nashville: Abingdon, 2007), pp. 11-27.

[106]Ricoeur's interest in the term pertains more to possibilities for multiple readings and multiple voices in texts. He uses this phrase throughout his writings, but of special help would be the third essay in Paul Ricoeur, *Interpretation Theory: Discourse and the Surplus of Meaning* (Fort Worth: Texas Christian University Press, 1976); Paul Ricoeur, *From Text to Action* (Evanston, IL: Northwestern University Press, 2007), pp. 159-62.

[107]Ronald J. Allen, "The Social Function of Language in Preaching," in *Preaching as a Social Act: Theology and Practice*, ed. Arthur Van Seters (Nashville: Abingdon, 1988), p. 182.

unsaid communicate important information to listeners. If the heroes of the stories/illustrations are always white, then perhaps this implies that the stories of nonwhite heroes are not worth telling. If they are always men, what does that say to the women of the congregation? If they are always adults, are children being told they are always learners and adults are always teachers? Listening to and critically reflecting on how and why we use some illustrations and not others is an important and necessary practice.

Emphasize respectful listening through a 360-degree feedback loop. In every course I teach, I use a "360-degree feedback loop" to encourage class participation and careful listening during the feedback process. Homiletician André Resner suggests there are two main types of feedback: "violent" feedback and critically constructive feedback. "Violent forms of post-sermon evaluation are typically dominated by one authoritarian voice that offers some 'good' comments before signaling the turn to harsh critique with a 'but.'"[108] In order to facilitate (nonviolent) critically constructive feedback, the key to better evaluation does not lie in training preachers to preach, but in training listeners to listen. When student listeners learn how to reflect theologically on sermons, Resner argues, their listening is richer, their theological feedback is deeper, and, by extension, their sermons are stronger.

The 360-degree feedback loop is a simple way to train both preachers and listeners theologically and interculturally while also democratizing the evaluation process. The feedback loop is straightforward in that it begins and ends with the student preacher. First, I invite the student to speak with simple questions such as, *What did you like or dislike about the sermon,* or *What was it like for you to preach this sermon—how did you feel?* or some other open-ended, dialogically oriented statement such as, *Tell us about what it was like for you to prepare this sermon and to deliver it.*

Then I invite the members of the class to speak through asking more open-ended questions as a way to guide them through the feedback

---

[108]See André Resner, "No Preacher Left Behind: A New Prerequisite for the Introductory Preaching Course" (paper presented at the Annual Academy of Homiletics Conference, Washington, D.C., 2009), p. 40. Cf. also Daniel E. Harris's chapter on assessing sermons, "Methods of Assessment," in *Teaching Preaching as a Christian Practice: A New Approach to Homiletical Pedagogy,* ed. Thomas G. Long and Leonora Tubbs Tisdale (Louisville: Westminster John Knox, 2008).

process. I usually start with a positive question such as, *What did you appreciate about Maria's sermon?* before moving on to an improvement question such as, *What would make Maria's sermon better or stronger?*[109] At this point, I am still just a facilitator and nothing more. If the preacher is the first to identify a weakness in the sermon similar to those I have identified, then this can ease the feedback process. If the class offers something valuable that they noticed that the instructor didn't notice, then they are adding insight and co-constructing the feedback.

In a diverse classroom, if students have cultural, ethnic, or ecclesial blind spots, these are usually uncovered in this part of the feedback loop through such comments as, "I thought this sermon sounded too much like a performance," if the preacher has a poetic style; or "I thought the sermon was way too over the top," if the preacher has more of a pathos style. When students make such judgmental comments, these become occasions to practice respect and responsibility, to acknowledge their concerns as real to them while also creating an open space for the student preacher to educate the class as to why a poetic style, pathos appeals, or other aspects of their preaching are normative in their context. The student preacher may be eager to educate the class, or he may be timid. If the student is timid, then the professor can try to adjudicate these ethnic, cultural, or ecclesial tensions by exposing as pastorally as possible any cultural blind spots. Asking questions designed to name difference as an asset rather than a liability assists students in learning.

Only after the student preacher and members of the class have spoken do I offer constructive feedback on the sermon. This process is made simpler when the preacher and the class have already identified the same strengths and weaknesses that I wrote down. I discuss in a nonthreatening, nonjudgmental way what I observed concerning the student's content and delivery. Then I invite the student to have the last word in order to complete the 360-degree process. They might have a question, a comment based on an observation a fellow student made, or, as is

---

[109]Both André Resner and Thomas G. Long frame the places-for-improvement question in the following way: *What is the "growing edge" of this sermon?* Using the language of "growing edge," they argue, helps to frame the question in a constructive (nonjudgmental) way rather than a violent way. See Resner's discussion and his citation of Long in Resner, "No Preacher Left Behind," pp. 43, 46.

sometimes the case, they might have nothing to add. In adopting a 360-degree model of feedback, the goal is that the student preacher and the members of the class will have spaces in which they're given the power to speak and to reflect on preaching. The professor adopts the stance of a facilitator, a side coach, who assists students in speaking about and reflecting on preaching through careful and critical listening. To borrow an exhortation from Scripture, the educator is "quick to listen, slow to speak" (Jas 1:19).

Engage. The second interculturally proficient strategy is to *engage*, more specifically to engage in encounters across racial, ethnic, and ecclesial difference. This strategy belongs to the third A of the 3A Framework of Intercultural Competence Proficiency: action. Intercultural engagement requires intercultural inter*action*. In chapter one, we saw that Taylor crossed over racial and cultural divides as a preacher and pastor. He led predominantly white secular and religious organizations, built strategic friendships with white mainline preachers in New York, preached at predominantly white conferences, taught at predominantly white theological institutions, offered hospitality to white preachers at Concord, and practiced performative pastiche. In chapter four, we observed that his childhood influences, choices during his college years, and commitment to ecumenical cooperation shaped his intercultural competence. These are all different ways of stating that Taylor engaged with difference, that engagement helped him foster improvisational and intercultural proficiency. He crossed over established boundaries and transgressed borders of difference.

Educators who challenge students to engage in encounters across racial, ethnic, and ecclesial difference assist their students in IC proficiency development. According to Prue Holmes and Gillian O'Neill, ongoing engagement with a "cultural other" is crucial to the development of intercultural competence proficiency.[110] It is almost if not entirely impossible to develop intercultural competence *without* intercultural ex-

---

[110]Holmes and O'Neill lift up the "PEER model" of IC development: Prepare, Engage, Evaluate, and Reflect. For their discussion of the importance of engagement with a "Cultural Other," see Prue Holmes and Gillian O'Neill, "Developing and Evaluating Intercultural Competence: Ethnographies of Intercultural Encounters," *International Journal of Intercultural Relations* 36, no. 5 (September 2012): 711.

periences with cultural others. One way to engage students with difference is to celebrate diverse traditions. But celebration is not the only
way. Sometimes celebrating diversity is superficial because it avoids the
hard antiracism work of naming the beliefs and values beneath the
surface of cultural assumptions. So how do we encourage students to
engage with difference at a deeper level than celebration? One possible
answer is through in-class and out-of-class activities designed to dislocate ethnocentric vantage points.

Engage with difference through in-class activities. Some classroom activities can facilitate engagement with difference. In their book *Intercultural Training*, Richard Brislin and Tomoko Yoshida describe a simple
classroom exercise that helps students understand the difference between individualist and collectivist cultures.[111] The imagined scenario: six
office workers receive an unexpected $1 million profit. Some workers
contributed more than others to the project. In small groups, students
determine how to divide the money. Students who come from individualist cultures usually want to divide the money unequally since, in their
judgment, unequal work should result in unequal pay. By contrast, students from collectivist cultures usually recommend dividing the money
equally, since they are more concerned about the primacy of relationships, the long-term benefits of group harmony, and the prospect that
those who contributed less in the past will contribute more in the future.
When students observe the various results of the activity, it becomes an
opportunity for them to talk about the cultural assumptions they bring
to concepts like fairness, parity, equity, and harmony. In another section,
Brislin and Yoshida approach the same individualist-collectivist question
from a different angle. They ask: "If you went out to a restaurant with a
group of friends, would you split the cost evenly, would one person take
the tab, or would you pay only for what you have eaten?"[112]

Activities like these highlight the dissonances that emerge when the
beliefs and values that undergird cultural identities collide. One way to
uncover these differences in the homiletical classroom has already been

---

[111]Richard W. Brislin and Tomoko Yoshida, *Intercultural Communication Training: An Introduction*
(Thousand Oaks, CA: Sage, 1994), p. 183.
[112]Ibid., p. 55.

mentioned: listen to alternative readings. Although reading Scripture in community helps students improve their listening skills, it also helps them engage with their own cultural beliefs and values. One idea related to reading could be to ask students to break into small groups. Assign them all the same text, but give each group a different audience to whom this text will be preached. Then the one main question to ask is, *How might this text be heard in/by . . . ?* For example, How might this text be heard in an individualist culture versus a collectivist culture? By the poor? By immigrant communities? By affluent teenage Americans? By teenage gang members? By single mothers? The point of the exercise is simple: to get students talking about the cultural beliefs and values that shape their and others' reading strategies and to help them think interculturally as preachers. Students who experience cognitive dissonance concerning their own interpretive lens and recognize the provisional nature of that lens become more adept at engaging difference.

Also, through other assignments, teachers can help students engage with difference. In the collaboration section of this chapter, we saw that students have a more rewarding educational experience in classrooms where they co-construct their learning and are given opportunities to be coeducators. One way to help students engage difference (in a collaborative manner) is to ask them to give presentations in which they answer the question: *What are the issues and challenges facing the ___ church in America generally and preaching among ___ churches particularly?* For a question like this, it is okay to give students a lot of leeway. The fact that a number of choices are available allows them to pursue their own interests. Students may want to highlight generational differences by delivering a presentation on issues and challenges among Latin@ Pentecostal churches in the United States in general and preaching among first-generation and second-generation Latin@s in particular. Perhaps they want to highlight gender differences: issues facing African American Baptists generally and preaching by women in African American Baptist settings in particular. Through presentations, students educate the class about their traditions, cultural backgrounds, and ecclesial practices. In a sense, they function as live reporters giving an account to the class about what is taking place "on the ground" in the churches where they serve.

Engage with difference through out-of-class activities. In addition to in-class activities, out-of-class activities also help students engage difference. In *The Cultural Intelligence Difference*, David Livermore recommends various ways to study a "culture up close." Practices like studying non-verbal gestures through people-watching, attending cultural celebrations such as holidays, wedding ceremonies, or rights of passage, immersing oneself in art museums when in a foreign country, going to foreign movies, or reading foreign novels are just a few of the ways one can improve cultural intelligence.[113]

In *Intercultural Training*, Brislin and Yoshida recommend additional practices such as spending a day with an international student, attending a coming-of-age or national celebration with someone from a different culture, visiting a language school, or dining at a number of "ethnic" restaurants. Brislin and Yoshida cite two academic studies in which "the number of visits to various ethnic restaurants was found to be significantly correlated with intercultural sensitivity [my term is IC]" and a person's "willingness to change one's typical behaviors."[114]

How does one tailor these out-of-class activities for a typical preaching course? One idea is for students to interview international students about their various experiences of preaching. Some training in what subjects to broach and to avoid might be required for an assignment like this so that American students don't insult international students or make them feel pressure to speak on behalf of all people from their home nation. Another idea would be for students to observe preaching practices in an immigrant church setting, or, if they come from an immigrant church, a setting that is markedly different from their own. For an assignment like this, students might ask the following questions:

1. What does preaching sound like in this context and why?

2. What image is most appropriate to describe how the preacher is seen by the congregation?

---

[113]David A. Livermore, *The Cultural Intelligence Difference: Master the One Skill You Can't Do Without in Today's Global Economy* (New York: American Management Association, 2011), pp. 78-84. For more ideas like these, cf. also Duane Elmer, *Cross-Cultural Connections: Stepping Out and Fitting In Around the World* (Downers Grove, IL: InterVarsity Press, 2009).

[114]Brislin and Yoshida, *Intercultural Communication Training*, p. 186.

3. What are the nonverbal cues I observe of the preacher and the listeners in this context?

4. How are biblical texts interpreted in this context?

5. How is language used in this context?

Develop pedagogical strategies that enhance intercultural competence proficiency. Another idea is for homileticians to rethink existing pedagogical strategies.[115] In a diverse classroom, one way to help students engage with difference is by giving reading assignments that acknowledge their diverse backgrounds and interests. Even in classes that are more monocultural, offering students a wide range of books and articles is still beneficial in that it exposes them to diverse interpretive strategies, theologies, and preaching practices. Recall that the first of the three A's is knowledge *acquisition.* Students who read about practices in other ecclesial-cultural settings acquire knowledge that aids in enhancing their IC proficiency. One of the goals of an IC proficient professor should be to familiarize students with expressions of preaching outside their own context. Exposing students to diverse academic readings is one way to accomplish this goal.

Educational theorist Barbara Gross Davis contends that simple adjustments to a teacher's pedagogical strategy can also enhance intercultural competence. Here is a representative sample of Davis's ideas for planning and teaching courses that are more culturally inclusive:[116]

- Be aware of misinterpreting students' nonverbal behaviors.

- Use inclusive language and examples in class.

- Learn to pronounce names correctly.

- Try to select texts and readings whose language is gender neutral and free of stereotypes.

---

[115] Faculty participants in other disciplines, and in partnership with the Teachers College at Columbia University, are already doing important work in intercultural pedagogy. Geneva Gay has developed an intercultural approach to higher education known as culturally responsive teaching, or CRT. See Geneva Gay, *Culturally Responsive Teaching: Theory, Research, and Practice* (New York: Teachers College Press, 2010).

[116] This list is a representative, paraphrased sample of Davis's ideas for educators rather than an exhaustive list. See Barbara Gross Davis, *Tools for Teaching* (San Francisco: Jossey-Bass, 2009), pp. 59-67.

- Do not assume that all students will recognize cultural, literary, or historical references familiar to you.
- Bring in guest lecturers.
- Do not treat students as spokespersons for their demographic group.
- Use a variety of names in classroom examples and test questions.

As an amendment to Davis, remember that some students come from cultures in which it is rude to speak up in class unless invited to do so by the professor. For such students, raising one's hand or talking too much might be seen as a sign of disrespect. These students almost never raise their hands unless an IC proficient professor calls on them. By contrast, other students are so used to speaking up regularly in class that the professor's responsibility in this situation might be to help these students learn to listen more and speak less.

Discover ways to help students apprentice themselves to preachers outside their tradition. The definition of "outside" might mean a preacher who is racially or ethnically different, or it might mean one who is ecclesially different. What would happen if students listened to preaching outside their own ethnic, racial, or ecclesial tradition on a semiregular basis in preaching class? Taking it a step further, what would happen if students apprenticed themselves to a preaching mentor outside their ecclesial tradition either formally in a mentoring relationship or informally through listening to a preacher's audio or video sermons regularly? The latter option might be a less intimidating step than the former. The point is to take *a* step. Continued exposure to an accomplished preacher outside one's tradition would not only enrich a student's preaching; it would also expand their definition of what constitutes "good" preaching: what it is, what it isn't, and what it sounds like. Recall that Taylor was willing to do this as early as his college years at Oberlin. Reading preachers from *outside* his tradition aided his development and enhanced his intercultural competence.

This next option might prove more valuable in a classroom setting: students can benefit from listening to and studying crossover preachers, that is, preachers who excel at being both improvisational and intercultural and who are able to negotiate difference effectively in diverse

preaching contexts. If one of our pedagogical goals is enhanced intercultural competence, then students will only benefit from listening to
and studying preachers who demonstrate IC proficiency. The possibilities for reflection and research are numerous and extend beyond
Gardner C. Taylor. For instance, students could compare and contrast
a James Forbes sermon delivered at the Hampton Institute Minister's
conference with a sermon delivered at the Riverside Church, the National Cathedral, or the Princeton University Chapel. Likewise, students could compare and contrast an Elizabeth Condé-Frazier sermon
delivered at an affluent, white, evangelical women's conference with a
sermon delivered at a Latin@ Pentecostal church in a poor, urban
neighborhood. Or students could employ a different tactic and study
preachers at interculturally diverse churches in order to research what
preaching strategies are effective in these settings. These are just three
examples. The point is this: students can gain knowledge about how
crossover preaching works through listening to and conducting research
on IC proficient crossover preachers.

Assess. The third interculturally competent proficient strategy is to
assess. Assessment assists professors and students in gaining knowledge
acquisition, the first of the three A's. The assessment strategy I recommend
in this section is not drawn from Taylor's preaching per se. Most of the
tools used in IC assessment have been developed in the last twenty
years—in other words, after Taylor retired. The data presented here are
drawn from recent developments in intercultural competence theory.

If one of the goals of IC proficiency attainment is progress over time,
then this makes assessment invaluable. It quantifies progress. Especially
at educational institutions that focus on measurable learning outcomes,
quantifiable data are important. Assessment can look a lot of different
ways in IC pedagogy. One way to assess IC proficiency is through conducting interviews with students. Another way is through written assignments like journals, case studies, or reflection papers.

The best empirical method for assessing IC proficiency is through
an *intercultural competence assessment test (ICAT).* The acronym ICAT
is not common in IC theory. I use it as shorthand to describe written
assessment tests of IC proficiency. Professors can offer these tests at

the beginning *and* the end of the semester as a way to gauge a student's individual progress in IC proficiency. If the student enrolls in classes for more than one semester, the professor can stretch ICATs out to a year or more. For obvious reasons, student scores on this test are not part of their overall grade. The instructor's job is not to reward the students whose scores are high and penalize the students whose scores are low, but to note their progress in becoming more interculturally proficient over time. The primary benefit of assessing students through an ICAT is that it gives us "hard data" to measure where students are when the semester/year begins and whether they have made progress by the time it ends.

Some intercultural competence theorists have brief assessments that cover a particular subarea in IC theory, such as communication strategies, low-context and high-context differences, tolerance for ambiguity, and perceptions of time. Students complete these assessments in a short period of time and can discuss one particular aspect of intercultural competence awareness. For example, in *Improving Intercultural Interactions: Modules for Cross-Cultural Training Programs*, one finds various shorter ICATs pertaining to cultural awareness, individualism-collectivism, and knowledge of nonverbal cues.[117] In *Bridging Differences*, William B. Gudykunst has thirty different shorter ICATs covering topics such as empathy, conflict resolution, listening, gender, national identity, and generational interaction, along with many other subjects.[118]

A number of longer ICATs are available through business organizations and educational institutes. In fact, at least ten *major* tests exist at present.[119] Two tests in particular are professional, widely used, and available in university and graduate school settings. The first test is a fifty-four-question free assessment found in the appendix to Christopher P. Earley, Soon Ang, and Joo-Seng Tan's *Cultural Intelligence:*

---

[117]See Richard W. Brislin and Tomoko Yoshida, *Improving Intercultural Interactions: Modules for Cross-Cultural Training Programs* (Thousand Oaks, CA: Sage, 1994).

[118]William B. Gudykunst, *Bridging Differences: Effective Intergroup Communication* (Thousand Oaks, CA: Sage, 1998).

[119]For the latest survey and evaluation of the ten major tests offered, see David Matsumoto and Hyisung C. Hwang, "Assessing Cross-Cultural Competence: A Review of Available Tests," *Journal of Cross-Cultural Psychology* 44, no. 6 (August 2013): 849-73.

Individual Interactions Across Cultures.[120] The test is called "A Self Assessment of Your CQ." CQ is shorthand for cultural intelligence, the designation Earley, Ang, and Tan use when describing "a person's capability for successful adaptation to new cultural settings, that is, for unfamiliar settings attributable to cultural context," the same phenomenon I (and others) refer to as intercultural competence.[121] The cultural intelligence "CQ" model is divided according to three main competencies: knowledge CQ (also called "cultural strategic thinking"), motivational CQ, and behavioral CQ.[122] Knowledge CQ refers to the "general thinking skills that you use to understand how and why people act as they do in a new culture."[123] This first competency is guided by the question, *How and why do people do what they do here?* The second competency, motivational CQ, pertains to the level of a person's volition in intercultural contexts, especially in the face of adverse situations.[124] This second competency is guided by the question, *Am I motivated to do something here?* The third competency, behavioral CQ, pertains to the "capability of an

---

[120]Cf. also P. Christopher Earley, Soon Ang, and Joo-Seng Tan, *CQ: Developing Cultural Intelligence at Work* (Stanford, CA: Stanford Business Books, 2006), pp. 217-27. Cf. also P. Christopher Earley and Soon Ang, *Cultural Intelligence: Individual Interactions Across Cultures* (Stanford, CA: Stanford Business Books, 2003).

[121]Earley and Ang, *Cultural Intelligence*, p. 59.

[122]See Earley and Ang, *Cultural Intelligence*. In their earlier work, Earley and Ang instead organize their model according to four competencies: metacognitive CQ, cognitive CQ, motivational CQ, and behavioral CQ. Fons J. R. Van de Vijver and Kwok Leung provide an excellent summary of each of these core competencies: "*Metacognitive CQ* refers to the mental capability to acquire and understand cultural knowledge. *Cognitive CQ* refers to the general knowledge and knowledge structures about culture. *Motivational CQ* refers to the capability for an individual to direct energy toward learning about and functioning in intercultural situations. Finally, *behavioral CQ* refers to the capability of an individual to exhibit appropriate verbal and nonverbal actions in culturally diverse settings." Fons J. R. Van de Vijver and Kwok Leung, "Methodological Issues in Researching Intercultural Competence," in *The Sage Handbook of Intercultural Competence*, ed. Darla K. Deardorff (Thousand Oaks, CA: Sage, 2009), p. 407 (emphasis added).

[123]Earley, Ang, and Tan, *CQ*, p. 5.

[124]Several communication theorists have pointed to the importance and even indispensability of motivation in acquiring intercultural competence. Brian Spitzberg and William Cupach suggest that motivation is one of three main components of communicative competence. Fiora Biagi et al. argue that "personal motivation affects in a considerable way the acquisition of RIC" (RIC stands for reflective intercultural competence). See Brian H. Spitzberg and William R. Cupach, *Interpersonal Communication Competence* (Beverly Hills, CA: Sage, 1984), as cited in Gudykunst, *Bridging Differences*, p. 105. See also Fiora Biagi et al., "Reflective Intercultural Competence (RIC) and Its Assessment: The RICA Model," in *Intercultural Horizons: Best Practices in Intercultural Competence Development*, ed. Eliza J. Nash, Nevin C. Brown, and Lavinia Bracci (Newcastle upon Tyne, UK: Cambridge Scholars Publishing, 2012), p. 63.

individual to exhibit appropriate verbal and nonverbal actions in culturally diverse settings."[125] The relevant question for this third competency is, *Am I able to do the right thing culturally in specific situations?* A
high-CQ leader possesses knowledge, motivation, and behavior across
differences in culture without being disingenuous or artificial among
those with whom he or she interacts.

In *Cultural Intelligence,* students are granted access to a free ten-page
self-assessment test designed to measure their CQ. After they complete
the test, they tabulate their overall CQ score, and they tabulate their
scores in the three subareas of knowledge, motivation, and behavior. On
the last two pages of the test students interpret their overall score and
their subarea scores in order to find out where they excel, where they
have moderate skills, and where they need improvement. In *The Cultural
Intelligence Difference,* published five years later in 2011, David Livermore
draws on Earley, Ang, and Tan's research. He offers an *online* CQ assessment to anyone who purchases his book. He divides his online test
into four interrelated areas instead of three: CQ drive (motivation), CQ
knowledge, CQ strategy, and CQ action.[126]

The second test is known as the "Intercultural Development Inventory"
(IDI), and it has been developed according to Milton J. Bennett's Developmental Model of Intercultural Sensitivity (DMIS).[127] Bennett's
DMIS model is a developmental model.[128] It is a progressive, step-
oriented system that consists of six phases: (1) denial, (2) defense/reversal,
(3) minimization, (4) acceptance, (5) adaptation, and (6) integration.
Bennett's larger metabehavioral aim is to move the student learner from
ethnocentrism (steps one to three) to ethno-relativism (steps four to six).
His thesis is that as "one's experience of cultural difference becomes more

[125] Van de Vijver and Leung, "Methodological Issues in Researching Intercultural Competence," p. 407.

[126] Livermore, *Cultural Intelligence Difference.*

[127] At present Bennett is the executive director of the Intercultural Development Research Institute (IDRI) in Hillsboro, Oregon. He does business and education trainings through the Institute and makes some of his research available on www.intercultural.org. Bennett also maintains an additional IDR Institute in Milan, Italy. For an overview of the genesis and development of the IDI, see Hammer, Bennett, and Wiseman, "Measuring Intercultural Sensitivity."

[128] In the words of Bennett, "A developmental model, then, should both illustrate 'improvement' in the ability to comprehend and experience difference, and it should imply the strategies that will impede such experience." See Bennett, "A Developmental Approach to Training for Intercultural Sensitivity," p. 181.

complex and sophisticated, one's potential competence in intercultural relations increases."[129] The student learner who progresses to step six can be characterized as displaying a high level of what Bennett refers to as "intercultural sensitivity": the desired outcome of the DMIS model.[130] The IDI is a fifty-item questionnaire designed according to Bennett's DMIS Model. (Although it is based on and measured according to Bennett's model, it was prepared over a several-year span through the research of Mitchell R. Hammer, Milton J. Bennett, and Richard Wiseman.[131]) When students take the IDI, they are invited to answer questions on a scale of 1 to 5, with 1 being "disagree," 5 being "agree." The numbers 2, 3, and 4 represent the various possibilities between these two extremes. Student results on the IDI place them in one of the five categories mentioned previously: defense-denial, reversal, minimization, acceptance-adaptation, and encapsulated marginality. Since Bennett's model is progressive and developmental, the data from the IDI can be used to help students gauge their progress in moving from one step to another no matter where they are on the scale.

ICATs are also useful for professors to take. When teachers are willing to subject themselves to the same level of cultural self-scrutiny to which their students are subjected, they signal to students their ongoing commitment to being a colearner in intercultural competence, and they signal to themselves (and each other) that they are in no way exempt from succumbing to similar cultural blind spots.

Decenter. The final strategy is to *decenter*. In particular, the goal is decentering from ethnocentricity. In many ways, decentering requires an equal commitment to all three A's: acquisition, aptitude, and action. Remember that the goal of Bennett's DMIS model is to help students move from ethnocentrism to ethno-relativism.[132] This should also be a major goal of an interculturally competent pedagogy. Moving out of ethnocentrism is, by definition, a process of decentering. For the Christian, this process is not only psychological, but also *kenotic* (Phil 2:5-11).

---

[129]Hammer, Bennett, and Wiseman, "Measuring Intercultural Sensitivity," p. 423.

[130]Bennett, "A Developmental Approach to Training for Intercultural Sensitivity," p. 179.

[131]Hammer, Bennett, and Wiseman, "Measuring Intercultural Sensitivity: The Intercultural Development Inventory."

[132]Ibid., p. 423.

Recall what Miroslav Volf states in *Exclusion and Embrace*: that, in order for the self to create space for the other, it must be "decentered" in order to be "recentered" on the only person who should occupy the central place, namely, Jesus Christ. True centeredness is found by "participating in the death and resurrection of Christ through faith and baptism."[133] The absence of centeredness leads to the exclusion of others. The presence of it leads to the embrace of others.[134]

Decentering is integral to our identity as Christian pilgrims. Historically, the church is diasporic and migratory. We belong to a "pilgrim church." As missiologist David Bosch puts it,

> The church is a pilgrim not simply for the practical reason that in the modern age it no longer calls the tune and is everywhere finding itself in a diaspora situation; rather, to be a pilgrim in the world belongs intrinsically to the church's ex-centric position. It is *ek-klesia*, "called out" of the world, and sent back into the world. Foreignness is an element of its constitution.[135]

Decentering reminds us that "foreignness is an element of [our] constitution." Through decentering, we are disoriented from being ethnocentric for the sake of reorienting our identity as Christian pilgrims.

It is clear that Taylor committed himself to decentering even though he didn't use this exact language. Being improvisational requires being protean, that is, not being fixed to only one form of expression. Being interculturally competent requires being curious about other cultures, engaging with people from other cultures, and not allowing the enclosure of one's identity within a hermetically sealed cultural marker.[136] Recall Taylor's point that culture is important, but it is not a prison—"it does not have to circumscribe us." Culture is a "secondary identity over

---

[133]Miroslav Volf, *Exclusion and Embrace: A Theological Exploration of Identity, Otherness, and Reconciliation* (Nashville: Abingdon, 1996), p. 70.

[134]See Volf's discussion of centeredness in Jesus Christ as the prerequisite for denouncing exclusion and practicing embrace in ibid., p. 78.

[135]David J. Bosch, *Transforming Mission: Paradigm Shifts in Theology of Mission* (Maryknoll, NY: Orbis Books, 1991), pp. 373-74.

[136]Sharan B. Merriam recommends that Western pedagogies also need to be decentered so that non-Western practices of learning and knowing can emerge and take root among educators. See Sharan B. Merriam, ed., *Non-Western Perspectives on Learning and Knowing* (Malabar, FL: Krieger, 2007).

which we rank the demands of God."[137] This is arguably similar to the process Volf describes: decentering for the sake of recentering on the one who has the right to occupy the central place, Jesus Christ.

Decentering is an important value to embrace, but as a concept, it is also abstract. What does it look like on the ground? What are some concrete ways to encourage students to decenter? Let me recommend two possible answers: critical self-study and reflective immersion.

Encourage critical self-study. The primary question here for the student to reflect on critically is, *What are the beliefs, values, and thought patterns that exist in my culture at the unconscious level?* In laying out his Intercultural Communicative Competence model (ICC), Michael Byram argues that the highest level of IC is "critical cultural awareness" (*savoir s'engager*). Those with high levels of critical cultural awareness not only have an ability to communicate effectively with people of other cultures; they also have an ability to reflect critically on the "practices and products" of their own culture.[138] Persons with high levels of critical cultural consciousness are willing to shine the mirror back on their own culture—its beliefs, values and thought patterns—just as frequently as they hold up a magnifying glass to other cultures. Because Byram's primary audience is foreign language teachers, he focuses more on linguistic competence across cultural difference. Yet his insights on cultural self-awareness should not be overlooked as constructive for homiletical pedagogy just because he writes to a different audience. Byram reminds us that, in addition to engaging with the "language (varieties) and culture(s) of others," people with high levels of critical cultural awareness also seek to understand their own language, thought patterns, and cultural values at both the macro and micro levels.[139] Drawing pri-

---

[137]WGT 5:53.

[138]According to Byram, persons with high levels of *savoir s'engager* have an understanding of the relationship between their own language and language varieties in their own culture *and* cultures of different social groups in their society, on the one hand, and the language (varieties) and culture(s) of others, between (inter) which they find themselves acting as mediators (Michael Byram, *Teaching and Assessing Intercultural Communicative Competence* [Philadelphia: Multilingual Matters, 1997], p. 53).

[139]James Nieman and Thomas Rogers suggest that knowing one's own culture is an important step in being able to negotiate difference effectively in a multicultural congregation. See James R. Nieman and Thomas G. Rogers, *Preaching to Every Pew: Cross-Cultural Strategies* (Minneapolis: Fortress, 2001), pp. 140-41.

marily from Edward T. Hall, Gary M. Weaver uses the analogy of an iceberg to argue the same point. A person's internal culture, Weaver claims, can be compared to an iceberg: 10 percent of it is above the surface and the other 90 percent resides under the surface, as it were, at the unconscious level. "When one enters another culture," writes Weaver, "it is somewhat like two icebergs colliding—the real clash occurs beneath the water where values and thought patterns conflict."[140] What exists underwater, where the clashes take place, is what Hall means by a person's internal culture. Through the process of intercultural communication and crosscultural engagement, new knowledge of the self emerges. A person becomes "more aware or conscious of his or her own internal culture . . . [and can] raise to the conscious level that part of culture which is internal or unconscious."[141] Put differently, the way to enhanced IC proficiency comes not only through knowledge of other cultures but also through knowledge of one's own culture; it comes not only by acculturation, but by enculturation. As Terry Ford writes, "critical self-reflection is the action through which individuals become more conscious of themselves, and more understanding of how others also operate in the world."[142]

At present, homileticians do not discuss the importance of critical self-study in-depth, at least the kind of *cultural* self-study that enhances intercultural competence. The literature is limited. Thomas H. Troeger and Leonora Tubbs Tisdale have a number of reflection exercises for individuals and small groups that highlight the various expectations and assumptions that preachers bring to the preaching task.[143] James R. Nieman and Thomas G. Rogers discuss the importance of "knowing yourself" through doing "self-reflective cultural work." In fact, they claim

---

[140]Gary R. Weaver, "Understanding and Coping with Cross-Cultural Adjustment Stress," in *Culture, Communication, and Conflict*, ed. Gary R. Weaver (Boston: Pearson Learning Solutions, 2000), p. 190. In *Beyond Culture*, Edward T. Hall makes a similar point to Byram's: that a person must be able to identify his or her internal culture in order to engage effectively with external culture. See Edward T. Hall, *Beyond Culture* (Garden City, NY: Anchor, 1976), pp. 79-101.

[141]Weaver, "Understanding and Coping with Cross-Cultural Adjustment Stress," p. 190.

[142]Terry Ford, *Becoming Multicultural: Personal and Social Construction Through Critical Teaching* (New York: Falmer, 1999), p. 23.

[143]See "Hallmarks of Preaching" exercise and "Diversity of Our Preaching Expectations" exercise in Troeger and Tisdale, *A Sermon Workbook*, pp. 10, 17.

that such work can be "profoundly liberating" to a preacher.[144] Lisa Washington Lamb claims that preachers must recognize their own social location and ethnic identity as integral to the work they do in multi-ethnic churches.[145] However, none of these homileticians offers concrete ideas for how to do this important work.

Critical self-study *can* become a core value in overt ways in the preaching classroom, particularly through assignments in which students identify, name, and bring to consciousness their cultural beliefs, values, and thought patterns. Homiletics professors can ask their students how preaching shaped them growing up, what blind spots they might bring to preaching, how their denominational affiliations shape their expectations of preaching, and how their unique voice and vantage point contribute to preaching.

There are also covert pedagogical ways to bring about critical self-study. Especially in diverse classrooms, the feedback loop after students preach is fertile soil for critical self-study. We can ask questions like: *How do you think you preach similarly or differently from your past preaching mentors? How do you think your sermon would be received at your field education site versus here in the classroom (explain your answer)? How do you think your denominational affiliations shape your preaching style? What does preaching "success" look like in your context?*[146] Of course, questions like these (and others) would not need to be directed only to the student preacher. They could also be directed to the class, especially when other students give feedback that sounds ethnocentric.

Finally, instructor-based cultural self-reflection is integral to the practice of critical self-study.[147] Recall Robert C. Weigl's claim that cul-

---

[144]Nieman and Rogers, *Preaching to Every Pew*, pp. 140-41.

[145]Lisa Washington Lamb, *Blessed and Beautiful: Multiethnic Churches and the Preaching That Sustains Them* (Eugene, OR: Cascade, 2014), pp. 132, 178.

[146]This question was adapted from a similar question David Livermore suggests for conducting critical self-study. See Livermore, *Cultural Intelligence Difference*, p. 95.

[147]In a book written to Western-trained Christian educators, Judith E. Lingenfelter and Sherwood A. Lingenfelter describe the importance of cultural self-reflection: "All of us [teachers] are people of a culture, and we carry our cultural heritage and practices, including our practice of faith, with us into every situation of life. Unless we have a clear understanding of our cultural self and how that self restricts our acceptance of and service to others, we will not readily reach an understanding of others or be able to serve them effectively." See Judith Lingenfelter and Sherwood G. Lingenfelter, *Teaching Cross-Culturally: An Incarnational Model for Learning and Teaching* (Grand Rapids: Baker Academic, 2003), p. 9.

tural self-study is vital to intercultural competence.[148] Instructors are not exempt from Weigl's challenge. In *Teaching Inclusively in Higher Education*, Susan C. Brown claims: "Inclusive college instructors wishing success for all students embrace diversity not just as a nice idea, but as a working condition. To do this, they first need to examine themselves and their teaching to see how their beliefs, values, attitudes and behaviors influence the students' learning." In this book, Brown provides a thirty-question self-assessment called "Instructor Self-Assessment in Multicultural and Global Education" for instructors who desire to become more inclusive as educators.[149] As Barbara Gross Davis reminds us, instructors in higher education must be willing to ask themselves difficult cultural self-reflection questions if they expect to build inclusive classrooms.[150]

Mindful IC educators are cultural colearners with their students. Professors who do not engage in critical-cultural self-reflection for the purpose of unveiling (in some capacity) their own cultural identity markers and cultural blind spots will always risk teaching in exclusive rather than inclusive ways. According to educational theorists Susan C. Brown and Moira A. Fallon, the absence of critical-cultural self-reflection among instructors often leads to "cultural mismatches" between professors and students in which students suffer rather than thrive.[151] Preachers who value cultural inclusivity in their classes work hard at doing self-critical spadework in order to avoid these mismatches.

Promote reflective immersion. Still another possible way to engage stu-

---

[148]Robert C. Weigl, "Intercultural Competence Through Cultural Self-Study: A Strategy for Adult Learners," *International Journal of Intercultural Relations* 33 (2009).

[149]Susan C. Brown, "Students as Cultural Beings," in *Teaching Inclusively in Higher Education*, ed. Susan C. Brown and Moira A. Fallon (Charlotte, NC: Information Age Publishing, 2010), pp. 20-21.

[150]In her book *Tools for Teaching*, Barbara Gross Davis recommends these six questions (which she compiled from various articles and books) as prompts to help instructors reflect on their classroom practices: "1) Do you interact with men and women in ways that manifest double standards, 2) Do you inadvertently undervalue comments made by speakers whose English is accented differently from your own?, 3) Do you assume that students of some racial or ethnic groups will need additional help? Or that students of some racial or ethnic group will do better than others?, 4) Are you comfortable around people whose racial, ethnic, or sexual identity differs from your own?, 5) Are you comfortable disclosing your knowledge of and experiences with diversity?, 6) How do you handle your own doubts or ambivalence about multicultural issues?" See Davis, *Tools for Teaching*, p. 57.

[151]Susan C. Brown and Moira A. Fallon, "A Student-Centered Approach to College Classrooms," in Brown and Fallon, eds., *Teaching Inclusively in Higher Education*, pp. 8-9.

dents interculturally is through *reflective immersion*. What would happen if professors provided students with at least one opportunity to take a preaching course in a crosscultural context either here in the United States or in an overseas setting, and to reflect on what they learned? Although the preference would be for students to travel overseas, some places in the United States might suffice quite well. For instance, an instructor could take rural seminary students to an urban setting, urban students to a rural setting, or white students to a predominantly non-white setting. In settings like these, students have an opportunity to experience preaching in a cultural milieu radically different from their own. Ideally, they would also be in conversation with other seminary students and preachers from the country or place they visit so as to facilitate peer interaction and evaluation. Such dialogue creates space for students to practice intercultural competence proficiency together.

Formal education in a traditional classroom only takes a student to a certain level of IC proficiency. At some point, real-life experience interacting with people who are culturally different is required. David Livermore claims: "Any formal education in cultural intelligence or the like must include immersion in various cultural contexts."[152] The courses that are best suited for enhancing IC proficiency include "some kind of immersion in various cultural contexts where you actually spend time with people from that culture."[153]

In a 2004 study on the impact of study-abroad experiences on undergraduates and their levels of IC, Tracy Rundstrom Williams was able to demonstrate that "students who study abroad exhibit a greater change in intercultural communication skills after their semester abroad than students who stay on campus."[154] The two specific skills Williams was able to identify through data assessments were intercultural adaptability and intercultural sensitivity. Students who studied abroad, especially

---

[152]David A. Livermore, *Cultural Intelligence: Improving Your CQ to Engage Our Multicultural World* (Grand Rapids: Baker Academic, 2009), p. 252.

[153]David A. Livermore, *Leading with Cultural Intelligence: The New Secret to Success* (New York: AMACOM, 2010), p. 174.

[154]Tracy Rundstrom Williams, "Exploring the Impact of Study Abroad on Students' Intercultural Communication Skills: Adaptability and Sensitivity," *Journal of Studies in International Education* 9, no. 4 (2005): 356.

those exposed to various foreign cultures rather than one foreign culture, displayed greater intercultural competence proficiency. After their study-abroad experience, they could more easily adapt and were more interculturally sensitive than their non–study abroad counterparts.

As important as immersion is to enhancing intercultural competence, an additional pedagogical step is also needed. Two recent studies indicate that cultural immersion alone does not guarantee high levels of IC proficiency. According to these recent studies, courses in which the instructor does not take an active, intentional, and strategic role in teaching about intercultural competence before, during, and after immersion experiences tend to produce students with lower levels of IC proficiency.[155] This is why critical *reflection* is so crucial.[156] The emphasis in courses like these should be on reflective immersion as opposed to

---

[155]In a 2012 study conducted in the United States, academic researchers Elizabeth Root and Anchalee Ngampornchai analyzed eighteen reflective papers of students who had recently returned from study abroad experiences and concluded that, "while experiences abroad have an obvious impact on students' cognitive, affective, and behavioral skills, they do not necessarily help to develop deeper levels of intercultural competence . . . immersion into the culture alone may not increase intercultural competence." See Elizabeth Root and Anchalee Ngampornchai, "'I Came Back as a New Human Being': Student Descriptions of Intercultural Competence Acquired Through Education Abroad Experiences," *Journal of Studies in International Education* 17, no. 5 (2012): 513. In a 2013 study conducted in Australia, academic researchers Franziska Trede, Wendy Bowles, and Donna Bridges were able to demonstrate a connection between unreflective, unstrategic intercultural pedagogies in study-abroad programs (in Australia) and poor returns on investment, that is, universities producing students with low levels of IC proficiency. An international experience without a strong pedagogical framework to interpret it had the potential to reinscribe rather than eradicate ethnocentric and even racist ways of thinking. As Trede, Bowles, and Bridges explain, "Immersion in culture is not, on its own, an assurance of intercultural learning. Providing international experiences without a pedagogical framework that helps students to reflect on self and others can be a wasted opportunity and runs the risk of reinforcing stereotypical thinking and racist attitudes." See Franziska Trede, Wendy Bowles, and Donna Bridges, "Developing Intercultural Competence and Global Citizenship Through International Experiences: Academics' Perceptions," *Intercultural Education* 24, no. 5 (2013): 442. For a recent discussion of students' study-abroad experiences, one that broadly covers subjects such as what students are learning, what they're not learning, and the role of the instructor in learning, see Michael Vande Berg, R. Michael Paige, and Kris Hemming Lou, eds., *Student Learning Abroad: What Our Students Are Learning, What They're Not, and What We Can Do About It* (Sterling, VA: Stylus Publishing, 2012).

[156]According to educational theorist Stephen D. Brookfield, students' ability to identify and reflect on the assumptions that influence their actions and ways of thinking is a crucial step on the road toward higher-level critical thinking. Brookfield suggests that students must be able to do at least four things when it comes to their own assumptions about the world around them: "hunt" out assumptions, check assumptions, see things from different perspectives, and take informed action. See Stephen D. Brookfield, *Teaching for Critical Thinking: Tools and Techniques to Help Students Question Their Assumptions* (San Francisco: Jossey-Bass, 2012), pp. 1, 11-14.

unexamined, uncritical, nonreflective immersion. Biagi and others argue that students who do not engage in critical reflection lack "deep understanding."[157] However, when students reflect on why they do what they do and are self-aware regarding the limitations and benefits of their own culture and other cultures, they develop "critical cultural awareness," to use Byram's phrase.[158] Any preaching course in which immersion is a major component also requires reflective elements such as journaling, reflection paper assignments, or group reflection.

For obvious reasons, it is not possible to make travel courses a requirement for seminary students. Also, these courses tend to attract students who are already convinced that intercultural competence is beneficial rather than those whose IC scores are remedial. Reflective immersion courses would be an option that professors could make available but could not require. If a travel course is not an option, perhaps the homiletics instructor could create assignments that immerse students in unfamiliar church settings a few times per semester or year. Students could participate in church services at immigrant churches and dialogue with pastors in these churches, or perhaps these church visits could be added to the requirements of the seminary's field education department.

CONCLUSION

The strategies we recommended in this chapter converge with practices latent in Taylor's homiletical approach in many ways. However, in other ways, they diverge. Some strategies are a creative attempt to go beyond what we can learn from Taylor. His preaching practices are one conversation partner, but improvisational theory and intercultural theory are equal partners (if not lead partners).

While these theories refine and deepen our understanding of Taylor's homiletical approach, in many ways they take us beyond Taylor. Recent

---

[157]Biagi et al., "Reflective Intercultural Competence (RIC) and Its Assessment: The RICA Model," pp. 62-64.

[158]Byram argues that those with high levels of critical cultural awareness not only have an ability to communicate with people of other cultures; they also have an ability to reflect critically on the "practices and products of their own culture." See Byram, *Teaching and Assessing Intercultural Communicative Competence*, p. 53.

developments in improvisational and intercultural theory are the ground for the strategies I recommended. PACE and LEAD are inspired by Taylor's preaching, but they are not exactly derived from it. What we can conclude about Taylor, however, is this: latent in his preaching practices one observes the firstfruits of an improvisational-intercultural approach that highlights his unique contribution and, more important for contemporary discussion, illumines his contemporary significance to churches and seminary classrooms in the present and the future. It is in these places that a crossover homiletic inspired by Taylor's approach and deepened and refined by improvisational and intercultural theory has the potential to take root and to flourish.

CROSSING *LA FRONTERA* (THE BORDER)

*I have always felt that the action most worth watching
is not at the center of things but where the edges meet . . . often,
if you stand at the point of tangency, you can see both sides
better than if you were in the middle of either one.*

Anne Fadiman
The Spirit Catches You and You Fall Down

*You never want to have a gospel that you
can only preach on one side of town.*

Manuel L. Scott Sr.
The Quotable Manuel Scott Sr.

◆

It was a spring day in Princeton, New Jersey, in April 2014, thirteen years removed from Andrew F. Walls delivering the Stone Lectures at Princeton Theological Seminary. This time, the speakers were minoritized Princeton University undergraduate students wanting to speak out against racism by means of a collaborative online photo essay that they titled "We, Too, Are Princeton. We, Too, Are Human."[1] In each photo

---

[1]Their manifesto reads as follows: "In the wake of a post-racial ideology circulating in our society today, it is imperative that the light of the struggles that categorize this nation is not erased. With this circulation also comes the muting of the voices that make up the sound of the U.S. This is an

essay, a student held a placard with one or two sentences designed to reveal his or her pain, to render visible that which was invisible, and to complexify reified constructions of identity. A male student voiced this complaint: "When did speaking properly become a 'white thing'?" A female student's read: "I'm not 'acting white.' My actions are not a color." Another male student's sign revealed his ongoing frustration with ste- reotypes: "Don't tell me I 'dress white.' My clothes do not invalidate my identity as a black male." Still another female student's sign revealed her frustrations with racialized microagression. It read: "My value at this institution lies within my intelligence, accomplishments, and who I am as a person; not my skin color." And still another male student's sign read: "No, I am not a waiter here, I actually go here."

The list of students is long in this photo essay, much longer than stated here, and the experiences they articulate on their placards reveal the trou- bling realities of persistent, perennial racism in an era of so-called post- racial ideology. More pertinent to this book, their experiences also reveal complex and variegated identity constructions that are fluid instead of static, hybridized rather than essentialized, definable instead of defined.[2] Their protest is a public declaration that they are rooted in, but not re- stricted by, the confinements of cultural or societal categorization.

The students' refusal to be circumscribed, that is, enclosed through imposed or volitional designation, is arguably the central reason why Taylor's contribution is so relevant to the US ecclesial landscape and to contemporary homiletical discussion. The reason he is an ideal case study is *not* because he was one of the twentieth century's premier preachers

---

opportunity to turn the volume back up. We hope to offer the opportunity to build a stage on which men and women of color can be included in the atmosphere of this campus. Most of all, we want to continue the momentum pushed forth by other I Am movements across the nation and the world. We strive to inspire and motivate other marginalized peoples in all communities to push through invisible boundaries and make their voices heard. We, Too, Are Princeton. We, Too, Are Human." See http://itooamprinceton.tumblr.com.

[2] In the area of psychology, Bernando Ferdman discusses the move toward hybridized constructions of identity. Ferdman suggests that we inhabit a world in which "more and more of us confound and defy systems of social classification and are constantly crossing and often blurring cultural boundar- ies." See Bernardo Ferdman, "'Why Am I Who I Am?' Constructing the Cultural Self in Multicul- tural Perspective," *Human Development* 43 (2000): 19. Cf. also Kathryn Tanner's discussion of the ways that culture resists enclosure into "self-contained and clearly bounded units," in Kathryn Tanner, *Theories of Culture: A New Agenda for Theology* (Minneapolis: Fortress, 1997), p. 38.

in the United States or because of significant gaps between public acclaim and homiletical reflection. Neither is it because every dimension of his homiletic is worthy of emulation. In fact, some younger African American preachers reject his emphasis on perfect grammar as out of touch with the current landscape. Further, the fact that he failed to account for the ways that *his* understanding of and articulation of the gospel was culturally conditioned also remains somewhat puzzling. Rather, what makes him an ideal case study is this: latent in his preaching practices one finds the proficiencies of improvisation and intercultural competence, the same proficiencies that assist preachers and homileticians in preparing for the churches and seminaries that are now emerging. These proficiencies help preachers to break free from being hermetically sealed and to rupture enclosure, that is, to be crossover preachers.

It is not surprising that the US context is complex and paradoxical: churched and churchless, immigrant and anti-immigrant, secularized while also being permeated with off-the-radar religious revival. Despite these seeming contradictions, the signs are more encouraging than the current rhetoric of "the church in rapid decline" seems to suggest. Unlike in Europe, where Christianity is dwindling and even disappearing in many places, much of the growth in the population of the United States is coming from the same places where Christianity is expanding at an exponential rate. The age of the pulpit prince, neo-Gothic architecture, and internationally prominent radio preachers may be gone, but the age of an intercultural church with an intercultural future is emerging. Preachers and homiletics professors who learn to be improvisationally-interculturally proficient crossover preachers can play an important part in that future and may yet have opportunities to lead us toward it in fresh, innovative, and faithful ways.

In the Princeton lectures, Walls referred to "the demographic transformation of the church" as a way of describing Christianity's global shift to the south and the east. Again, no one would deny that this *has taken place* and will continue to take place.[3] What we have failed to see, however, is that the same phrase also describes what is taking place at

---

[3]Andrew F. Walls, "From Christendom to World Christianity: Missions and the Demographic Transformation of the Church," *The Princeton Seminary Bulletin* 22, no. 3 (2001): 306.

present in the United States. Consequently, I disagree with Diana Butler Bass's research-based assertions that, in the United States, "Christian belief and practice" are experiencing a precipitous decline and "general belief in God has eroded in the last thirty years."[4] Recall Bass's claims that the first decade of the twenty-first century in the United States "could rightly be called the Great Religious Recession."[5] To a certain extent, her assertions are accurate and descriptive, but only for a subset of the population: traditional mainline denominations are struggling, as are some evangelical denominations, Americans are increasingly disassociating themselves from the word *religious*, and according to recent *USA Today* polls, the number of religiously unaffiliated and agnostics/atheists is increasing compared to one generation ago. Yet, it is also true that *USA Today* polls are not always the best indicators of realities on the ground. Perhaps we should ask, *Who controls the narrative for religious growth and decline in the United States?* and, *With whom are those controlling the narrative speaking?*

When one hears of the precipitous decline of the church in the United States, perhaps the better question to ask would be, *Whose church is declining, and why?* Does the phrase "Great Religious Recession" really describe what is taking place overall, or does it describe a subset of churches? Plenty of congregations are not only surviving but thriving and even flourishing. There are good reasons for American Christians to think and talk about refiguring the concept of the denomination in the United States, recasting reductive labels and binaries, or even assessing Christianity's recession from the center to the margins of American civic life, but to say that Christianity in the United States is undergoing a Great Religious Recession is misguided. I wonder: How many Portuguese-speaking Pentecostals in Boston take *USA Today* polls? How

---

[4]Diana Butler Bass bases her argument not only on data collected by *USA Today*, but also notes: "Since the mid 1990s . . . observers of contemporary religion have increasingly argued that Christian belief and practice are eroding even in the United States" (p. 14). Later in the same chapter, she also points to the statistical rise of unaffiliated atheists (p. 16). The peak of Christian influence and expression in the United States, claims Bass, was during the Jesus Movement in the 1970s, what she also calls the "Fourth Great Awakening" (pp. 2-7, 217-24). See Diana Butler Bass, *Christianity After Religion: The End of the Church and the Birth of a New Spiritual Awakening* (New York: HarperOne, 2012).

[5]Ibid., p. 20.

many Nigerian Christians in Detroit? How many Mandarin-speaking Chinese Christians in New York? How many undocumented Latin@ Christians in most if not all metropolitan cities?

A groundswell of church growth is taking place that, though difficult to quantify, will reveal itself with increasing force in the future, especially given the demographic changes already in motion. At present, in Washington, D.C., there are approximately 250,000 Ethiopian immigrants and thirty-five different Christian churches where they worship.[6] New York is home to over 150 African immigrant churches. As Mark R. Gornik reminds us, "In New York City, you don't have to travel to another country to experience African Christianity; all you need to do is get on the subway."[7] In Boston, the number of immigrant churches has grown so large and with such speed over the last few decades that some refer to this movement as "The Quiet Revival."[8] Manoj Shrestha, a Nepali pastor in Maryland and a recent PhD graduate in homiletics from Princeton Theological Seminary, reports that whereas in 2008 there were five Nepali immigrant churches in the United States, now, in 2015, there are at least 150 Nepali churches.[9] Twenty years ago, in 1990, there were approximately two thousand Korean churches. Recent estimates place that number at over four thousand.[10] As of 2014, there are more Latin@ Protestants in the United States than there are Episcopalians.[11]

---

[6]Statistics found in Wesley Granberg-Michaelson, *From Times Square to Timbuktu: The Post-Christian West Meets the Non-Western Church* (Grand Rapids: Eerdmans, 2013), p. xiv.

[7]Mark R. Gornik, *Word Made Global: Stories of African Christianity in New York City* (Grand Rapids: Eerdmans, 2011), p. 3.

[8]For more on the Quiet Revival in Boston, see the ongoing work of the Emmanuel Gospel Center at http://egc.org/quietrevival. On their website, they provide the following definition/description for what is taking place in Boston and the ongoing work they are trying to do: "The Quiet Revival is an unprecedented and sustained period of Christian growth in the city of Boston beginning in 1965 and persisting for nearly five decades. The number of churches in Boston has doubled during this period, though the population is about the same now as then. Today, Boston's Christian church community is characterized by a growing unity, increased prayer, maturing church systems, and a strong and trained leadership. The spiritual vitality of churches birthed during the Quiet Revival has spread, igniting additional church development and social ministries in the region and across the globe."

[9]Personal conversation with Manoj Shrestha, April 2014.

[10]Statistics found in Rebecca Y. Kim, "Migration and Conversion of Korean American Christians," in *The Oxford Handbook of Religious Conversion*, ed. Lewis R. Rambo and Charles E. Farhadian (New York: Oxford University Press, 2014), p. 191.

[11]Granberg-Michaelson, *From Times Square to Timbuktu*, p. 93.

Noting the significance of these and other trends, Jehu Hanciles observes:

> The overwhelming majority of post-1965 immigrants are of non-European stock and come from over 150 countries. The non-Western origins and incomparable diversity of post-1965 immigrants are *crucial considerations* in estimating their *long-term impact* on America's religious landscape. So is the indication that the majority are *Christian*.[12]

These new realities are the reason why Taylor's homiletical approach becomes more rather than less significant to our contemporary situation. The demographic transformation of the church is not just a Global South phenomenon; it is a US phenomenon. The voices of those who recognize and embrace this reality and who understand its importance for theological education will become more rather than less relevant to theological discussion and, with respect to my discipline, relevant to homiletical reflection.

By contrast, churches and seminaries that fail to account for and engage with racial, ethnic, and ecclesial difference either through isolation or entrenchment are at far greater risk. As Association of Theological Schools executive director Daniel Aleshire revealed in a recent interview, the "scale and cultural presence of communities of color" are likely "the most compelling issue for the American church and for the seminaries related to the American church." If churches and seminaries refuse to wake up to this reality and to the implications of it, they are destined to establish what Aleshire calls a "boutique culture" that is out of step and out of touch with the daily lived experiences (*lo cotidiano*) of twenty-first-century American Christianity.[13] Do we want our institutions to be historical artifacts from a bygone era, or living organisms in a broader ecology? Are we preparing women and men for the church of 1985, or preparing them for a church that has emerged and is emerging?

---

[12]Jehu Hanciles, *Beyond Christendom: Globalization, African Migration, and the Transformation of the West* (Maryknoll, NY: Orbis Books, 2008), p. 286. For the word *Christians*, emphasis original. For the other italicized phrases, emphasis added.

[13]Norman Jameson, "Shifting Sands: Seminaries Are at a Crossroads (Interview with Daniel Aleshire)," *Baptist World News*, October 28, 2014, http://baptistnews.com/ministry/organizations /item/29429-shifting-sands-seminaries-are-at-a-crossroads.

OPPORTUNITIES FOR FURTHER RESEARCH

No doubt some of the questions raised in this book require further exploration, reflection, and refinement. Even what is presented with respect to Gardner C. Taylor is just a partial rather than complete landscape. Many questions remain for those wishing to pursue further research. Some are explicitly theological: In what ways does Taylor's theology of proclamation shape his practice of proclamation? How does Taylor's Christology reveal itself in his preaching practices since Taylor believed that "Calvary ought to be in all of our sermons, explicit or implicit"?[14] How might Taylor's otherworldly eschatological appeals counteract and even challenge a commonly held belief in some circles of black theology that appeals to eschatology slow down the cause of justice and are inherently escapist?

Other questions are more rhetorical and biographical. On the matter of rhetoric, are there any clues in Taylor's preaching that might lead to new inroads in a conversation between homiletics and rhetoric? Or, if we place Taylor's biography in conversation with that of Henry H. Mitchell, what might we uncover through comparing and contrasting their approaches and even their alternative visions of preaching when they delivered the Lyman Beecher Lectures in the 1970s?

Another opportunity for further research relates to my twofold emphasis on improvisation and intercultural competence as descriptive practices in Taylor's preaching and as recommended practices for preachers and homileticians. In order to delimit the research, this book has been preacher-centered and not congregation-centered. Work in congregational studies could pose questions such as: (1) How do Christian communities practice faithful improvisation not only in the context of formal Christian proclamation, but also in wider contexts such as formal worship, music, Bible study, various informal practices, and through the evangelistic commitment to being the church in the world?[15] (2) If intercultural competence proficiency is so important in the future, how might congregations demonstrate not only adeptness at

---

[14]From Taylor's lecture "Great Preachers Remembered," WGT 5:116.

[15]To a certain extent, Samuel Wells tries to answer this question in *Improvisation: The Drama of Christian Ethics* (Grand Rapids: Brazos, 2004).

intercultural competence, but also a commitment to developing inter-cultural competence proficiency over time? (3) How might Christian communities practice improvisation and intercultural competence in their interfaith actions, maintaining a commitment to Christ while also respecting what British rabbi Jonathan Sacks describes as "the dignity of difference"?[16]

Another broader question that needs to be discussed not only in hom-iletics but more broadly in other disciplines is the ongoing need for racial reconciliation. Minoritized and racialized communities often hear a message, sometimes tacitly and other times overtly, from those who teach them that their ecclesial traditions are not valuable contributors to the broader theological community. This is what Taylor heard at one point at Oberlin and at various places where he lectured, and this is why decentering is so important. Perhaps we should ask: Which voices need to be moved closer to the center? Who needs to be mentored by whom? What can theological educators do to be rooted in but not restricted by their own cultural situatedness? Are we willing to cede our place through encountering and being encountered by cultural others, or would we rather be restricted and hermetically sealed?

Ample opportunities also exist to engage more deeply with improvi-sational theory in performance studies as well as race theory and inter-cultural competence theory. The questions I have posed and the research areas I have identified provoke opportunities for homileticians, practical theologians in other fields, rhetoricians, and systematic theologians to move forward the conversation that I have begun here into exciting and stimulating new terrain. As was mentioned, I have provided the reader with only a partial landscape.

This book is an attempt to begin a conversation and thus to cross a *frontera*, or border. The strategies recommended in chapter five are *one* possible way forward to move across this border. My aim is to point toward *a* path so as to spark dialogue, not to lay down hard-and-fast fundamentals. That stated, ideas from a conversation such as this one are not only necessary, but also urgent given the current and projected

---

[16]Jonathan Sacks, *The Dignity of Difference: How to Avoid the Clash of Civilizations* (New York: Continuum, 2003).

changes to the national, educational, and ecclesial landscape. I fear that if preachers, homileticians, and other church practitioners and theologians do not begin a dialogue soon and thus fail to develop creative and innovative strategies for meeting the needs these changes will induce, then the churches they serve and the students they teach will suffer on account of their shortsightedness and inaction. If the church is changing, which, of course, it is, and the seminary classroom is changing, which, of course, it is—so must we.

ON ADOPTING A DISPOSITIONAL STANCE

All of the great movements in preaching begin with an entrance into previously unchartered territory, with stepping across borders. Crossover preachers are willing to take necessary steps, to be improvisationally and interculturally proficient in order to transgress these borders. The willingness to do so extends beyond the deployment of strategies; it requires adopting a stance—*a disposition*—a generative way of being-in-the-world among those who are racially, ethnically, and ecclesially different, what systematic theologian Nathan Crawford refers to as a "disposition of openness."[17] Then the next logical question becomes: *How does one adopt this generative way of being?* Put differently, in what way does a dispositional stance reveal itself in one's knowledge, skills, and habits? What does that look like? Before concluding, let me suggest five proposals as a way of answering these questions and tying together seemingly disparate strands. Granted, these are tentative and provisional instead of definitive and final.

1. Crossover preachers reject reified and essentialized categorization. The second commandment in the Decalogue in Exodus 20:3, "You shall have no other gods before me," calls into question even our most cherished markers of identity. It subjects the gods we have made to the God who has made us. The reason this commandment calls these markers into question is because it calls all of our priorities into

---

[17] According to Nathan Crawford, the practice of theological reflection must be preceded by a "disposition of openness." He writes: "We only become attuned to an other if we have a disposition of openness that allows the other to come, to encounter us, and to change us . . . only the theologian who is rightly disposed will be able to be attuned to the other." Nathan Crawford, *Theology as Improvisation: A Study in the Musical Nature of Theological Thinking* (Boston: Brill, 2013), pp. 201-2.

question. Are the markers with which we identify like the sun, or are they like the planets that orbit around the sun? If our answer is the former rather than the latter, we risk becoming propagators of dangerous and even *idolatrous* reification through enclosed categorization. Succumbing to this temptation is one of the reasons Victor Anderson and Cornel West sound the alarm with such vehemence. Anderson reminds us: "When race is made total, then ontological blackness is idolatrous."[18] Central to West's vision of "prophetic Christianity" is a "deep suspicion of any form of idolatry."[19] It is important to realize, however, that rejection of hermetically sealed categorization does not require the supersessionism of the identity makers that one values, but rather the jettisoning of idolatrous reification. In other words, one does not need to abandon all markers of categorization; one needs to reorient them. One can still be rooted in but not restricted by imposed or volitional classification.

2. Crossover preachers perform homiletically and ecclesially faithful improvisation. The word *perform* comes from the Old French *parfounir*, which means "to complete, accomplish, or carry through."[20] To perform the gospel according to this definition of the term, then, is to "go public" with Christian faith, that is, to accomplish its significance in action, and to carry it through in a manner of preaching that lives and in a manner of living that preaches. Both the preacher and the church are summoned to this task: *to envision and enact faithful performances of the gospel in the world.* Here again is why improvisation-as-intercultural-negotiation is so significant. Because the scene of the performance has changed, the form of the performance must also change. Systematic theologian Kevin Vanhoozer writes: "The church cannot rest content with identical repetitions." Rather, it must "take the gospel into new situations." To do this, that is, to be faithful while enacting new performances in new situations, claims Vanhoozer, "the church must constantly be different. Indeed, at

---

[18]Victor Anderson, *Beyond Ontological Blackness: An Essay on African American Religious and Cultural Criticism* (New York: Continuum, 1995), p. 92.

[19]Cornel West, *Prophesy Deliverance! An Afro-American Revolutionary Christianity* (Louisville: Westminster John Knox, 2002), p. 8.

[20]See Michael Brothers's discussion of the term in *Distance in Preaching: Room to Speak, Space to Listen* (Grand Rapids: Eerdmans, 2014), p. 5.

times it must even improvise."[21] Faithful improvisation is clerical and communal. It actualizes itself in the life of the preacher and the daily practices of the *ekklēsia*. The *ek-klēsia* is called out from among the nations so that the nations might be called back in to covenant relationship with God.

3. Crossover preachers decenter Western homiletical discourse from hegemonic and totalitarian constriction. Hegemonic impulse among Western Christians is not a new phenomenon. When Chilean Jesuit priest Gonzalo Arroyo was invited to the United States to speak to a group of North American theologians, he appeared before the conference and posed this question: "Why is it that when you speak of *our* theology you call it 'Latin American theology,' but when you speak of *your* theology you call it 'theology'?"[22]

In a recent article, missiologist Craig Ott describes the phenomenon that Arroyo illustrates in greater detail: "Western churches may acknowledge in theory that they have much to learn from Majority World [non-Western] brothers and sisters but in practice a spirit of superiority generally prevails."[23] Jehu Hanciles also observes this proclivity in *Beyond Christendom* when he writes: "The fundamental assumption that Western paradigms have universal validity contaminates understanding of non-Western realities."[24] Not only are existing accounts of the religiosity of non-Western societies and non-Western immigration to Western societies inadequate to account for quotidian realities on the ground, according to Hanciles, they are in fact "unsustainable, even misleading" accounts. The charge to resist a totalitarian penchant and hegemonic impulse may prove difficult for homileticians in the United States, and more broadly for theological educators, as most were trained in

---

[21]Kevin Vanhoozer, *The Drama of Doctrine: A Canonical-Linguistic Approach to Christian Theology* (Louisville: Westminster John Knox, 2005), p. 128.

[22]Story in Robert McAfee Brown, *Gustavo Gutierrez: An Introduction to Liberation Theology* (Maryknoll, NY: Orbis Books, 1990), p. xix. Emphasis in original. Cf. also Justo González's observation in his book *Mañana*: "What is said in Manila is meant for the Philippines. What is said in Tübingen, Oxford, or Yale is meant for the entire church." See Justo L. González, *Mañana: Christian Theology from a Hispanic Perspective* (Nashville: Abingdon, 1990), p. 52.

[23]Craig Ott, "Globalization and Contextualization: Reframing the Task of Contextualization in the Twenty-First Century," *Missiology: An International Review* 43, no. 1 (2014): 12.

[24]Hanciles, *Beyond Christendom*, pp. 375-76.

Western theological schools. The call here is not for wholesale rejection of Western models of education, but the repudiation of discursive constriction. At the practical level, the time is *now* to learn from preaching practices in nonmajority contexts and among immigrant churches, to attend to the theologies and preaching methodologies emerging from the Global South, to reverse unhelpful rhetoric of "the church" in steep decline, and to renounce the North American tendency to speak for all churches everywhere.

4. Crossover preachers embrace a Christocentric focus vis-à-vis their identity. One of the most compelling accounts for a radically inclusive reordering of human identity is found in Galatians 3:28-29: "There is no longer Jew or Greek, there is no longer slave or free, there is no longer male and female; for all of you are one in Christ Jesus. And if you belong to Christ, then you are Abraham's offspring, heirs according to the promise." Those who are in Christ, no matter their lot or station, belong to Abraham's seed. They are "children of God through faith" (Gal 3:26). As a result of this new identity, closed and antiquated accounts of existence are ruptured by union with Christ, by being "in Christ," the one who "is all and in all" (Col 3:11).

Interestingly, J. Kameron Carter lifts up a similar vision for reframing reality throughout his book *Race: A Theological Account.* The breaking free of "tyrannical self-enclosure" takes place through "reconstituting [one's] identity in Christ." Every language, Carter writes, "has the language of Jesus as its destiny." Again, Christ reopens human nature "so that it is no longer hermetically sealed in upon itself."[25] What is my point here? It is simple: Christ reorders one's former and current designations. Christocentric focus necessitates the perpetual recognition of a reframed and reoriented constitution as a consequence of one's union with Christ.[26] Perhaps not surprisingly, one of the Christian Princeton University students who participated in the photo essay understood the implications of this orientation when she put the following sentence on her placard:

---

[25]J. Kameron Carter, *Race: A Theological Account* (Oxford: Oxford University Press, 2008), pp. 235, 311, 351, 366.

[26]For a compelling account of "union with Christ" and what it means to be "in Christ" from a biblical-theological vantage point, see Constantine R. Campbell, *Paul and Union with Christ: An Exegetical and Theological Study* (Grand Rapids: Zondervan, 2012).

"Although I love being a black Princetonian . . . I am the righteousness of God in Christ (2 Cor 5:21)."

5. Crossover preachers cross borders of difference for the sake of the gospel. That is to say, they embrace border crossing as a sign of gospel fidelity and as a marker of their obedience to Jesus the border crosser. Following Christ over the walls of difference is at one and the same time a pneumatological, eschatological, and spiritually formative practice. First, it is pneumatologically attuned with the ongoing work of the Holy Spirit. The Pentecost event signals the rupture rather than reification of enclosed circumscriptions of classification. As Ajith Fernando observes, "[At Pentecost] the barriers that divided the human race have been broken down so that a new humanity is on the way to being created."[27] Through the pouring out of the Spirit, writes Michael Welker, "God effects a world-encompassing, multilingual, poly-individual testimony."[28] Crossing over also takes place *con un acento escatológico*, that is, with an eschatological accent. It moves *toward* rather than *away from* apocalyptic reality, from the kingdom that has come, is come, and will come. In the heavenly vision of the book of Revelation, the church's witness is described as a mosaic of "people of every tribe and language and people and nation." This phrase appears no less than seven times (Rev 5:9; 7:9; 10:11; 11:9, 13:7; 14:16; 17:15 NIV) and in many ways is an intentional reversal of the cultural absolutism and arrogance found in the tower of Babel in Genesis 11.[29] Transgressing borders in the eschatological sense means rejecting Babel and embracing parousia. Finally, crossing over is a spiritually formative practice, what Peter C. Phan calls a "spirituality of missionary border crossing."[30] Those who risk going beyond cultural confinement by deciding to be a stranger or a guest elsewhere abide by the "theological imperative of Christian life as *imitatio Christi*."[31] Believers in the "new way" of Christianity, claims Virgilio P. Elizondo, adopt a "constant defiance and

---

[27]Ajith Fernando, *The NIV Application Commentary: Acts* (Grand Rapids: Zondervan, 2010), p. 91.
[28]Michael Welker, *God the Spirit* (Minneapolis: Fortress, 1994), p. 235.
[29]For an analysis of these passages in the book of Revelation and their significance for racial reconciliation, see J. Daniel Hays, *From Every People and Nation: A Biblical Theology of Race* (Downers Grove, IL: InterVarsity Press, 2003). For a discussion of the tower of Babel as a metaphor for cultural absolutism and exclusion, see Hanciles, *Beyond Christendom*, p. 142.
[30]Peter C. Phan, *In Our Own Tongues: Perspectives from Asia on Mission and Inculturation* (Maryknoll, NY: Orbis Books, 2003), p. 146.
[31]Ibid., p. 147.

crossing of borders for the sake of the new human family."[32] By transgressing divides, they imitate Christ.

CONCLUDING THOUGHTS

In 1819, Washington Irving published a short story called "Rip Van
Winkle."[33] In this story, Irving invites us to imagine a man living in a
tiny village at the foot of the Catskill Mountains during colonial times.
One day, he meanders up a mountainside on a walk with his dog, and
after enjoying a bit too much wine he falls asleep on the hillside. When
he awakes, he is drowsy and disoriented. His beard is overgrown and his
dog is missing. He enters the village and discovers that nothing is the
same as he recalls it: the villagers are different; his wife is dead; his
friends are gone. When he goes inside the local tavern and looks up at
what was supposed to be a familiar portrait on the wall, he notices that
the painting of King George has been replaced with a painting of George
Washington. "What in the world is happening?" he wonders. Upon
leaving, so the story goes, an elderly villager recognizes him and explains
to him what he is already beginning to suspect: he had been sleeping
much longer than a single night. Not only had life changed in his tiny
village in the twenty years he was asleep—the world had changed! At
that moment, Rip Van Winkle came to the stunning realization that he
had been sleeping through a great revolution.

This book helps homileticians and pastors in the United States to
"remain awake through a great revolution," to use Martin Luther King
Jr.'s phrase, rather than to remain asleep at the time the tide is turning.
It prepares them to meet the needs of a church that already exists and
will soon exist: a "church we cannot yet envision."[34]

---

[32]Virgilio P. Elizondo, "Transformation of Borders: Border Separation or New Identity," in *Theology: Expanding the Borders*, ed. María Pilar Aquino and Roberto S. Goizueta (Mystic, CT: Twenty-
Third Publications, 1998), p. 35.

[33]Washington Irving, *Rip Van Winkle* (Utrecht: The Catharijne Press, 1987).

[34]At McCormick Theological Seminary in Chicago, a school that is embracing the power and
promise of multicultural theological education, scholars like Anna Case-Winters and others use
the following phrase in the school's promotional material: "preparing leaders for a church we
cannot yet envision." See Anna Case-Winters, "Multicultural Theological Education: On Doing
Difference Differently," in *Shaping Beloved Community: Multicultural Theological Education*, ed.
David Esterline and Ogbu Kalu (Louisville: Westminster John Knox, 2006), p. 45.

Crossover preachers take the risk of transgressing *fronteras* (borders). They become border crossers by virtue of their commitment to gospel fidelity, in obedience to the one who was and is a border crosser *pro nobis*, namely Jesus Christ. What is needed now more than ever is women and men who are willing to take this risk, to be improvisational and intercultural not only in the strategic but the dispositional sense of these words—women and men who are eager to be and to become crossover preachers.

BIBLIOGRAPHY

◆

2000-14 Annual Data Tables. Pittsburgh: Association of Theological Schools, 2014. www
.ats.edu/resources/institutional-data/annual-data-tables.

"72nd Convocation Set at Bangor Seminary." *Bangor Daily News*. January 21, 1977.

"Aid Offered to Church." *New York Times*, October 4, 1952.

Aleshire, Daniel. *Community and Diversity*. Report presented at the ATS Biennial Meeting,
Pittsburgh, June 2012. www.ats.edu/resources/publications-and-presentations.

Allen, Ronald J. *Hearing the Sermon: Relationship, Content, Feeling*. St. Louis: Chalice,
2004.

———. *Preaching and the Other: Studies of Postmodern Insights*. St. Louis: Chalice,
2009.

———. "The Social Function of Language in Preaching." In *Preaching as a Social Act:
Theology and Practice*, edited by Arthur Van Seters, pp. 167-204. Nashville: Abingdon,
1988.

Alperson, Philip. "On Musical Improvisation." *Journal of Aesthetics and Art Criticism* 43,
no. 1 (Autumn 1984): 17-29.

Alterhaug, Bjorn. "Improvisation on a Triple Theme: Creativity, Jazz Improvisation, and
Communication." *Studia Musicologica Norvegica* 30 (2004): 97-118.

"American Preaching: A Dying Art?" *Time*, December 31, 1979.

Ames, Russell. *The Story of American Folk Song*. New York: Grosset & Dunlap, 1960.

Anderson, Victor. *Beyond Ontological Blackness: An Essay on African American Religious
and Cultural Criticism*. New York: Continuum, 1995.

Anzaldúa, Gloria. *Borderlands=La Frontera*. San Francisco: Aunt Lute Books, 1999.

Appadurai, Arjun. *Modernity at Large: Cultural Dimensions of Globalization*. Minneapolis:
University of Minnesota Press, 2005.

Aquino, María Pilar, and Maria José Rosado-Nunes, eds. *Feminist Intercultural Theology:
Latina Explorations for a Just World*. Maryknoll, NY: Orbis Books, 2007.

Aristotle. *On Rhetoric: A Theory of Civic Discourse*. Edited by George A. Kennedy. New
York: Oxford University Press, 2007.

Artaud, Antonin. *Ouevres Complète*. Paris: Gallimard, 1980.

Augustine. *On Christian Teaching*. Translated by R. P. H. Green. New York: Oxford University Press, 2008.

Austin, J. L. *How to Do Things with Words*. The William James Lectures 1955. New York: Oxford University Press, 1965.

———. "Performative Utterances." In *Philosophical Papers*, pp. 220-39. Oxford: Clarendon Press, 1961.

Bantum, Brian. *Redeeming Mulatto: A Theology of Race and Christian Hybridity*. Waco, TX: Baylor University Press, 2010.

Barba, Eugenio. "The Deep Order Called Turbulence: The Three Faces of Dramaturgy." *The Drama Review* 44, no. 1 (Winter 2000): 56-66.

Barna, George, and David Kinnaman. *Churchless: Understanding Today's Unchurched and How to Connect with Them*. Austin, TX: Tyndale Momentum, 2014.

Barrett, Frank J., and Ken Poplowski. "Minimal Structures Within a Song: An Analysis of 'All of Me.'" *Organization Science* 9, no. 5 (October 1998): 558-60.

Barth, Karl. *Church Dogmatics*. Translated by Geoffrey William Bromiley. Edinburgh: T & T Clark, 1936.

———. "Evangelical Theology in the Nineteenth Century." In *The Humanity of God*, translated by Thomas Wieser, pp. 11-33. Atlanta: John Knox, 1978.

Bartow, Charles L. *God's Human Speech: A Practical Theology of Proclamation*. Grand Rapids: Eerdmans, 1997.

Bartula, Malgorzata, Stefan Schroer, and Roberto Ciulli. *On Improvisation: Nine Conversations with Roberto Ciulli*. Translated by Geoffrey V. Davis. New York: Peter Lang, 2003.

Bass, Diana Butler. *Christianity After Religion: The End of the Church and the Birth of a New Spiritual Awakening*. New York: HarperOne, 2012.

Bateson, Mary Catherine. *Peripheral Visions: Learning Along the Way*. New York: Harper-Collins, 1994.

"Baylor Names the 12 Most Effective Preachers." *Baylor University Media Communications*. February 28, 1996. Last modified April 23, 2012. www.baylor.edu/mediacommunications/news.php?action=story&story=1036.

Begbie, Jeremy. *Theology, Music, and Time*. Cambridge: Cambridge University Press, 2000.

Bell, Elizabeth. *Theories of Performance*. Thousand Oaks, CA: Sage, 2008.

Belloc, Hilaire. *Europe and the Faith*. Rockford, IL: TAN Books and Publishers, 1992.

Bennett, Milton J. "Becoming Interculturally Competent." In *Toward Multiculturalism: A Reader in Multicultural Education*, edited by Jaime S. Wurzel, pp. 62-77. Newton, MA: Intercultural Resource Corporation, 2004.

———. "A Developmental Approach to Training for Intercultural Sensitivity." *International Journal of Intercultural Relations* 10 (1986): 179-96.

———. "Towards Ethnorelativism: A Developmental Model of Intercultural Sensitivity."

In *Education for the Intercultural Experience*, edited by R. Michael Paige, pp. 21-71. Yarmouth, ME: Intercultural Press, 1993.

Benson, Bruce Ellis. "The Improvisation of Hermeneutics: Jazz Lessons for Interpreters." In *Hermeneutics at the Crossroads*, edited by Kevin J. Vanhoozer, James K. A. Smith, and Bruce Ellis Benson, pp. 193-210. Bloomington: Indiana University Press, 2006.

———. "Improvising Texts, Improvising Communities: Jazz, Interpretation, Heterophany, and the Ekklesia." In *Resonant Witness: Conversations Between Music and Theology*, edited by Jeremy Begbie, Steven R. Guthrie, and Bruce Ellis Benson, pp. 295-319. Grand Rapids: Eerdmans, 2011.

Berger, Peter L. *The Desecularization of the World: Resurgent Religion and World Politics*. Grand Rapids: Eerdmans, 1999.

———. *The Heretical Imperative*. New York: Doubleday, 1979.

Berliner, Paul. *Thinking in Jazz: The Infinite Art of Improvisation*. Chicago: University of Chicago Press, 1994.

Beyer, Peter, and Lori Beaman, eds. *Religion, Globalization and Culture*. Boston: Brill, 2007.

Bhargava, Rajeev, ed. *Secularism and Its Critics*. New York: Oxford University Press, 1998.

Biagi, Fiora, Lavinia Bracci, Juan Carlos Ruiz-Coll, and Jules Martin Bella Owona. "Reflective Intercultural Competence (RIC) and Its Assessment: The RICA Model." In *Intercultural Horizons: Best Practices in Intercultural Competence Development*, edited by Eliza J. Nash, Nevin C. Brown, and Lavinia Bracci, pp. 61-82. Newcastle upon Tyne, UK: Cambridge Scholars Publishing, 2012.

"Billy Graham: Heaven Won't Let Racists In." *New York Amsterdam News*, July 20, 1957.

Birch, Bruce C. *Let Justice Roll Down: The Old Testament, Ethics, and Christian Life*. Louisville: Westminster John Knox, 1991.

Black, J. Stewart, Hal B. Gregersen, and Mark E. Mendenhall. *Global Assignments: Successfully Expatriating and Repatriating International Managers*. San Francisco: Jossey-Bass, 1992.

Blatner, Adam, ed. *Interactive and Improvisational Drama: Varieties of Applied Theatre and Performance*. Lincoln, NE: iUniverse, 2007.

Boal, Augusto. *Games for Actors and Non-Actors*. New York: Routledge, 2002.

———. *The Rainbow of Desire: The Boal Method of Theatre and Therapy*. New York: Routledge, 2003.

Bok, Derek. *Our Underachieving Colleges: A Candid Look at How Much Students Learn and Why They Should Be Learning More*. Princeton, NJ: Princeton University Press, 2008.

Bond, L. Susan. *Contemporary African American Preaching: Diversity in Theory and Style*. St. Louis: Chalice, 2003.

———. "To Hear the Angel's Wings: Apocalyptic Language and the Formation of Moral Community with Reference to the Sermons of Gardner C. Taylor." PhD diss., Vanderbilt University, 1996.

Bond, Michael Harris. *Working at the Interface of Culture: Eighteen Lives in Social Science.* New York: Routledge, 1997.

Bosch, David J. *Transforming Mission: Paradigm Shifts in Theology of Mission.* Maryknoll, NY: Orbis Books, 1991.

Bourbouhakis, Emmanuel C. "Rhetoric and Performance." In *The Byzantine World*, edited by Paul Stephenson, pp. 175-87. New York: Routledge, 2010.

Bourdieu, Pierre. *The Logic of Practice.* Stanford, CA: Stanford University Press, 1990.

———. *Outline of a Theory of Practice.* New York: Cambridge University Press, 1977.

Boyd, Neva L., and Paul Simon. *Play and Game Theory in Group Work: A Collection of Papers.* Chicago: University of Illinois at Chicago, 1971.

Branch, Taylor. *Parting the Waters: America in the King Years, 1954–63.* New York: Simon and Schuster, 1988.

Brett, Mark, ed. *Ethnicity in the Bible.* Leiden: Brill, 1996.

Brislin, Richard W., and Tomoko Yoshida. *Improving Intercultural Interactions: Modules for Cross-Cultural Training Programs.* Thousand Oaks, CA: Sage, 1994.

———. *Intercultural Communication Training: An Introduction.* Thousand Oaks, CA: Sage, 1994.

Brookfield, Stephen D. *Teaching for Critical Thinking: Tools and Techniques to Help Students Question Their Assumptions.* San Francisco, CA: Jossey-Bass, 2012.

"Brooklyn Tests Racial Exchange." *New York Times*, December 12, 1955.

"Brooklyn's Exceptional Preacher." *The New York Times.* June 30, 1990. Last modified January 22, 2009. www.nytimes.com/1990/06/30/opinion/brooklyn-s-exceptional-preacher.html.

Brothers, Michael. *Distance in Preaching: Room to Speak, Space to Listen.* Grand Rapids: Eerdmans, 2014.

Brown, Robert McAfee. *Gustavo Gutierrez: An Introduction to Liberation Theology.* Maryknoll, NY: Orbis Books, 1990.

Brown, Stuart. *Play: How It Shapes the Brain, Opens the Imagination, and Invigorates the Soul.* New York: Penguin, 2009.

Brown, Susan C. "Students as Cultural Beings." In *Teaching Inclusively in Higher Education*, edited by Susan C. Brown and Moira A. Fallon, pp. 17-37. Charlotte, NC: Information Age Publishing, 2010.

Brown, Susan C., and Moira A. Fallon. "A Student-Centered Approach to College Classrooms." In *Teaching Inclusively in Higher Education*, edited by Susan C. Brown and Moira A. Fallon, pp. 3-15. Charlotte, NC: Information Age Publishing, 2010.

Brueggemann, Walter. *Cadences of Home: Preaching Among Exiles.* Louisville: Westminster John Knox, 1997.

Buechner, Frederick. *Telling the Truth: The Gospel as Tragedy, Comedy, and Fairy Tale.* San Francisco: Harper & Row, 1977.

Byram, Michael. "On Being 'Bicultural' and 'Intercultural.'" In *Intercultural Experience and Education*, edited by Geof Alred, Michael Byram, and Mike Fleming, pp. 50-66. Tonowanda, NY: Multilingual Matters, 2002.

———. *Teaching and Assessing Intercultural Communicative Competence*. Philadelphia: Multilingual Matters, 1997.

Campbell, Charles L. *Preaching Jesus: New Directions for Homiletics in Hans Frei's Post-liberal Theology*. Grand Rapids: Eerdmans, 1997.

———. *The Word Before the Powers: An Ethic of Preaching*. Louisville: Westminster John Knox, 2002.

Campbell, Constantine R. *Paul and Union with Christ: An Exegetical and Theological Study*. Grand Rapids: Zondervan, 2012.

Carter, J. Kameron. *Race: A Theological Account*. Oxford: Oxford University Press, 2008.

Carter, Jerry M. "The Audible Sacrament: The Sacramentality of Gardner C. Taylor's Preaching." PhD diss., Drew University, 2007.

Cartledge, Mark J., and David Cheetham, eds. *Intercultural Theology: Approaches and Themes*. London: SCM Press, 2011.

Case-Winters, Anna. "Multicultural Theological Education: On Doing Difference Differently." In *Shaping Beloved Community: Multicultural Theological Education*, edited by David Esterline and Ogbu Kalu, pp. 43-55. Louisville: Westminster John Knox, 2006.

Cassady, Jerrell C., and Mourad Ali Eissa, eds. *Emotional Intelligence: Perspectives from Educational and Positive Psychology*. New York: Peter Lang, 2008.

Chanda, Nayan. *Bound Together: How Traders, Preachers, Adventurers, and Warriors Shaped Globalization*. New Haven, CT: Yale University Press, 2008.

Choi, Woosung Calvin. "Preaching to the Multiethnic Congregation: Positive Marginality as a Homiletical Paradigm." PhD diss., London School of Theology, 2013.

Chow, Rey. *The Protestant Ethnic and the Spirit of Capitalism*. New York: Columbia University Press, 2002.

Christie, Ron. *Acting White: The Curious History of a Racial Slur*. New York: Thomas Dunne Books/St. Martin's Press, 2010.

Cleage, Albert B. *The Black Messiah*. New York: Sheed and Ward, 1968.

"Concord Pastor Sworn in as School Board Member." *New York Amsterdam News*, May 7, 1949.

"Concord to Mark 110th Anniversary." *New York Amsterdam News*, May 4, 1957.

Cone, James H. *A Black Theology of Liberation*. Maryknoll, NY: Orbis Books, 1990.

———. *God of the Oppressed*. New York: Seabury Press, 1975.

Conquergood, Dwight. "Beyond the Text: Toward a Performative Cultural Politics." In *The Future of Performance Studies: Visions and Revisions*, edited by Sheron J. Dailey, pp. 25-36. Annandale, VA: National Communication Association, 1998.

———. "Rethinking Ethnography: Towards a Critical Cultural Politics." *Communication Monographs* 58 (June 1991): 179-94.

Cooke, Mervyn, and David Horn, eds. *The Cambridge Companion to Jazz*. New York: Cambridge University Press, 2002.

"Copenhagen Minister Preaches Sunday at Concord." *New York Amsterdam News*, August 26, 1950.

Corbett, Jim. "Robert Griffin III Refuses to Be Defined by Race." *USA Today*, December 12, 2012. www.usatoday.com/story/sports/nfl/redskins/2012/12/12/robert-griffin-iii-washington-redskins-race/1765701/.

Coughlan, Sean. "US Schools to Have Non-White Majority." *BBC News*, August 26, 2014. www.bbc.com/news/education-28937660.

Cox, Harvey. *The Future of Faith*. New York: HarperOne, 2009.

———. *The Secular City: Secularization and Urbanization in Theological Perspective*. New York: Macmillan, 1965.

Craddock, Fred B. *As One Without Authority*. St. Louis: Chalice, 2001.

———. *Preaching*. Nashville: Abingdon, 1985.

Crawford, Evans E., and Thomas H. Troeger. *The Hum: Call and Response in African American Preaching*. Nashville: Abingdon, 1995.

Crawford, Nathan. *Theology as Improvisation: A Study in the Musical Nature of Theological Thinking*. Boston: Brill, 2013.

———. "Theology as Improvisation: Using the Metaphor of Attunement to Think Theologically." PhD diss., Loyola University Chicago, 2011.

Crossan, Mary, and Marc Sorrenti. "Making Sense of Improvisation." In *Advances in Strategic Management*, edited by J. Walsh and A. Huff, 14:155-80. Greenwich, CT: Jai Press, 1997.

Dabney, Robert Lewis. *Sacred Rhetoric: Or, a Course of Lectures on Preaching*. Richmond, VA: Presbyterian Committee of Publication, 1870.

Davis, Barbara Gross. *Tools for Teaching*. San Francisco: Jossey-Bass Publishers, 2009.

Davis, Gerald L. *I Got the Word in Me and I Can Sing It, You Know: A Study of the Performed African American Sermon*. Philadelphia: University of Pennsylvania Press, 1985.

De Vet, Thérèse. "Context and the Emerging Story: Improvised Performance in Oral and Literate Societies." *Oral Tradition* 23, no. 1 (2008): 159-79.

Deardorff, Darla K. "Implementing Intercultural Competence Assessment." In *The Sage Handbook of Intercultural Competence*, edited by Darla K. Deardorff, pp. 477-91. Thousand Oaks, CA: Sage, 2009.

———. "In Search of Intercultural Competence." *International Educator* 13, no. 2 (Spring 2004): 13-15.

DeBose, Charles E. "Codeswitching: Black English and Standard English in the African-American Linguistic Repertoire." *Journal of Multilingual and Multicultural Development* 13 (1992): 157-67.

Deichmann Edwards, Wendy J. "Forging an Ideology for American Missions: Josiah Strong and Manifest Destiny." In *North American Foreign Missions, 1810–1914: The-*

ology, Theory, and Policy, edited by Wilbert R. Shenk, pp. 163-91. Grand Rapids: Eerdmans, 2004.

Dennis, James S. *Foreign Missions After a Century*. Students' Lectures on Missions, Princeton Theological Seminary 1893. New York: Fleming H. Revell, 1893.

Department of Homeland Security. *Table 2: Persons Obtaining Legal Permanent Resident Status by Region and Selected Country of Last Residence: Fiscal Years 1820 to 2013*. Last modified June 16, 2014. www.dhs.gov/yearbook-immigration-statistics-2013-lawful-permanent-residents.

Dewey, John. *Democracy and Education: An Introduction to the Philosophy of Education*. New York: Macmillan, 1916.

Diognetus. *The Epistle to Diognetus*. Edited by Lewis Bostock Radford. New York: Society for Promoting Christian Knowledge, 1908.

Dixon, Christa Klingbeil. *Negro Spirituals: From Bible to Folk Song*. Philadelphia: Fortress, 1976.

"Dr. Taylor on Radio Pulpit for 13 Weeks." *New York Amsterdam News*, June 27, 1959.

"Dr. Taylor Speaking at Riverside Ch." *New York Amsterdam News*, July 30, 1960.

"Dr. Taylor Will Preach on Radio." *The Washington Afro-American*, April 21, 1959.

Duffy, Margaret M. "The Roots of American Improvisation: Play, Process, and Pedagogy." PhD diss., City University of New York, 2011.

Dugan, George. "Churches Scored as Race Conscious." *New York Times*, May 26, 1953.

Dumouchel, Réjean. "Le Spectateur et le Contactile." *Revuecinemas.info*, 1.3.Web. October 2010.

Dunn, James D. G. *Romans*. Word Biblical Commentary 38A-38B. Dallas: Word Books, 1988.

Dykstra, Robert C. *Discovering a Sermon: Personal Pastoral Preaching*. St. Louis: Chalice, 2001.

———. "Unrepressing the Kingdom: Pastoral Theology and Aesthetic Imagination." *Pastoral Psychology* 61 (2012): 391-409.

Dyson, Michael Eric. *Between God and Gangsta Rap: Bearing Witness to Black Culture*. New York: Oxford University Press, 1996.

———. "Gardner Taylor: Poet Laureate of the Pulpit." *Christian Century* 112, no. 1 (January 4, 1995): 12-16.

———. *Open Mike: Reflections on Philosophy, Race, Sex, Culture and Religion*. New York: Basic Civitas Books, 2003.

———. "Tour(é)ing Blackness." In *Who's Afraid of Post-Blackness? What It Means to Be Black Now*, by Touré, pp. xi-xvii. New York: Free Press, 2011.

Earley, P. Christopher, and Soon Ang. *Cultural Intelligence: Individual Interactions Across Cultures*. Stanford, CA: Stanford Business Books, 2003.

Earley, P. Christopher, Soon Ang, and Joo-Seng Tan. *CQ: Developing Cultural Intelligence at Work*. Stanford, CA: Stanford Business Books, 2006.

Eberstadt, Mary. *How the West Really Lost God: A New Theory of Secularization*. Radnor, PA: Templeton, 2013.

Edwards, Jonathan. "Extraordinary Gifts of the Spirit Are Inferior to Graces of the Spirit." In *The Works of Jonathan Edwards: Religious Affections*, edited by John E. Smith, 2:279-312. New Haven, CT: Yale University Press, 1959.

Edwards, O. C. *A History of Preaching*. Nashville: Abingdon, 2004.

El Nasser, Haya. "U.S. Hispanic Population to Triple by 2050." *USA Today*, February 12, 2008. www.usatoday.com/news/nation/2008-02-11-population-study_N.htm.

Elizondo, Virgilio P. "Transformation of Borders: Border Separation or New Identity." In *Theology: Expanding the Borders*, edited by María Pilar Aquino and Roberto S. Goizueta, pp. 22-39. Mystic, CT: Twenty-Third Publications, 1998.

Elmer, Duane. *Cross-Cultural Connections: Stepping Out and Fitting In Around the World*. Downers Grove, IL: InterVarsity Press, 2009.

Emmerling, Robert J., Vinod K. Shanwal, and Manas K. Mandal, eds. *Emotional Intelligence: Theoretical and Cultural Perspectives*. New York: Nova Science, 2008.

Engelsviken, Tormod. *The Church Going Glocal: Mission and Globalisation*. Eugene, OR: Wipf & Stock, 2011.

Erez, Miriam, and P. Christopher Earley. *Culture, Self-Identity, and Work*. New York: Oxford University Press, 1993.

Ericsson, K. Anders. "The Influence of Experience and Deliberate Practice on the Development of Superior Expert Performance." In *The Cambridge Handbook of Expertise and Expert Performance*, edited by K. Anders Ericsson, Neil Charness, Robert R. Hoffman, and Paul J. Feltovich, pp. 685-705. New York: Cambridge University Press, 2006.

Escobar, Samuel E. *Changing Tides: Latin America and World Mission Today*. Maryknoll, NY: Orbis Books, 2002.

Eslinger, Richard L. *A New Hearing: Living Options in Homiletic Method*. Nashville: Abingdon, 1987.

———. *The Web of Preaching: New Options in Homiletic Method*. Nashville: Abingdon, 2002.

Espín, Orlando O. *Grace and Humanness: Theological Reflections Because of Culture*. Maryknoll, NY: Orbis Books, 2007.

———. *Idol and Grace: On Traditioning and Subversive Hope*. Maryknoll, NY: Orbis Books, 2014.

Esterline, David, and Ogbu Kalu, eds. *Multicultural Theological Education: On Doing Difference Differently*. Louisville: Westminster John Knox, 2006.

Evans, Donald D. *The Logic of Self-Involvement: A Philosophical Study of Everyday Language with Special Reference to the Christian Use of Language About God as Creator*. London: SCM Press, 1963.

Fadiman, Anne. *The Spirit Catches You and You Fall Down: A Hmong Child, Her Doctors, and the Collision of Two Cultures*. New York: Farrar, Straus and Giroux, 1997.

Fee, Gordon D. *The First Epistle to the Corinthians.* Grand Rapids: Zondervan, 1987.

Feltovich, Paul J., Michael J. Prietula, and K. Anders Ericsson. "Studies of Expertise from Psychological Perspectives." In *The Cambridge Handbook of Expertise and Expert Performance,* edited by K. Anders Ericsson, Neil Charness, Robert R. Hoffman, and Paul J. Feltovich, pp. 41-68. New York: Cambridge University Press, 2006.

Ferdman, Bernardo. "'Why Am I Who I Am?' Constructing the Cultural Self in Multicultural Perspective." *Human Development* 43 (2000): 19-23.

Fernando, Ajith. *The NIV Application Commentary: Acts.* Grand Rapids: Zondervan, 2010.

Fischlin, Daniel, and Ajay Heble, eds. *The Other Side of Nowhere: Jazz, Improvisation, and Communities in Dialogue.* Middletown, CT: Wesleyan University Press, 2004.

Florence, Anna Carter. *Preaching as Testimony.* Louisville: Westminster John Knox, 2007.

Folio: Diversity in Theological Education. Pittsburgh: Association of Theological Schools, March 2002. Last modified January 30, 3014. www.ats.edu/resources/publications-and-presentations.

Fontanier, Pierre. *Les Figures Du Discours.* Paris: Flammarion, 1968.

Ford, Terry. *Becoming Multicultural: Personal and Social Construction Through Critical Teaching.* New York: Falmer Press, 1999.

Foucault, Michel. "Preface to Transgression." In *Language, Counter-Memory, Practice: Selected Essays and Interviews,* pp. 29-52. Ithaca, NY: Cornell University Press, 1977.

Fox, Patricia D. *Being and Blackness in Latin America: Uprootedness and Improvisation.* Gainesville: University Press of Florida, 2006.

Freire, Paulo. *Learning to Question: A Pedagogy of Liberation.* Geneva: WCC Publications, 1989.

———. *Pedagogy of the Oppressed.* New York: Continuum, 1993.

Frey, William H. "The Census Projects Minority Surge." *The Brookings Institution,* August 18, 2008. Accessed January 23, 2015. www.brookings.edu/research/ opinions/2008/08/18-census-frey.

Friedli, Richard, Jan A. B. Jongeneel, Klaus Koschorke, Theo Sundermeier, and Werver Ustorf, eds. *Intercultural Perceptions and Prospects of World Christianity.* Frankfurt am Main: Peter Lang, 2010.

Frost, Anthony, and Ralph Yarrow. *Improvisation in Drama.* New York: St. Martin's Press, 1990.

Fulkerson, Mary McClintock. *Places of Redemption: Theology for a Worldly Church.* Oxford: Oxford University Press, 2007.

Fullwood, Alfonza W. "A Study of Gardner C. Taylor's Theology of Preaching as a Decisive Factor Shaping His Theory of Preaching: Implications for Homiletical Pedagogy." PhD diss., Southeastern Baptist Theological Seminary, 2012.

Gadamer, Hans Georg. *Truth and Method.* New York: Continuum Books, 2004.

"Gardner Calvin Taylor: Oral History Memoir, Interview 1." Interview by Joel C. Gregory. Baylor University Institute for Oral History, January 22, 2007.

"Gardner Calvin Taylor: Oral History Memoir, Interview 2." Interview by Joel C. Gregory. Baylor University Institute for Oral History, March 17, 2008.

"Gardner Calvin Taylor: Oral History Memoir, Interview 3." Interview by Joel C. Gregory. Baylor University Institute for Oral History, March 17, 2008.

Gardner, Howard. *Multiple Intelligences: New Horizons*. New York: BasicBooks, 2006.

Gates, Henry Louis, Jr. "'Blackness of Blackness': A Critique of the Sign and the Signifying Monkey." *Critical Inquiry* 9, no. 4 (June 1983): 685-723.

———. *The Signifying Monkey: A Theory of Afro-American Literary Criticism*. New York: Oxford University Press, 1988.

Gay, Geneva. *Culturally Responsive Teaching: Theory, Research, and Practice*. New York: Teachers College Press, 2010.

George, Timothy. "Introduction: Honor to Whom Honor Is Due." In *Our Sufficiency Is of God: Essays on Preaching in Honor of Gardner C. Taylor*, edited by Timothy George, James Earl Massey, and Robert Smith Jr., pp. ix-xxxii. Macon, GA: Mercer University Press, 2010.

George, Timothy, James Earl Massey, and Robert Smith Jr., eds. *Our Sufficiency Is of God: Essays on Preaching in Honor of Gardner C. Taylor*. Macon, GA: Mercer University Press, 2010.

Gerkin, Charles V. *An Introduction to Pastoral Care*. Nashville: Abingdon, 1997.

———. *The Living Human Document: Re-Visioning Pastoral Counseling in a Hermeneutical Mode*. Nashville: Abingdon, 1984.

———. *Prophetic Pastoral Practice: A Christian Vision of Life Together*. Nashville: Abingdon, 1991.

———. *Widening the Horizons: Pastoral Responses to a Fragmented Society*. Philadelphia: Westminster Press, 1986.

Gilbert, Christopher J., and Jonathan P. Rossing. "Trumping Tropes with Joke(r)s: The Daily Show Plays the 'Race Card.'" *Western Journal of Communication* 77, no. 1 (February 2013): 92-111.

Gilbert, Kenyatta R. *The Journey and Promise of African American Preaching*. Minneapolis: Fortress, 2011.

Giroux, Henry A. "The Hope of Radical Education: A Conversation with Henry A. Giroux." In *What Schools Can Do: Critical Pedagogy and Practice*, edited by Kathleen Weiler and Candace Mitchell, pp. 13-26. Albany: SUNY Press, 1992.

———. "The Hope of Radical Education: A Conversation with Henry Giroux." *Journal of Education* 170, no. 2 (January 1, 1988): 91-101.

Goffman, Erving. *The Presentation of Self in Everyday Life*. Garden City, NY: Doubleday Anchor Books, 1959.

Goleman, Daniel. *Emotional Intelligence*. New York: Bantam Books, 2005.

González, Justo L. *Mañana: Christian Theology from a Hispanic Perspective*. Nashville: Abingdon, 1990.

Gornik, Mark R. *Word Made Global: Stories of African Christianity in New York City.* Grand Rapids: Eerdmans, 2011.

Gorski, Philip S. "Historicizing the Secularization Debate: An Agenda for Research." In *Handbook of the Sociology of Religion*, edited by Michele Dillon, pp. 110-22. New York: Cambridge University Press, 2003.

Graham, Elaine L. *Transforming Practice: Pastoral Theology in an Age of Uncertainty.* London: Mowbray, 1996.

Granberg-Michaelson, Wesley. *From Times Square to Timbuktu: The Post-Christian West Meets the Non-Western Church.* Grand Rapids: Eerdmans, 2013.

Great Preachers Series: Gardner C. Taylor. Video recording. Distributed by Gateway Films/ Vision Video; Odyssey Productions Ltd, 1997.

Greenberg, Chris. "Rob Parker on RG3: ESPN 'First Take' Host Asks If Robert Griffin III Is a 'Cornball Brother.'" *Huffington Post*, December 13, 2012. www.huffingtonpost .com/2012/12/13/rob-parker-robert-griffin-race-first-take_n_2295726.html.

Groody, Daniel G., and Gioacchino Campese. *A Promised Land, A Perilous Journey: Theological Perspectives on Migration.* South Bend, IN: University of Notre Dame Press, 2008.

Guay, Louis-Martin. "Theatre of the Unexpected: When the Spectator Becomes Actor." Translated by Jacqueline Dinsmore. *Canadian Theatre Review* 143 (Summer 2010): 6-10.

Gudykunst, William B. *Bridging Differences: Effective Intergroup Communication.* Newbury Park, CA: Sage, 1991.

———. *Bridging Differences: Effective Intergroup Communication.* Thousand Oaks, CA: Sage, 1998.

Gudykunst, William B., and Young Yun Kim. *Communicating with Strangers: An Approach to Intercultural Communication.* New York: McGraw-Hill, 1997.

Gundry Volf, Judith M., and Miroslav Volf. *A Spacious Heart: Essays on Identity and Belonging.* Valley Forge, PA: Trinity Press International, 1997.

Hajdu, David. "Wynton's Blues." *The Atlantic Monthly*, March 2003.

Hall, Edward T. *Beyond Culture.* Garden City, NY: Anchor, 1976.

Hamilton, Charles V. *Adam Clayton Powell Jr.: The Political Biography of an American Dilemma.* New York: Atheneum, 1991.

Hammer, Mitchell R., Milton J. Bennett, and Richard Wiseman. "Measuring Intercultural Sensitivity: The Intercultural Development Inventory." *International Journal of Intercultural Relations* 27 (2003): 421-33.

Hanciles, Jehu. *Beyond Christendom: Globalization, African Migration, and the Transformation of the West.* Maryknoll, NY: Orbis Books, 2008.

Harris, Daniel E. "Methods of Assessment." In *Teaching Preaching as a Christian Practice: A New Approach to Homiletical Pedagogy*, edited by Thomas G. Long and Leonora Tubbs Tisdale, pp. 191-204. Louisville: Westminster John Knox, 2008.

Harris, James Henry. *Preaching Liberation*. Minneapolis: Fortress, 1995.

———. *The Word Made Plain: The Power and Promise of Preaching*. Minneapolis: Fortress, 2004.

Hauerwas, Stanley. *Against the Nations: War and Survival in a Liberal Society*. Minneapolis: Winston, 1985.

Hayakawa, S. I. *Language: In Thought and Action*. London: George Allen & Unwin, 1964.

Hays, J. Daniel. *From Every People and Nation: A Biblical Theology of Race*. Downers Grove, IL: InterVarsity Press, 2003.

Hearlson, Adam W. "Finding Ourselves There: Martin Heidegger's Notions of Place and What They Might Mean for Preaching." Paper presented at the Annual Academy of Homiletics Conference, Washington, D.C., 2009.

———. "Preaching as Sabotage: Power, Practice, and Proclamation." PhD diss., Princeton Theological Seminary, 2013.

Heltzel, Peter. *Resurrection City: A Theology of Improvisation*. Grand Rapids: Eerdmans, 2012.

Hodgson, John, and Ernest Richards. *Improvisation*. New York: Grove, 1979.

Hofstede, Geert H., Gert Jan Hofstede, and Michael Minkov. *Cultures and Organizations: Software of the Mind: Intercultural Cooperation and Its Importance for Survival*. New York: McGraw-Hill, 2010.

Hogan, William L. "White Guys Can't Preach: What I Have Learned from African American Preachers." Paper presented at the Evangelical Homiletics Society Conference, South Hamilton, Massachusetts, 1996.

Hollenweger, Walter J. *Interkulturelle Theologie*. 3 vols. Munich: Kaiser, 1979–1988.

Holmes, Prue, and Gillian O'Neill. "Developing and Evaluating Intercultural Competence: Ethnographies of Intercultural Encounters." *International Journal of Intercultural Relations* 36, no. 5 (September 2012): 707-18.

Holmes, Seth M. *Fresh Fruit, Broken Bodies: Migrant Farmworkers in the United States*. Berkeley: University of California Press, 2013.

Holt, Nora. "Abyssinian Baptist Largest Protestant Church in the World." *New York Amsterdam News*, December 2, 1950.

hooks, bell. *Teaching Community: A Pedagogy of Hope*. New York: Routledge, 2003.

———. *Teaching to Transgress: Education as the Practice of Freedom*. New York: Routledge, 1994.

Howard, Gary. "Whites in Multicultural Education: Rethinking Our Role." In *Multicultural Education, Transformative Knowledge, and Action: Historical and Contemporary Perspectives*, edited by James A. Banks, pp. 323-34. New York: Teachers College Press, 1996.

Huizinga, Johan. *Homo Ludens: A Study of the Play Element in Culture*. Boston: Beacon, 1970.

Hyams, Barry. "Spolin Game Plan for Improvisational Theater." *Los Angeles Times*. May 26, 1974.

Irving, Washington. *Rip Van Winkle*. Utrecht: The Catharijne Press, 1987.

Isasi-Díaz, Ada María. *La Lucha Continues: Mujerista Theology*. Maryknoll, NY: Orbis Books, 2004.

Izzo, Gary. *The Art of Play: The New Genre of Interactive Theatre*. Portsmouth, NH: Heinemann, 1997.

Jameson, Norman. "Shifting Sands: Seminaries Are at a Crossroads (Interview with Daniel Aleshire)." *Baptist World News*, October 28, 2014. http://baptistnews.com/ministry/organizations/item/29429-shifting-sands-seminaries-are-at-a-crossroads.

Jenkins, Philip. *The Next Christendom: The Coming of Global Christianity*. New York: Oxford University Press, 2002.

Jennings, Willie James. *The Christian Imagination: Theology and the Origins of Race*. New Haven, CT: Yale University Press, 2010.

Jeter Jr., Joseph R., and Ronald J. Allen. *One Gospel, Many Ears: Preaching for Different Listeners in the Congregation*. St. Louis: Chalice, 2002.

Joh, Anne, and Dori Baker. *Time to Choose, Time to Change: A Report on the 2013 FTE Consultation on Doctoral Theological Education*. Decatur, GA: The Forum for Theological Exploration, October 2013. Last modified February 13, 2014. http://fteleaders.org/resources/Doctoral-Report.

Johnson, Todd M., and Kenneth R. Ross, eds. *Atlas of Global Christianity: 1910–2010*. Edinburgh: Edinburgh University Press, 2009.

Johnstone, Keith. *Impro for Storytellers*. New York: Routledge, 1999.

———. *Impro: Improvisation and the Theatre*. New York: Routledge, 1992.

Jones, Carolyn M. "The Task of African American Biblical Hermeneutics." In *Yet with a Steady Beat: Contemporary U.S. Afrocentric Biblical Interpretation*, edited by Randall C. Bailey. Atlanta: Society of Biblical Literature, 2003.

Jones, Kirk Byron. *The Jazz of Preaching: How to Preach with Great Freedom and Joy*. Nashville: Abingdon, 2004.

Kay, James F. *Preaching and Theology*. St. Louis: Chalice, 2007.

Kealey, Daniel. "The Challenge of International Personnel Selection." In *Handbook of Intercultural Training*, edited by Dan R. Landis and Rabi S. Bhagat, pp. 81-105. Thousand Oaks, CA: Sage, 1996.

Kelsey, David H. *The Uses of Scripture in Recent Theology*. Philadelphia: Fortress, 1975.

Kennedy, George A. *A New History of Classical Rhetoric*. Princeton, NJ: Princeton University Press, 1994.

Kim, Eunjoo Mary. *Preaching in an Age of Globalization*. Louisville: Westminster John Knox, 2010.

Kim, Rebecca Y. "Migration and Conversion of Korean American Christians." In *The Oxford Handbook of Religious Conversion*, edited by Lewis R. Rambo and Charles E. Farhadian, pp. 191-208. New York: Oxford University Press, 2014.

King, Martin Luther, Jr. *The Papers of Martin Luther King, Jr.* Edited by Clayborne Carson. Vol. 3. Berkeley: University of California Press, 1992.

Kinnaman, David. *You Lost Me: Why Young Christians Are Leaving Church—and Rethinking Faith.* Grand Rapids: Baker Books, 2011.

Kirchner, Bill, ed. *The Oxford Companion to Jazz.* New York: Oxford University Press, 2000.

Klyukanov, Igor. *Principles of Intercultural Communication.* New York: Pearson, 2005.

Knowlton, Dave S. "A Constructivist Pedagogue's Personal Narrative of Integrating Faith with Learning: Epistemological and Pedagogical Challenges." *Journal of Research on Christian Education* 11, no. 1 (Spring 2002): 33-57.

Kohlberg, Lawrence, Charles Levine, and Alexandra Hewer. *Moral Stages: A Current Formulation and a Response to Critics: Contributions to Human Development.* Basel: Karger, 1983.

Kreiser, Chris. "'I'm Not Just Making This Up as I Go Along': Reclaiming Theories of Improvisation for Discussions of College Writing." *Pedagogy* 14, no. 1 (Winter 2014): 81-106.

Lamb, Lisa. *Blessed and Beautiful: Multiethnic Churches and the Preaching That Sustains Them.* Eugene, OR: Cascade, 2014.

Lanham, Richard A. *A Handlist of Rhetorical Terms.* Berkeley: University of California Press, 1991.

Lanzetta, Beverly J. *The Other Side of Nothingness: Toward a Theology of Radical Openness.* Albany: SUNY Press, 2001.

LaRue, Cleophus J. *The Heart of Black Preaching.* Louisville: Westminster John Knox, 2000.

———. *I Believe I'll Testify: The Art of African American Preaching.* Louisville: Westminster John Knox, 2011.

———, ed. *Power in the Pulpit: How America's Most Effective Black Preachers Prepare Their Sermons.* Louisville: Westminster John Knox, 2002.

———. "Two Ships Passing in the Night." In *What's the Matter with Preaching Today?*, edited by Mike Graves, pp. 127-44. Louisville: Westminster John Knox, 2004.

Lash, Nicholas. *Theology on the Way to Emmaus.* London: SCM Press, 1986.

Law, Eric H. F. *The Word at the Crossings: Living the Good News in a Multicontextual Community.* St. Louis: Chalice, 2004.

Lawrence, William B. *Sundays in New York: Pulpit Theology at the Crest of the Protestant Mainstream, 1930–1955.* Lanham, MD: Scarecrow, 1996.

Lefebvre, Henri. *The Production of Space.* Translated by Donald Nicholson-Smith. Malden, MA: Blackwell, 1991.

Lévi-Strauss, Claude. *The Savage Mind.* Chicago: University of Chicago Press, 1966.

Lévinas, Emmanuel. *Is It Righteous to Be? Interviews with Emmanuel Lévinas.* Edited by Jill Robbins. Stanford, CA: Stanford University Press, 2001.

———. *Time and the Other and Additional Essays.* Pittsburgh: Duquesne University Press, 1987.

Lincoln, C. Eric, and Lawrence H. Mamiya. *The Black Church in the African American Experience*. Durham, NC: Duke University Press, 1990.

Lindbeck, George A. *The Nature of Doctrine: Religion and Theology in a Postliberal Age*. Louisville: Westminster John Knox, 2009.

Lingenfelter, Judith, and Sherwood G. Lingenfelter. *Teaching Cross-Culturally: An Incarnational Model for Learning and Teaching*. Grand Rapids: Baker Academic, 2003.

Lischer, Richard. "Gardner Taylor." In *Concise Encyclopedia of Preaching*, edited by William H. Willimon and Richard Lischer, pp. 465-67. Louisville: Westminster John Knox, 1995.

———. *The Preacher King: Martin Luther King Jr. and the Word That Moved America*. New York: Oxford University Press, 1995.

Livermore, David A. *The Cultural Intelligence Difference: Master the One Skill You Can't Do Without in Today's Global Economy*. New York: American Management Association, 2011.

———. *Cultural Intelligence: Improving Your CQ to Engage Our Multicultural World*. Grand Rapids: Baker Academic, 2009.

———. *Leading with Cultural Intelligence: The New Secret to Success*. New York: AMACOM, 2010.

Lloyd-Jones, D. Martyn. *Preaching and Preachers*. London: Hodder and Stoughton, 1971.

Lockford, Lesa, and Ronald J. Pelias. "Bodily Poeticizing in Theatrical Improvisation: A Typology of Performative Knowledge." *Theatre Topics* 14, no. 2 (September 2004): 431-43.

Loder, James E. *The Transforming Moment*. Colorado Springs: Helmers & Howard, 1989.

Logan, Christie. "Improvisational Pedagogy." In *The Future of Performance Studies: Visions and Revisions*, edited by Sheron J. Dailey, pp. 181-85. Annandale, VA: National Communication Association, 1998.

Long, Beverly Whitaker, and Mary Frances Hopkins. *Performing Literature: An Introduction to Oral Interpretation*. Englewood Cliffs, NJ: Prentice-Hall, 1982.

Long, Thomas G. "Out of the Loop." In *What's the Shape of Narrative Preaching? Essays in Honor of Eugene L. Lowry*, edited by Mike Graves and David J. Schlafer, pp. 115-30. St. Louis: Chalice, 2008.

Lonner, Walter J., and Susanna A. Hayes. "Understanding the Cognitive and Social Aspects of Intercultural Competence." In *Culture and Competence: Contexts of Life Success*, edited by Robert J. Sternberg and Elena L. Grigorenko, pp. 89-110. Washington, DC: American Psychological Association, 2004.

Lord, Albert B. "Characteristics of Orality." *Oral Tradition* 2, no. 1 (1987): 54-72.

———. *The Singer of Tales*. Cambridge, MA: Harvard University Press, 1960.

Loritts, Bryan. *Right Color, Wrong Culture: The Type of Leader Your Organization Needs to Become Multiethnic*. Chicago: Moody Press, 2014.

Lose, David J. *Preaching at the Crossroads*. Minneapolis: Fortress, 2013.

Lowry, Eugene L. *The Homiletical Beat: Why All Sermons Are Narrative*. Nashville: Abingdon, 2012.

———. *The Sermon: Dancing on the Edge of Mystery*. Nashville: Abingdon, 1997.

Lustig, Myron W., and Jolene Koester. *Intercultural Competence: Interpersonal Communication Across Cultures*. Boston: Allyn & Bacon, 2009.

Magee, Michael. *Emancipating Pragmatism: Emerson, Jazz, and Experimental Writing*. Tuscaloosa: University of Alabama Press, 2004.

Massey, James Earl. "Composing Sermons That Sing!" In *Our Sufficiency Is of God: Essays on Preaching in Honor of Gardner C. Taylor*, edited by Timothy George, James Earl Massey, and Robert Smith Jr., pp. 11-22. Macon, GA: Mercer University Press, 2010.

———. *The Responsible Pulpit*. Anderson, IN: Warner Press, 1974.

———. *Stewards of the Story: The Task of Preaching*. Louisville: Westminster John Knox, 2006.

Matsumoto, David, and Hyisung C. Hwang. "Assessing Cross-Cultural Competence: A Review of Available Tests." *Journal of Cross-Cultural Psychology* 44, no. 6 (August 2013): 849-73.

McClain, William B. "African American Contexts of Narrative Preaching." In *What's the Shape of Narrative Preaching? Essays in Honor of Eugene L. Lowry*, edited by Mike Graves and David J. Schlafer, pp. 55-67. St. Louis: Chalice, 2008.

McClure, John S. "Preaching Theology." Paper presented at the Annual Academy of Homiletics Conference, Memphis, 2004.

———. *The Roundtable Pulpit: Where Leadership and Preaching Meet*. Nashville: Abingdon, 1995.

McClure, John S., Ronald J. Allen, Dale P. Andrews, and L. Susan Bond, eds. *Listening to Listeners: Homiletical Case Studies*. St. Louis: Chalice, 2004.

McGrath, Alister E. *The Future of Christianity*. Malden, MA: Wiley-Blackwell, 2002.

McIntosh, Gary L., and Alan McMahan. *Being the Church in a Multi-Ethnic Community: Why It Matters and How It Works*. Indianapolis: Wesleyan Publishing House, 2012.

McMickle, Marvin A. *Preaching to the Black Middle Class: Words of Challenge, Words of Hope*. Valley Forge, PA: Judson Press, 2000.

Melde, Wilma. *Zur Integration von Landeskunde und Kommunikation im Fremdsprachenunterricht*. Tübingen: Gunter Narr Verlag, 1987.

Merriam, Sharan B., ed. *Non-Western Perspectives on Learning and Knowing*. Malabar, FL: Krieger, 2007.

Miller, Keith D. *Voice of Deliverance: The Language of Martin Luther King, Jr., and Its Sources*. New York: Free Press, 1992.

Minnow, Martha. *Making All the Difference: Inclusion, Exclusion, and American Law*. Ithaca, NY: Cornell University Press, 1991.

Mitchell, Henry H. "African American Preaching." In *Concise Encyclopedia of Preaching*, edited by William H. Willimon and Richard Lischer. Louisville: Westminster John Knox, 1995.

———. "African American Preaching." *Interpretation* 51, no. 4 (October 1997): 371-83.

———. *Black Belief: Folk Beliefs of Blacks in America and West Africa.* New York: Harper & Row, 1975.

———. *Black Preaching.* New York: Harper & Row, 1979.

———. *Celebration and Experience in Preaching.* Nashville: Abingdon, 1990.

———. "The Holy Spirit: A Folk Perspective." *The Living Pulpit* 5, no. 1 (March 1996): 40-41.

———. "Preaching as Experience of the Gospel: An Insight with Roots in the Wisdom of Gardner C. Taylor." In *Our Sufficiency Is of God: Essays on Preaching in Honor of Gardner C. Taylor,* edited by Timothy George, James Earl Massey, and Robert Smith Jr., pp. 139-50. Macon, GA: Mercer University Press, 2010.

Mitchell, Jolyon P. *Visually Speaking: Radio and the Renaissance of Preaching.* Edinburgh: T & T Clark, 1999.

Moltmann, Jürgen. *The Spirit of Life: A Universal Affirmation.* Minneapolis: Fortress, 1992.

Monson, Ingrid T. *Saying Something: Jazz Improvisation and Interaction.* Chicago: University of Chicago Press, 1996.

Moreau, A. Scott, Evvy Hay Campbell, and Susan Greener. *Effective Intercultural Communication: A Christian Perspective.* Grand Rapids: Baker, 2014.

Morello, Carol, and Ted Mellnik. "Census: Minority Babies Are Now Majority in United States." *The Washington Post,* May 17, 2012, sec. Local. www.washingtonpost.com/local/census-minority-babies-are-now-majority-in-united-states/2012/05/16/gIQAiWY8UU_story.html.

Morse, Christopher. *Not Every Spirit: A Dogmatics of Christian Disbelief.* New York: Continuum, 2009.

Mott, John R. "Report of Commission: World Missionary Conference, Edinburgh 1910." In *The History and Records of the Conference, Together with Addresses Delivered at the Evening Meetings,* vol. 9. Des Moines, IA: LBS Archival Products, 1990.

Moyd, Olin P. *The Sacred Art: Preaching & Theology in the African American Tradition.* Valley Forge, PA: Judson Press, 1995.

Muyumba, Walton M. *The Shadow and the Act: Black Intellectual Practice, Jazz Improvisation, and Philosophical Pragmatism.* Chicago: University of Chicago Press, 2009.

Nachmanovitch, Stephen. *Free Play: Improvisation in Life and Art.* New York: Jeremy P. Tarcher/Putnam, 1990.

Nanko-Fernández, Carmen. *Theologizing En Espanglish: Context, Community, and Ministry.* Maryknoll, NY: Orbis Books, 2010.

Napier, Mick. *Improvise: Scene from the Inside Out.* Portsmouth, NH: Heinemann, 2004.

Narayan, Uma, and Sandra Harding, eds. *Decentering the Center: Philosophy for a Multicultural, Postcolonial, and Feminist World.* Bloomington: Indiana University Press, 2000.

"Negro Pastor Honored: Legion Post Gives Award to Dr. Taylor of Brooklyn." *New York Times,* September 15, 1958.

Neuliep, James W. *Intercultural Communication: A Contextual Approach*. Thousand Oaks, CA: Sage, 2012.

Neuner, Gerhard. *Intercultural Competence*. Edited by Michael Byram. Strasbourg: Council of Europe, Language Policy Division, 2003.

Newbigin, Lesslie. *Foolishness to the Greeks: The Gospel and Western Culture*. Grand Rapids: Eerdmans, 1986.

Niebuhr, H. Richard. *The Social Sources of Denominationalism*. Hamden, CT: Shoe String Press, 1954.

Nieman, James R., and Thomas G. Rogers. *Preaching to Every Pew: Cross-Cultural Strategies*. Minneapolis: Fortress, 2001.

Nimmo, Paul T. *Being in Action: The Theological Shape of Barth's Ethical Vision*. London: T & T Clark, 2007.

Norgaard, Martin. "Descriptions of Improvisational Thinking by Artist-Level Jazz Musicians." *Journal of Research in Music Education* 59, no. 2 (2008): 109-27.

Old, Hughes Oliphant. *The Reading and Preaching of the Scriptures in the Worship of the Christian Church: The Modern Age*. Vol. 6. Grand Rapids: Eerdmans, 2007.

Ostransky, Leroy. *The Anatomy of Jazz*. Seattle: University of Washington Press, 1960.

Ott, Craig. "Globalization and Contextualization: Reframing the Task of Contextualization in the Twenty-First Century." *Missiology: An International Review* 43, no. 1 (2014): 1-16.

Palmer, Parker J. *The Courage to Teach: Exploring the Inner Landscape of a Teacher's Life*. Hoboken, NJ: Wiley, 2010.

Paris, Peter J. *Black Religious Leaders: Conflict in Unity*. Louisville: Westminster John Knox, 1991.

Pew Forum on Religion and Public Life. "Faith on the Move: The Religious Affiliation of International Migrants." March 8, 2012. Last modified February 19, 2014. www .pewforum.org/2012/03/08/religious-migration-exec/.

Phan, Peter C. *In Our Own Tongues: Perspectives from Asia on Mission and Inculturation*. Maryknoll, NY: Orbis Books, 2003.

Pipes, William H. *Say Amen, Brother!: Old-Time Negro Preaching, a Study in American Frustration*. Detroit: Wayne State University Press, 1992.

Powell Jr., Adam Clayton. *Adam by Adam: the Autobiography of Adam Clayton Powell Jr*. New York: Dial, 1971.

Powell, Mark Allan. *What Do They Hear? Bridging the Gap Between Pulpit and Pew*. Nashville: Abingdon, 2007.

Powery, Luke A. *Dem Dry Bones: Preaching, Death, and Hope*. Minneapolis: Fortress, 2012.

———. *Spirit Speech: Celebration and Lament in Preaching*. Nashville: Abingdon, 2009.

Poynton, Robert. *Do Improvise: Less Push. More Pause. Better Results. A New Approach to Work (and Life)*. Cardigan, Wales: Do Book Company, 2013.

Preminger, Alex, and TVF Brogan, eds. *The New Princeton Encyclopedia of Poetry and Poetics*. Princeton, NJ: Princeton University Press, 1993.

Premnath, D. N., ed. *Border Crossings: Cross-Cultural Hermeneutics.* Maryknoll, NY: Orbis Books, 2007.

Proctor, Samuel D. *The Certain Sound of the Trumpet: Crafting a Sermon of Authority.* Valley Forge, PA: Judson Press, 1994.

Proctor, Samuel D., and Gardner C. Taylor. *We Have This Ministry: The Heart of the Pastor's Vocation.* Valley Forge, PA: Judson Press, 1996.

Raboteau, Albert J. *A Fire in the Bones: Reflections on African-American Religious History.* Boston: Beacon, 1995.

———. *Slave Religion: The "Invisible Institution" in the Antebellum South.* Oxford: Oxford University Press, 2004.

Rainey, Brian P. "Non-Peoples and Foolish Nations: Xenophobia and Ethnic Foreigners in the Hebrew Bible and Mesopotamia." PhD diss., Brown University, 2014.

Raper, Arthur F. *Preface to Peasantry; a Tale of Two Black Belt Counties.* Chapel Hill: University of North Carolina Press, 1936.

Rawlins, Robert, and Nor Eddine Bahha. *Jazzology: The Encyclopedia of Jazz Theory for All Musicians.* Edited by Barrett Tagliarino. Milwaukee: Hal Leonard, 2005.

Ray, Sandy F. *Journeying Through a Jungle.* Nashville: Broadman, 1979.

Ray, Stephen. "E-Racing While Black." In *Being Black, Teaching Black*, edited by Nancy Lynn Westfield, pp. 39-59. Nashville: Abingdon, 2008.

Resner, André. "No Preacher Left Behind: A New Prerequisite for the Introductory Preaching Course." Paper presented at the Annual Academy of Homiletics Conference, Washington, D.C., 2009.

Ricoeur, Paul. *From Text to Action.* Evanston, IL: Northwestern University Press, 2007.

———. *Interpretation Theory: Discourse and the Surplus of Meaning.* Fort Worth: Texas Christian University Press, 1976.

———. *Oneself as Another.* Chicago: University of Chicago Press, 1992.

Roberts, Bob, Jr. *Glocalization: How Followers of Jesus Engage the New Flat World.* Grand Rapids: Zondervan, 2007.

Robertson, Roland. *Globalization: Social Theory and Global Culture.* Thousand Oaks, CA: Sage, 1992.

Root, Elizabeth, and Anchalee Ngampornchai. "'I Came Back as a New Human Being': Student Descriptions of Intercultural Competence Acquired Through Education Abroad Experiences." *Journal of Studies in International Education* 17, no. 5 (2012): 513-32.

Rose, Lucy Atkinson. *Sharing the Word: Preaching in the Roundtable Church.* Louisville: Westminster John Knox, 1997.

Rudlin, John. *Jacques Copeau.* Cambridge: Cambridge University Press, 1986.

Sacks, Jonathan. *The Dignity of Difference: How to Avoid the Clash of Civilizations.* New York: Continuum, 2003.

Saldine, Kristin Emery. "Preaching God Visible: Geo-Rhetoric and the Theological

Appropriation of Landscape Imagery in the Sermons of Jonathan Edwards." PhD diss., Princeton Theological Seminary, 2004.

Sawyer, R. Keith. *Creating Conversations: Improvisation in Everyday Discourse*. Cresskill, NJ: Hampton Press, 2001.

———. "Creative Teaching: Collaborative Discussion as Disciplined Improvisation." *Educational Researcher* 33, no. 2 (March 2004): 12-20.

———. "The Emergence of Creativity." *Philosophical Psychology* 12, no. 4 (1999): 447-69.

———. *Group Genius: The Creative Power of Collaboration*. New York: Basic Books, 2007.

———. *Improvised Dialogues: Emergence and Creativity in Conversation*. Westport, CT: Ablex, 2003.

———. "Improvised Lessons: Collaborative Discussion in the Constructivist Classroom." *Teaching Education* 15, no. 2 (June 2004): 189-201.

———. *Social Emergence: Societies as Complex Systems*. New York: Cambridge University Press, 2005.

Scheuerer, Franz Xaver. *Interculturality: A Challenge for the Mission of the Church*. Bangalore, India: Asian Trading Corp, 2001.

Schreiter, Robert J. *The New Catholicity: Theology Between the Global and the Local*. Maryknoll, NY: Orbis Books, 1997.

Scott, Manuel L., Jr. *The Quotable Manuel Scott Sr.: Words From a Gospel Genius*. Los Angeles: Manuel Scott Jr. Ministries, 2010.

Searle, John R. *Speech Acts: An Essay in the Philosophy of Language*. London: Cambridge University Press, 1969.

Seham, Amy. "Play Fair: Feminist Tools for Teaching Improv." In *Radical Acts: Theatre and Feminist Pedagogies of Change*, edited by Ann Elizabeth Armstrong and Kathleen Juhl, pp. 135-51. San Francisco: Aunt Lute Books, 2007.

Seham, Amy E. *Whose Improv Is It Anyway? Beyond Second City*. Jackson: University Press of Mississippi, 2001.

Sensing, Tim. "African American Preaching." *Journal of the American Academy of Ministry* 7 (Winter/Spring 2001): 38-53.

Simmons, Martha J., and Frank A. Thomas, eds. *Preaching with Sacred Fire: An Anthology of African American Sermons, 1750 to the Present*. New York: W. W. Norton, 2010.

Simpson, Lorenzo Charles. *The Unfinished Project: Towards a Postmetaphysical Humanism*. New York: Routledge, 2001.

Sisko, John E. "Phronesis." In *Encyclopedia of Ethics: P-W*, edited by Lawrence C. Becker and Charlotte B. Becker, pp. 1314-16. New York: Routledge, 2001.

Smith, Robert C., Jr. *Doctrine That Dances: Bringing Doctrinal Preaching and Teaching to Life*. Nashville: B & H Academic, 2008.

Sparks, Kenton L. *Ethnicity and Identity: Prolegomena to the Study of Ethnic Sentiments and Their Expression in the Hebrew Bible*. Winona Lake, IN: Eisenbrauns, 1998.

Spencer, Jon Michael. *Sacred Symphony: The Chanted Sermon of the Black Preacher*. New York: Greenwood, 1987.

Spencer, Raymond Bernard. "Imagery and Improvisation in African American Preaching: Resources for Energizing the Protestant Pulpit." PhD dissertation, Southwestern Baptist Theological Seminary, 2001.

Spitzberg, Brian H., and Gabrielle Changnon. "Conceptualizing Intercultural Competence." In *The Sage Handbook of Intercultural Competence*, edited by Darla K. Deardorff, pp. 2-52. Thousand Oaks, CA: Sage, 2009.

Spitzberg, Brian H., and William R. Cupach. *Interpersonal Communication Competence*. Beverly Hills, CA: Sage, 1984.

Spolin, Viola. *Improvisation for the Theater*. Evanston, IL: Northwestern University Press, 1999.

———. *Theater Games for Rehearsal: A Director's Handbook*. Evanston, IL: Northwestern University Press, 1985.

———. *Theater Games for the Classroom: A Teacher's Handbook*. Evanston, IL: Northwestern University Press, 1986.

Steiner, George. *Real Presences*. Chicago: University of Chicago Press, 1989.

Stowe, Harriet Beecher. *Uncle Tom's Cabin, Or, Life Among the Lowly*. Cambridge, MA: Belknap, 1962.

Strong, Josiah. *Our Country: Its Possible Future and Its Present Crisis*. New York: Baker & Taylor, 1885.

Sundermeier, Theo. "Erwägungen zu einer Hermeneutik interkulturellen Verstehens." In *Konvivenz und Differenz: Studien zu einer verstehenden Missionswissenschaft*, edited by Volker Küster, pp. 87-101. Erlangen: Verlag der Ev.-Luth. Mission, 1995.

Swartz, David. *Culture & Power: The Sociology of Pierre Bourdieu*. Chicago: University of Chicago Press, 1997.

Sweet, Jeffrey. *Something Wonderful Right Away*. New York: Hal Leonard, 2000.

Tanner, Kathyrn. *Christ the Key*. New York: Cambridge University Press, 2010.

———. *Theories of Culture: A New Agenda for Theology*. Minneapolis: Fortress, 1997.

Taylor, Charles. *A Secular Age*. Cambridge, MA: Belknap Press of Harvard University Press, 2007.

———. "Understanding the Other: A Gadamerian View on Conceptual Schemes." In *Gadamer's Century: Essays in Honor of Hans-Georg Gadamer*, edited by Jeff Malpas, Ulrich von Arnswald, and Jens Kertscher, pp. 279-98. Cambridge, MA: MIT Press, 2002.

Taylor, Clarence. *The Black Churches of Brooklyn*. New York: Columbia University Press, 1994.

"Taylor Completes Decade at Concord." *New York Amsterdam News*, May 31, 1958.

Taylor, Edward L. "Introduction." In *The Words of Gardner Taylor*, vol. 1, *NBC Radio Sermons, 1959–1970*, edited by Edward L. Taylor. Valley Forge, PA: Judson Press, 2004.

Taylor, Gardner C. *Essential Taylor Audio CD*. Valley Forge, PA: Judson Press, 2001.

———. *How Shall They Preach? The Lyman Beecher Lectures and Five Lenten Sermons.* Elgin, IL: Progressive Baptist Publishing House, 1977.

———. Personal interview. March 5, 2012.

———. Personal interview with Joel C. Gregory. September 2006.

———. "Shaping Sermons by the Shape of Text and Preacher." In *Preaching Biblically*, edited by Don M. Wardlaw, pp. 137-52. Philadelphia: Westminster Press, 1983.

———. "The Sweet Torture of Sunday Morning (Interview)." *Leadership* II, no. 3 (Summer 1981): 16-29.

———. *The Words of Gardner Taylor*, vol. 1, *NBC Radio Sermons, 1959–1970*. Edited by Edward L. Taylor. Valley Forge, PA: Judson Press, 2004.

———. *The Words of Gardner Taylor*, vol. 2, *Sermons from the Middle Years, 1970–1980*. Edited by Edward L. Taylor. Valley Forge, PA: Judson Press, 2004.

———. *The Words of Gardner Taylor*, vol. 3, *Quintessential Classics, 1980–Present*. Edited by Edward L. Taylor. Valley Forge, PA: Judson Press, 2004.

———. *The Words of Gardner Taylor*, vol. 4, *Special Occasion and Expository Sermons*. Edited by Edward L. Taylor. Valley Forge, PA: Judson Press, 2004.

———. *The Words of Gardner Taylor*, vol. 5, *Lectures, Essays, and Interviews*. Edited by Edward L. Taylor. Valley Forge, PA: Judson Press, 2004.

———. *The Words of Gardner Taylor*, vol. 6, *50 Years of Timeless Treasures*. Edited by Edward L. Taylor. Valley Forge, PA: Judson Press, 2004.

———. "Why I Believe There Is a God." In *Why I Believe There Is a God; Sixteen Essays by Negro Clergymen*, edited by Howard Thurman, pp. 102-8. Chicago: Johnson, 1965.

Taylor, Mark L. *The Theological and the Political: On the Weight of the World.* Minneapolis: Fortress, 2011.

Thomas, Frank A. *They Like to Never Quit Praisin' God: The Role of Celebration in Preaching.* Cleveland: United Church Press, 1997.

Thomas, Gerald Lamont. *African American Preaching: The Contribution of Dr. Gardner C. Taylor.* New York: Peter Lang, 2004.

———. "African American Preaching: The Contribution of Gardner C. Taylor." PhD diss., Southern Baptist Theological Seminary, 1993.

Thomson, Lynn M. "Teaching and Rehearsing Collaboration." *Theatre Topics* 13, no. 1 (March 2003): 117-28.

"Ties Sought in City by Baptist Groups." *New York Times*, July 31, 1958.

Tisdale, Leonora Tubbs. *Preaching as Local Theology and Folk Art.* Minneapolis: Fortress, 1997.

Toft, Monica Duffy, Daniel Philpott, and Timothy Samuel Shah. *God's Century: Resurgent Religion and Global Politics.* New York: W. W. Norton, 2011.

Tomasi, Gabriele. "On the Spontaneity of Jazz Improvisation." In *Improvisation: Between Technique and Spontaneity*, edited by Marina Santi, pp. 77-102. Newcastle upon Tyne, UK: Cambridge Scholars Press, 2010.

Touré. *Who's Afraid of Post-Blackness? What It Means to Be Black Now.* New York: Free Press, 2011.

———. "Wynton Marsalis." *Icon Thoughtstyle Magazine*, August 1997.

Trede, Franziska, Wendy Bowles, and Donna Bridges. "Developing Intercultural Competence and Global Citizenship Through International Experiences: Academics' Perceptions." *Intercultural Education* 24, no. 5 (2013): 442-55.

Troeger, Thomas H., and Leonora Tubbs Tisdale. *A Sermon Workbook: Exercises in the Art and Craft of Preaching.* Nashville: Abingdon, 2013.

Turner, William C. "The Musicality of Black Preaching." *Journal of Black Sacred Music* 2, no. 1 (Spring 1988): 21-27.

Van de Vijver, Fons J. R., and Kwok Leung. "Methodological Issues in Researching Intercultural Competence." In *The Sage Handbook of Intercultural Competence*, edited by Darla K. Deardorff, pp. 404-18. Thousand Oaks, CA: Sage, 2009.

Vande Berg, Michael R., Michael Paige, and Kris Hemming Lou, eds. *Student Learning Abroad: What Our Students Are Learning, What They're Not, and What We Can Do About It.* Sterling, VA: Stylus Publishing, 2012.

Vanhoozer, Kevin J. *The Drama of Doctrine: A Canonical-Linguistic Approach to Christian Theology.* Louisville: Westminster John Knox, 2005.

———. *Faith Speaking Understanding: Performing the Drama of Doctrine.* Louisville: Westminster John Knox, 2014.

Vera, Dusya, and Mary Crossan. "Improvisation and Innovative Performance in Teams." *Organization Science* 16, no. 3 (June 2005): 203-24.

———. "Theatrical Improvisation: Lessons for Organizations." *Organization Studies* 25, no. 5 (2004): 727-49.

Vico, Giambattista. *The Art of Rhetoric: (Institutiones Oratoriae, 1711–1741).* Translated by Giorgio A. Pinton and Arthur W. Shippee. Atlanta: Rodopi, 1996.

Vinet, Alexandre. *Homiletics.* Translated by Thomas H. Skinner. New York: Ivison and Phinney, 1870.

Volf, Miroslav. *Exclusion and Embrace: A Theological Exploration of Identity, Otherness, and Reconciliation.* Nashville: Abingdon, 1996.

Walker, John A. *Glossary of Art, Architecture, and Design Since 1945.* Boston: G. K. Hall, 1992.

Walls, Andrew F. "Christian Scholarship and the Demographic Transformation of the Church." In *Theological Literacy in the Twenty-First Century*, edited by Rodney L. Petersen and Nancy M. Rourke, pp. 166-84. Grand Rapids: Eerdmans, 2002.

———. *From Christendom to World Christianity: The Demographic Transformation of the Church [Audio Recording].* Students' Lectureship on Missions: Lecture 4. Princeton, NJ: Princeton Theological Seminary, Educational Media, 2001.

———. *The Cross-Cultural Process in Christian History: Studies in the Transmission and Appropriation of Faith.* Maryknoll, NY: Orbis Books, 2002.

Ward, Richard F. *Speaking of the Holy: The Art of Communication in Preaching*. St. Louis: Chalice, 2001.

Warner, Michael, Jonathan VanAntwerpen, and Craig J. Calhoun, eds. *Varieties of Secularism in a Secular Age*. Cambridge, MA: Harvard University Press, 2010.

Weaver, Gary R. "Understanding and Coping with Cross-Cultural Adjustment Stress." In *Culture, Communication, and Conflict*, edited by Gary R. Weaver, pp. 177–94. Boston: Pearson Learning Solutions, 2000.

Webb, Stephen H. *The Divine Voice: Christian Proclamation and the Theology of Sound*. Grand Rapids: Brazos, 2004.

Weigl, Robert C. "Intercultural Competence Through Cultural Self-Study: A Strategy for Adult Learners." *International Journal of Intercultural Relations* 33 (2009): 346–60.

Weimer, Maryellen. *Learner-Centered Teaching: Five Key Changes to Practice*. San Francisco: Jossey-Bass, 2002.

Welker, Michael. *God the Spirit*. Minneapolis: Fortress, 1994.

Wells, Samuel. *Improvisation: The Drama of Christian Ethics*. Grand Rapids: Brazos, 2004.

West, Cornel. *The Cornel West Reader*. New York: Basic Civitas Books, 1999.

———. *Prophesy Deliverance!: An Afro-American Revolutionary Christianity*. Louisville: Westminster John Knox, 2002.

———. *Race Matters*. Boston: Beacon, 1993.

Wheeler, Barbara G. "Consultation Address." In *Time to Choose, Time to Change: A Report on the 2013 FTE Consultation on Doctoral Theological Education*, ed. Anne Joh and Dori Baker. Decatur, GA: The Forum for Theological Exploration, October 2013. Last modified February 13, 2014. http://fteleaders.org/resources/Doctoral-Report.

Wheeler, Barbara G., and Anthony T. Ruger. "Sobering Figures Point to Overall Enrollment Decline." *In Trust* 24, no. 2 (Spring 2013): 5–11.

White, V. Hayden. *Metahistory: The Historical Imagination in Nineteenth-Century Europe*. Baltimore, MD: Johns Hopkins University Press, 1975.

Wicklein, John. "Taylor to Preach for Australians." *New York Times*, July 26, 1959.

Wiemann, John M., and Clifford W. Kelly. "Pragmatics of Interpersonal Competence." In *Rigor and Imagination: Essays from the Legacy of George Bateson*, edited by C. Wilder-Mott and John H. Weakland, pp. 283–97. New York: Praeger, 1981.

Wilkerson, Barbara, ed. *Multicultural Religious Education*. Birmingham, AL: Religious Education Press, 1997.

Williams, Rowan. *Christ on Trial: How the Gospel Unsettles Our Judgment*. London: Fount, 2000.

Williams, Tracy Rundstrom. "Exploring the Impact of Study Abroad on Students' Intercultural Communication Skills: Adaptability and Sensitivity." *Journal of Studies in International Education* 9, no. 4 (2005): 356–71.

Wills, Lawrence M. *Not God's People: Insiders and Outsiders in the Biblical World*. Lanham, MD: Rowman & Littlefield, 2008.

World Population to 2300. New York: The United Nations Department of Economic and Social Affairs: Population Division, 2004. Last modified March 2, 2014. www.un.org/esa/population/publications/longrange2/WorldPop2300final.pdf.

Wright, David. "The Mythopoetic Body: Learning Through Creativity." In *Pedagogies of the Imagination: Mythopoetic Curriculum in Educational Practice*, edited by Timothy Leonard and Peter Willis, pp. 93-106. New York: Springer Books, 2010.

Wright, N. T. *The Epistles of Paul to the Colossians and to Philemon: An Introduction and Commentary.* Grand Rapids: Eerdmans, 1986.

Wu, Frank H. *Yellow: Race in America Beyond Black and White.* New York: Basic Books, 2002.

Wuthnow, Robert. *After the Baby Boomers: How Twenty- and Thirty-Somethings Are Shaping the Future of American Religion.* Princeton, NJ: Princeton University Press, 2007.

Yee, Gale A. "Yin/Yang Is Not Me: An Exploration into an Asian American Biblical Hermeneutics." In *Ways of Being, Ways of Reading: Asian American Biblical Interpretation*, edited by Mary F. Foskett and Jeffrey K. Kuan, pp. 152-63. St. Louis: Chalice, 2006.

Yong, Amos. *The Future of Evangelical Theology : Soundings from the Asian American Diaspora.* Downers Grove, IL: IVP Academic, 2014.

———. *Hospitality and the Other: Pentecost, Christian Practices, and the Neighbor.* Maryknoll, NY: Orbis Books, 2008.

Young, Vershawn Ashanti, Rusty Barrett, Y'Shanda Young-Rivera, and Kim Brian Lovejoy. *Other People's English: Code-Meshing, Code-Switching, and African American Literacy.* New York: Teachers College Press, 2013.

Zauenbrecher, Nicolas J. "The Elements of Improvisation: Structural Tools for Spontaneous Theatre." *Theatre Topics* 21, no. 1 (March 2011): 49-60.

AUTHOR AND SUBJECT INDEX

STRATEGIC INITIATIVES IN EVANGELICAL THEOLOGY

IVP Academic presents a series of seminal works of scholarship with significant relevance for both evangelical scholarship and the church. Strategic Initiatives in Evangelical Theology (SIET) aims to foster interaction within the broader evangelical community and advance discussion in the wider academy around emerging, current, groundbreaking or controversial topics. The series provides a unique publishing venue for both more senior and younger promising scholars.

While SIET volumes demonstrate a depth of appreciation for evangelical theology and the current challenges and issues facing it, the series will welcome books that engage the full range of academic disciplines from theology and biblical studies, to history, literature, philosophy, the natural and social sciences, and the arts.

Editorial Advisory Board

Published Volumes

Addiction and Virtue, Kent Dunnington

The Analogy of Faith, Archie J. Spencer

The God of the Gospel, Scott R. Swain

Incarnational Humanism, Jens Zimmerman

Rethinking the Trinity & Religious Pluralism, Keith E. Johnson

Theology's Epistemological Dilemma, Kevin Diller

The Triumph of God Over Evil, William Hasker

Finding the Textbook You Need